VILENSKY

ILENSKY

Published Books by Mordecai Richler

Fiction

The Acrobats

Son of a Smaller Hero

A Choice of Enemies

The Apprenticeship of Duddy Kravitz

The Incomparable Atuk

Cocksure

St. Urbain's Horseman

Joshua Then and Now

Solomon Gursky Was Here

Barney's Version

Stories

The Street

Nonfiction

Hunting Tigers under Glass

Shovelling Trouble

Notes on an Endangered Species and Others

Great Comic Book Heroes and Other Essays

Home Sweet Home

Broadsides

Oh Canada! Oh Quebec!

This Year in Jerusalem

Belling the Cat

On Snooker

Dispatches from the Sporting Life

Children's Books

Jacob Two-Two Meets the Hooded Fang

Jacob Two-Two and the Dinosaur

Jacob Two-Two's First Spy Case

Anthologies [Editor]

The Best of Modern Humour

Canadian Writing Today

Writers on World War II

MORDECAI RICHLER WAS HERE

Selected Writings

EDITED BY JONATHAN WEBB

ILLUSTRATIONS BY AISLIN | INTRODUCTION BY ADAM GOPNIK

BLACK WALNUT

ISBN-13: 978-1-897330-33-3
ISBN-10: 1-897330-33-2

Library and Archives Canada Cataloguing in Publication
Available upon request to the publisher.

Every effort has been made to remain faithful to the original text from which these
excerpts were taken. Since spelling and punctuation vary greatly among different
editions and books, some adjustments were made for the sake of consistency.

This edition published in 2008 by Black Walnut Books,
an imprint of Madison Press Books.

Madison Press Books
1000 Yonge Street, Suite 303
Toronto, Ontario, Canada
M4W 2K2
madisonpressbooks.com

Printed in Canada

Front-cover photo: © CP / Toronto Star (Andrew Stawicki).
Back-cover photo: © CP / Toronto Star (Dick Loek).

CONTENTS

Introduction

GROWING UP IN MONTREAL — growing up, especially, as an emancipated but still ethnically unmistakable Jew, and growing up, even more especially, as someone who Wanted To Write — the novelist Mordecai Richler was the single powerful local presence, the one with whom one had to deal. To read his novels — *Cocksure* or *The Apprenticeship Of Duddy Kravitz* — was to recognize with a thrill that someone had *got it down* right, had made of streets and smells and accents something shapely and satirically exact. It wasn't that you had never known before that your experience was worth writing about. It was that you had never known before that you were living in a book. Even if, as I did, you saw the material secondhand and at a distance, and just as it was disappearing, St. Urbain Street already on its way to being Rue St. Urbain, it didn't matter. The Montreal he knew had become the books that he had already written.

Yet there was, in the arc of his career, something interestingly double, complicatedly ambiguous. He was *there*. If Leonard Cohen was the one who got away, Richler was the one who got away and then got back, the one who came home to Montreal. (Where, odd personal history, for many years his large and avid family lived across a courtyard from my own slightly larger and no less avid one). This made him a central local figure — for some, almost too central a figure — a subject of Montreal lore and wonder to whom legends and (mostly imaginary) scandals stuck. (I recall that he once quoted to me, with approval, Chekhov's remark that the worst thing in the world is a provincial celebrity.) But it also provided him with that ambiguity, or double message, expressed as clearly in his life as in his work. Choosing to get away and then choosing to go home again, one sensed in his character a motivation more complicated than the obvious one that Montreal was cheap and familiar.

The lure of place and home was powerful for him because he was, in the best nineteenth-century sense, a local novelist, one who owned a place. Montreal was not his only place — he wrote well wherever he went; his first novel was set in Spain — but it was his chief place, the place where his experience spoke most eagerly to his imagination. And not all or even most of Montreal even. He was a specific, not an encyclopaedic, novelist. Montreal around St. Lawrence Boulevard and then over into the conquered territories of Westmount and the other richer Jewish areas across the mountain — just to write these names down is to recall how wonderfully he imprinted their peculiar presences in his fiction.

Local bad makes boy; local boy makes good. It is a familiar story, though never a dull one. But it may make us miss the other, larger and more international story going on in his work.

The importance of locale is one of the many things that separate Richler's work from that of the American Jewish novelists with whom he is often, and wrongly, conflated. When he died, there was a condescending sense, in the American press anyway, that he was a lesser northern light of the American Jewish sensibility — but, in fact, his tastes and talents could not have been more unlike those of Roth and Bellow and Malamud and Stern. They were vast cosmic meteors headed for Stockholm — poets of identity, writers whose dramas were inside the self, not out in the neighbourhood. (Roth is Newark and New York but might be Oak Park and Chicago.) Richler had a great regard for those novelists, but also a slightly amused feeling about the insistent largeness, the American grandiosity, that infected them. His own tastes and style had been, I believe — or at least sensed in the brief time that I "edited" him at a monthly magazine in the mid-eighties, when I was a pup and he was a lion, in no need of editing at all — most affected by his long years in London in the fifties and sixties. Evelyn Waugh was to him what Melville was to the Americans, his adopted grandfather and model-novelist. Richler was drawn to Waugh, for all Waugh's rabid anti-Semitism and petty snobberies, because he was a comic master who showed a way to be elegant without being "tasteful" — a combination Richler found powerful, and, no small thing, because Waugh did his work through dialogue, not monologue. (Richler is a dialogue-and-image, not a monologue-and-idea, writer — a cinematic, rather than a philosophical, novelist.)

There was, in his personal presence, as well as in his work, always a certain kind of fifties-black-and-white, drinking-club-and-broadsheet-newspaper, BBC (the old cultured BBC) English sensibility present — that grim gaiety, born in a cozy but austere cold-water London, that runs through Braine and Amis to the novels of Bradbury and Lodge. In many ways, it was the English satiric novelists of that generation who were his real contemporaries, far more than their cosmically minded Jewish Americans. He shares with Braine and Amis, Sharpe and Bradbury a balloon-puncturing, self-mocking sound — well-read but frightened of seeming pretentious, allergic to metaphor or self-consciously poetic language, with a willingness to render life as it is without trying to make more of it than can be made. It is a form of satiric realism, deliberately circumscribed of obvious ambition — rooted in a desire not to buy into it all, to make fun of petty grandiosity by refusing to be grandiose oneself. (This Englishness, very different from provincial Anglophilia, was still manifest after he came home: his last published book was on snooker.)

And yet it seems to me that he achieved something larger as a novelist than his English contemporaries mostly did. Theirs was a small subject, the shrinking of England, its power, and its optimism and the range of its writing, and that shrinkage was present in their smallness of tone, and of subject. Although the last thing in the world Richler would have imagined himself as is any kind of Third World writer, still his real affinities are with the other Commonwealth wits — with Australians of the Clive James generation and particularly with the Caribbean V.S. Naipaul. (*A House For Mr. Biswas* could have been a Richler novel, in weather fifty or so degrees colder.) Richler had, by luck, a larger subject than his English contemporaries, and, though he would have eschewed anything as pretentious as a Big Theme, he had one: the transformation of a post-colonial culture in a post-modern age, the comedy of emergence from a cultural cringe at the price of vulgarity in cultural assertion. It was not exactly the usual Canadian subject — survival, the play between the vast nature and minor signs of human persistence — but, in its urban-Jewish specificity, in some ways more truly universal.

Provincial narrowness was what he hated; but provincial narrowness was also the source of his comedy, particularly the comedy of how, by insisting on being neither provincial nor narrow, one was usually both. Where the American Jewish novelists were American first of all — "I am an American, Chicago born" is how Augie March greets us — and could lay claim to a whole literature (to Melville and Whitman as much as to their parents' jokes), Richler, like the Australian and Caribbean writers, had first to show that what he was writing about existed at all. He had to show that a language and lore existed before he could attach it to anyone else's tradition.

The satiric, deprecatory tone that he shared with Amis and Braine was therefore allied in his writing to a larger ambition — he had to write about a city (and country) that didn't quite know it was one, about the manners of a tribe who hadn't been told they had them. The urge to inventory a reality that everyone else thought was merely a dependency, one that didn't really count, is present everywhere in his novels, and it creates an unwilled expansiveness, an appetite for setting down experience, that feels less claustrophobic than the worlds of his English contemporaries. It was the same tone, but they were describing a world shrinking inward. He was describing one pushing out.

Richler had to give form to a world before he could make fun of it, and the two ambitions were so closely allied — the affectionate urge to inventory a city and tribe already vanishing as he wrote of them; the satiric urge to mock their narrowness and pretensions — that they became indistinguishable. Reading *Duddy* or *St. Urbain's Horseman* one feels not that "tender affection," which small-town novelists are supposed to have for their subjects, but something better, a knowledge so deep and uncensored that it becomes a kind of love. It was having the two things at once — a relish for absurdity, a need to get this style of absurdity exactly right — that made his later fiction, and particularly his masterpiece, *Solomon Gursky Was Here*, resonate in ways usually unavailable to narrowly satiric fiction. *Solomon Gursky*, in which the renegade "Bronfman" Montreal Jew is also mythologized as a Native American trickster (so that the life of the little immigrants clinging to the narrow southern shelf of cities is magically tied to the mysteries of vast tundra above), is what makes the book, for this reader, the closest thing we have to a truly great Canadian novel.

Richler was no small writer, no secondary figure. But he was not a cloistered artist either. Like Naipaul and James he wrote, of necessity, a lot of journalism. Some of it was written as a way to make money, the most honourable of writerly reasons. But most of it he took dead seriously, because it was a way of articulating clearly themes that his scruples as an artist would only allow him to dramatize, ambiguously, in his novels. His journalism was good-humoured, witty, acerbic, and above all *observant*. He had no mind for theory, but he had an eye for folly as good as any writer of his time, and he put it down, sometimes pitilessly.

He became famous — notorious, I suppose — for his attacks on Quebec nationalism and on the language laws that it brought with it. In retrospect, it is possible that, though he misunderstood his targets, they also misunderstood him. If, by upbringing and language, he did not know the French-Canadian world that surrounded his subjects as well as he might have, he recognized in their nationalism the same stubborn provincialism disguised as "pride" and "identity" that exasperated him in his St. Urbain Street past. The only times he went wrong were when he still saw them too narrowly through the lens of an exasperated Anglophone, rather than seeing how much they revealed the same pattern — of ethnic insecurity, grandiose over-assertion and provincialism — that he had charted so coolly in his own neighbourhood.

He was above all, and in everything he wrote, including his journalism, a real writer, not a show-off or time-server. He was not an artist who boasted of his sensitivities, but a writer, through and through, who hated everything pretentious and academic and fake in the literary world, yet who had an unshakeable reverence for literature. He believed in books, wanted to write one great one, and did. A provincial boy determined to live by writing, he became a cosmopolitan man who had. He loved his family, lived by his wits, and left behind a book that will last. It's hard to imagine anyone, in any city, doing more.

— *Adam Gopnik*

A Note about the Selection

In selecting the excerpts and arranging them for this book, the editor was guided by the material itself. The themes around which the parts have been constructed spring directly from the texts. Running through them, there can be discerned a rough trajectory that mirrors Richler's life. Certainly, everything starts in the Montreal of his youth. The expatriate years are both a stage in his life and a source of material for his writing. Even his keen interest in sports reflects life changes: baseball and hockey begin when he is small; fishing comes later. And so on. In general, in the arrangement of excerpts, an attempt has been made to show how the life and the writing reflect each other.

The fiction and nonfiction reflect each other too. When Richler is writing about either Montreal or family, whether in fiction or memoir, the voice is virtually the same. The overlap does not end there. Richler happily acknowledged that magazine assignments yielded useful material that he refashioned as art. So fiction and nonfiction, excerpts from novels, and chunks of magazine pieces are laid side by side in these pages in the hope that each will illuminate and enrich the other.

An attempt has been made to keep editorial intervention to a minimum. Where it might prove useful, a line or two has been inserted at the head of an excerpt to provide context. (The few footnotes are transcribed from the original works: none has been added by the editor.) Overall, the aim has been to let Richler speak for himself.

— *Jonathan Webb*

On Writing

Unanswerable questions still surface at parties.

"What kind of novels do you write?"

Legendary. Seminal. Filthy.

"Should I know your name?"

To which I usually reply, eyes modestly lowered, "Not necessarily," but, riding sufficient scotch, I become equally capable of a bellicose "Yes, if you're literate," after which my wife usually points out it is time to go home.

Strangers who accept without question a man who has put together a life dealing in pork-belly futures or manufacturing zippers demand to know *why you did it*. Such a weighty query begs for an appropriately pretentious answer. Something about artistic compulsions. Muses. Inspiration. But the truth is, everybody I knew in high school who wasn't going to be another Hank Greenberg or Barney Ross or Maurice "The Rocket" Richard was willing to settle for being a writer. As far as we could make out, Hemingway set his own hours. He seemed to go fishing whenever he felt like it. He was on first-name terms with Ingrid Bergman and Marlene Dietrich. It had to be a good life.

What I find more intriguing than why anybody became a writer is how some of the boys at school grew up to be caterers, or frozen-chicken-breast packagers, or distributors of plate-glass windows. When we were sitting on the stoop together and I was dreaming of diving out of my hotel window to swim across the Grand Canal like Byron, or drinking too much in Hollywood like Scott Fitzgerald, were they secretly pledged to catering the Great American Bar Mitzvah? Or freezing the most tasteless chicken breast? Or installing the ultimate plate-glass window? The boy who grew up to be the plate-glass window distributor, incidentally, is worth further mention. When a sufficient number of orders were not forthcoming, he took to creating instant demand, speeding around Montreal in the early-morning hours and heaving bricks through his latest installations. Alas, his initiative earned him three years in the slammer.

The boys I grew up with are not taken in by my published novels.

"I remember you at school."

"You were short for your age."

"I had better-looking girls."

"You were nothing."

"I can't understand why anybody would pay any attention to you now."

The first writers I warmed to were George Alfred Henty, H. G. Wells, O. Henry and, for the hot stuff, Tiffany Thayer. I was only fourteen when I acquired a pipe and a lined notebook and began to write short stories that unfailingly began in a British club as Sir Bertram Digby-Howard reminisced with a chum.

"I say, Sir Archibald, do you believe in ghosts?"

"By Jove, no, old boy."

"Then let me acquaint you with what happened to me one night at Raffles Hotel. The clock had just struck twelve when…."

In another story, I tried my first experiment with irony. An anti-Semitic bully is saved from drowning by a total stranger.

"I owe you my life," the bully says, "but I don't even know your name."

"My name," the stranger reveals in the last sentence of the story, "is Isadore Lipschitz. But you can call me Izzy."

Looking back, I fear that to begin with I did not so much want to write as to be a writer, on first-name terms, if not with Ingrid Bergman, then at least with Ruth Roman. When I drifted into the Algonquin Hotel, out-of-towners would gawk, nudging each other. "Look, it's him!"

Nowadays, when I read reviews of my work, I secretly believe the worst, but at the time it never occurred to me that I might fail.

Fortunately, every neophyte writer is armoured with arrogance. So, however, is many an overlooked middle-aged writer.

We have read a good deal in literary journals about the unjustly neglected novelist, but seldom a word about the many who are justly neglected, the scratch players, brandishing their little distinctions (a translation into Icelandic, a rave review in the *University of British Columbia Alumni News*), so I would like to say something about Harry. Harry and I were in Paris together in the early fifties, two happy scribblers, equally awash in rejection slips, yet both confident that everything was possible. Over the years, however, I won a certain recognition. He didn't. Mind you, his novels are still published, if only in Canada, where he sells maybe 1,500 copies and in one interview after another explains, "Nothing would make me set my novels in Chicago or New York in order to pursue whorish best-sellerdom. I'm proud to be a Canadian."

As impoverished in his fifties as we once were in Paris, he subsists on literary scraps: a Canada Council reading tour in the Northwest Territories, a term as literary resource person at an obscure Nova Scotia college, putting together an anthology of Canadian writing for Radio Finland. He is also a constant rebuke to me.

"Do you think Kafka or Martin Buber would have published in *Playboy?*"

"Certainly not."

"Then how come I saw your name in the June issue right under the cover girl's left nipple?"

Or after the publication of *Joshua Then and Now*: "You, you still call yourself an artist, and you let *People* take your picture."

To which I could at least counter, "Don't tell me you read *People* now?"

"Kitsch enriches my work."

I am always careful to take Harry to a second-rate restaurant so as not to flaunt my bourgeois affluence. I drink beer. I don't order cognac or pay with my credit card. I feed him all the bad things that have happened to me recently. But in the end he nabs me.

"There is a magazine in Bulgaria doing a special Canadian issue. The editor is a great admirer of mine. If you let me have a story,

I'll send it to him. But they only pay $1.75 a page, so you probably aren't interested."

"Of course I'm interested. I'll send you something as soon as I get home."

"*You own it!*"

"What?"

"The mansion in Westmount."

"It's not a mansion, and there's a hell of a big mortgage on it."

In the end, he will leave me a copy of his latest novel, with xeroxed endorsements by various professors.

"With your connections, maybe you can place it for me in New York. I haven't got your knack for marketing myself."

In 1951, at the age of nineteen, I dropped out of college and sailed for England on the *Franconia*. After two weeks in London, I moved on to Paris. Devoured Malraux, Hemingway, Céline, Sartre, Camus. Determined to be a real literary man, I was scornful of my own natural material, St. Urbain Street, considering it far too commonplace for fiction. I mean, I *knew* people like that. I didn't want to *write* about them. I wanted to write like Malraux or Hemingway and, unfortunately, that's exactly what I tried in my first novel, *The Acrobats*, which I published three years later and have cunningly kept out of print ever since. The British publisher, André Deutsch, paid me an advance of £100 and Putnam's forked out $750 for the American rights. When I applied for a new passport, I no longer described myself as "STUDENT," but under "occupation" printed "WRITER," though to myself I added "of sorts." I had to force two more novels through the hothouse before I found my own voice and wrote *The Apprenticeship of Duddy Kravitz*, for which the pillars of Montreal's Jewish community have never forgiven me.

"Why," I was once asked, "couldn't you have given the boy an Italian name?"

"Why," I was asked after I had lectured at a suburban synagogue, "does everybody adore Sholem Aleichem, but hate your guts?"

For all that, the novel was hardly noticed when it appeared. It sold fewer than 1,000 copies in Canada, maybe 1,200 in the United States and something like 3,000 in England. But twenty-one years later, after I published *Joshua Then and Now*, the critic who blasted it in

The New York Review of Books redeemed himself to me by observing in passing that *Duddy Kravitz* was a comic classic.

Graham Greene once said that, so far as critics were concerned, you were a young writer until you were forty and thereafter a writer who had never fulfilled his early promise. But in this game, he might have added, there is also nothing like patience.

I'm fifty-nine years old now. Only yesterday, it seems, my tonsils were plucked out on a dining-room table, but now the trendy operation for my age group is open-heart surgery. The triple bypass. An ordeal, I suspect, that is not followed by mounds of ice cream consumed on the doctor's orders. The sports and film stars of my adolescence, once indestructible, are now either gone (Peter Reiser, Rita Hayworth) or are wheeled out for television commercials promoting Preparation H, Grecian Formula, or Polident. If you're an actor or an athlete, given the right agent, even the body's betrayals can be turned to a profit. The residual's residuals.

I belong to a generation that sprang to adolescence during World War II. Too young to fight, we were forever shaped by the war all the same. The headlines. The battles. The casualties. We could never wear the flag as underwear or respect those who did. Or, come to think of it, be surprised that many who did are today's stockbrokers and supply-side economists. I can remember, and bore your children and mine, with tales of the good old days, when chicken tasted of something more than sawdust, actors didn't run for high office, hockey was a winter sport, nobody had ever heard of acid rain, doctors made house calls, mail was delivered, department stores would accept cash.

We were, and remain by today's standards, a rather inhibited bunch. A friend of mine, far too proper to walk into a porn movie house to watch *Deep Throat* or *Swedish Fly Girls*, told me that he had recently stayed at a hotel in Toronto that offered on Channel C a decidedly saucy film beginning at 11 p.m. But to have it appear on his television set, he had to dial a number and provide his name and room number. "I picked up the phone. I was about to do it. Then I hung up. I was sure if I requested the film, it would be my mother on the other end of the line. *'Bobby, whatever are you up to?'*"

After all these years, writing has become a habit. I no longer question why I do it any more than a welder wonders why he turns up at the shop every morning. Which is to say, of course we all endure our bad days, but we do get on with it. I wouldn't know what to do with myself until 4 p.m., my usual quitting time, if I couldn't sit down at my portable typewriter. Even so, I'm stuck with my original notion, which is to be an honest witness to my time, my place, and to write at least one novel that will last, that will make me remembered after death. So I'm compelled to keep trying.

Meanwhile, there are satisfactions. Fame, for instance. One year I had a letter from a university all the way out in Australia, inviting me to be writer-in-residence. But there was a problem. The invitation was addressed to Ms. Mordecai Richler. I wrote back saying I'd love to come but I just wouldn't know what to wear.

Another time, pulling into a Montreal parking lot, the car jockey began to wave me off, indicating the "FULL" sign, but then he looked at me more closely and smiled.

"Hey, I know you. I love your books."

Recognition at last.

"You're Farley Mowat, aren't you?"

"Damn right."

"Let me park your car for you, sir."

On my way back to Canada from Paris in 1953, I stopped off in London and left the manuscript of my first novel with an agent whose name had been passed to me by a poker-playing crony. After a couple of rejections, she placed it, and ever since, unpublished or disappointed writers have accused me of luxuriating in connections, an ever-broadening cabal made up of the right literary people. Their point is well taken. I have been to dinner with more than one influential critic. The trouble is, the critics I know, far from boosting a dinner companion, will bend over backward to prove their purity in print. Critics should be read but not seen.

Envy is not unknown among writers; there are jealousies, there are resentments. And I'm not immune. This year, I wouldn't lose any sleep if John Updike didn't win anything. I don't want to read any more about Norman Mailer's $4 million contract. But, on balance,

I think writers are a much-maligned group. I have never been to a dentist who did not fiercely denounce the last man to slip a filling into your mouth, but from my earliest days, I have benefited from the generosity of other writers. Beyond the cocktail-party sniping, there is a commitment to the craft, a tendency to help, in Norman Mailer's phrase, anybody who is trying to add an inch to the house.

All the same, I could do with less self-pity, less dollar-a-word complaining about the lonely craft and how hell is a blank sheet of paper. We weren't drafted, we volunteered. And even as I suspected in high school, you can set your own hours. You can go fishing when you feel like it. My father, a failed scrap dealer, worked a lot harder than I do without anything like the satisfactions. On bad days, it's good to remember that.

—*Broadsides,* "Hemingway Set His Own Hours," pp. 1–8

A shaded yellow light hung low over each
of the eight tables in the Royal Billiard
Room. Smoke, eight clouds for eight suns,
thickened under and around the bulbs. The
long and narrow room reeked of french fried
potatoes, the walls were heavy with soot.
Men watched the players from the benches
that flanked the walls.

PART I

ST. URBAIN
THEN AND NOW

Mordecai Richler was born in Montreal on January 27, 1931. His mother's father was Rabbi Judah Yudel Rosenberg, Montreal's chief Hasidic rabbi, a scholar and author. His father, the oldest of fourteen children, was the son of an Orthodox Jew who emigrated from Poland to Montreal where he established a junk business. The marriage between Lily Rosenberg and Moses Richler was arranged by their parents. They were not well matched: she was strong-willed and cultured; he was easygoing, his interests parochial. Under the stress of poverty brought on by the Depression, the marriage failed.

Their circumstances, when Mordecai was growing up, were dire, but the neighbourhood and community of which they were a part were well established, closely knit, and supportive. Mordecai, a lean, restless, and inquisitive youth, found it oppressive. He rebelled against it, first by refusing to observe the rituals of the Orthodox faith, and then by joining Habonim, a socialist Zionist organization. Later, after dropping out of Sir George Williams College — another rebellion — he would try to escape the Jewish ghetto altogether. But, as he explained in a CBC television documentary years later, "the further I got away from it, the closer I came to it." The street where he grew up, St. Urbain, and the streets around it became the territory he would claim for himself and explore in his novels, stories, and essays.

— J. W.

No matter how long I continue to live abroad, I do feel forever rooted in Montreal's St. Urbain Street. That was my time, my place, and I have elected myself to get it right.

— *Shovelling Trouble*, "Why I Write," p. 19

"Why do you want to go to university?" the student counselor asked me.

Without thinking, I replied, "I'm going to be a doctor, I suppose."

A doctor.

One St. Urbain Street day cribs and diapers were cruelly withdrawn and the next we were scrubbed and carted off to kindergarten. Though we didn't know it, we were already in pre-med school. School-starting age was six, but fiercely competitive mothers would drag protesting four-year-olds to the registration desk and say, "He's short for his age."

"Birth certificate, please?"

"Lost in a fire."

On St. Urbain Street, a head start was all. Our mothers read us stories from *Life* about pimply astigmatic fourteen-year-olds who had already graduated from Harvard or who were confounding the professors at MIT. Reading *Tip-Top Comics* or listening to *The Green Hornet* on the radio was as good as asking for a whack on the head, sometimes administered with a rolled-up copy of the *Canadian Jewish Eagle*, as if that in itself would be nourishing. We were not supposed to memorize baseball batting averages or dirty limericks. We were expected to improve our Word Power with the *Reader's Digest* and find inspiration in Paul de Kruif's medical biographies. If we didn't make doctors, we were supposed to at least squeeze into dentistry. School marks didn't count as much as rank. One wintry day I came home, nostrils clinging together and ears burning cold, proud of my report. "I came rank two, Maw."

"And who came rank one, may I ask?"

Mrs. Klinger's boy, alas. Already the phone was ringing. "Yes, yes," my mother said to Mrs. Klinger, "congratulations, and what does the eye doctor say about Riva, poor kid, to have a complex at her age, will they be able to straighten them…."

Parochial school was a mixed pleasure. The old, underpaid men who taught us Hebrew tended to be surly, impatient. Ear-twisters and knuckle-rappers. They didn't like children. But the girls who handled the English-language part of our studies were charming, bracingly modern, and concerned about our future. They told us about *El Campesino*, how John Steinbeck wrote the truth, and read Sacco's speech to the court aloud to us. If one of the younger, unmarried teachers started out the morning looking weary, we assured each other that she had done it the night before. Maybe with a soldier. Bareback.

From parochial school, I went on to a place I call Fletcher's Field High in the stories and memoirs that follow. Fletcher's Field High was under the jurisdiction of the Montreal Protestant School Board, but had a student body that was nevertheless almost a hundred per-cent Jewish. The school became something of a legend in our area. Everybody, it seemed, had passed through FFHS: Canada's most famous gambler. An atom bomb spy. Boys who went off to fight in the Spanish Civil War. Miracle-making doctors and silver-tongued lawyers. Boxers. Fighters for Israel. All of whom were instructed, as I was, to be staunch and bold, to play the man, and, above all, to

> Strive hard and work
> With your heart in the doing.
> Up play the game,
> As you learnt it at Fletcher's.

Again and again we led Quebec province in the junior matriculation results. This was galling to the communists among us, who held we were the same as everyone else, but to the many more who knew that for all seasons there was nothing like a Yiddish boy, it was an annual cause for celebration. Our class at FFHS, Room 41, was one of the few to boast a true Gentile, an authentic white Protestant. Yugoslavs and Bulgarians, who were as foxy as we were, their potato-filled mothers sitting just as rigid in their corsets at school concerts, fathers equally prone to natty straw hats and cursing in the mother tongue, did not count. Our very own WASP's name was Whelan, and he was no less than perfect. Actually blonde, with real blue eyes, and a tendency to sit with his mouth hanging open. A natural hockey player, a born first-baseman. Envious students came from other classrooms to look him over and put questions to him. Whelan, as was to be expected, was not excessively bright, but he gave Room 41 a certain tone, some badly needed glamour, and in order to keep him with us as we progressed from grade to grade, we wrote essays for him and slipped him answers at examination time. We were enormously proud of Whelan.

Among our young schoolmasters, most of them returned war veterans, there were a number of truly dedicated men as well as some sour and brutish ones, like Shaw, who strapped twelve of us one afternoon, ten on each hand, because we wouldn't say who had farted while his back was turned. The foibles of older teachers were well known to us, because so many aunts, uncles, cousins, and elder brothers had preceded us at FFHS. There was, for instance, one master who initiated first-year students with a standing joke: "Do you know how the Jews make an 's'?"

"No, Sir."

Then he would make an "s" on the blackboard and draw two strokes through it. The dollar sign.

Among us, at FFHS, were future leaders of the community. Progressive parents. Reform-minded aldermen. Antifallout enthusiasts. Collectors of early French Canadian furniture. Boys who would actually grow up to be doctors and lecture on early cancer warnings to ladies' clubs. Girls who would appear in the social pages of the

Montreal *Star*, sponsoring concerts in aid of retarded children (regardless of race, colour, or creed) and luncheon hour fashion shows, proceeds to the Hebrew University. Lawyers. Notaries. Professors. And marvelously with-it rabbis, who could not only quote Rabbi Akiba but could also get a kick out of a hockey game. But at the time who would have known that such slouchy, aggressive girls, their very brassieres filled with bluff, would grow up to look so serene, such honeys, seeking apotheosis at the Saidye Bronfman Cultural Centre, posing on curving marble stairwells in their bouffant hairstyles and strapless gowns? Or that such nervy boys, each one a hustler, would mature into men who were so damn pleased with what this world has to offer, epiphanous, radiating self-confidence at the curling or country club, at ease even with potbellies spilling over their Bermuda shorts? Who would have guessed?

Not me.

Looking back on those raw formative years at FFHS, I must say we were not a promising or engaging bunch. We were scruffy and spiteful, with an eye on the main chance. So I can forgive everybody but the idiot, personally unknown to me, who compiled our criminally dull English reader of prose and poetry. Nothing could have been calculated to make us hate literature more unless it was being ordered, as a punishment, to write *Ode to the West Wind* twenty-five times. And we suffered that too.

Graduation from FFHS meant jobs for most of us, McGill for the anointed few, and the end of an all but self-contained world made up of five streets: Clark, St. Urbain, Waverly, Esplanade, and Jeanne Mance, bounded by The Main, on one side, and Park Avenue, on the other.

—*Notes on an Endangered Species,* "Going Home," pp. 179–83

The March of the Fletcher's Cadets

Lance Corporal Boxenbaum led with a bang bang bang on his big white drum and Litvak tripped Cohen, Pinsky blew on his bugle, and the Fletcher's Cadets wheeled left, reet, left, reet, out of Fletcher's Field, led by their Commander-in-chief, that snappy five-footer W. E. James (that's 'Jew' spelt backwards, as he told each new gym class). Left, reet, left, reet, powdery snow crunching underfoot, Ginsburg out of step once more and Hornstein unable to beat his drum right because of the ten-on-each Mr. Coldwell had applied before the parade. Turning smartly right down Esplanade Avenue they were at once joined and embarrassed on either side by a following of younger brothers on sleighs, little sisters with running noses, and grinning delivery boys stopping to make snowballs.

"Hey, look out there, General Montgomery, here comes your mother to blow your nose."

"Lefty! Hey, Lefty! Maw says you gotta come right home to sift the ashes after the parade. No playing pool she says. She's afraid the pipes will burst."

Tara-boom, tara-*boom*, tara-BOOM-BOOM-BOOM, past the Jewish Old People's Home where on the balcony above, bedecked with shawls and rugs, a stain of yellowing expressionless faces, women with little beards and men with sucked-in mouths, fussy nurses with thick legs and grandfathers whose sons had little time, a shrunken little woman who had survived a pogrom and two husbands and three strokes, and two followers of Rabbi Brott the Miracle Maker, watched squinting against the fierce wintry sun.

"Jewish children in uniform?"

"Why not?"

"It's not nice. For a Jewish boy a uniform is not so nice."

Skinny, lumpy-faced Boxenbaum took it out on the big white drum, and Sergeant Grepsy Segal, who could burp or break wind at will, sang,

> BULLSHIT, that's all the band could play,
> BULLSHIT, it makes the grass grow green.

Mendelsohn hopped to get back into step and Archie Rosen, the FFHS Cadet Corps Quartermaster, who sold dyed uniforms at $8.00 each, told Naturman the one about the rabbi and the priest and the bunch of grapes. "Fun-ny," Naturman said. Commander-in-chief W. E. James, straight as a ramrod, veteran of the Somme, a swagger stick held tight in his hand, his royal blue uniform pressed to a cutting edge and his brass buttons polished perfect, felt a lump in his throat as the corps bugles blowing approached the red brick armory of the Canadian Grenadier Guards. "Eyes...RIGHT," he called, saluting stiffly.

Duddy Kravitz like the rest turned to salute the Union Jack, and the pursuing gang of kid brothers and sisters took up the chant,

> Here come the Fletcher's Cadets,
> smoking cigarettes,
> the cigarettes are lousy
> and so are the Fletcher's Cadets.

Crunch, crunch, crunch-crunch-crunch, over the powdery snow ears near frozen stiff the FFHS Cadet Corps marched past the Jewish Library, where a poster announced,

Wednesday Night
ON BEING A JEWISH POET
IN MONTREAL WEST
A Talk by H. I. Zimmerman, B.A.
Refreshments

and smack over the spot where in 1933 a car with a Michigan license plate had machine-gunned to death the Boy Wonder's uncle. They stopped in front of the YMHA to mark time while the driver of a KIK KOLA truck that had slid into a No. 97 streetcar began to fight with the conductor.

"Hip, hip," W. E. James called. "*HUP-HIP-HIP.*"

A bunch of YMHA boys came out to watch.

"There's Arnie. Hey, Arnie! Where's your gun? Wha'?"

"Hey, Sir! Mr. James! You know what you can do with that stick?"

"Boxenbaum. Hey! You'll get a rupture if you carry that drum any further."

"Hip, hip," W. E. James called. "HIP-HIP-HIP."

Geiger blew on his bugle and Sivak goosed Kravitz. A snowball knocked off Sergeant Heller's cap, Pinsky caught a frozen horse bun on the cheek, and Mel Brucker lowered his eyes when they passed his father's store. Monstrous icicles ran from the broken second floor windows of his home into the muck of stiff burnt dry goods and charred wood below. The fire had happened last night. Mel had expected it because that afternoon his father had said cheerfully, "You're sleeping at grandmaw's tonight," and each time Mel and his brother were asked to sleep at grandmaw's it meant another fire, another store.

"Hip. Hip. Hip, hip, hip."

To the right Boxenbaum's father and another picketer walked up and down blowing on their hands before the Nu-Oxford Shoe Factory, and to the left there was Harry's War Assets Store with a sign outside that read, IF YOU HAVEN'T GOT TIME TO DROP IN — SMILE WHEN YOU WALK PAST. Tara-boom, tara-*boom*, tara-BOOM-BOOM-BOOM, past the Hollywood Barbershop where they removed blackheads for 50¢, around the corner of Clark where Charna Felder lived, the FFHS Cadet Corps came crunch-crunch-crunch. Tansky started on his drum, Rubin dropped an icicle down Mort Heimer's back, and the cadets wheeled left, reet, left, reet, into St. Urbain Street. A gathering of old grads and slackers stepped out of the Laurier Billiard Hall, attracted by the martial music.

"Hey, Sir. Mr. James! Is it true you were a pastry cook in the first war?"

"We hear you were wounded grating latkas."

"There's Stanley. Hey, Stan! Jeez, he's an officer or something. Stan! It's OK about Friday night but Rita says Irv's too short for her. Can you bring Syd instead? Stan! STAN?"

Over the intersection where Gordie Wiser had burned the Union Jack after many others had trampled and spit on it the day Ernest Bevin announced his Palestine policy, past the house where the Boy

A Victory Day parade in Fletcher's Field, 1945.

Wonder had been born, stopping to mark time at the corner where their fathers and elder brothers armed with baseball bats had fought the frogs during the conscription riots, the boys came marching. A little slower, though, Boxenbaum puffing as he pounded his drum and thirteen or thirty-five others feeling the frost in their toes. The sun went, darkness came quick as a traffic-light change, and the snow began to gleam purple. Tansky felt an ache in his stomach as they slogged past his house and Captain Bercovitch remembered there'd be boiled beef and potatoes for supper but he'd have to pick up the laundry first.

"Hip. HIP. Hip, hip, hip."

To the right the AZA clubhouse and to the left the poky Polish synagogue where old man Zabitsky searched the black windy street and saw the cadets coming towards him.

"Label. Label, come here."

"I can't, zeyda, it's a parade."

"A parade. *Narishkeit*. We're short one man for prayers."

"But zeyda, please."

"No buts, no please. Rosenberg has to say kaddish."

Led by the arm, drum and all, Lionel Zabitsky was pulled from the parade.

"Hey, Sir. A casualty."

"Chic-*ken!*"

Past Moe's warmly lit Cigar Store where you could get a lean on rye for 15¢ and three more cadets defected. Pinsky blew his bugle faint-heartedly and Boxenbaum gave the drum a little bang. Wheeling right and back again up Clark Street five more cadets disappeared into the darkness.

"Hip. Hip. HIP, HIP, HIP."

One of the deserters ran into his father, who was on his way home from work.

"Would you like a hot dog and a Coke before we go home?"

"Sure."

"OK, but you mustn't say anything to Maw."

Together they watched the out-of-step FFHS Cadet Corps fade under the just starting fall of big lazy snowflakes.

"It's too cold for a parade. You kids could catch pneumonia out in this weather without scarves or rubbers."

"Mr. James says that in the first world war sometimes they'd march for thirty miles without stop through rain and mud that was knee-deep."

"Is that what I pay school fees for?"

— *The Apprenticeship of Duddy Kravitz,* pp. 41–45

BAD NEWS. They're closing Baron Byng High School. Our Baron Byng. I speak of a legendary Montreal school, founded in 1921, that resembles nothing so much as a Victorian workhouse. Architecturally, the loss will be minimal (the building's a blight), but emotionally…ah, that's something else. If the Battle of Waterloo was won on the playing fields of Eton, then the character of Montreal's diminishing Jewish community was hammered into shape in the smelly classrooms of that big brown brick building.

> Themistocles, Thermopylae,
>   the Peloponnesian War,
> X^2, Y^2, H_2SO_4,
>   One, two, three, four,
> Who are we for?
>   Byng! Byng! Byng!

Today's Jewish community in Montreal is a group riddled with apprehension. Nobody is signing a long lease, every family has its own contingency plans. Once, however, many of us were at BBHS together. Everything possible. September 1944. Even as our elder brothers and cousins were thrusting into Holland, with the Canadian army battling on the Hitler Line, we stood in rows in the BBHS gym, raw and pimply, but shiny trousers freshly pressed. New boys we were. Rambunctious thirteen-year-olds, charged with hope. We were told, "I suppose most of you expect to go on to McGill University four years from now. Well, you will have to work hard. McGill entrance calls for a sixty-five percent average in the matriculations, but Jewish boys seeking admission will require seventy-five percent."

Baron Byng was being shut down because its student body, now largely Greek in origin, numbered only 405, but once those classrooms reverberated with the ambition of 1,000 strivers. Scrappy, driving boys and girls who led the province of Quebec in matriculation results year after year.

Baron Byng lies right out there on St. Urbain Street in what used to be the heart of Montreal's swirling Jewish quarter. In my day, St. Urbain Street was the lowest rung on a ladder we were all hot to climb. No, St. Urbain wasn't the lowest rung, for one street below came Clark, where they had no lane and had to plunk their garbage out on the street. Parked right before the front door. Immediately below Clark there came the fabled Main or, more properly, Boulevard St. Laurent. Levitt's delicatessen. Moishe's steak house. Richstone's bakery. The editorial offices of the *Canadian Jewish Eagle*. The

Canada, where you could take in three movies for a quarter, but sometimes felt grey squishy things nibbling at your ankles. The Roxy and the Crystal Palace, where they showed only two movies, but offered a live show as well. A forlorn parade of pulpy strippers. "Put on your glasses, boys," the MC would say, "for here come the Hubba-Hubba Girls." It was to The Main we repaired for zoot trousers, ducktail haircuts, and free auto parts calendars that showed leggy girls, their skirts blown high by the wind. If the calendar was vintage, the real stuff, you could just make out the girl's nipples *straining against her blouse*, as they wrote in the best stories that appeared in *True Detective*.

Our world was largely composed of the five streets that ran between Park Avenue and The Main: Jeanne Mance, Esplanade, Waverly, St. Urbain, and Clark. Standing tippy-toe on St. Urbain's next-to-the-bottom rung, you could just peer over Park Avenue —

A section of The Main, as it looked in 1950.

Park Avenue, the dividing line — into blessed Outremont, with its tree-lined streets and parks and skating rinks and (oh my God) furnished basements. Outremont, where the girls didn't wear shiny discount dresses and gaudy shell necklaces, but frocks that had been bought retail and pearls, yes, strands of pearls that had not been pilfered from Kresge's grab-all counter, but paid for at Birks maybe. Outremont fathers, in their three-piece suits and natty fedoras, were in property or sweaters or insurance or (the coming thing) plastics. They were learning how to golf. They thought nothing of driving down to New York to "take in the shows" or of renting a summer cottage on the lakeside in Ste-Agathe-des-Monts. For the children's sake, they bought sets of *The Book of Knowledge*, sheltering them in a prominently displayed glass-doored bookcase. *King's Row* or *Forever Amber*, on the other hand, was kept in the bottom desk drawer. Locked.

Outremont, our heart's desire, was amazing. Kids our own age there didn't hang out at the corner cigar store or poolroom, they had their very own quarters. *Basement playrooms, Ping-Pong tables.* There were heated towel racks in the bathrooms. In each kitchen, a Mixmaster. No icebox, but a refrigerator. I had a school friend up there whose mother wore a *pince-nez*, and had hired a maid to answer the door, and even the telephone.

We would ring the house again and again, crowding round the receiver, stifling giggles, if only to hear the maid chirp, "This is the Feigelbaum residence."

But on St. Urbain, our fathers worked as cutters or pressers or scrap dealers and drifted into cold-water flats, sitting down to supper in their freckled Penman's long winter underwear, clipping their nails at the table. Mothers organized bazaars, proceeds for the Jewish National Fund, and jockeyed for position on the ladies' auxiliary of the Talmud Torah or the Folkshule, both parochial schools. Visiting aunts charged into the parlour, armed with raffle books, ten cents a ticket. Win an RCA Victor radio. Win a three-volume *History of the Jews*, slipcover case included. The ladies had a favourite record. It was Jan Peerce, one of ours, singing "The Bluebird of Happiness." "The poet with his pen/ The peasant with his plow/ It's all the same somehow."

We preferred Artie Shaw's "Stardust," which gave us a chance to dance close, or any boogie-woogie, an opportunity to strut. After supper, I had to sift the ashes before stoking the furnace for the night, emerging prematurely grey from the shed. I attended parochial school (studying English, modern Hebrew, and French), and after classes, three afternoons a week, I knuckled down to the Talmud with Mr. Yalofsky's class in the back room of the Young Israel Synagogue.

— If a man tumbles off the roof of an eight-story building and four stories down another man sticks a sword out of the window and stabs him, is that second man guilty of murder? Or not?

— Rabbi Menasha asks, did he fall or was he pushed off the roof?

— Rabbi Yedhua asks, was he already dead of heart failure before he was stabbed?

— Were the two men related?

— Enemies?

— Friends?

— Was the sword already sticking out of the window or was it thrust into the falling body?

— Would the man have died from the fall in any event?

Who cared? Concealed on our laps, below the table, at the risk of having our ears twisted by Mr. Yalofsky, was the *Herald*, opened at the sports pages. What concerned us, children of the new world, was would the Punch Line (Maurice "the Rocket" Richard, Elmer Lach, Toe Blake) finish one-two-three in the scoring race, and would the Canadiens thrash the dreaded Toronto Maple Leafs in the Stanley Cup Finals?

Our parents were counting on us — a scruffy lot, but, for all that, the first Canadian-born generation — to elbow our way into McGill, not so much Cardinal Newman's notion of a university as the block and tackle that would hoist the family into blessed Outremont. Many of us, but certainly not all, made it not only into Outremont, which turned out to be no more than a way station, but into the once *judenfrei* Town of Mount Royal, and even Westmount. *Above the Boulevard.*

Bliss, yes, but at a price.

En route, Schneider was anglicized to Taylor; Putterschnit was born again Patterson; Krashinsky, Kane. Children were no longer named Hershl or Muttel or Malke or Zippora, but, instead, Stuart, Byron, Melinda, and Vanessa. Rather than play jacks under a winding outside staircase after school, the girls in their trainer bras from New York, New York, were driven to the nose-job doctor and ballet class and the ortho-dontist in Mommy's Mercedes. The boys, instead of delivering for the drugstore after classes, saving up for their very own CCM bike, took ten-nis lessons, which would help them to meet the right people.

And then (surprise, surprise) suddenly the old neighbourhood, *the starting line*, became modish and some of the children, the ungrateful ones, the know-it-alls, moved back into those yucky moldering cold-water flats on St. Urbain, nudging out the new tenants: Greeks, Italians, Portuguese. And there, on St. Urbain, where it was whispered that they smoked pot and didn't even remove their Frye boots to screw on those filthy sheets, they filled the front windows not with rubber plants of the old days, but with protest posters. Those play-poor kids in designer jeans were against nukes, acid rain, and herpes, and for organically grown, good multiple orgasms, and the Parti Québécois.

The Parti Québécois?

"You exploited the French," they lectured grandfathers who used to eke out a living bent over a sewing machine, fathers who remem-bered flying into street battles against the followers of Adrian Arcand, armed with lengths of lead pipe.

"You've got to learn to identify with the real Québécois," they argued.

"What, at my age, I should acquire a taste for Mae Wests or sugar pie or french fries soaked in vinegar?"

"That's a racist remark."

"Listen, kid, they don't have to fast with me on Yom Kippur, I don't need to march in the St. Jean Baptiste parade."

Red-letter days on St. Urbain.

Sent to Jack and Moe's barbershop, corner of Park Avenue and Laurier, for my monthly haircut, a quarter clutched in my hand, I had grown accustomed to the humiliation of waiting for Moe to slide the board over the barber chair's arms, which raised me high enough to be shorn. But this day of glory, Moe merely jerked his head at me and snarled, "Siddown." There was no board. I was now tall enough to sit in the actual chair. On the St. Urbain Street standard, my manhood had been certified. From this day forward anything was possible.

Another day, at Baron Byng High School, I came of political age.

Ramsay MacDonald's number-one son Malcolm, the British colonial secretary, came to address us in the gym, but those of us who were members of the Labour Zionist Movement absolutely refused to stand up to sing "God Save the King." We greeted MacDonald with hostile silence. Why, that bastard had cut off immigration to Palestine. Leaking tubs overflowing with emaciated concentration-camp survivors were being turned back or led to Cyprus.

On St. Urbain, we were either very observant Orthodox Jews, dedicated Labour Zionists, or red-hot communists. There were a few suspected homosexuals in the neighbourhood, that is to say, young men who read poetry and smoked cork-tipped cigarettes; there was at least one professional hooker that I knew of; but nobody, certainly, who would admit to being a member of the Conservative Party.

Communist conundrums on St. Urbain were sometimes resolved in a peculiar fashion.

A cousin of mine, then a communist firebrand but now a computer consultant, canvassed votes door-to-door for Labour–Progressive Party MP Fred Rose. Standing on one supposedly communist doorstep, expounding on Marx and Engels, the worker's sorry plight in Montreal, he was cut short by the irate housewife. "What you say may be true," she allowed, "but this time I don't vote for him, you can count on it."

"Why?"

"When his niece got married last April, we were invited to the ceremony but not to the dinner. The hell with him."

In my last year at Baron Byng High School, I worked nights in a Park Avenue bowling alley, spotting pins. A year later, enrolled at Sir George Williams College, I found work reporting on college events for the *Montreal Herald* on space rates. The bowling alley paid me three cents a line, the *Herald* only two, but I chucked being a pin boy

Richler (second row, centre photo) was president of his graduating class.

and stuck with the *Herald*, revealing, I think, a precocious dedication to letters no matter what the cost.

St. Urbain.

Like many another old boy of my generation, I still wander down there on occasion, tramping through the lanes where we once played hockey — lanes still thick with garbage and abandoned mattresses bleeding stuffing. I make the obligatory stop at the Bagel Factory on St. Viateur near Park Avenue. In deference to the French Language Charter, Bill 101, it is now called La Maison du Bagel, Boulangerie. The YMHA, on Mount Royal, where we used to box, hoping to qualify for the Golden Gloves, has become the Pavillon Mont-Royal of the Université de Montréal. My old parochial school, the Talmud Torah, where we once stumbled over Hebrew grammar, has happily maintained a connection of sorts with Zion. It is now École Primaire Nazareth. Only a block away, on Laurier, the Stuart

Biscuit Company, where we used to be able to buy a bag of broken biscuits for two cents, is still there. But immediately across the street, my father's favourite old cigar & soda, Schacter's, has become an overpriced antique shop, haunted — I like to think — by the ghosts of gin rummy games past. Laurier, above Park Avenue, is no longer a tacky street of bicycle and auto-parts shops. It has been transmogrified into a street of elegant restaurants, boutiques, fine-food shops, and bookstores. My God, my God, these days, only two blocks away from hot bagel heaven and Mehadrin's Marché de Viande Kosher, you can feast on hot croissants and espresso.

Jack and Moe's barbershop, where you could once also lay down two bucks on a horse, has been displaced by a more reliable investment house, a branch of the Banque Nationale de Grèce. The Young Israel Synagogue is no longer on Park Avenue. The Regent Theatre — where I sat through at least four double features in the balcony before I dared slip my arm (slowly, slowly) around Riva Tannenbaum's bony shoulders, my heart thumping as I actually kissed her cheek in the dark — has, given such a start, slid into undreamed-of depravity. It has become le Beaver, where you can now catch HOT LEGS, "The Ups and Downs of the Stocking and Garter Industry Fully Exposed!" The Rialto, on the corner of Bernard, has also become a porn palace, this one showing the hot stuff in Greek. Indeed, this familiar chunk of Park Avenue, a street where our mothers used to comparison-shop for odd cups and saucers an avenue where the nearest you could come to sin was to flip hastily through the latest *Esquire* at the corner newsstand, searching for the Vargas girl — is now totally disreputable. Where once it was a scandal for a neighbourhood girl to be seen out for a stroll, wearing a tight sweater, acknowledging what she had there, you can now drop into SECRET SUPER SEXE, *danseuses nues*, as well as EXPO SEXE, both establishments serving hamburgers for lunch. To go with, as they say. But for all that, Park Avenue is still a street of Hasidic rabbis and their progeny. Immediately around the corner from Park Avenue, on Jeanne Mance, the two-fisted followers of the Satmar rabbi are rooted, and also in the neighbourhood there are still many adherents of the

Lubavitcher rabbi. Boys, wearing skullcaps and long sidecurls, who gather together to sing:

> "We only eat a kosher diet,
> Nonkosher food we'd never try it.
> To be healthy Jews is our main goal
> Nonkosher food is harmful for body and soul."

Nobody who was raised on St. Urbain ventures into the old neighbourhood without stopping for a special at Wilensky's, corner of Clark and Fairmount. A special, I should point out, is made up of cuts of different kinds of salami, grilled in a delicious roll. Traditionally, it is washed down with a nonvintage cherry Coke, mixed at the fountain.

Wilensky's, which has been serving the neighbourhood since 1931, is now presided over by Moe, son of the original proprietor. During World War II days, we gathered at the soda fountain for heated political disputes. Should the Allies OPEN UP A SECOND FRONT NOW, relieving pressure on the hard-pressed Russians but risking the life of many a St. Urbain urchin who had enlisted?

—*Home Sweet Home*, "St. Urbain Street Then and Now," pp. 106–14

TANSKY'S BEAT-UP brown phone booth was an institution in our neighbourhood. Many who didn't have phones of their own used it to summon the doctor. "I'd rather pay a nickel here than be indebted to that cockroach downstairs for the rest of my life." Others needed the booth if they had a surreptitious little deal to transact or if it was the Sabbath and they couldn't use their own phones because they had a father from the stone ages. If you had a party line you didn't dare use the phone in your own house to call the free loan society or the exterminator. Boys who wanted privacy used the phone to call their girlfriends, though the regulars were particularly hard on them.

Between two and four in the afternoon the horse players held a monopoly on the phone. One of them, Sonny Markowitz, got an incoming call daily at three. Nat always took it for him. "Good afternoon," he'd say, "Morrow Real Estate. Mr. Morrow. One moment, please."

Markowitz would grab the receiver, his manner breathless. "Glad you called, honey. But I've got an important client with me right now. Yes, doll. You bet. Soon as I can. *Hasta la vista.*"

Anxious callers had long ago picked the paint off one wall of the booth. Others had scratched obscenities into the exposed zinc. Somebody who had been unable to get a date with Molly had used a key to cut MOLLY BANGS into the wall. Underneath, Manny had written ME TOO, adding his phone number. Doodles tended toward the expansively pornographic, they were boastful too, and most of the graffiti was obvious. KILROY WAS HERE. OPEN UP A SECOND FRONT. PERLMAN'S A SHVANTZ.

After each fight with Joey, Sadie swept in sobbing, hysterical, her housecoat fluttering. She never bothered to lower her voice. "It's happened again, Maw. No, he wasn't wearing anything. He wouldn't. Sure I told him what the doctor said. *I told him.* He said what are you, the B'nai Jacob Synagogue, I can't come in without wearing a hat? How do I know? I'm telling you, Maw, he's a beast, I want to come home to you. *That's not true.* I couldn't stop him if I wanted to. Yes, I washed before Seymour. A lot of good it does. All right, Maw. I'll tell him."

Sugarman never shuffled into Tansky's without first trying the slot in the booth to see if anyone had left a nickel behind. The regulars seldom paid for a call. They would dial their homes or businesses, ring twice, hang up, and wait for the return call.

Tansky's was not the only store of its sort on St. Urbain. Immediately across the street was Myerson's.

Myerson had put in cushions for the card players, he sold some items cheaper than Tansky, but he was considered to be a sour type, a regular snake, and so he did not do too well. He had his regulars, it's true, and there was some drifting to and fro between the stores out of pique, but if a trucker or a peddler stopped at Myerson's it was an accident.

Myerson had a tendency to stand outside, sweeping up with vicious strokes, and hollering at the men as they filed into Tansky's. "Hey, why don't you come over here for once? I won't bite you. Blood poisoning I don't need."

Myerson's rage fed on the refugees who began to settle on St. Urbain during the war years. "If they come in it's for a street direction," he'd say, "or if it's for a Coke they want a dozen glasses with." He wasn't kind to kids. "You know what you are," he was fond of saying, "your father's mistake."

If we came in to collect on empty bottles, he'd say, "We don't deal in stolen goods here. Try Tansky's."

—The Street, pp. 16–18

MY HEART WENT OUT, however grudgingly, to the Brooklyn Dodgers, if only because so many of their players had served their apprenticeship with our Montreal Royals. One autumn afternoon I joined a concerned knot of fans outside Jack and Moe's barbershop, on the corner of Park Avenue and Laurier, to listen to the radio broadcast of the infamous 1941 World Series game, wherein catcher Mickey Owen dropped that third strike, enabling the dreaded Yankees to trample the jinxed Dodgers yet again.

When we were St. Urbain Street urchins, Hank Greenberg, the Detroit Tigers' first baseman, was our hero. Proof positive that not all Jews were necessarily short, good at chess, but unable to swing a bat.

—Dispatches from a Sporting Life, "Writers and Sports," p. 99

St. Lawrence Boulevard, The Main, was the Jewish ghetto's commercial thoroughfare. Here the community met, shopped, traded gossip, and found entertainment in restaurants, theatres, and pool halls. Occasionally there were confrontations with other communities as well.

TWO STREETS BELOW our own came The Main. Rich in delights, but also squalid, filthy, and hollering with stores whose wares, whether furniture or fruit, were ugly or damaged. The signs still say FANTASTIC DISCOUNTS or FORCED TO SELL PRICES HERE, but the bargains so bitterly sought after are illusory — and perhaps they always were.

The Main, with something for all our appetites, was dedicated to pinching pennies from the poor, but it was there to entertain, educate, and comfort us too. Across the street from the synagogue you could see THE PICTURE THEY CLAIMED COULD NEVER BE MADE. A little further down the street there was the Workman's Circle and, if you liked, a strip show. Peaches, Margo, Lili St. Cyr. Around the corner there was the ritual baths, the *shvitz* or *mikva*, where my grandfather and his cronies went before the High Holidays, emerging boiling red from the highest reaches of the steam rooms to happily flog each other with brushes fashioned of pine tree branches. Where supremely orthodox women went once a month to purify themselves.

It was to The Main, once a year before the High Holidays, that I was taken for a new suit (the itch of the cheap tweed was excruciating) and shoes (with a built-in squeak). We also shopped for fruit on The Main, meat and fish, and here the important thing was to watch the man at the scales. On The Main, too, was the Chinese Laundry — "Have you ever seen such hard workers?" — the Italian hat-blocker — "Tony's a good goy, you know. Against Mussolini from the very first." — and strolling French Canadian priests "Some of them speak Hebrew now." "Well, if you ask me, it's none of their business. Enough's enough, you know." Kids like myself were dragged along on shopping expeditions to carry parcels. Old men gave us snuff, at the delicatessens we were allowed salami butts, card players pushed candies on us for luck, and everywhere we were poked and pinched by the mothers. Absolutely the best that could be said of us was, "He eats well, knock wood," and later, as we went off to school, "He's a rank-one boy."

— The Street, pp. 50–51

WE WERE A RUDE, aggressive bunch round The Main. Cocky too. But bring down the most insignificant, pinched WASP fire insurance inspector and even the most arrogant merchant on the street would dip into the drawer for a ten spot or a bottle and bow and say, "Sir."

After school we used to race down to The Main to play snooker at the Rachel or the Mount Royal. Other days, when we chose to avoid school altogether, we would take the No. 55 streetcar as far as St. Catherine Street, where there was a variety of amusements offered. We could play the pinball machines and watch archaic strip-tease movies for a nickel at the Silver Gameland. At the Midway or the Crystal Palace we could see a double feature and a girlie show for as little as thirty-five cents. The Main, at this juncture, was thick with drifters, panhandlers, and whores. Available on both sides of the street were "Tourist Rooms by Day and Night," and everywhere there was the smell of french fried potatoes cooking in stale oil. Tough, unshaven men in checked shirts stood in knots outside the taverns and cheap cafés. There was the promise of violence.

As I recall it, we were always being warned about The Main. Our grandparents and parents had come there by steerage from Rumania or by cattleboat from Poland by way of Liverpool. No sooner had they unpacked their bundles and cardboard suitcases than they were planning a better, brighter life for us, the Canadian-born children. The Main, good enough for them, was not to be for us, and that they told us again and again was what the struggle was for. The Main was for *bummers*, drinkers, and (heaven forbid) failures.

— *The Street*, pp. 54–55

I ONCE READ somewhere that Billy Graham said he first found God on a golf course. He did not specify on which hole it was that he discovered he had a calling, not that it matters. In fact, I mention this bizarre epiphany not to mock the evangelist, but in self-defense. For just as Billy Graham connected with his Maker on the links, so I first broke with my faith at the age of thirteen — not due to a precocious reading of Voltaire or Darwin, which would have done me credit, but by frequenting poolrooms, snooker my liberation.

I was raised in an ultra-Orthodox home where we didn't switch on the lights, answer the phone, or light the wood stove in the kitchen on the Sabbath. Why, in my paternal grandfather's home across the street — ten of his fourteen children were still rooted there in those days — an aunt estimated how much toilet paper would be required over the Sabbath, and tore and stacked the sheets on Friday afternoons, because ripping off perforated paper was considered work, which was forbidden after sundown. With hindsight, I must admit that some of our religious practices were not that far removed from voodoo. Several days before Yom Kippur, for instance, I had to rotate a live rooster over my head (quickly, ever fearful of being shat on) while reciting a blessing that transferred a year's sum of masturbations, shoplifting expeditions, farting into my older brother's pillow in the bedroom we shared, and lesser sins, to that unfortunate bird. My God, think of what People for the Ethical Treatment of Animals would have to say about such an outrage today. The mind boggles.

Anyway, one Friday evening shortly after my bar mitzvah, I tempted God's wrath, daring to slip into the Laurier poolroom to challenge a stranger to a game of snooker. The heavens failed to open. I was not struck by lightning. Becoming a Friday evening regular at the Laurier, I had joined an alternative Jewish culture of sorts, where guys only a few years older than me — guys who were going nowhere — guys who would never discover the cure for cancer and didn't give a shit — smoked and drank beer on the Sabbath, swore, gobbled nonkosher hot dogs, and dated shiksas with impunity. Obviously snooker was a hell of a lot more fun than Talmud classes with Mr. Yalofsky in a back room of the Young Israel Synagogue. I hid my phylacteries under a pile of shirts in my bottom dresser drawer, where I also hid copies of the *Police Gazette* and *Sunbathing*, and never put them on again. Instead, I resolved to improve my cue work. It may have taken me more than fifty years, but that's what propelled me from St. Urbain Street to my vigil in a hotel bar in Kill, County Kildare [site of a snooker competition].

— On Snooker, pp. 80–82

A SHADED YELLOW LIGHT hung low over each of the eight tables in the Royal Billiard Room. Smoke, eight clouds for eight suns, thickened under and around the bulbs. The long and narrow room reeked of french fried potatoes, the walls were heavy with soot. Men watched the players from the benches that flanked the walls. Occasionally they made derogatory remarks: but otherwise they did not talk much. The snooker balls clacked together again and again making a hard, clean sound. Shloime, who was also known as Kid Lightning, was playing The Sleeper on the second table. The game was for five dollars. Shloime, who was a good player, was up twenty-two points and they were already on the coloured balls. The Sleeper, who in his wakeful hours had been arrested four times, once for arson, twice for petty larceny, and another time for shoplifting, cursed each time he shot and always watched to make sure that Shloime kept one foot on the floor. Each time Shloime made a run he accused him of fluking. Shloime was excited. Not because of the five dollars, no, but because he was being watched by Lou The Hook Edelman. Each time he sunk a difficult shot Shloime looked up at The Hook and grinned. The Hook had his boys with him. It could mean anything, Shloime thought.

"You waitin' for Christmas? Shoot," The Sleeper said.

Shloime took aim patiently, and sunk the green ball in the side pocket. The cue ball swerved back and rolled into perfect position behind the brown ball. Shloime knocked the brown hard into the corner pocket and the cue ball zoomed fast down the cloth, nearly scratched in the far corner pocket, jumped clear and rolled lazily up towards the blue ball which was frozen against the band. Shloime leaned his cue against the table and rubbed the chalk off his hand. "Pay up," he said.

"You blind? Dey're still three balls on the table."

"This jerk believes in miracles yet," Shloime said, turning to the others.

The Sleeper flung his cue down on the table and rushed towards Shloime. "Who's a jerk, eh?"

"You tell me. I'm lissnink."

The Hook got up and came between them. He turned to The Sleeper. "You're a jerk. Okay? Now give the kid his five fish."

"Dis is our business," The Sleeper said, beating his chest.

"I just made it mine. Okay, *jerk*. I'll count ten."

The Sleeper flung a five-dollar bill down on the table and then grabbed his coat and rushed towards the door. He stopped in the doorway. "You can't count no higher'n ten, Hook. You ex-con you. Hankink is too good fur you." Then he slammed the door and rushed down the street.

"Heroes." The Hook shrugged his shoulders and turned to Shloime. "You play me now. Okay, pal?"

"Sure. But it's on me, Hook. I'll pay."

"Naw. We'll play for the fin. But you and me, we're pals. We got business to talk to you after de game. Me, and the boys."

"I'll be right back."

Shloime washed the chalk off his hands and combed his hair in the toilet. Various comments had been scrawled over the urinals.

"The next Guy who comes in may be Barefoot!"

"JEANNE SA 2146."

And written in yellow chalk:

"A MERRY XMAS TO ALL OUR READERS."

Shloime hurried back to the table and chalked up his cue joyously. A whole new world seemed to be opening up to him.

—*Son of a Smaller Hero,* pp. 53–55

FOR YEARS NOW many sophisticated French Canadians have maintained that their Jewish problem stems from the fact that we integrated long ago into the province's Anglophone minority — insofar as this was tolerated — rather than its French majority. The standard Jewish response to this complaint is that we were not welcome in the French Catholic school system. An answer that is certainly true, but also disingenuous. We would have identified with the English-speaking community in any event. We were the progeny of hardworking, sometimes even driven, immigrants, who were counting on us, the first Canadian-born generation, to catapult them into a better life, and the glory road to self-improvement was clearly paved with English, French an obvious cul-de-sac. Look at it this way. Back there on St. Urbain Street, during World War II, we were poor, but the French were poorer. I still carry with me the image of a spunky French Canadian kid, maybe ten years old, who was

St. Urbain Street in the 1930s.

often seen on St. Urbain Street, searching the gutter for cigarette butts, pulling a wagon in which sat his even scrawnier older brother, a victim of rickets, a disease that I expect is unheard of today, except in the Third World.

— *Oh Canada! Oh Quebec!*, p. 98

THE JEWS OF CRAIG STREET, I should explain, though few in number, were pawnshop proprietors, and our section of St. Lawrence, or The Main, as we called it, was triumphantly Jewish. It was where working-class Jewish families went to buy their food, haberdashery, and furniture. And in my experience none of these families, my own included, could afford French Canadian maids or other employees. In fact, if my brother did become fluent in French, it was because, in the forties, he was a student at the Université de Montréal. My own initial experience of French Canadians was far from unpleasant. I had, along with a couple of school friends, acquired a chemistry set, and once a week the three of us went to visit a French Canadian pharmacist to present him with a list of our requirements. I can no longer remember the man's name, but he ran a drugstore at the corner of Park Avenue and St. Viateur, in the very heart of the city's Jewish quarter, and he could not have treated a Nobel laureate with more courtesy, nicely commingled with *gravitas*, than he did three scruffy kids determined to create the ultimate stink bomb. He would unfailingly invite us into a back room, where chemicals were stored in large jars, weighing our purchases on a delicate scale, contriving never to charge us more than a token thirty-five or fifty cents for whatever we needed.

— *Oh Canada! Oh Quebec!*, pp. 79–80

WE WOULD RETURN to The Main once more when we wanted a fight with the pea-soups. Winter, as I recall it, was best for this type of sport. We could throw snowballs packed with ice or frozen horse buns and, with darkness falling early, it was easier to elude pursuers. Soon, however, we developed a technique of battle that served us well even in the spring. Three of us would hide under an outside staircase while the fourth member of our group, a kid named Eddy, would idle provocatively on the sidewalk. Eddy was a good head-and-a-half shorter than the rest of us. (For this, it was rumoured, his mother was to blame. She wouldn't let Eddy have his tonsils removed and that's why he was such a runt. It was not that Eddy's mother feared surgery, but Eddy sang in the choir of a rich synagogue, bringing in some thirty dollars a month, and if his tonsils were removed it was feared that his voice would go too.) Anyway, Eddy would stand out there alone and when the first solitary pea-soup passed he would kick him in the shins. "Your mother fucks," he'd say.

The pea-soup, looking down on little Eddy, would naturally knock him one on the head. Then, and only then, would we emerge from under the staircase.

"Hey, that's my kid brother you just slugged."

And before the bewildered pea-soup could protest, we were scrambling all over him.

These and other fights, however, sprang more out of boredom than from racial hatred, not that there were no racial problems on The Main.

—*The Street,* pp. 52–53

THE FURNITURE SHOP on Saint Lawrence Boulevard was owned by a man called Steinberg, who had once owned a furniture store on the Theatinerstrasse in Munich. There he had sold hideous modern furniture on the instalment plan to a hard-pressed but Aryan clientele. When the hard-pressed Aryans had smashed his shop and burned his account books in '36 Steinberg had fled to London. He had been interned there in a camp as an enemy alien and then he had been sent to Canada, where after a short period in another camp he had been released. Now Steinberg once more sold hideous modern furniture on the instalment plan to hard-pressed Aryans. He even had a few of his old customers back. But this time he kept his account books locked in a fireproof safe.

—*A Choice of Enemies,* pp. 238–39

SMITH FIRST DRIFTED to Montreal in 1948. Answering a want ad in the *Star*, scraping bottom, he actually found himself working for a Jew. Hornstein's Home Furniture on The Main. Smith's first day on the job, he discovered that he was one of six rookies on the floor. Gordy Hornstein gathered them together before opening the doors to the crowd that was already churning outside, jostling for position, rapping on the plate-glass windows. "You see that three-piece living-room set in the window? I took a half-page ad in the *Star* yesterday advertising it for $125 to our first fifty customers. Anybody who sells one of those sets is fired. Tell those bargain-hunters outside what-ever you want. Delivery is ten years. The cushions are stuffed with rat shit. The frames are made of cardboard. Tell them anything. But it's your job to shift them into pricier lines and to sign them to twelve-month contracts.

Mordecai Richler
on St. Urbain Street.

Now some words of advice because you're new here and only three of you will still be working for Hornstein's once the week is out. We get all kinds here. French Canadians, Polacks, guineas, Jews, hunkies, niggers, you name it. This isn't Ogilvy's or Holt Renfrew. It's The Main. You sell a French Canadian a five-piece set for $350, ship him only four unmatched pieces from cheaper sets he won't complain, he's probably never been into a real store before and he buys from a Jew he expects to be cheated. I trust you have memo-rized the prices from the sheets I gave you because none are marked on the actual items. You are selling to Italians or Jews, you quote them double, because they don't come in their pants unless they can beat you down to half-price. One thing more. We don't sell to DPs here."

In those days DP was the Canadian coinage for Displaced Persons, that is to say, the trickle of European survivors that had recently been allowed into the country.

"Why don't we sell to refugees?" one of the rookies asked.

"Oh shit, a DP by me isn't a *greener*, it's a nigger. We call them DPs because all that interests them is the Down Payment. They fork out for that, load my furniture on to their stolen pickup, and it's goodbye Charlie. Tell them we're out of anything they want. Whisper they can get it cheaper at Greenberg's, he does the same to me, may he rot in

hell. But do not sell to them. Okay, hold your noses. I'm now gonna open up dem golden gates. Good luck, guys."

—*Solomon Gursky Was Here,* pp. 170–71

BUT MANY OF OUR GRANDPARENTS, the very same people who assured us The Main was only for *bummers* and failures, will not get out. Today when most of the children have made good, now that the sons and daughters have split-level bungalows and minks and West Indian cruises in winter, many of the grandparents still cling to The Main. Their children cannot in many cases persuade them to leave. So you still see them there, drained and used up by the struggle. They sit on kitchen chairs next to the Coke freezer in the cigar store, dozing with a fly swatter held in a mottled hand. You find them rolling their own cigarettes and studying the obituary columns in the *Star* on the steps outside the Jewish Library. The women still peel potatoes under the shade of a winding outside staircase. Old men still watch the comings and goings from the balcony above, a blanket spread over their legs and a little bag of polly seeds on their lap. As in the old days the sinking house with the crooked floor is right over the store or the wholesaler's, or maybe next door to the scrap yard. Only today the store and the junkyard are shut down. Signs for Sweet Caporal cigarettes or old election posters have been nailed in over the missing windows. There are spider webs everywhere.

—*The Street,* p. 10

There was, of course, a city outside the Jewish ghetto. Beyond St. Urbain Street, Westmount's leafy streets were chiselled into the side of Mount Royal. South of Sherbrooke lay the old city and Montreal's downtown core. And beyond Montreal, another world beckoned, a world to which Richler was soon drawn.

MONTREAL IS CLEANLY DEFINED on cold autumn nights. Each building, each tree, seems to exist as a separate and shivering object, exposed to the winds again after a flabby summer. Downtown the neon trembles like fractures in the dark. Fuzziness, bugs, groups of idlers blurring cigar-store windows, have all retreated together. Whores no longer stroll up and down St. Lawrence Boulevard, but beckon from the shelter of doorways or linger longer at nightclub bars. The mountain, which all summer long had seemed a gentle green slope, looms up brutal against the night sky. Streets seem longer, noises more hard.

Autumn is stingy, Noah thought unhappily.

Walking back to his room, down St. Catherine Street, he stopped several times to blow on his hands. He peered into the window of Dinty Moore's restaurant where sporty men sat around telling masculine jokes and cleaning their fingernails. Later, he thought, they will move on to various nightclubs where they'll drink cool drinks with bored, anonymous women. But they won't drink too much.

A man yelled: "GZET! Layst noos! GZET! Payph! GZET! GZET!"

Bums sprawled on the concrete seats on Phillips Square, and across the street in Morgan's windows, cool mannequins like all our next-door neighbours prepared to pass this and every night on Beautyrest mattresses.

—*Son of a Smaller Hero,* p. 45

THE BOYS, THE BOYS. He remembered them loping down *their* Boulevard on a Friday afternoon in spring, exploring, puffing Turrets, itchy in their Grover Knit-to-Fit sweaters, brash voices hushed for once, their manner subdued, because they were in Westmount. Where, according to Morty, everyone had a maid, some even a butler as well, and there was a buzzer under the dining-room table to bring them coming on the trot. Where, Izzy swore, property values couldn't be beat. And what about the snatchola, Seymour wanted to know.

Sssh. Not for you, *bubbele.* This is Westmount. Mothers didn't bargain here, or fathers cheat at pinochle. The daughters were blonde and leggy, they were taught horseback riding early, if only to break their cherries with impunity, and the sons didn't collect butcher bills on Sunday mornings to earn enough to buy their own two-wheel bikes, but instead were given sports cars. British. The best.

The boys stood in front of Selwyn House amazed, as cars, some of them chauffeured, came to collect the students. "If they actually had to *walk* home," Joshua ventured, "they'd only get dusty, like."

Rosy-cheeked they were, wearing navy-blue blazers and grey flannel trousers, and they didn't give St. Urbain's interlopers so much as a glance.

"Have you ever seen such pricks?" Joshua asked. "I mean, would you get into that sissy suit every morning?"

"It's not your problem," Max replied. "They don't want Jews here."

Not in Westmount, with a cricket pitch, and its own police force. Where the snow was cleared instantly, and if even a crack, never mind a real pothole, opened on the streets a French Canadian came running with a shovel of hot tar — "Yes, sir. Right away, boss." But where, on the other hand, nobody had a bar mitzvah.

Eli's father, a hot Zionist, showed a documentary on life on the kibbutz for the boys' party at his bar mitzvah. They showed Charlie Chaplin two-reelers at Max's party. For Seymour's, his father shovelled them all into his fruit-and-vegetable truck that stank of rotting cabbages and drove them to a doubleheader at Delorimier Downs. They laid on a Bud Abbott and Lou Costello movie for Izzy's bar mitzvah, and a day later he was peddling the gifts he didn't want. Everybody was treated to a party at Levitt's Delicatessen for Morty Zipper's celebration. Yet, surprisingly, the bar mitzvah that none of them would ever forget was Joshua Shapiro's.

— Joshua Then and Now, pp. 92–93

CANADIAN MYTHOLOGY has it that until very recently the true movers and shakers in this country were the dour Scotch Presbyterians of the incomparably affluent Montreal suburb of Westmount. If this was in fact once the case, it hasn't been true for years. All the same, a popular French Canadian variation on this theme is enriched by the conviction that, even today, the quintessential Westmount man — a banker — is chauffeured each morning to his office on St. James Street, where, in need of a daily hee-haw, he will foreclose on an impecunious habitant and then hurry home to mount the ravishing but innocent Francophone maid, throwing her off the roof if she gets pregnant. The women shop at Holt Renfrew and then repair to the neighbouring Ritz-Carlton Hotel for drinks and, providing they are not hopelessly frigid, assignations as well. And once a year the Westmount men and women convene at the Ritz in their tribal finery for St. Andrew's Ball, their champagne-laden tables attended by the white niggers of North America, *Québécois pure laine*, whose parents live in an unheated East End flat, owned by a short fat Jew slumlord, the mother suffering from consumption and the father bound to die without ever once wintering in Hollywood, Florida, a lifelong dream.

— Oh Canada! Oh Quebec!, p. 71

WELCOMED INTO NEIGHBOURHOODS hitherto unknown to me by my new friends, I found that "among them" living rooms were not out of bounds, kept clean for special occasions, and that it was not the rule to maintain cellophane wrappings around lampshades. But my emancipation, as it were, came with culinary penalties. Invited to dinners here and there in Montreal's Presbyterian redoubt of Notre Dame de Grâce, I learned to tolerate tinned soup into which, in lieu of kasha or *kreplach*, you were expected to break Ritz crackers that quickly turned to slush. This was invariably followed by a leathery toast, untainted by garlic, served with potatoes boiled beyond the crumbling point. To my astonishment, anecdotes about my Hasidic childhood were considered entertaining. I had been raised on the dictum that it was hard to be a Jew (*siz shver tzu zein a Yid*) but, at least in some quarters, it was also considered a novelty. A story I burnished into a real knee-slapper was the one about how I used to be sent, as a child, to the home of a *shammes* (sexton) on City Hall Street, to pick up our Passover wine. The old man would bundle the bottles into newspapers before slipping them into a heavy-duty brown bag — not to ensure them against breakage, but to make them proof against the evil eye. If a *goy* so much as glanced at an uncovered bottle in passing, it was instantly rendered *trayf*, unclean, and had to be poured down the sink. Another tale that went over big was the one about how, late one afternoon during the Ten Days of Awe which culminate in Yom Kippur, I had to rotate a squawking chicken over my head while pronouncing a blessing that enabled me to shift all my previous year's sins onto the bird. This led to a discussion of *The Golden Bough*, Aztec rituals, and voodoo rites. Walking home alone, I felt that I was the one who was now *trayf*.

— *This Year in Jerusalem*, pp. 42–43

BEFORE THE REST of us had even graduated from Baron Byng High School, Jerry scampered out west to seek his fortune. After graduation, Myer elected not to continue with his studies. Instead, he took a job as an usher at the Rialto, and I hardly ever saw him any more. Hershey went on to McGill, where he hoped to major in English literature. McGill's Jewish quota was still intact in those days and my matriculation results weren't nearly good enough for me to seek

Mordecai Richler (left) at Wilensky's, a well-known neighbourhood diner.

admission; I had to settle for the less desirable Sir George Williams College. Hershey and I, no longer Friday night regulars at Habonim or students at the same school, made an effort to remain friends all the same. One evening I went to his place for a beer. "Obviously," I allowed, "McGill has more prestige, but Sir George is truer to our working-class origins and socialist beliefs."

Hershey said that his most stimulating course, conducted by a professor with a degree from Oxford, dealt with nineteenth-century English poetry. "But the other day I had to admit to him that I was unable to respond to the poetry of William Wordsworth. However, I suspect it may not be that his poetry is *passé*. I fear it could be some inadequacy in me."

Months passed before I ran into Hershey again, this time at the Café André on Victoria Street, then a favoured student haunt. He wore a white sweater with a big red felt M sewn onto it and sat drinking beer with a bunch of fraternity boys. Thumping the table, they sang:

> If all the young ladies were little white rabbits,
> and I was a hare,
> I'd teach them bad habits....

I was wearing a navy blue beret (the real McCoy, made in France) and had already written my first poem in lowercase letters. Hershey and I waved at each other, but he didn't come to my table, and I didn't go to his.

—*This Year in Jerusalem,* pp. 39–40

WHENEVER NORMAN thought of his country he did not, as Americans were supposed to do, recall with a whack of joy the wildest rivers and fastest trains, fields of corn, skyscrapers, and the rest of it. There were all these things in his country. There were magical names in abundance. A town called Trois-Rivières; a mountain pass named Kicking Horse; Saskatchewan — a province. But there was no equivalent of the American dream to boost or knock. The Canadian dream, if there was such a puff, was how do I get out?

—*A Choice of Enemies,* p. 4

A Minor-league Catskills

In an essay on Catskill Mountain resorts, Richler reports on a visit to Grossinger's, the granddaddy of them all. There, he spoke to its "guiding genius," Arthur Winarick, who once coyly asked the actor Zero Mostel what more could be added to the resort's amenities. Mostel replied: "An indoor jungle, Arthur. Hunting for tigers under glass."

Montreal's Jews fled the summer heat, not by heading to the Catskills, but to the Laurentians. There they coexisted more or less uneasily with their French-Canadian neighbours in hotels like the fictional Rubin's in The Apprenticeship of Duddy Kravitz. *The facilities were more modest than those offered at Grossinger's but, as Richler describes them, they were ample and comfortable. It was while working at Rubin's that Duddy first set eyes on the hills and lake that would make him a man of property. And it was in this region that Solomon Gursky confounded the Anglo anti-Semites by purchasing one of their exclusive hotels.*

ANY ACCOUNT OF THE CATSKILL Mountains must begin with Grossinger's. The G. On either side of the highway out of New York and into Sullivan County, a two-hour drive north, one is assailed by billboards. DO A JERRY LEWIS — COME TO BROWN'S. CHANGE TO THE FLAGLER. I FOUND A HUSBAND AT THE WALDEMERE. THE RALEIGH IS ICIER, NICIER, AND SPICIER. All the Borscht Belt billboards are crisscrossed with lists of attractions, each hotel claiming the ultimate in golf courses, the latest indoor and outdoor pools, and the most tantalizing parade of stars. The countryside between the signs is ordinary, without charm. Bushland and small hills. And then finally one comes to the Grossinger billboard. All it says, *sotto voce*, is GROSSINGER'S HAS EVERYTHING.

"On a day in August, 1914, that was to take its place among the red-letter days of all history," begins a booklet published to commemorate Grossinger's 50th anniversary, "a war broke out in Europe. Its fires seared the world.... On a summer day of that same year, a small boarding house was opened in the Town of Liberty." The farm house was opened by Selig and Malke Grossinger to take in nine people at nine dollars a week. Fresh air for factory workers, respite for tenement dwellers. Now Grossinger's, spread over a thousand acres, can accommodate fifteen hundred guests. It represents an investment of fifteen million dollars. But to crib once more from the anniversary booklet, "The greatness of any institution cannot be measured by material size alone. The Taj Mahal cost a king's ransom but money in its intrinsic form is not a part of that structure's unequalled beauty."

Grossinger's, on first sight, looks like the consummate kibbutz. Even in the absence of Arabs there is a security guard at the gate. It has its own water supply, a main building — in this case Sullivan County Tudor with picture windows — and a spill of outlying lodges named after immortals of the first Catskill Aliya, like Eddie Cantor and Milton Berle.

I checked in on a Friday afternoon in summer and crossing the terrace to my quarters stumbled on a Grossinger's Forum of The Air in progress. Previous distinguished speakers — a reflection, as one magazine put it, of Jennie Grossinger, in whom the traditional reverence for learning remains undimmed — have included Max Lerner and Norman Cousins. This time out the lecturer was resident hypnotist Nat Fleischer, who was taking a stab at CAN LOVE SURVIVE MARRIAGE? "I have a degree in psychology," Fleischer told me, "and am now working on my doctorate."

"Where?"

"I'd rather not say."

There were about a hundred and fifty potential hecklers on the terrace. All waiting to pounce. Cigar-chumpers in Bermuda shorts and ladies ready with an alternative of the New York *Post* on their laps. "Men are past their peak at twenty-five," Fleischer shouted into the microphone, "but ladies reach theirs much later and stay on a plateau, *while the men are tobogganing downhill.*" One man hooted, another guffawed, but many ladies clapped approval. "You think," Fleischer said, "the love of the baby for his momma is natural — *no!*" A man, holding a silver foil sun reflector to his face, dozed off. The lady beside him fanned herself with *From Russia, With Love*. "In order to remain sane," Fleischer continued, "what do we need? ALL OF US. Even at sixty and seventy. LOVE. A little bit of love. If you've been married for twenty-five years you shouldn't take your wife for granted. Be considerate."

A lady under a tangle of curlers bounced up and said, "I've been married twenty-nine years and my husband doesn't take me for granted."

This alarmed a sunken-bellied man in the back row. He didn't join in the warm applause. Instead he stood up to peer at the lady. "I'd like to meet her husband." Sitting down again, he added, "The *shmock*."

There was to be a get-together for singles in the evening, but the prospects did not look dazzling. A truculent man sitting beside me in the bar said, "I dunno. I swim this morning. I swim this afternoon — indoors, outdoors — my God, what a collection! When are all the beauties checking in?"

I decided to take a stroll before dinner. The five lobbies at Grossinger's are nicely panelled in pine, but the effect is somewhat undermined by the presence of plastic plants everywhere. There is plastic sweet corn for sale in the shop beside the Olympic-size outdoor pool and plastic grapes are available in the Mon Ami Gift and

Sundry Shop in the main building. Among those whose pictures hang on The Wall Of Fame are Cardinal Spellman and Yogi Berra, Irving Berlin, Governors Harriman and Rockefeller, Ralph Bunche, Zero Mostel, and Herman Wouk. The indoor pool, stunningly simple in design, still smelled so strongly of disinfectants that I was reminded of the more modest "Y" pool of my boyhood. I fled. Grossinger's has its own post office and is able to stamp all mail "Grossinger, NY." There is also Grossinger Lake, "for your tranquil togetherness"; an 18-hole golf course; stables; an outdoor artificial ice rink; a ski trail and toboggan run; a His 'n' Hers health club; and of course a landing strip adjoining the hotel, the Jennie Grossinger Field.

The ladies had transformed themselves for dinner. Gone were the curlers, out came the minks. "Jewish security blankets," a guest, watching the parade with me, called the wraps, but fondly, with that sense of self-ridicule that redeems Grossinger's and, incidentally, makes it the most slippery of places to write about.

I suppose it would be easiest, and not unjustified, to present the Catskills as a cartoon. A Disneyland with knishes. After all, everywhere you turn the detail is bizarre. At the Concord, for instance, a long hall of picture windows overlooks a parking lot. There are rooms that come with two adjoining bathrooms. ("It's a gimmick. People like it. They talk about it.") All the leading hotels now have indoor ice skating rinks because, as the lady who runs The Laurels told me, our guests find it too cold to skate outside. True, they have not yet poured concrete into the natural lakes to build artificial filtered pools above, but, short of that, every new convenience conspires to protect guests from the countryside. Most large hotels, for instance, link outlying lodges to the main building through a system of glassed-in and sometimes even subterranean passages, all in the costly cause of protecting people from the not notoriously fierce Catskills outdoors.

What I'm getting at is that by a none too cunning process of selected detail one can make Grossinger's, the Catskills, and the people who go there, appear totally grotesque. One doesn't, because there's more to it than that. Nothing, on the other hand, can prevent Sullivan County from seeming outlandish, for outlandish it certainly is, and it would be condescending, the most suspect sort of liberalism, to overlook this and instead celebrate, say, Jennie Grossinger's maudlin "warmth" or "traditional reverence" for bogus learning.

Something else. The archetypal Grossinger's guest belongs to the most frequently fired-at class of American Jews. Even as *Commentary* sends out another patrol of short-story writers, the *Partisan Review* irregulars are waiting in the bushes, bayonets drawn. Saul Bellow is watching, Alfred Kazin is ruminating, Norman Mailer is ready with his flick-knife, and who knows what manner of trip wires the next generation of Jewish writers is laying out at this very moment. Was there ever a group so pursued by such an unsentimental platoon of chroniclers? So plagued by moralists? So blamed for making money? Before them came the *luftmensh*, the impecunious dreamers — tailors, cutters, corner grocers — so adored by Bernard Malamud. After them came Phillip Roth's confident college boys on the trot, Americans who just happen to have had a Jewish upbringing. But this generation between, this unlovely spiky bunch that climbed with the rest of middle-class America out of the Depression into a pot of prosperity, is the least liked by literary Jews. In a Clifford Odets play they were the rotters. The rent collectors. Next Jerome Weidman carved them up and then along came Budd Schulberg and Irwin Shaw. In fact in all this time only Herman Wouk, armed with but a slingshot of clichés, has come to their defense. More of an embarrassment, I'd say, than a shield.

An aerial view of Grossinger's in 1954.

Well now here they are at Grossinger's, sitting ducks for satire. Manna for sociologists. Here they are, breathless, but at play, so to speak, suffering sour stomach and cancer scares, one Israeli bond drive after another, unmarriageable daughters and sons gone off to help the Negroes overcome in Mississippi. Grossinger's is their dream of plenty realized, but if you find it funny, larger than life, then so do the regulars. In fact there is no deflating remark I could make about minks or matchmaking that has not already been made by visiting comedians or guests. Furthermore, for an innocent *goy* to even think some of the things said at Grossinger's would be to invite the wrath of the B'nai Brith Anti-Defamation League.

—*Hunting Tigers under Glass*, "The Catskills," pp. 115–19

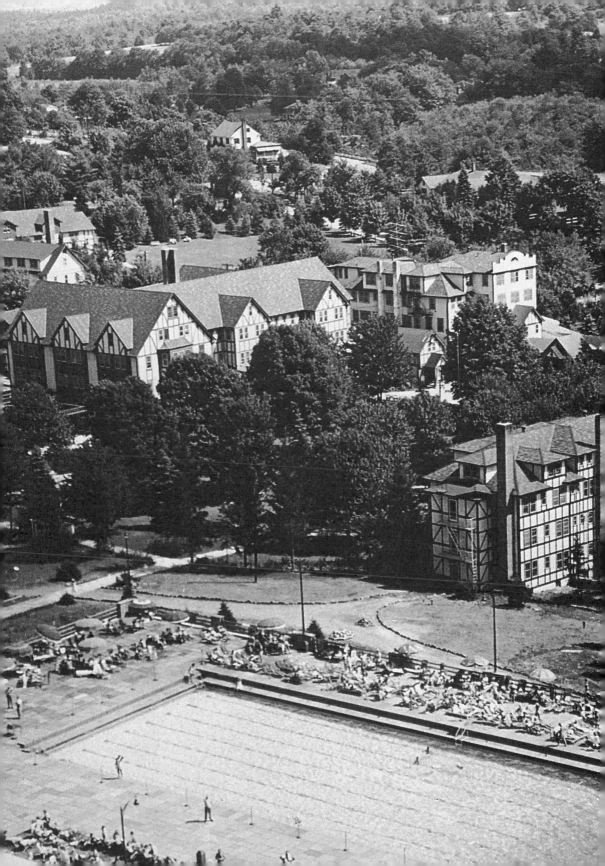

SOON AFTER ST. JEROME, a prosperous French Canadian mill town with a tall grey church, the horizon widens and the highway begins to rise, rise and dip, rise again from the valley and into higher hills. Sloping easily on all sides are the slow, pine-rumpled hills. Old and shrivelled cliffs appear like bruised bones here and there, and in the valleys below, the fertile fields are yellow and green and brown. There is the occasional unpainted barn or silo — blackened by the wind and the rain — rising out of the landscape as natural as rocks. Billboards, more modern, stick out of the earth incongruously. The slim and muddy river, sheltered from the sun by birch and bush, winds northwards drowsily but insistent between the still hills. Cottages — a mess strewn on a hilltop or a pile of them spilled sloppily into a valley — appear every ten miles or so. From time to time, as the highway climbs higher north, some ambitious cliff or hill pokes into the soft underbelly of a low grey cloud. These higher hills, sometimes called mountains, are often ribbed by ski tows, trails, and the occasional derelict jump. Bears, the stray deer or two, are often rumoured in these parts, but, like the pretty girls who beckon from the travel brochures, they are seldom seen.

About forty-five miles north of Montreal a side road turns up off into Ste-Adèle en-haut. It's about three miles to the lake. Ste-Adèle is the retreat of Montreal's aspiring middle class, and, as a resort town, is prone to all the faults and virtues of that group. The cottages are clean but prosaic: no Jews are wanted, but, on the other hand, they are dealt with diplomatically. The French Canadians tolerate the Presbyterians from the city because they have brought prosperity to their village, and the Presbyterians find that the French Canadians add spice to their holiday: they accept their haughtiness as philosophically as rain on Sundays. Few on either side are bilingual.

—*Son of a Smaller Hero,* p. 109

SHUNNED BY the college-boy waiters, Duddy began to investigate Ste-Agathe on his own when he had time off.

Some sixty miles from Montreal, set high in the Laurentian hills on the shore of a splendid blue lake, Ste-Agathe-des-Monts had been made the middle-class Jewish community's own resort town many years ago. Here, as they prospered, the Jews came from Outremont to build summer cottages and hotels and children's camps. Here, as in the winter in Montreal, they lived largely with their neighbours. Friends and relatives bought plots of land and built their cottages and boat houses competitively, but side by side. There were still some pockets of Gentile resistance, it's true. Neither of the two hotels that were still in their hands admitted Jews but that, like the British raj that still lingered on the Malabar Coast, was not so discomforting as it was touchingly defiant. For even as they played croquet and sipped their gin and tonics behind protecting pines they could not miss the loud, swarthy parade outside. The short husbands with their outrageously patterned sports shirts arm in arm with purring wives too obviously full for slacks, the bawling kids with triple-decker ice-cream cones, the squealing teenagers, and the trailing grandfather with his beard and black hat. They could not step out of their enclaves and avoid the speeding cars with wolfcall horns. The lake was out of the question. Sailboats and canoes had no chance against speedboats, spilling over with relatives and leaving behind a wash of empty Pepsi bottles. Even the most secluded part of the lake was not proof against the floating popsicle wrapper, and the moonlight canoe trip ran the risk of being run down by a Cuckoo Kaplan-led expedition to the island. Boatloads full of honeymooners and office girls and haberdashery salesmen singing, to the tune of "Onward, Christian Soldiers":

> Onward, Rubin's boarders,
> Onward, to the shore,
> With sour cream and latkas,
> We're staying two weeks more.

—*The Apprenticeship of Duddy Kravitz*, pp. 70–71

CUCKOO [KAPLAN] WAS BILLED as Montreal's Own Danny Kaye and his name and jokes often figured in *Mel West's What's What*. Short and wiry, with a frantic, itchy face, Cuckoo was ubiquitous. At

For years, Richler summered at Lake Memphremagog in Quebec's Eastern Townships.

breakfast he'd pop up from under a table to crack an egg on a bald man's head and at midnight he'd suddenly race through the dance hall in a gay nineties bathing suit and dive through a window into the lake. He always had a surprise for lunch too. Once he'd chase the cook through the dining room with a meat cleaver and later in the week chances were he'd hold up two falsies, saying he had found them on the beach, and ask the owner to claim them. Aside from organizing games when it rained and his regular nightly act — his Romeo and Juliet Capelovitch skit was a knockout — Cuckoo had some special routines for the winter season and was good at getting publicity. He got his picture in the paper on the first sub-zero day of winter by sawing a hole in the ice and taking a dip. For this annual picture, with Rubin's Hotel Lac des Sables prominent in the background, Cuckoo wore an hilarious wig, blackened two front teeth, and put on a long black woollen bathing suit. Once, after his annual dip, he was in bed with a fever for two weeks.

Cuckoo's father couldn't understand him. "What is it with you, Chaim? For a lousy ninety dollars a week," he said, "to make a fool of yourself in front of all those strangers."

But Cuckoo was not without hope. He had once been held over for three weeks in a night club in Buffalo and another time he had stopped the show at the Pink Elephant in New Jersey. Each year on his vacation he went to New York and walked from one agent's office to another with a large folio under his arm. Meanwhile, he was adored in Ste-Agathe. Guests from all the other hotels came to Rubin's on Saturday night to catch his act.

— *The Apprenticeship of Duddy Kravitz*, pp. 71–72

"SOLOMON'S JOKES were always at somebody else's expense," Callaghan said, "but he was indifferent to the damage. Take the prank of buying the Chalet Antoine in Ste-Adèle, for instance. Far from being overjoyed, the bunch from Fancy Finery were intimidated the minute they came spilling out of those chartered buses and saw what kind of hotel they were being put up at. Tennis courts. Lawn bowling. Croquet. Canoes. Instead of a bottle of seltzer at each table, a snobby waiter presenting them with a wine list and a menu they couldn't understand. *Pâté de fois gras. Ris de veau. Tournedos.* A couple of the more enterprising husbands piled into a pickup truck, drove out to Prévost, and came back with a sack of kosher chickens and briskets, gallon jars of sour pickles, stacks of rye bread and so forth, and their wives took over the kitchen. But then there were those bastards who gathered in boats offshore, come to gawk at the fat ladies taking the sun in their bras and bloomers and the men playing pinochle in their underwear. So the beneficiaries of Solomon's largesse, confined to the hotel for the most part, longed for nothing so much as the corner cigar & soda or the familiar front-door stoop."

— *Solomon Gursky Was Here*, pp. 397–98

I CAN WELL IMAGINE what the Curé Labelle would have thought, because in the immediate postwar years Ste-Agathe became a veritable

Jewish paradise. A minor-league Catskills. Indigenous comics played a flourishing hotel circuit that included Greenberg's, the Castle des Monts, Levine's, the Hotel Vermont, Rabiner's, the Chalet, and many others. Children's camps proliferated on small neighbouring lakes: Camp Hiawatha, Pripstein's, Pine Valley. A Jewish baker set up in town, and there was of course a synagogue and a kosher butcher. On Saturdays in July the rue Principale and the rue Tour de Lac swelled with noisy Jewish families parading in their finery, tooting the horns of their newly acquired Buicks, lining up for a midnight medium-fat smoked meat on rye at the local deli. At the time, it occurred to me that it was surprising that French Canadians and Jews did not get on better. Certainly we had a good deal in common. A lust for life. A love of display. A fear for the survival of the *mameloshn*, French or Yiddish, and an inner conviction that only our society was truly distinctive. Sadly, however, abrasiveness continued to be the rule.

From the balcony of my mother's modest little inn the old men in their yarmulkes, gossiping in Yiddish, could just make out the sign on the outside wall of the Hotel Chez Maurice, immediately across the dirt road. It read: RESTRICTED CLIENTELE ONLY. Three blocks away, equally boorish WASPs played lawn bowls behind the sheltering cedar hedge of the Laurentide Inn, which was also restricted to Gentiles only. At the time, I was a hot-blooded teenager — a *New Statesman* reader who actually believed justice would be served in this world — so these twin signposts of the gut feelings of our "two founding races" outraged me. With hindsight, however, I am bound to admire the goofy stance of these two doomed hotel proprietors, determined to protect their Alamos of bigotry, refusing to acknowledge that they were already surrounded by cavorting, cigar-chewing men, pinochle mavens in Hawaiian shirts, and fat ladies plopping into the lake, squealing, "It's a *mechaiah*, Bessie! I swear it's a *mechaiah*!" And neighbouring hotel loudspeakers that crackled before bellowing, "Long-distance call for Moishe Tannenbaum," or "Mrs. Bishinsky, your niece Jewel from Turrono is at the train station and needs a lift."

Looking back, it is now clear to me that Ste-Agathe-des-Monts, like Oxford, was once a champion of lost causes and, furthermore, what happened there in the late forties is a metaphor for what ails Canada now.

Examined closely, what really exercises our two founding races today is the recent intrusion into this privileged and still largely empty land of so many southern Europeans and wogs from Asia, Central and South America, the West Indies, and North Africa. In Montreal, where the French are officially eager for more French-speaking immigrants, their bourgeoisie is unofficially fleeing the city — its schools contaminated by the children of Moroccans, Haitians, Lebanese, and Vietnamese — for the etiolated suburbs, say Laval, which is still purportedly racially pure. And out there in Vancouver the indolent natives, who once tied Chinese coolies together by their queues and tossed them over cliffs into the sea, are scared stiff of the many new and obviously astute arrivals from Hong Kong, certain to run circles around them before breakfast. And when the middle classes of both our founding races open their newspapers in June and see that most of the high school scholarship students have Asian faces, they tend to feel a chill, even as they once winced at the photographs of all those hot-to-trot Jewish prize winners with unpronounceable names. Hence the plaintive racial cry in the streets of Montreal of "*Le Québec aux Québécois!*" and out west the revolt of the nerds, that is to say, the sudden rise of the equally xenophobic Reform Party, and the emergence in Orangeman's Ontario of APEC and screwy, paranoid books like *Bilingual Today, French Tomorrow*, claiming sales of 110,000 copies. Put plainly, the most insecure members of our two founding races — failed, according to Conrad Black, by their elites — have seen the Canadian future and grasped that it won't work as well as the past for them.

—*Oh Canada! Oh Quebec!*, pp. 99–101

All at once, it was spring.

One day shopkeepers were wretched, waiters surly, concierges mean about taking messages, and the next, the glass windows encasing café terraces were removed everywhere, and Parisians were transmogrified: shopkeepers, waiters, concierges actually spoke in dulcet tones.

I TRIED
MY VERY BEST
TO ESCAPE

Richler set off from Montreal for Liverpool on board the ocean liner Franconia *in the late summer of 1950. He was nineteen years old. After just two weeks in England, he moved on to Paris, where he settled into a Left Bank hotel and was soon assimilated into the expatriate community.*

Over the next few years, he established the disciplined writing regimen to which he adhered all his life, starting work early in the day, setting aside the evening for the company of friends. He moved around as his means permitted, living cheaply on the island of Ibiza, visiting Valencia, Munich, and other European destinations, and sharing rented accommodation on the Cote d'Azur. He returned to Canada for a few months in 1952, but upon learning that his novel, The Acrobats, *had been accepted for publication by André Deutsch, he headed happily back to London.*

The Acrobats *was not Richler's first attempt at sustained fiction. An earlier manuscript, referred to in a letter to his friend William Weintraub as "The Rotten People," was never published. Spain figures as a backdrop in a number of the early works. Paris is a significant presence only in* Barney's Version. *But Richler lived among the British for some seventeen years, from the mid-1950s until 1972, and his wry commentary on things British is a recurrent motif.*

—J. W.

JAKE RECALLED standing with Luke at the ship's rail, afloat on champagne, euphoric, as Quebec City receded and they headed into the St. Lawrence and the sea.

"I say! I say! I say!" Jake had demanded, "what's beginning to happen in Toronto?"

"Exciting things."

"And Montreal?"

"It's changing."

Tomorrow country then, tomorrow country now. And yet — and yet — he felt increasingly claimed by it, especially in the autumn, the Laurentian season, and the last time he had sailed the tranquil St. Lawrence into swells and the sea, it was with a sense of loss, even deprivation, and melancholy, that he had watched the clifftop towns drift past. Each one unknown to him.

Circles completed, he thought.

As a St. Urbain Street boy he had, God forgive him, been ashamed of his parents' Yiddish accent. Now that he lived in Hampstead, Sammy (and soon Molly and Ben too, he supposed) mocked his immigrant's twang. Such, such are the trendy's dues, Jake thought, as he added a couple of pieces to Sammy's unfinished Popeye jigsaw puzzle on the table, found the cards, and sat down to play solitaire. If I win, he thought, I'll be acquitted. If I lose, it's the nick for me.

— *St. Urbain's Horseman,* pp. 13–14

NORMAN, UNLIKE THE OTHER ÉMIGRÉS, had taken London to his heart. It didn't yield itself to strangers with nearly so much ease as Paris, but in the end the city's beneficence, its quality of being used, feasible, sane, took you prisoner. New York was more spectacular, but London, perhaps because you were not the saint or irresistible lover you longed to be, was the more reassuringly human. Greatness and power and youth had passed: the city, like you, was relieved.

—*A Choice of Enemies*, p. 5

Barney Panofsky (Barney's Version) *is not an artist, but as a young man in Paris in the 1950s, he hangs out with writers, painters, and poets. He lives there with Clara, who subsequently becomes the first Mrs. Panofsky.*

I DUNNO. I JUST DUNNO. The past is a foreign country, they do things differently there, as E. M. Forster* once wrote. Anyway, those, those were the days. We had not so much arrived in the City of Light as escaped the constraints of our dim provincial origins, in my case the only country that declared Queen Victoria's birthday a national holiday. Our lives were unstructured. Totally. We ate when we were hungry and slept when we were tired, and screwed whoever was available whenever it was possible, surviving on three dollars a day. Except for the always elegantly dressed Cedric, a black American who was the beneficiary of a secret source of funds about which the rest of us speculated endlessly. Certainly it wasn't family money. Or the pathetic sums he earned for stories published in the *London Magazine or Kenyon Review*. And I dismissed as a canard the rumour rife among some other Left Bank black Americans that, in those days of crazed anti-communism, Cedric received a monthly stipend from the FBI, or CIA, to inform on their activities. Whatever, Cedric wasn't hunkered down in a cheap hotel room but ensconced in a comfortable

* Actually, it was L. P. Hartley in *The Go-Between*, p. 1. London: Hamish Hamilton, 1953.

apartment on the rue Bonaparte. His Yiddish, which he had acquired in Brighton Beach, where his father worked as an apartment-building janitor, was good enough for him to banter with Boogie, who

addressed him as the *shayner* Reb Cedric, the *shvartzer gaon* of Brooklyn. Ostensibly without racial hang-ups, and fun to be with, he went along with Boogie's jest that he was actually a pushy Yemenite trying to pass as black because it made him irresistible to young white women who had come to Paris to be liberated, albeit on a monthly allowance from their uptight parents. He also responded with a mixture of warmth and deference whenever Boogie, our acknowledged master, praised his latest short story. But I suspected his pleasure was simulated. With hindsight, I fear that he and Boogie, constantly jousting, actually disliked each other.

—*Barney's Version*, pp. 26–27

A young Richler, passport in hand, 1950s.

ANYWAY, BACK IN OUR LEFT BANK DAYS, Cedric was seldom seen without a white girl on his arm. Clara, simulating jealousy, usually greeted him with, "How long before I get my ticket punched?"

She took a different tack with Terry. "For you, honey-child, I'd be willing to dress as a boy."

"But I much prefer you as you are, Clara. Always tricked out like a harlequin."

Or, an avid Virginia Woolf reader, Clara would pretend to espy a tell-tale stain on his trousers. "You could go blind, Terry. Or haven't they heard about that in Canada yet?"

Clara not only did troubled nonfigurative paintings, but also frightening ink drawings, crowded with menacing gargoyles, prancing little devils, and slavering satyrs attacking nubile women from all sides. She committed poetry as well, inscrutable to me, but published in both *Merlin* and *Zero*, earning her a request from James Laughlin of New Directions Press to see more. Clara shoplifted. Sliding things under her voluminous shawls. Tins of sardines, bottles of shampoo, books, corkscrews, postcards, spools of ribbon. Fauchon was a favourite haunt, until she was denied entry. Inevitably, she was once caught snatching a pair of nylon stockings at the MonoPrix, but got off, she said, by allowing the fat, greasy *flic* to drive her to the Bois de Boulogne and come between her breasts. "Just like my dear uncle Horace did when I was only twelve years old. Only he didn't boot me out of a moving car, laughing as I tumbled head over heels, calling me filthy names, but presented me with a twenty-dollar bill each time to keep our secret."

Our room, in the Hôtel de la Cité, on the Île de la Cité, was perpetually dark, its one small window looking out on an interior courtyard as narrow as an elevator shaft. There was a tiny washbasin in the room, but the communal toilet was down a long hallway. It was a squatter, no more than a hole in the floor, with elevated grips for your shoes, and a clasp fixed to the wall offering paper squares scissored out of the politically relevant *L'Humanité* or *Libération*. I bought a Bunsen burner and a small pot, so that we could hard-boil eggs to eat in baguette sandwiches for lunch. But the crumbs attracted mice, and she wakened screaming when one skittered over her face during the night. Another time she opened a dresser drawer to retrieve a shawl and stumbled on three newly born mice nesting there, and began to shriek. So we gave up eating in our room.

We languished in bed a good deal of the time, not making love but in search of warmth, dozing, reading (me into Jacques Prévert's *Paroles*, which she scorned), comparing difficult childhoods and congratulating each other on our amazing survivals. In the privacy of our refuge, far from the café tables where she felt compelled to shock or, anticipating criticism, to pick at the scabs of other people's weaknesses, she was a wonderful storyteller, my very own Scheherazade. I, in turn, entertained her with tales of the exploits of Detective Inspector Izzy Panofsky.

Clara abhorred her mother. In a previous life, she said, Mrs. Chambers must have been an ayah. Or, in another spin of the reincarnation wheel, Chinese, her feet bound in childhood, taking little mincing steps in The Forbidden City during the days of the Ming Dynasty. She was the ultimate wifey. "*Très mignonne*. Hardly a virago," said Clara. Her husband's philandering she took to be a blessing, as it meant she no longer had to suffer him between the sheets. "It is astonishing to what lengths a man will go," she once said to Clara, "to achieve thirty seconds of friction." Having provided Mr. Chambers with a son, Clara's younger brother, she felt that her duty was done, and was delighted to move into her own bedroom. But she continued to thrive as an exemplary chatelaine, managing their Gramercy Park brownstone and Newport mansion with panache. Mrs. Chambers was a member of the Metropolitan Opera Company board. Giuseppe di Stefano had sung at one of her soirées. Elisabeth Schwarzkopf was a frequent dinner guest. Mrs. Chambers had made a point of taking Kirsten Flagstad to lunch at Le Pavillon after the Jews had taken against her. "My mother would suffer a stroke if she knew I was living with a Jew," said Clara, tickling my nose with one of her ostrich boas. "She thinks you're the poison contaminating America's bloodstream. What have you got to say to that?"

Her father, she once told me, was a senior partner in John Foster Dulles's old law firm. He kept Arabian horses and once a year flew over to Scotland to fly-fish for salmon on the Spey. But another time I heard her say that he was a Wall Street broker and a cultivator of rare orchids, and when I asked her about that, once we were alone together, she countered, "Oh, you're so fucking literal. What does it matter?" and she ran off, disappearing round a corner of the rue de Seine, and didn't return to our room that night. "As a matter of interest," I asked, when she showed up at the Pergola the next evening, "where did you stay last night?"

"You don't own me, you know. My pussy's my own."

"That's no answer."

"It just so happens my aunt Honor is staying at the Crillon. She put me up. We ate at Lapérouse."

"I don't believe you."

"Look," she said, and digging into her skirts, she produced a wad of one-thousand-franc notes, and threw them at me. "Take whatever I owe you for room and board. I'm sure you've been keeping track."

"Is it all right if I charge interest?"

"I'm taking the train to Venice with my aunt tonight. We're staying with Peggy Guggenheim."

Shortly after one o'clock in the morning a week later, Clara returned to our room, undressed, and slid into bed with me. "We drank endless Bellinis at Harry's Bar with Tennessee Williams. Peggy took us to Torcello for lunch one day. For your sake, I visited the Campo del Ghetto Nuovo. Had you lived there back then you wouldn't have been allowed out after ten o'clock at night. I was going to send you a postcard from the Rialto," she said, "to say there's no news to report, but I forgot."

In the morning, I couldn't help noticing the angry scratches running down her back. A veritable trail. "Peggy keeps Russian greyhounds," said Clara. "They got overexcited when I wrestled with them on the rug."

"Nude?"

"We should try everything. Isn't that what your mentor said?"

"Boogie's not my mentor."

"Look at you. Raging inside. You want to kick me out, but you won't. Because you enjoy showing me off, your crazy, upper-middle-class *shiksa*."

"It would help if you bathed occasionally."

"You're not an artist, like the rest of us here. You're a voyeur. And when you go home to make money, which is inevitable, given your character, and you've married a nice Jewish girl, somebody who shops, you'll be able to entertain the guys at the United Jewish Appeal dinner with stories about the days you lived with the outrageous Clara Chambers."

"Before she became famous."

"If you don't enjoy me now, you will in retrospect. Because what you're doing here is loading up your memory bank. Terry McIver has got you down pat."

"Oh yeah? What does that creep have to say about me?"

"If you want to know what Boogie was thinking yesterday, listen to Barney today. He calls you Barney like the player piano. Always playing somebody else's music because you have none of your own."

Stung, I belted her one, hard enough to bang her head against the wall. And when she came at me with her fists, I knocked her to the bed. "Were you with a guy called Carnofsky?" I asked.

"I don't know what you're talking about."

"I'm told somebody by that name has been showing a photograph of you here and there, making inquiries."

"I know no such person. I swear to God, Barney."

"Have you been shoplifting again?"

"No."

"Passing bad cheques? Anything I should know about?"

Paris in the early spring.

"Oh, wait. Now I've got it," she said, her eyes filled with guile. "I had an art teacher in New York called *Charnofsky*. A real sicko. He used to follow me to my loft in the Village and stand outside and watch the window. There were obscene phone calls. Once he exposed himself to me in Union Square."

"I thought you didn't know anybody called Carnofsky."

"I just remembered, but it was *Charnofsky*. It has to be him, that pervert. He mustn't find me, Barney."

A week passed before she would leave our hotel room again, and even then she was furtive, her face obscured by shawls, and avoiding our usual haunts. I knew she was lying about Carnofsky, or Charnofsky, but I didn't twig to what was going on. Had I understood, I might have been able to save her. *Mea culpa* yet again. Shit. Shit. Shit.

—*Barney's Version,* pp. 61–65

My room at the Grand Hotel Excelsior, off Boul' Mich, was filled with rats, rats and a gratifyingly depraved past, for the hotel had once functioned as a brothel for the Wehrmacht. Before entering my room, I hollered, and whacked on the door, hoping to scatter the repulsive little beasts. Before putting on my sweater, I shook it out for rat droppings. But lying on my lumpy bed, ghetto-liberated, a real expatriate, I could read the forbidden, outspoken Henry Miller, skipping the windy cosmic passages, warming to the hot stuff. Paris in the fabled twenties, when luscious slavering

American school teachers came over to seek out artists like me, begging for it. Waylaying randy old Henry in public toilets, seizing him by the cock. Scratching on his hotel room door, entering to gobble him. Wherever I travel I'm too late. The orgy has moved elsewhere.

My father wrote, grabbing for me across the seas to remind me of my heritage. He enclosed a Jewish calendar, warning me that Rosh Hashonnah came early this year, even for me who smoked hashish on the Sabbath. Scared even as I smoked it, but more terrified of being put down as chicken-shit. My father wrote to say that the YMHA *Beacon* was sponsoring a short-story contest and that the *Reader's Digest* was in the market for "Unforgettable Characters." Meanwhile, *The New Yorker* wouldn't have me, neither would the *Partisan Review*.

—*Shovelling Trouble,* "A Sense of the Ridiculous," p. 29

ONE NIGHT AN EXUBERANT TERRY caught up with me at the Café Royal St-Germain. "George Whitman read my story," he said, "and has asked me to read at his bookshop."

"Why, that's terrific," I said, feigning enthusiasm. But I was in a foul mood for the rest of the day.

Boogie insisted on accompanying Clara and me to the bookshop opposite Notre Dame Cathedral. "Unmissable," said Boogie, obviously stoned. "Why, in years to come people will ask, where were you the night Terry McIver read from his *chef d'oeuvre*? Less fortunate men will be bound to say, I was cashing in my winning Irish Sweepstakes ticket, or I was screwing Ava Gardner. Or Barney will be able to boast he was there the night his beloved Canadiens won yet another Stanley Cup. But I will be able to claim I was present on the night literary history was being made."

"You're not coming with us. Forget it."

"I shall be humble. I will gasp at his metaphors and applaud each use of *le mot juste*."

"Boogie, I want your word that you're not going to heckle him."

"Oh, stop being such a *kvetch*," said Clara. "You're not Terry's mother."

Folding chairs had been provided for forty, but there were only nine people there when Terry began to read, a half-hour late.

"I believe Edith Piaf is opening somewhere on the Right Bank tonight," said Boogie, *sotto voce*, "otherwise there would surely have been a better turnout."

Terry was in mid-flight when a bunch of Letterists barged into the bookshop. They were supporters of *Ur, Cahiers Pour Un Dictat Culturel*, which was edited by Jean-Isador Isou. The redoubtable Isou was also the author of *A Reply to Karl Marx*, a slender riposte that was peddled to tourists by pretty girls on the rue de Rivoli and outside American Express — tourists under the tantalizing illusion that they were buying the hot stuff. The Letterists believed that all the arts were dead and could be resurrected only through a synthesis of their collective absurdities. Their own poems, which they usually recited in a café on the Place St-Michel, consisted of grunts and cries, incoherent arrangements of letters, set to an antimusical background and, for a time, I was one of their fans. And now, as Terry continued to read in a monotone, they played harmonicas, blew whistles, pumped the rubber bulb of a klaxon, and, hands cupped under armpits, made farting noises.

Deep down, I'm a homer. I root for the Montreal Canadiens and, when they were still playing ball in Delorimier Downs, our Triple-A Royals. So I instinctively sprang to Terry's defense. "*Allez vous faire foutre! Tapettes! Salauds! Petits merdeurs! Putes!*" But this only served to spur on the rowdies.

A flushed Terry read on. And on. And on. Seemingly in a trance, his fixed smile chilling to behold. I felt sick. *Hold the phone.* Yes, I was truly concerned for him, but, bastard that I am, I was equally relieved that he hadn't drawn a crowd. Or won acclaim. Afterwards, I told Boogie and Clara I would catch up with them at The Old Navy, but first I was taking Terry out for a drink. Before we parted, Boogie startled me by saying, "I've heard worse, you know."

Terry and I met at a café on the boulevard St-Michel, and sat on the terrace, the only people there, a couple of Canucks who didn't mind the cold. "Terry," I said, "those clowns were out for blood and wouldn't have behaved any differently had Faulkner been reading there tonight."

"Faulkner is overestimated. He won't endure."

"All the same, I'm sorry for what happened. It was brutal."

"Brutal? It was absolutely wonderful," said Terry. "Don't you know that the first performance of Mozart's *Marriage of Figaro* was booed in Vienna and that when the Impressionists first showed their work they were laughed at?"

"Yeah, sure. But —"

"…you ought to know," he said, obviously quoting somebody, "that What is Grand is necessarily obscure to Weak men. That which can be made Explicit to the Idiot is not worth my care."

"And just who said that, may I ask?"

"William Blake wrote that in a letter to the Reverend John Trusler, who had commissioned some watercolours from him and then criticized the results. But what did you think, not that it matters?"

"Who could hear in all that racket?"

"Don't be evasive with me, please."

Sufficiently irritated by now to want to crack his carapace of arrogance, I knocked back my cognac and said, "All right, then. Many are called, but few are chosen."

"You're pathetic, Barney."

"Right. And you?"

"I'm surrounded by a confederacy of dunces."

That prompted a laugh from me.

"Now why don't you just settle the bill, because after all it was you who invited me, and move on to wherever you're meeting your oafish Trilby and foul-mouthed Paphian?"

"My foul-mouthed what?

"Harlot."

The Second Mrs. Panofsky once observed that in the absence of heart there was a knot of anger swirling inside me. And now, my blood surging, I leapt up, lifted Terry out of his chair, and smashed him hard in the face, his chair toppling over. Then I stood over him, crazed, fists ready to fly. Murder in my heart. But Terry wouldn't fight back. Instead he sat on the pavement, smirking, nursing his bleeding nose with a handkerchief. "Good night," I said.

"The bill. I haven't got enough money on me. Settle the bill, damn you."

I threw some franc notes at him, and was just about to flee when he began to tremble and sob brokenly. "Help me," he said.

"What?"

"…my hotel…"

I managed to get him to his feet and we started to walk, his teeth chattering, his legs rubbery. We had only gone a block when he began to shake. No, vibrate. He sank to his knees and I held his head, as he vomited again and again. Somehow or other, we made it back to his room on the rue Saint-André-des-Arts. I got him into bed, and when he started to tremble again, I piled whatever clothes I could find on top of his blankets. "It's the flu," he said. "I'm not upset. This has nothing to do with my reading. You're not saying anything."

"What should I say?"

"There's no doubting my talent. My work will last. I know that."

"Yes."

Then his teeth began to chatter at such a rate I feared for his tongue. "Please don't go yet."

I lit a Gauloise and passed it to him, but he couldn't handle it. "My father can hardly wait for me to fail and to join him in misery."

He began to weep again. I grabbed the wastepaper basket and held his head, but for all his heaving he could bring up nothing but a string of green slime. As soon as the retching stopped, I brought him a glass of water. "It's the flu," he said.

"Yes."

"I'm not upset."

"No."

"If you tell any of the others you saw me like this, I'll never forgive you."

"I won't say a word to anybody."

"Swear it."

I swore it, and sat with him until his body stopped jerking, and he fell into a troubled sleep. But I had been a witness to his cracking and that, dear reader, is how you make enemies.

—*Barney's Version,* pp. 93–96

DEAR BILL: You don't really deserve a long letter. after all i'm still starving and writing on the cote while you are able to drop into ben's for a sandwich every night. today i installed myself in a lovely apartment in haut-de-cagnes…. a huge window here overlooks a wonderful view of the "picturesque" hills and the sea and every now and then i get up from my typewriter and overlook…. another window overlooks jimmy's bar and barefooted existentialist sex. every now and then i reach my arm out for a cognac or an existentialist breast. life, as you see, has its problems. i finished the rotten people about ten days ago. protter was down here with various other inscrutable intellectual types and they read parts of the book. protter & co. have come around: they think i'm stupendous and young and brilliant. but they also think i'll have one hell of a time selling the book (the conventional publishers wouldn't read past page three). it seems i could get the book done by new directions if i was a homosexual and slept with jimmy. hurray for the literary life. everybody thinks if i made my next opus a bit more digestible for the tender bourgeois stomachs i should be able to sell. all of which — really — is not too much comfort. anyway the rotten people has been mailed to creative age press…. eric thinks my book is 500% better than my stories and on the basis of this i ran home and wrote a new story which he says he will consider very carefully…. enough about writing and richler. i just thought i'd keep you informed…. in two weeks — after i have completed several stories — i move to italy for a month. i shall work out a presentable draft of my new novel there and with one hundred pages of copy present it to the doubleday agent in paris…. i shall be back in paris in mid-october and stay there until i go broke…. i hope — before such ill luck materializes — i will have an advance on my second book (it will be my first great novel)…. i found your letter thoroughly amusing. glad you liked mama. write soon.

Mordy

p.s. can you lend me $25?

—Letter to William Weintraub, August 30, 1951,
Getting Started, pp. 71–72

ALL AT ONCE, IT WAS SPRING.

One day shopkeepers were wretched, waiters surly, concierges mean about taking messages, and the next, the glass windows encasing café terraces were removed everywhere, and Parisians were transmogrified: shopkeepers, waiters, concierges actually spoke in dulcet tones.

Afternoons we took to the Jardins du Luxembourg, lying on the grass and speculating about Duke Snider's arm, the essays in *The God That Failed*, Jersey Joe Walcott's age, whether Salinger's *The Catcher in the Rye* could be good *and* a Book-of-the-Month, how far Senator Joe McCarthy might go, was Calder Willingham overrated, how much it might set us back to motorcycle to Seville, was Alger Hiss lying, why wasn't Nathaniel West more widely read, could Don Newcombe win thirty games, and was it disreputable of Max Brod to withhold Kafka's "Letter To My Father."

Piaf was big with us, as was Jacques Prévert's *Paroles*, the song "*Les Feuilles mortes*," Trenet, and the films of Simone Signoret. Anything by Genet, or Samuel Beckett was passed from hand to hand. I tried to read *La Nausée* in French, but stumbled and gave it up.

Early one Sunday morning in May, laying in a kitbag filled with wine, *pâté*, hardboiled eggs, guiches and salamis and cold veal from the charcuterie, cheeses, a bottle of armagnac and baguettes, five of us squeezed into a battered Renault quatre-chevaux and set off for Chartres and the beaches of Normandy. 1952 it was, but we soon discovered that the rocky beaches were still littered with the debris of war. Approaching the coast we bumped drunkenly past shelled-out, crumbling buildings, VERBOTEN printed on one wall and ACHTUNG! on another. This moved us to incredulous laughter, evoking old Warner Brothers films and dimly recalled hit parade tunes. But, once on the beaches, we were sobered and silent. Incredibly thick pill boxes, split and shattered, had yet to be cleared away. Others, barely damaged, clearly showed scorch marks. Staring into the dark pill boxes, through gun slits that were still intact, was chilling, even though gulls now squawked reassuringly overhead. Barefoot, our trousers rolled to the knees, we roamed the beaches, finding deep pits and empty shell cases here and there. As the tide receded, concrete teeth were revealed still aimed at the incoming tanks and landing craft. I stooped to retrieve a soldier's boot from a garland of seaweed. Slimy, soggy, already sea-green, I could still make out the bullet hole in the toe.

— *Shovelling Trouble,* "A Sense of the Ridiculous," pp. 33–34

ON BALANCE, our weekend in Paris was more unsettling than satisfying. Seated at the Dôme, well-dressed, consuming double scotches rather than nursing a solitary beer on the lookout for somebody who had just cashed his GI cheque on the black market, I realized I appeared just the sort of tourist who would have aroused the unfeeling scorn of the boy I had been in 1951. A scruffy boy with easy, bigoted attitudes, encouraging a beard, addicted to T-shirts, the obligatory blue jeans and, naturally, sandals. Absorbed by the Tarot and trying to write in the manner of Céline. Given to wild pronouncements about Coca-Cola culture and late nights listening to Sydney Bechet at the Vieux Colombier. We had not yet been labelled beats, certainly not hippies. Rather, we were taken for existentialists by *Life,* if not by Jean-Paul Sartre, who had a sign posted in a jazz cellar warning he had nothing whatsoever to do with these children and that they hardly represented his ideas.

— *Shovelling Trouble,* "A Sense of the Ridiculous," pp. 25–26

"YOU CROSS THE PYRENEES," Peabody said, "and you're leaving Europe behind you. Those mountains are a time machine. On the other side, it's a hundred years ago. Much more in some places."

Spain beckoned. Yes. But by this time he had already blown most of his stake, some of it on the horses at Longchamps and Maison Lafitte, the biggest chunk in one wild drunken night with Peabody at the roulette tables in a club near l'Opéra. So he set out for London instead, where he would at least be able to find work without a labour permit. Clippings in hand, he made the rounds. Reuters, UP, AP, CP. He filled in on somebody's vacation on a desk here, subbed somewhere else for a fortnight, and served as a stringer for a number of Canadian newspapers, filing the obligatory crap. If, for instance, a dumpy Canadian actress had a walk-on part in a play on Shaftesbury Avenue, he would write TORONTO BEAUTY DAZZLES WEST END. He also turned to plagiarism. Ripping a short story with a twist in its tail from *Collier's*, he rewrote it, setting it in Calgary, and sent it off to the Toronto *Star Weekly* with a covering letter saying he was a struggling Canadian artist, who simply refused to sell his proud heritage for a fistful of Yankee dollars. The enclosed story had been accepted by the *Saturday Evening Post*, if only he agreed to make the place-names American. This, he wrote, would be a violation of his integrity; he would rather accept less money from a Canadian publication. And, to his surprise, the story earned him a cheque for $300, and a request for more. Then he was asked by a Montreal editor to go to Cambridge and send them 750 words on Canadian students for an educational supplement.

Cambridge. Everywhere he looked, bats on bicycles. Rotten teeth. But there, on a wet misty Saturday morning in the Market Square, he first encountered Murdoch, literally bumping into him as they were both riffling David's Bookstall for early Penguins, ancient Everymans, costing no more than sixpence each. In those days the yet-to-be-published Murdoch still read other people's novels in anticipation of pleasure, and Joshua did not yet take them as fodder for his scabrous reviews, outbidding everybody in invective. Joshua picked up a hardback, a novel published in 1934, and the reviewers' quotes on the faded jacket were dazzling. "Not to be missed." "A minor masterpiece." "Brilliant." He had never heard of the author.

Murdoch, with his gift for anticipating what others thought, grinned at him. "It's a mug's game," he said.

Joshua read the first paragraph aloud, they both guffawed, and repaired to Morley's for a pint.

Soul mates.

Murdoch was still wiry then, National Health steel-rims riding his fussy nose, mop of greasy black hair, brown eyes amazed, his tweed jacket the standard utility wear. Already pumping wild-eyed energy and malice out of every pore. "Now tell me, who is this Adlai Badly chap they are all talking about so much over there?"

A council schoolboy from Bradford, a scholarship lad, Murdoch was to earn a double first at King's. Once, when they stopped there to collect his mail, he asked Joshua to wait outside the porter's gate. "Sorry," he said. "But you're not a member of the college. Indeed, you are my social inferior in every respect."

"A rare advantage for you, that, Sidney."

"If you only knew," he replied, grinning.

But later he retreated into melancholy. "Do you think there'll be a place for us?" he asked.

"Where?"

"In this world, is where. I won't stand in queues. I am not going to eat in restaurants that accept luncheon vouchers. Or keep a post office account. I want everything."

"We're going to have it, Sidney."

"You don't understand this wretched country. It's not enough to win a double first. It's pushy."

"We're special."

"Bless you. But you don't understand. If I won a Nobel Prize, the *Times* headline would read, 'Newsagent's Boy Wins...' And where, in God's name," he asked, rounding on Joshua, "do you get your confidence?"

Joshua unbuttoned his shirt to reveal a long thin key hanging from a silvery chain.

"What's that?"

"It's the key to a box which is in the Royal Bank of Canada on the main street of Cornwall just across the Ontario border."

"Seriously, Joshua, how come you're so sure of yourself?"

Me, sure of myself. He had to laugh. "Well," he said, "I'll tell you. When I was a kid, my father used to take me out walking downtown, and whenever we ran into somebody he knew, he'd stop him and say, 'I'd like you to meet my son, Joshua. This is my boy.' And when I was old enough, he took me to meet Colucci in the La Scala Barbershop, and he said, 'Your days are numbered, Sonny.' 'How come?' Colucci asked. 'This is my boy, Joshua, now you just feel that muscle.' My father wasn't in town for my bar mitzvah, he had business elsewhere, but when he got back he took me into his

A back street in Barcelona, 1951.

poolroom, marched me over to the rack, handed me a key, and said, 'This will unlock our cue. It's yours. Nobody else can use it.' Then he turned to the boss and said, 'Off your ass, Stash, and rack 'em up for me and my son here.'"

—*Joshua Then and Now,* pp. 103–05

I FIRST SAW SPAIN in the winter of 1951, grudgingly journeying down to Barcelona from civilized Paris, a young and unpublished writer, ridden with scurvy of all things, in disgruntled need of some sun on the cheap. I had intended to endure exile from the excitements of Montparnasse for no more than two weeks, but, to my astonishment, the country captured my heart. I remained rooted there, on the enchanting island of Ibiza, in the Balearics, for almost a year, venturing onto the peninsula again and again, for Semana Santa in Madrid, the diversions offered by Barcelona's raunchy *barrio chino* on any night of the year, and the *Fallas* in Valencia.

Ah, I remember Valencia, the *Fallas*, being twenty years old in the spring, an underachiever with holes in my socks and no plans for the future but more travel.

Valencia, lying on the banks of the Río Turia, is in the heart of the orange country, its fruit succulent beyond compare.

Founded by the Greeks, overrun in turn by the Carthaginians, the Romans, Visigoths, and Arabs, Valencia is, above all, the city of El Cid, the Campeador or Champion of Castile, more properly known as Rodrigo Diaz de Vivar. El Cid, leading an army of 7,000 men, mostly Muslims, captured Valencia after a bitter nine-month siege in 1094. And since then, no rumour of war, no insurrection, has come to Spain without touching the volatile port of Valencia.

Festival fireworks light up the night sky in Valencia.

In 1808, Valencia rose against the French. In 1843, there was yet another rebellion, this one to restore the regency of María Cristina of Naples. During the Spanish Civil War, after the fall of Madrid, Valencia became the last stronghold of the tattered republican forces.

In 1952, you could still see destroyed or bomb-damaged buildings in the old town, but I had come for the *Fallas*, my first experience of a fiesta. I had also come, as it turned out, to see my first western dubbed in Spanish, big Joel Macrea moseying up to the saloon bar in Tombstone and demanding, "*Un coñac, por favor.*"

Armed with Mr. Hemingway's *Death in the Afternoon*, my ticket to passing for an *aficionado*, I was eager to see Litri, Aparicio, and the young Luis Miguel Dominguín fight bulls, necessarily brave, in the Plaza de Toros. Having once studied Hemingway's splendid glossary, I had absorbed enough to holler *¡anda!*, go on, at any picador who was reluctant to charge the bull, and *camelo*, or fake, at any bullfighter "who by tricks tries to appear to work close to the bull while in reality never taking any chances."

The fiesta was rooted in the Middle Ages when, on St. Joseph's Day, the carpenters' brotherhood burned their accumulated wood shavings in bonfires known as *fallas*. It is marked not only by *corridas*, but also by parades; madness the rule rather than the exception. Fantastic *papier-mâché* floats, most of them satiric in nature, are produced by different quarters of the town in fierce competition and paraded through the Plaza del Caudillo and the adjoining streets. Then, on the evening of March 19, everything goes up in flames.

Suddenly, as I recall it, all the street lights were extinguished and the fireworks display began.

A thin nervous line of red light shot up into the sky, ripping the darkness, exploding into shivering streaks of red and orange and green. Another scratch of light darted skywards, shattering itself in mid-air and momentarily illuminating the plaza in an eerie yellow light. The crowd sighed. Some people recoiling, others tittering. Soon the sky was exploding in multi-coloured grandeur, bleeding a myriad of trickling stars, shot through with gaping holes and oblique pin-lines of firecracker lights.

The giant *falla* of a pot-bellied gypsy burst into flames.

Another send-off of rocket lights wooshed upward, blossoming over the flames of burning *falla*, spluttering and hissing, pumping more angry rents into the sky.

Still another flurry zoomed heavenwards, rattling, spluttering, dribbling coloured stars on the plaza, and then there were still more explosions, more lights and all the other *fallas* went up in flames.

It was, to come clean, a far cry from the staid Queen Victoria Day celebrations of my childhood, the only other fireworks display I was familiar with.

Yes, indeed.

And those flames in Valencia consumed not only a pot-bellied gypsy, after all, a stranger, but also a host of personal devils. The most wintry of my Canadian baggage as well as some of the more stultifying Jewish injunctions I had grown up with. Gone with the flames went the guilt acquired by leaving college without a degree. Not going on to medicine or law, which would have delighted my parents. Up with the smoke went the need to squirrel something away for a rainy day. The compulsion to be sensible above all. Into the ashes went the obligation to endure Canadian winters, simply because I had been born there. Or the necessity, this one more recently acquired, to understand *Finnegan's Wake* or adjudge myself shallow.

I'm a slow learner. But walking away from that fire I grasped, for the first time, that I was a free man. I owed no apologies. My life was mine to spend as I pleased.

—*Images of Spain,* pp. 21–23

THE MORE LIBERATING the drunk, the greater the hangover.

What, after all, was I doing in Spain, I wondered, even as I sailed back to Ibiza.

Coming from Canada, born to reticence in general and Montreal in particular, it seemed to me, even in those irresponsible days, that England and France, not to say the Babylonian Talmud, were a justifiable part of my heritage, but Spain, the country I had come to cherish, was utterly foreign. A dangerous indulgence.

I was only twenty then, impulsive, inexperienced, certainly not well travelled. Since 1952, however, I have lived in countries that certainly boasted more civilized forms of government, a more beneficial literary past, incomparably better food and wine, and yet — and yet — there remains to this day no land in Europe I find more compelling than Spain.

—*Images of Spain,* p. 23

THEY BEGAN TO ASSEMBLE sober and even shy on the corners and plazas and alleyways shortly after midnight. Wooden bandstands had been erected on the street corners, and for a long time the jerky music of *pasodobles* swelled in the slums. Old men who had been searching the gutters for butts, pickpockets, beggar children, plump mothers nursing bawling babes in their arms, pimps, ragged soldiers far away from home, aged cripples and the blind sellers of lottery tickets, unemployed workers and young girls — all the discarded junk and wonderful humanity of the slums joined hands for the dancing. Drunks tumbled out of *bodegas* to join in or at least harangue the womenfolk. The noise was tremendous, booming, wonderful, and crazy. Empty bottles crashed to the pavement, wineskins were flung up into the air. The shouting of one band soon got mixed up with another and nobody knew what kind of dance was being played. As long as there was noise, and shouting, and laughter.

Finally the whores showed themselves as well — dressed in sheer black gowns or formfitting sweaters or slit skirts, drinking and joking and belching, just to show the wives how much they gave a damn. The gypsy boys appeared, cheap guitars slung over their shoulders, and they sat down on the kerb to play a *flamenco* or a *jota*.

"It is very colourful," Mrs. Ira Birks — *visiting dignitary from the United States, wife of a Harvard Law School graduate, apple-cheeked, native of Little Oak, Conn., aged fifty-three, sexually incompatible with Mr. Birks, antivivisectionist, Vassar, class of '22, member — DAR, SPCA, wrote poetry from 1920 to 1924 and still does the occasional watercolour, virginity lost in the back seat of a '19 Ford, favourite poet, John Keats — said, turning to Cardinal Megura y Paenz, Archbishop of Valencia.* "I simply adore your fiesta! If only I weren't obliged to attend the bullfights...."

The Ambassador laughed heartily.

The Archbishop smiled his thin and malodorous smile.

"Mrs. Birks is only joking," *the Ambassador said.*

They stood by one of the huge windows in the Exchange Building overlooking the Plaza del Mercado. The ball they were attending was in honour of the Fallera Mayor, *and the twenty-five-piece orchestra was playing the* Merry Widow *waltz.*

Red-eyed drunk now, mad with the *flamenco* wail, the whores began to dance. Bleached blondes, jerking, twisting their bodies angrily; blackhaired bitches lifting their arms overhead and clapping desperately; old sluts shaking themselves into a frenzy and stamping their feet down on the pavement; giggling novices scream-singing until they soaked themselves in sweat. All for the dance, all for the song, all for the music.

Moaning guitarists, their hands ripping up and down the twanging strings and beating on the hard wood of their instruments, made with their magic joy or sorrow of the maddening mob.

Ai-aiii-ai-aii,
Oooh aii yooii,
En cárcel,
En cárcel.

"*It is a good thing there is a strong hand over them,*" *General Mellado —* *veteran of the Blue Division, son of a parish priest, first officer into* *Guernica — said. "Otherwise... No, I won't talk politics in the presence of* *such a beautiful and distinguished lady.*"

"*Oh, but I adore politics, don't I, Henry?*"

The Ambassador laughed heartily.

Sweaty hands clapping, swelling hands clapping. Voices upgoing, high, high. Soul music reeling on, on, on, tumbling, jerking, screaming:

Fuego! Fuego! Fuego!
Como huele a chamusquina!
Fuego! Fuego! Fuego!
Ay que no, que son sardina!

Bodies rattling with spiritpain, cavorting on the alive street. (A man grabs a woman and retreats into the shadows.) Eyes crave-filling, paining. (A girl bites the neck of her partner.) Mouths of disbelief and hunger, heads filling with blood and want. (A young girl swoons.) Veins of the neck swelling purplish, chests thumping and sweatful. (Pedro quells his quaking wife with a slap, and holds her to him.)

Fuego! Fuego! Fuego!
Mundos y planetas en revolución
con el fuego! De me corazón!

"What do you think of Graham Greene, Cardinal??"
"Greene...?"
"Oh, it is nothing," the Ambassador said quickly, "just a writer. Mrs. Birks is something of an intellectual. She often addresses clubs...."

...and the guitarist slaps his guitar bang bang bang bang, and all is quiet. The buildings are quiet, the streets are quiet. So quiet, so still. Only the sound of breathing and only the stink of sweat. Even the clouds don't move, even God is wondering. (I shall walk up to heaven and turn off the stars one by one. I shall rub out the Milky Way with my heel and paint the moon in black. I shall kick the sun sizzling into the sea and I shall spit comets on all of Spain. If God is in I shall tell him why.) And the guitarist laughs. Laughs madly and like a devil. *Dinero*, he says, *dinero*. A crippled child moves among the crowd, collecting *centimos*. The people rest and drink.

"Oh, but they dance divinely!"
The General laughed jovially. "Men will be men."
Mrs. Birks smiled.
The Ambassador laughed heartily.
"God bless them," said the Archbishop.

They danced until their bodies ached from excess of pleasure (and they thought the earth had fallen out of the sky), they danced until their eyes were swollen with need of sleep (and they saw the buildings were of gold and the streets of soft silk and the lampposts lit by glowing diamonds), they danced until they were too drunk to stand (and they believed the sun was hot and the earth was friendly and the grass was green in spring), they danced until Sunday's dawn filled the sky gloomily and without promise (and they believed in the day and God and they were no longer afraid).

— The Acrobats, pp. 37–40

TOURISTS, JOSHUA DISCOVERED, were rare in Spain in 1952, especially footloose young Canadians, and he was amazed, after having endured the grasping French, to find himself treated as a guest everywhere he wandered in Almeria, even bartenders standing him to drinks. *Como su casa.*

Barcelona.

There seemed, at first glance, to be a few of the very, very rich in Barcelona, many who were unspeakably poor, but hardly any middle class to speak of. The rich, he discovered, were for the most part vastly entertaining fellows who had never done a day's work in their lives and were offended by the very notion of it. Oblomovs abounded. Among them, the engaging but mindless Antonio, who wore a Savile Row suit and drove a sparkling white Austin-Healey. "Given the benefit of a couple of drinks," Antonio said, "we're all republicans here. A few more stiff ones, and we're Communists. But come four o'clock in the morning, man, every self-respecting Spaniard is an anarchist. So, we need Franco, don't you see?"

People gathered at the harbour in Ibiza.

Yes. Certainly. And the next evening Joshua sailed for Ibiza.

—*Joshua Then and Now,* pp. 107–08

IN THE WATERFRONT CAFÉ, where he was to become a regular, Ibiza's blind lottery-ticket seller would come wandering through the beaded door, tapping his cane, in hazard. The fishermen were fond of luring him into the rear of the café and then swiftly but surreptitiously shifting the tables and chairs around to block his passage out. As the old man lashed left and right with his cane, desperately trying to find a way out of the constantly shifting maze, the fishermen fell about laughing.

Ibiza, Ibiza.

Not him, no, no, but somebody else called Joshua Shapiro, a boy he blushed even to recall, had once been rooted there, roaring.

And yet, and yet, he thought, even as he disowned this other Joshua, I'd give a good deal for a cup of his enthusiasm right now.

Ibiza.

There are four islands in the Balearic Archipelago: Majorca, Minorca, Ibiza, and Formentera.

Ibiza is an island of limestone hills, lush pine forests, fertile flatlands, and enticing stretches of sandy beach. There is also a salt marsh. Juniper and evergreen oak thrive there. The most gnarled of the olive, fig, and almond trees are reputed to be a thousand years old. Oranges are grown on Ibiza, but they are not nearly as sweet as those produced in the province of Valencia. The Ibizenco peasant, an obdurate man, is not highly adaptable. He survives, nothing more. Many of the island's sailors, however, mariners of prodigious skill, had travelled the world. And there was a time when Ibiza's fishing grounds were fabulously rich.

The island's capital is also called Ibiza, and is quite unforgettably approached by sea. Cubelike, sun-dappled white houses. The Upper Town and its surrounding wall, built in the sixteenth century, soaring above the natural harbour. There are passageways winding through the wall, and when the lookout signalled the appearance of a Barbary pirate ship on the horizon, the Ibizencos hastily took refuge within. Defenders assumed positions at the top of the wall, overlooking the passageway into the Upper Town, as if peering down into a well. No sooner did the *corsarios* appear at the bottom than they were bombarded with rocks. His father would have approved, Joshua thought. Real scrappers, he would have said.

Stepping down the gangplank of the *Jaime II* early one evening in 1952, an exhilarated twenty-one-year-old Joshua Shapiro was immediately hailed by a man who was to become his mentor on the island. Juanito Tur-Guerra, otherwise celebrated as Juanito Pus, owner of two battered fishing boats, a dockside *barraca*, or storage shed, and undisputed king of the waterfront.

"*Venga, hombre. Aquí.*"

Clapping Joshua on the back, Juanito summoned fishermen to help him with his kitbag; he booked him into the small, flaking hotel on the quay and propelled him into the bar for a glass of Fundador. He was a small lithe man, his face leathery, his blue eyes flecked with mockery. Juanito had more than energy, he was a furnace. They stood at the bar for hours, joined by still more rubber-booted fishermen, laughing a good deal. Joshua established that he was a *Canadiensi*.

"Yes, but what do you do?"

"I'm a reporter. Sort of."

Juanito, like Uncle Oscar an authority on all matters, wasn't having any of it. Biting into a fresh cheroot and spitting on the floor, he revealed to the others that Joshua was obviously a rich man's son, sent to Ibiza to avoid his being drafted for military service in Korea. Joshua protested that there was no draft in Canada, but unavailingly, and the story was to stick with him for the duration of his stay.

Come midnight — groggy, staggering drunk — Joshua pleaded fatigue and inquired after his room, but Juanito insisted that they all immediately repair to Casa Rosita.

Voices subdued to whispers lest wives overhear them, they clambered over an incredibly narrow and twisting rock passageway that ran between the overhanging whitewashed houses in Sa Penya, the fishermen's quarter built on a rock promontory at the harbour mouth. Casa Rosita was the local bordello, and the arrival of Juanito and his band was greeted with whoops of delight from the girls. The girls, a frisky bunch, wore soiled housecoats unbuttoned over torn slips or bra and panties. Ascending to an upstairs bedroom with one or another of the drunken fishermen, they lugged a slopping pail of hot water, a bar of strong soap, and a freshly boiled but frayed towel.

"Is that a religious medal?" the girl asked, reaching for the long, thin key that was suspended from the silver chain round his neck.

"It's my inheritance."

The keys to the kingdom of Shapiro.

"If anything happens to me," Reuben had said, seeing him off, "everything you find in that box is yours. Do you mind if I kiss you?"

"Of course not."

"You never know. So I thought I'd ask first."

Arriving on the island, Joshua had been surprised to see the waterfront churning with strollers, but he soon came to appreciate that the weekly visit of a ship from Barcelona, Valencia, or Alicante was sufficient to bring out the crowds. An even more auspicious occasion, he discovered, was when Juanito let it out — the word flashing from bar to bar — that there would be a fresh shipment of girls for Casa Rosita on the incoming ship. The thin, pasty girls, their makeup garish, were unmistakable as they hobbled high-heeled and defiant down the gangplank, straining against the weight of cardboard suitcases bound with rope. The fishermen, stoked with Fundador, scrutinized them from the terrace of the waterfront café, staking claims and passing judgment on their promise. Impatient as they were to introduce themselves, the fishermen understood — even as Rosita hustled her charges off, respectable people creating a disdainful passage for them — that it would be early and alone to bed for the whores tonight. In the nature of things, they would have serviced the crew in the boiler room on their passage from the peninsula.

—Joshua Then and Now, pp. 124–27

SALLY WALKED.

It was a fine autumn day. Haverstock Hill was loud with Sunday afternoon strollers. Time out this was, reprieve, two hours' liberty from the bed-sitters. Tomorrow the battle; this afternoon the sun was a fact. There was the Heath, Tynan's column to read, and always the possibility that somebody might offer you a drive. Next week was plenty of time to start looking for a room where one could have guests after eleven. This evening at the Duke of York Beasley might turn up with the fiver he owed you. Later, if you were lucky, you might bring back a girl for tea and chocolate digestives.

Sally joined the crowd working up the hill to Hampstead Heath. There were corduroy boys with girls nicer than candies. A bearded man with a red fez spoke against Christ in front of Mence Smith's. Young-marrieds pushed prams before them. Thick, square Eastern Jews passed in groups of five and three. At every other corner a poky little man watched over a wide sweep of Sunday papers. Gilbert Harding will, for just a thruppence, tell you the most embarrassing incident of his life. Hitler's valet reveals all for the same price. So will Sabrina. At the next corner a West Indian in a shapeless fedora knelt tenderly over his little girl and gave her a lick of vanilla ice cream under an arrow which said, "To Keats' House."

Sally stopped off at the Duke of York and ordered a whisky and soda. Ordinarily she and Ernst avoided this pub because of the people who gathered there, but today Sally found the crowd reassuringly gay. She watched one group in particular, pretending to be one of them. There was a high man with a chalky British face and a silk scarf knotted round his neck who Sally was sure had contributed at least one poem to *Time and Tide*. He was talking to a girl who wore her hair in a ponytail. Wendy was her name, and she had turned in a bloody good performance on ITV last night. There were three others in the group. A squat red-faced bore, who, had he been Canadian would have been put down for an insurance salesman, but, being British, had probably won the MC for his part in organizing the partisans in lower Albania. The third man had obviously cultivated his Oxford stammer like a garden. The other girl, who had warned Dylan repeatedly that drink would be the end of him, was a spare blonde in toreador pants. All five pretended to abhor the pub and the people who frequented it. They gathered there, because like everyone else there, they found it droll to watch the others.

Sally squeezed out of the pub and continued up to the Heath. She felt numb. Something was dying inside her. A hope, perhaps, or a child's faith in the impossible. She watched for almost an hour as a man sailed an exact replica of the *Queen Mary* through the gales and lesser traffic of Hampstead Pond while his chauffeur leaned against the waiting Rolls Royce. The man, who sat on a canvas stool by the shore of the pond, controlled his ship by an electronic box. He often brought the Queen perilously close to the concrete shores before he made her turn sharply to the oohs and ahs of an apprehensive audience. Before long he shamed the adult owners of punier craft away from his sea. When Sally turned to go only the children's sailboats were left to dispute with the *Queen Mary*.

She descended into the Heath proper and counted all the boys with scarves and all the girls who wore glasses. She subtracted one sum from another, multiplied them by three and divided the new sum by two, and then she sank to the grass and wept long and bitterly. When she woke the first evening star was out. Walking down Haverstock Hill again she didn't realize that her eyes were red and that many of the passersby, particularly the older ones, eyed her with a not unkind concern. Running out on him, she thought, was a cowardly thing to do. Her steps quickened.

—*A Choice of Enemies*, pp. 126–28

IDLING ABT impotently on a cold night feeling damn depressed.... Just happened to pick up yr most recent letter and thought I'd write....

The book has slowed down on me. These things happen. I know they happen. But each day you sit vacant writing nothing but still a prisoner to the typewriter — each day like that is a special kind of hell. Questions come to you making small wounds. Why are you making this book? Does it matter? Do you believe in it? That's when you get up and have a cigarette and/or a cup of coffee. Then, a short walk. Then another cigarette. You pick up things. Books you can't concentrate on. Newspapers you can't understand. So on. Out again. Up to wander around the neighbourhood bookshops. So many books! Who — how — why are they written?? Back to the typewriter. You start again at the beginning, reading from P.1.... I thk art or attempts at art are born of despair. That, more than vanity or intimations of mortality.

I thk in writing there is no such thing as success. (I don't have to point out that publication is just a social hurdle and has nothing whatsoever to do with being a writer.) All writing is different levels of failure. Nothing really comes off. No. That's not exactly what I mean....

What I mean is once you go after a truth you can get only so close — closer yesterday than today, next week than this week, BUT never there — never the orgasm. Hope of excitement, sometimes even the excitement itself (inspiration?) but never the culminating death/birth....

Before I had my first bk accepted and until I began work on my second I wanted to be famous. Have position. Anecdotes told abt me. And the rest of it. But now I do not want or think abt these things very much. They are trifling in themselves. And, worse still, there is no fame big enough or money bribery enough to compensate for the

Richler in the streets of London during the sixties.

pain that goes into the making of a novel. (Even the mixed joy of publication is paltry, aspirins for cancer.) So why do I write? I really don't know. I can thk of a lot of reasons but all of them wd be "thought up" and only partly true. Nearest I can come to it is "I have to."

Elsewhere: Have ordered René Clair's book for you, shd get it on Tuesday. Was out drinking the other night with Louis MacNeice and wife, Kathleen Thomas and John Davenport. Mrs. Thomas is drinking like a fish. Has been ever since Dylan died. MacNeice says André Deutsch and Hart-Davis best post-war publishers. Read Orwell's *Homage to Catalonia* tonight. A man of commendable rages. I'll send it on if you haven't read it. There was a Cocteau festival at Everyman [cinema] in Hampstead recently. That man is a fraud of frauds. A poseur of the worst order. Marx Brothers festival begins on Monday (best news in wks!)....

Talking abt obscenities, there was a big fuss here. Printers refused to print [*The Acrobats*]. They got a lawyer. André [Deutsch] got a lawyer. Richler was called in, charged with obscenity, blasphemy, and worse. Bang bang bang. Several minor changes have been made; e.g., tits to breasts, kick you in the balls to kick you where it hurts, bloody christ to christ. Nothing important really. All most amusing.

Write.

Mort

—Letter to William Weintraub, January 29, 1954,
Getting Started, pp. 97–99

AT THE TIME, Murdoch and Margaret lived in Kentish Town and Joshua had a small flat in Chelsea.

In the seedy early fifties, long before London had been pronounced swinging, Chelsea's most celebrated tomcat was Eliot, a resident of Cheyne Walk, and the only boutiques worth seeking out on the King's Road were dark, smelly little places stacked with secondhand books. Joshua's modest flat on the then-tatty end of the King's Road lent him the use of place-names that matched his mood perfectly. His bus stop was Lot's Road; his local, the World's End. Stepping out in his baggy utility tweeds, he could, if he chose to, stroll toward squalid Fulham, lingering at smog-encrusted windows of row upon row of decrepit junk and secondhand furniture shops, munching fish and chips wrapped in a greasy *News of the World*. Or if he wandered the other way, toward Sloane Square, there were an abundance of foul Anglo-Indian and Chinese restaurants, secondhand bookshops, tobacconists, and barbershops with big flashing Durex signs in the window, and chemists, their dusty, faded window displays proffering rupture belts and salves that promised relief from itchy hemorrhoids.

Murdoch, whose first novel had been published to hosannas, was already famous as well as feared, though not yet in the money. He was still supplementing his income from royalties by reviewing here, pounding out a telly column there, and reading for a publisher somewhere else. Moved by his condition, even more parlous than his own, Joshua advised him to order all his food, even whatever clothes he required, from Harrods. "Open an account. Get your bloody publisher to sign for you, if necessary. And then, so far as gullible tradesmen are concerned, you are no longer a yabbo but a proper gentleman. The Harrods' accounts are sent out quarterly. When it comes, ignore it. A month will pass before you are sent a polite reminder. Then you run through the itemized account and query a jar of mustard here, a tin of sardines there. This creates unimaginable confusion. Wretched little clerks, who cycle to work from darkest Clapham, scurry from desk to desk in the basement. Files are pried open. Sales slips consulted. Ledgers double-checked. Months will pass before somebody comes up with the actual signed sales slip, including the mustard or sardines. The next step calls for a little guile. You write an indignant letter querying the authenticity of the signature on the sales slip. More confusion. Consternation in the very bowels of the emporium. Further delays. Six months will pass before you have to settle the account and by that time, I hope, you will have the necessary money. If not, keep the correspondence going."

—*Joshua Then and Now,* pp. 199–200

ALL THE GAY, SOPHISTICATED MEN gathered in his flat could be divided into two groups. Those who wore extravagant waistcoats and those who went in for extravagant moustaches. The first group, it seemed, was made up of journalists, advertising writers, assistant film and television directors, and nonfigurative painters. Most of them had been to minor public schools. They were, on the whole, amusing, clever, and with a tendency to get drunk as a matter of pride. The extravagant moustaches talked about their sports cars, past and present, with a mixture of energy, nostalgia, and passion that one usually associates with talk about one's mistresses. They wouldn't speak of their jobs. "You've got to earn a crust of bread somehow," was about as concrete as one of them got with Norman. But, it appeared, they were mostly businessmen of one sort or another and they were far more political. They thought the country was going to pot. There was a dream of a Northern Rhodesian farm, an Australian sheep ranch, or an oil job in Saudi Arabia in their futures. They were shorter, redder, and more inclined to corpulence than the others. Through their contact with the extravagant waistcoats they had acquired a taste for French salads, but nothing would make them give up tomato sauce. Most of the girls — actresses, models, dancers — were extremely attractive and, contrary to legend, far more decorative than their American or continental counterparts.

—*A Choice of Enemies,* pp. 245–46

BACK IN THE EARLY SIXTIES, we bought our first house on Kingston Hill, a London suburb. Ten rooms, it was, but come to think of it, it cost me less than it would to buy a new car today. In any event, I did hope that the purchase of the house would establish me as an unquestioned member of the Surrey bourgeoisie. We had only been installed on Kingston Hill a week, maybe two, when my wife sent me across the street to buy a large bag of peat. As I was about to hump it back across to Kingston Hill, a car slowed down, which I took for a courtesy, but then it stopped and the driver smiled and ·offered me something like ten shillings an hour if I would tend to his garden as well. Now my point is this — that could never happen to Robertson Davies. Most writers I know look like drug dealers, schoolmistresses who have been discharged for moral turpitude, card sharpers, barmaids or shoplifters. Robertson Davies, however, is not only a master of magic, but he also looks like one. He could never be mistaken for anything else.

—Robertson Davies, pp. 7–8

Jake Hersh (St. Urbain's Horseman)*, accused of sexual assault, requires legal advice.*

ORMSBY-FLETCHER.

When it became obvious, even to Jake, that there would be no stopping Ingrid's complaint and that the case would actually go to court, his first embarrassed thought was he did not want a Jewish lawyer, no twisting, eloquent point scorer, who would outwit judge and prosecutor, eat witnesses, alienate the jury, shine so foxily in court in fact as to ultimately lose him the case. No. Say what you like about the *goyim*, they had their uses. For his defense Jake required an upright plodding WASP; and, in his mind's eye, swishing cognac around in his glass night after night, Jake methodically fabricated his Identi-Kit champion. He would be unaggressively handsome, after the fashion of the British upper classes, that is to

London's Piccadilly Circus, 1949.

say, somewhat wanting, like an underdeveloped photograph. Without salt. He would commute, Jake imagined, from a detached in an unspoiled village in Surrey (nr. Guildford, 40 min. Waterloo), where on weekends he tended to the rose bushes and fought off encroaching crabgrass with his toothy wife. (If it isn't too much to hope for, Jake thought, fighting down the tears, we'll swap cuttings, my *goy* and I.) *England worries him.* Raised on the King James version, lemon squash, *Tom Brown's Schooldays*, hamsters from Harrods' pet shop, Daddy's Ceylon tea shares, Kaffirs, debentures, chocolate digestives, and duty, he would find today's swingers perplexing. He would approve of the court's decision on *Lady Chatterley's Lover*, but would argue — Jake hoped — that issuing the novel in paperback, thereby making it available to untutored minds, was going too far, rather, like MBEs for the Beatles. He would have been to a good but minor public school, doing his national service with a decent regiment, going on from there to Pembroke, Cambridge (his father's college) before being articled to a solicitor. He would not have crammed at university because his nagging parents had never had the chance *oy* and were doing without *oy oy*: he would have muddled through to a degree. He was a Tory, but no Blimp. While he felt, for instance, that black Africans were not quite ready for self-government, he could jolly well understand their point of view. His wife — "The vicar's daughter," Jake decided aloud — ordered a joint (tenderized) for Sunday and cleverly made do (colour supplement shepherd's pie, not-*too*-hot curry) until Tuesday. Waste not, want not. Instead of dinner on Wednesday they got by with high tea, cucumber and fish-paste sandwiches, bread and jam, while he helped his son with his Latin prep and she read *Mary Poppins* aloud to their little girl. Mnnn… I know, Jake added, clapping his hands, there is no central heating because they both agreed it was unhealthy. When she was having her menstrual period he was not so boorishly selfish as to hint at alternative forms of gratification: instead he came home bearing boxes of chocolates.

My *goy*'s wife, Jake thought, once the most feared leftwinger on the Girton hockey field, twice mentioned in Jennifer's Diary, drives him to his commuters' train each morning, both of them fastened into their seat belts, and — Jake added — if he makes a telephone call from my house he will offer me four pence. If she has stunning breasts she would keep them decently bound and cashmered: similarly, if her bottom was ravishingly round it would be squared into a tweed skirt.

We'll chat about politics, Jake thought, my *goy* and I, agreeing that while Harold Wilson was too clever by half and George Brown wasn't the sort of chap you'd send to see the Queen, they were, after all, entitled to their innings. Jake's solicitor would no more fiddle the tax inspector than cheat his mother at bezique; and what about the *Times* crossword? Yes, yes, of course he does it. Faithfully.

Perfect!

But where oh where, Jake wondered, consumed with ardour for his image, will I find such a limp prick? And then he remembered Ormsby-Fletcher. Stiff-collared, cherub-mouthed Ormsby-Fletcher, whom he had met at one of Luke's parties, finding him as abandoned as an empty beer bottle in a corner of the living room. "I daresay," Ormsby-Fletcher said, "I'm the only one here not connected with the arts. I'm Adele's cousin, you see."

So Jake located Ormsby-Fletcher and phoned him at his office. "Mr. Ormsby-Fletcher," he said, "I'm afraid you won't remember me. This is Jacob Hersh —"

"Indeed I do."

"I'm in trouble."

"I'm afraid I don't handle divorces myself, but I'd be glad to refer —"

"What about, um, criminal law?"

"I see," Ormsby-Fletcher said, faltering, retreating, already contriving excuses, Jake thought.

"Couldn't we meet," Jake cut in. "Informally, if you like."

They met at a pub, Jake arriving first, showily carrying a *Times* and *Punch*. "I fancy a long drink myself," Jake said, already tight. "What about you?" A gin, he said; and then Jake suffered chitchat and fortified himself with uncounted doubles before he risked saying, "This is probably not your cup of tea, Mr. Ormsby-Fletcher. I shouldn't have troubled you. You see, it's a sex charge."

The blood went from Ormsby-Fletcher's strawberry-coloured cheeks and he drew his long legs in from under the table tight as he could to his chair.

"Hold on. I'm not queer. It's —"

"Perhaps if you began at the beginning."

Brilliant. So Jake started to talk, circling close to repellent details, backpedalling furiously, hemming, hawing, hinting obliquely, retreating from the excruciating moment he would have to get down to concrete details, the crux, which would oblige him, just for openers, to use words such as penis and penetration…or, Jake wondered, hesitating again, was he expected to lapse into a gruffer idiom, something more forthrightly colonial? And then Ormsby-Fletcher, permanently endearing himself to Jake, volunteered, "I see. So then he led her into your room and, on her own initiative, she took hold of your roger..."

My roger, of course. "Yes," Jake said, igniting with drunken delight, "then the bitch took my roger in her hand...."

"But if that's the case, Mr. Hersh —"

Jake clapped his hand on Ormsby-Fletcher's shoulder and locked him in a manful heartfelt look. "Jake," he said.

"Edward," Ormsby-Fletcher responded without hesitation.

Unburdening himself now, Jake released the sewer gates. Careful not to incriminate Harry, he told all. Well, almost.

"I see."

"Well, Edward?"

"Can't promise anything, you understand, but I'll see what I can do."

"That's good enough for me," Jake said, compromising him, he hoped.

"I suggest you come to our offices first thing tomorrow morning," Ormsby-Fletcher said, and he called for a round-for-the-road.

"Sorry. No more for me," Jake said, immensely pleased with himself. "I'm driving, you see."

It was, as it turned out, the first of a seemingly endless run of conferences at offices, with ruinously expensive barristers, and at Jake's house.

Jake, doting on Ormsby-Fletcher, came to anticipate his needs. Five sugars and milk heated hot enough to make a fatty skin for his coffee. Brandy, yes, but not an ostentatiously sloshed three fingersful into a snifter: rather, a splash, British style, sufficient to dampen the bottom of the glass. Ormsby-Fletcher liked to relax with a cigar and natter about this island now. "I daresay, to your way of looking, we *are* hopelessly inefficient..."

"But living here, "Jake protested, looking deep, "is so much more civilized than it is in America. After all, man doesn't live by time-motion studies alone, does he?"

Encouraged, Ormsby-Fletcher asked, "Is it really true that corporations interview and grade executives' wives?"

"It's ghastly. Diabolical," Jake said, shaking his head. "I simply wouldn't know where to begin..."

Ormsby-Fletcher enjoyed sucking Smarties as he pondered his brief. Hooked on glitter, he liked to think Jake was on intimate terms with the stars, and Jake, lying outrageously, cribbing gossip from *Variety*, more than obliged. "Bloody Marlon," Jake began one evening, unaware that Nancy had just entered the room, "has done it again. He —"

"Marlon who?" Nancy asked.

"The baby's crying."

Suddenly Ormsby-Fletcher said, "If it doesn't sound too dreary, I wonder, well, Pamela thought if you had nothing better on, perhaps you'd both drive out to our place for dinner on Saturday night?"

"Why, that would be absolutely super," Jake said.

But he wakened ill-tempered, dubious, and he phoned Ormsby-Fletcher at his office. "Edward, about Saturday night —"

"You needn't explain. Something's come up."

"No. Not at all. It's, well — your wife — Pamela — does she know what I'm charged with?" Would I disgust her, he wanted to say.

"You mustn't even think like that, Jake. We'll expect you at eight."

Wednesday morning a postcard came, written in the most ornate hand and signed Pamela Ormsby-Fletcher. Were there any foods that didn't agree with either of them? Now there's breeding for you, Jake thought, and he wrote back to say all foods agreed with them. The next morning Ormsby-Fletcher phoned. "It's just, ah, well, are there any dietary laws…?" No, no, Jake said. Not to worry. But swinging out onto the Kingston bypass on Saturday night, Nancy in the car beside him, he began to worry more than a little himself. "Let's not have that smart-assed argument about pantos and homosexuality tonight, the principal boy being a girl…"

The Ormsby-Fletchers' cottage, overlooking the common in an unspoiled village in Surrey, exceeded Jake's fondest fantasies. It was Georgian, with magnificent windows and climbing red roses. Pulling into the driveway Jake braked immediately behind a black Humber with the license plate EOF 1, grateful that Nancy hadn't noticed the plate, because he did not want to admit to her that Edward's father, who had bought the original, had been called Ernest, and that Edward was so called because no other anything–OF 1 plate was available.

"Hullo, hullo," Ormsby-Fletcher said, and he led them through the house into the garden. Floribunda roses. Immense pink hydrangeas. Luscious dahlias...Pamela, a streaky blonde and very nice to look at, wore a Mary Quant sheath cut high above the knees and white crocheted stockings. There was another guest, a plump rumpled sybarite called Desmond — something in the City he was — waiting on the terrace, where drinks were served with cheese sticks and potato crisps. Suddenly a pale stammering boy called Edward was thrusting a book and pen at Jake. "What?" Jake asked, startled.

"It's the guest book," Nancy said. "You sign your name and birth date."

The *au pair* girl fetched Ormsby-Fletcher's other son, an unpleasant three-year-old called Eliot, to be kissed good night. This done, Pamela began to chat about the theatre: she was mad keen.

"But how do actors do it," Desmond asked Jake, "going on night after night, doing the same bloody thing...?"

"They're children, inspired children," Jake said triumphantly.

Pamela jumped up. "Would anybody like to wash their hands?" she asked.

"What?"

Nancy kicked Jake in the ankle.

"Oh, yes. Sure."

Pamela led Nancy to the downstairs toilet and Jake was directed upstairs. Passing Eliot's bedroom, he discovered the boy squatting on his potty, whining. The *au pair* girl was with him. "Anything wrong?" Jake asked.

The *au pair* girl looked up, alarmed. Obviously, she had seen Jake's picture in the newspapers. She knew the story. "He won't go to sleep without his golliwog," she said, "but he won't tell me where he put it."

Jake locked himself in the bathroom and immediately reached into his jacket pocket for the salami on rye Nancy had thoughtfully prepared for him. Munching his sandwich, he opened the medicine cabinet, but it yielded no secrets. Next he tried the laundry hamper. Shirts, socks, then at last, Pamela's smalls. Intricately laced black panties, no more than a peekaboo web. A spidery black bra, almost all filigree. You naughty thing, he thought.

Dinner commenced with hard-boiled eggs, sliced in half. Paprika had been sprinkled over the eggs and then they had been heated under the grill to suck out whatever moisture they still retained. Pamela flitted from place to place, proffering damp, curling white bread toast to go with the eggs. Jake washed down his egg with a glass of warm, sickeningly sweet, white Yugoslav wine, watching gloomily as Pamela brought in three platters. One contained a gluey substance in which toenail-size chunks of meat and walnuts and bloated onions floated; the next, a heap of dry lukewarm potatoes; and the third, frozen peas, the colour running. Pamela doled out the meat with two ice cream scoops of potatoes and an enormous spoonful of peas and then passed around the toast again.

"You *are* a clever thing," Desmond said, tucking in.

Next the cheese board came out, a slab of British Railways cheddar, which looked uncannily like a cake of floor soap. There was dessert too. A running pink blob called raspberry fool.

Desmond did most of the talking. The Tories, he admitted, seemed all played out at the moment, but one of these days another leader with fire in his belly would emerge and then we should see the last of that faceless little man in Number 10.

"We'll leave the men to their port now, shall we?" Pamela said, and, to Jake's astonishment, she led Nancy out of the dining room.

There actually was port, And cigars. Desmond apologized for the absence of his wife. She was in the hospital, he said, adding, "It's nothing. Just a plumbing job."

Ormsby-Fletcher recalled that when he had done his national service with the Guards on the Rhine he had occasionally gone to Hamburg on leave. "A chance to dip the wick, don't you know?"

Jake leaned back in his chair, aghast; Ormsby-Fletcher, he thought, you saucy fellow, dipping the wick on the Reeperbahn; and just as he was searching himself for an appropriate off-colour story, Desmond rode to the rescue with the one about the Duchess of Newbury. "On her wedding night," he said, "the Duke naturally decided to have a bash. The Duchess, it turned out, couldn't get enough. 'Is this what they call fucking?' she asked at last. 'Yes,' the Duke said. 'Well then,' she said, 'it's too good for the working classes.'"

Ho ho ho. Time to join the ladies. Jake excused himself, going to the upstairs toilet, his stomach rumbling, but when he finally rose to pull the chain nothing happened. This didn't surprise him at first, knowing British plumbing as well as he did, but again and again he pulled, and still nothing happened. Oh my God, Jake thought, a big fat stool staring him in the face. What to do? Ah, he thought, opening the toilet door softly. There was nobody in the hall. Jake slipped into the adjoining bathroom, found a plastic pail, filled it with water, tiptoed back to the toilet, and poured it into the bowl. Now the stool floated level with the toilet seat. Flood tide. Pig, Jake thought. Sensualist. Hirsute Jew.

Wait. Don't panic, Jake thought, opening the toilet window wide. There's a simple solution. Wrap the stool quickly in your underwear, lean back and heave it into the rose bushes. *Yes, yes*, Jake agreed, *but how do I pick it up?* It's yours, isn't it? Your very own bodily waste. Disgust for it is bourgeois. *Yes, yes, but how do I pick it up?* Sunshine soldier! Social democrat! Middlebrow! Unable to face life fully. Everything is holy, Jake. Holy holy. *Yes, but how do I pick it up?* With your underwear. Quickly. Zip, zoom. Then lean back and heave. The Hersh garbage ball, remember? Inimitable, unhittable. In an instant Jake stood resolutely over his stool, jockey shorts in hand, counting down: ten-nine-eight-seven-six-five-four — three — two — one-and-a-half — one! — three-quarters — *WHOAH! Voices in the garden*. Jake tottered backwards, relieved. I'm no bourgeois chicken, though, he thought. Another second and I would have done it.

Jake lit a cigarillo. So, they're all outside on the terrace again. Good, good, he thought, stepping into his underwear, sneaking out of the toilet, swiftly down the stairs, and then into the downstairs toilet. *Baruch ato Adonoi*, he said twice, before he pulled the chain. It flushed. Should I go upstairs again, fetch the stool, and...? No. Exhilarated, Jake flushed the toilet again, noisily, and then he began to pound on the door. Finally Ormsby-Fletcher came. "I seem to be locked in," Jake shouted.

"Oh, dear." Ormsby-Fletcher told Jake how to unlock the door and then he led him into the garden, where Pamela was exhibiting paintings. A landscape. A boat in the harbour. A portrait. All reminiscent of the jigsaw puzzles of Jake's childhood. He made loud appreciative noises.

"Now nobody tell him." Then Pamela, bursting with mischief, turned to Jake. "Would you say these pictures showed talent?"

"Absolutely."

"But amateur?" she asked enticingly.

Jake glanced imploringly at Nancy but her face showed nothing. Bitch. He stepped closer to the picture on display. "Mn," he said, gratefully accepting a brandy from Ormsby-Fletcher. "Professional. The brushwork," he added. "Oh, yes. Professional, I'd say."

Desmond clapped a pink hand to his mouth, stifling a laugh.

They're hers, Jake thought. Afternoons, wearing her spidery black bra and nearly nothing panties, she —

"Oh, for heaven's sake," Ormsby-Fletcher said. "Tell him."

Pamela waited, savouring the expectant silence. Finally, breathlessly, bosom heaving, she exclaimed, "All these pictures were executed by mouth and foot painting artists!"

Jake gaped; he turned pale.

"Didn't guess," Pamela said, shaking a finger at him, "did you?"

"...no..."

Ormsby-Fletcher explained with a certain pride that Pamela was a director of the Society for Mouth and Foot Painting Artists.

"And still finds time to make such sumptuous meals," Desmond said. "Oh, you are clever."

"This picture," Pamela said, holding up a seascape, "was done by a boy of seventeen, *holding the brush between his teeth*."

With trembling hand, Jake held out his brandy glass to Ormsby-Fletcher.

"He has been paralyzed for eight years."

"Amazing, " Jake said weakly.

Desmond felt the group's work should be publicized in America. Swinging London, decadence, and all that tosh. Here was a bunch of disabled people who refused to cadge on the welfare state. An example to all of us, especially the rundown-Britain brigade.

"This one," Pamela said, holding up a portrait of General Montgomery, "is a foot painting. It's one of a series done by a veteran of El Alamein." Next she showed another mouth painting, a still life, done by a street-accident victim.

Shamelessly holding out his glass for yet another brandy, Jake shouted, "I'll buy it."

Pamela's mouth formed an enormous reproachful O. "Now you'll go away thinking I'm frightful," she said.

"But it's for such a good cause," Jake said.

Pamela's enthusiasm ebbed. "You may only buy one if you really, really think it's good."

"Oh, but I do. I do."

"You mustn't condescend to disabled people," she said sulkily.

Jake pleaded and Pamela, all forgiveness now, allowed him to have the Montgomery portrait for twenty-five guineas. Then, bosom heaving again, she added, "And I'll tell you what I'm going to do for you. I'm going to take you to see the artist in his studio."

Jake shook his head, he waved his hands imploringly, no, but he didn't know what to say.

"It would be so encouraging for him to know," Pamela continued, "that somebody in your position admired his talents."

"Couldn't I just write him a letter?"

"But you'd adore Archie. He has such a wonderful sense of humour."

"He has?" Jake's voice quivered.

"And courage. Buckets of courage." Then Pamela started into what Jake figured must be her set piece for women's club luncheons. "If a man has the talent and urge to paint," she said, "he will paint. He will paint even if it means living in a back street garret on a near starvation diet. If he has no arms he will paint with the canvas on the floor and a brush between his toes. If both arms and feet are lost he will grip the brush between his teeth."

The upstairs light went on. Jake gripped his brandy glass tighter and hastily lit a cigarillo.

"Speaking as a creative person, wouldn't you say, Jake," Pamela asked heatedly, "that art thrives on difficulty?"

Another upstairs light was turned on. "You're goddamn right," Jake said.

The *au pair* girl raised her voice, a pause, then Eliot began to shriek. Ormsby-Fletcher leaped to his feet. "I'll see what it is, darling."

"It seems to me," Pamela said, "the sterner the trials of creation, the finer that which is created."

"My wife isn't feeling well," Jake said, shooting Nancy a fierce look. "Pardon?"

"I must take Nancy home immediately."

In the house again they ran into a flushed ill-tempered Ormsby-Fletcher; he was coming from the kitchen, carrying a pump.

"What is it?" Pamela asked.

Eliot sat at the top of the stairs, tears running down his cheeks. "Didn't do it," he wailed. "Didn't do it."

"He's been naughty," Ormsby-Fletcher said tightly.

"Don't be too hard on him," Jake pleaded compulsively.

Ormsby-Fletcher seemed to notice Jake for the first time. "Not going so soon, are you?"

"It's Nancy. She's unwell."

"Just an upset stomach," Nancy said, trying to be helpful.

"No. *Not a* —" Jake stopped himself. "What I mean is…she's being brave. Good night, everybody." He assured the Ormsby-Fletchers that they had had an absolutely super evening and, clutching his Montgomery portrait, he hurried Nancy to the car. Eliot's howling pursued him.

"What in the hell's got into you?" Nancy asked.

But Jake wouldn't talk until they reached the highway. "I've got a splitting headache, that's all."

"What do you think the child did?"

"Stuffed his bloody golliwog down the toilet, that's what."

While Nancy got ready for bed, Jake poured himself a stiff drink and sat down to contemplate his Montgomery portrait. What am I doing in this country, he thought? What have I got to say to these nutty, depraved people?

Well, Yankel?

—*St. Urbain's Horseman*, pp. 179–90

Richler's essay on the phenomenal appeal of Ian Fleming's James
Bond novels draws on his broad acquaintance with the English.

ENGLAND, ENGLAND.

James Bond is a meaningless fantasy cutout unless he is tacked to the canvas of diminishing England. After the war, Sir Harold Nicolson wrote in his diary, he feared his way of life was coming to an end; he and his wife, Victoria Sackville-West, would have to walk and live a Woolworth life. Already, in 1941, it was difficult to find sufficient gardeners to tend to Sissinghurst, and the Travellers' Club had become a battered caravanserai inhabited only by "the scum of the lower London clubs."

In 1945, Labour swept into office with the cry, "We are the masters now." Ten years later, in Fleming/Bond's time, the last and possibly the most docile of the British colonies, the indigenous lower middle and working-class, rebelled again, this time demanding not free medical care and pension schemes, already torn from the state by their elders, but a commanding voice in the arts and letters. Briefly, a new style in architecture. So we had Osborne, Amis, Sillitoe, and Wesker, among others.

The gentleman's England, where everyone knew his place in the natural order, the England John Buchan, Sir Harold Nicolson, Bobbety,* Chips,** and Boofy*** had been educated to inherit — "Good God," Hannay says, "what a damn task-mistress duty is!" — was indeed a war victim. Come Ian Fleming, there has been a metamorphosis. We are no longer dealing with gentlemen, but with a parody-gentleman.

Look at it this way. Sir Harold Nicolson collected books because he cherished them, Ian Fleming amassed first editions because, with Britain's place unsure and the pound wobbly, he grasped their market value. Similarly, if the Buchan's Own Annual cry of God, King,

* The 5th Marquess of Salisbury
** Sir Henry Channon
*** The Earl of Arran

and Empire, was now risible, it was also, providing the packaging was sufficiently shrewd, very, very saleable.

Sir Harold Nicolson was arrogantly anti-American, but after World War II a more exigent realism began to operate. Suddenly, an Englishman abroad had to mind his manners. Just as Fleming could not afford to be too overtly anti-Semitic, proffering a sanitized racism instead, so it wouldn't do for Bond to put down all things American. Ian Fleming was patronizing (Bond says of America, it's "a civilized country. More or less."), but whatever his inner convictions, there is an admixture of commercial forelock touching. Where once Englishmen bestrode the American lecture circuit with the insolence of Malcolm X, they now came as Sir Stepin Fetchits. The Bond novels were written for profit. Without the American market, there wouldn't be enough.

Little England's increasingly humiliating status has spawned a blinkered romanticism on the left and the right. On the left, this yielded CND (the touching assumption that it matters morally to the world whether or not England gives up the Bomb unilaterally) and anti-Americanism. On the right, there is the decidedly more expensive fantasy that this offshore island can still confront the world as Great Britain. If the brutal facts, the familiar facts, are that England has been unable to adjust to its shrivelled island status, largely because of antiquated industry, economic mismanagement, a fusty civil service, and reactionary trade unions, then the comforting right-wing pot dream, a long time in the making, is that virtuous Albion is beset by disruptive communists within and foreign devils and conspirators without.

"(If you) get to the real boss," John Buchan writes in *The Thirty-Nine Steps*, "then the one you are brought up against is a little white-faced Jew in a bathchair with an eye like a rattlesnake."

In Buchan's defence, his biographer, Janet Adam Smith, has observed that some of his best and richest friends were Jews. Yes, indeed. Describing a 1903 affair in Park Lane, Buchan wrote, "A true millionaire's dinner — fresh strawberries in April, plovers' eggs, hooky noses and diamonds." Elsewhere, Buchan went so far out on a limb as to write that it would be unfair to think of Johannesburg as

'Judasburg.' You will see more Jews in Montreal or Aberdeen, but not more than in Paris; and any smart London restaurant will show as large a Semitic proportion as a Johannesburg club." Furthermore, like many another promising young anti-Semite, Buchan mellowed into an active supporter of Zionism, perhaps in the forelorn hope that hooky-nosed gourmets would quit Mayfair for the Negev.

Alas, they still abounded in London in Sir Henry Channon's time. On January 27, 1934, Chips wrote in his diary, "I went for a walk with Hore-Belisha, the much advertised Minister of Transport. He is an oily man, half a Jew, an opportunist, with the Semitic flare for publicity." Then, only two months later, on March 18, Chips golfed with Diana Cooper at Trent, Sir Philip Sassoon's Kent house. "Trent is a dream house, perfect, luxurious, distinguished with the exotic taste to be expected in any Sassoon Schloss. But the servants

Sir Harold Nicolson (left) and his wife, Victoria Sackville-West, on board the S.S. Bremen, *bound for New York in 1933.*

are casual, indeed, almost rude; but this, too, often happens in a rich Jew's establishment."

Sir Harold Nicolson's Jewish problem bit deeper. On June 18, 1945, he wrote in his diary, "I do not think that anybody of any Party has any clear idea of how the election will run. The Labour people seem to think the Tories will come back…the Tories feel that the Forces will all vote for Labour, and that there may be a landslide towards the left. They say the *Daily Mirror* is responsible for this, having pandered to the men in the ranks and given them a general distrust of authority. The Jewish capacity for destruction is really illimitable. Although I loathe anti-Semitism, I do dislike Jews."

In a scrupulous, if embarrassed, footnote Nigel Nicolson, who edited his father's diaries, wrote, "H. N. had the idea that the Board of the *Daily Mirror* was mainly composed of Jews."

If Sir Harold Nicolson saw destructive Jews manipulating Churchill's defeat, then Ian Fleming, an even coarser spirit, sniffed plotters, either coloured or with Jewish blood, perpetually scheming at the undoing of the England he cherished. This, largely, is what James Bond is about.

— *Shovelling Trouble,* "Bond," pp. 60–63

YOU SIMPLY CAN'T TRUST THE BRITISH. With Americans (or Canadians, for that matter) what you see is what you get. But settle into your seat on a 749 flying out of Heathrow next to an ostensibly boring old Englishman with wobbly chins, the acquired stammer, obviously something in the City, intent on his *Times* crossword puzzle, and don't you dare patronize him. Mr. Milquetoast, actually a judo black belt, was probably parachuted into the Dordogne in 1943, blew up a train or two, and survived the Gestapo cells by concentrating on what would become the definitive translation of *Gilgamesh* from the Sin-Leqi-Inninni; and now — his garment bag stuffed with his wife's most alluring cocktail dresses and lingerie — he is no doubt bound for the annual convention of cross-dressers in Saskatoon.

— *Barney's Version,* p. 17

THE TRUTH WAS, I decided, weeks before leaving for Montreal, I no longer understood the idiom. Doomed to always be a foreigner in England, I was now in danger of finding Canada foreign too. After thirteen almost uninterrupted years abroad, I now realized the move I had made with such certainty at the age of twenty-three had exacted a considerable price. Some foggy, depressing nights it seemed to me that I had come full circle. Many years ago my parents emigrated from Poland to Canada, to Montreal, where I grew up ashamed of their Yiddish accents. Now I had seemingly settled in London, where my own children (spoiled, ungrateful, enjoying an easier childhood than I had, etc. etc.) found my American accent just as embarrassing.

—*Hunting Tigers under Glass,* "Expo 67," p. 24

O Canada!

On his return to Canada, Richler took seriously his responsibilities to the indigenous cultural community. Among other projects, the anthology of Canadian writing that he compiled for Penguin (Canadian Writing Today) was a substantial undertaking. But he also had fun at Canada's expense.

Barney Panofsky (Barney's Version) is a filmmaker, founder, and president of Totally Unnecessary Productions. His greatest financial success is a television series with archetypal Canadian content, that is to say, Mounties and Eskimos. As an attentive member of the Canadian Broadcasting Corporation's radio audience, especially when his third wife, Miriam, goes back to work there, he lampoons the sort of listener who writes in with a heartfelt musical request.

But perhaps the offhand remarks about Canadian culture are the most devastating. Richler was at home in Montreal after his return from England, but he continued to view the rest of Canada through the eyes of a worldly expatriate.

WHAT CHARACTERIZES CANADIAN CULTURE today is not so much energy and talent — though it is there at last, a real but tender shoot — as an astonishing affluence and beneficence. Happily, an enlightened beneficence. But as the British health plan, in its formative years, could be sniped at by reactionaries for handing out toupées to all comers, so our culture plan is vulnerable to the charge of staking just about all the alienated kids to committing their inchoate, but modish, complaints to paper or canvas. On the other hand, betting on fragile promise is a built-in hazard of art investment and the people who run the Canada Council could hardly be more decent and imaginative. It's a pity, then, that the Council's first eleven years could come to be noted for one conspicuous omission. Morley Callaghan has yet to be presented with its highest award, the Molson Prize.*

Which brings me to our ludicrous, newly minted honours system, an innovation that must be seen as the last snobbish gasp of our eldest generation, the unselective, slavish Anglophiles. Really, in these austerity-minded days it's high time the Queen dismissed her Canadian second-floor maid, the Governor-General, who is of course Chancellor of the Order of the Companions of Canada, which now entitles many a bore to write the initials "CC" after his name, a measure hitherto accorded only to bottles of medicine. But my immediate point is, once more Morley Callaghan was overlooked. And then insulted. For, on second thought it seems, he was asked to accept the also-ran Medal of Canada.

Meanwhile, lesser writers, all of them world-famous in Canada, are blowing the dust off early manuscripts and digging old letters out of the attic, mindful of the burgeoning market in raw Canadiana. Book-length studies of just about everybody in the house are threatened, operas are being commissioned, ballet companies subsidised, and townships sorely in need of tolerable restaurants and bars are being paid to erect theatres instead. If Canada was once loosely stitched together by railroads, such is the force of today's culture-boom that it may be reknit by art palaces coast to coast, though there hardly be plays or players, not to mention audiences,

---

* Callaghan was, in fact, awarded the Molson Prize in 1970.

to fill them. The promise of a Canadian film industry, backed by ten million dollars, alarms me for other reasons.

Even as in London, the movies have become increasingly, almost insufferably, fashionable among younger Canadian writers, intellectuals, and students. In fact, the sort of student who once used to help put out a snarling little magazine, everything in lowercase letters, writing poems about his revolt against crippling poverty, is nowadays more likely to be making a film with a handheld camera, all about his rebellion against suffocating affluence.

The dizzying prospect of a Canadian film industry frightens me when I dig into my own past experience of Toronto-based production companies. The archetypal Toronto film outfit has made indecently large profits out of TV commercials or has perhaps produced a puerile but money-spinning series about Indians or mounties, and has now set its sights higher, so to speak. They wish to make a "serious, yet commercially viable" film *with Canadian content.* That is to say, if *The Young Wantons* will look yet again at sex (unblinkingly, frankly, outspokenly) this time out it will be set in the palpitating streets of LSD-crazed, hippie-ridden, wife-swapping, transvestite-rich Toronto. Ontary-ary-ary-yo; with French Canadian tits being given equal exposure.

—*Shovelling Trouble,* "Maple Leaf Culture Time," pp. 144–46

EARLY IN APRIL, 1969, I discovered I was among the year's Governor-General's Award Winners for literature.

"You're accepting it," my Canadian publisher said, astonished.

"Yes."

"You're pleased, you're actually pleased."

"Yes, I am."

—*Shovelling Trouble,* "Êtes-vous canadien?" p. 150

I ACCEPTED THE AWARD at once, but with mixed feelings. As a writer I was pleased and richer, but as a father of five, mortified. When *Cocksure* was published in Canada, the reviewer in the

Montreal *Star* revealed that I had churned out an obvious potboiler with all the lavatory words. The man who pronounces on books in the New Brunswick *Daily Gleaner* put me down for a very filthy fellow and warned parents in Montreal that I would be teaching their children at Sir George Williams University, where I was to be writer-in-residence for a year. Others denounced me as a pornographer. And now the ultimate symbol of correctitude in our country, the GG himself, would actually reward me for being obscene. For the establishment's sake, I couldn't help but be ashamed.

> —*Shovelling Trouble,* "Êtes-vous canadien?" pp. 152–53

THE FACT THAT I AM a Canadian Jewish writer may seem so obvious as to be unworthy of comment, but, fifteen years ago, when I first began to publish, it troubled me enormously.

Because I didn't want to be taken for that pathetic provincial, the Canadian writer, I wouldn't allow my first novel to be compromised by the imprint of a Toronto publisher and went out of my way to have *The Acrobats* published in England.

Neither, I now recall with embarrassment, did I wish to be classified as a Jewish writer. No, no, I was, as I pompously protested to an interviewer, a writer who merely happened to be Jewish.

Fortunately for me, a Yiddish newspaper in Montreal saw the interview and swiftly cut me down to size: "The oven is big, the loaf is small."

> —*Hunting Tigers under Glass,* "Foreword," p. 8

"WHAT WAS IT LIKE in Siberia?" Moses once asked.

"Like Canada," Shloime Bishinsky said, shrugging, "what else?"

For them Canada was not yet a country but the next-door place. They were still this side of Jordan, in the land of Moab, the political quarterlies as well as the Yiddish newspapers they devoured coming out of New York.

> —*Solomon Gursky Was Here,* p. 14

WHEN CALLAGHAN RETURNED, he settled into his chair, reached for the bottle, and said, "Let me put it this way. Canada is not so much a country as a holding tank filled with the disgruntled progeny of defeated peoples. French Canadians consumed by self-pity; the descendants of Scots who fled the Duke of Cumberland; Irish, the famine; and Jews, the Black Hundreds. Then there are the peasants from the Ukraine, Poland, Italy, and Greece, convenient to grow wheat and dig out the ore and swing the hammers and run the restaurants, but otherwise to be kept in their place. Most of us are still huddled tight to the border, looking into the candy store window, scared by the Americans on one side and the bush on the other. And now that we are here, prospering, we do our damn best to exclude more ill-bred newcomers, because they remind us of our own mean origins in the draper's shop in Inverness or the *shtetl* or the bog. What was I talking about?"

"Solomon."

—*Solomon Gursky Was Here,* pp. 398–99

ATUK WAS SHOWN into Snipes's office.

"Well, well, lemme see," Snipes consulted a typewritten sheet on his desk. "Uh-huh...mm...Gore says you're quite a poet."

Atuk lowered his eyes modestly.

"Well, I've read your stuff, old chap. It's Georgian. Cornpoke." Snipes reached quickly into his desk, brought out a copy of his own most recent book of poems, *Ejaculations, Epiphanies, et etc.*, signed it, and handed it to Atuk. "You want to get with it. You want to make your poetry more gutsy."

Atuk promised he would try.

"That'll be three seventy-five, please."

Atuk paid up immediately.

"Good. Now lemme see...Are you familiar with the *Metro* image?"

"Yes."

"We're fighting for our life here. We stand for a Canadian national identity and the American mags are trying to drive us out of business. Like fiction?"

"Yes."

"Good. Now lemme see." Snipes lifted a copy of the Aug. 4, 1940 issue of *Collier's* off a stack of old magazines and neatly razored out a short story. "Here's a good one. I want you to re-set it in Moose Jaw in 1850. We haven't any western yarns for the May issue. But please remember to change more than the names. Play around with the physical descriptions and details. Use your imagination, Atuk. That's what we're paying you for."

—*The Incomparable Atuk,* pp. 5–6

Mordecai Richler, 1972. WHEN I WAS A STUDENT there was actually a course on Can. lit. at Sir George Williams U., but the text was mimeographed and a typical assignment was for a student to list all the books ever written about the Hudson's Bay Co., noting the dimensions, number of pages, and photographs. Now there are a number of books, most of them embarrassingly boosterish, about Canadian writing, and there is at least one serious quarterly, the bilingual *Canadian Literature*, edited by George Woodcock, that is exclusively — no, quixotically — devoted to the study of Canadian writing past and present. In the very first issue, Dwight Macdonald, asked to appraise a number of Canadian little magazines, was left with the impression of "a starved, pinched version of our own culture." Canada, he felt, was "a mingy version of the United States." That was 1959. Since then, a real Canadian book club has been formed, with monthly selections that run from Malcolm Lowry's *Ultramarine* to *Love and Peanut Butter* ("Lesley Conger's warm and lively account of the trials of being a wife, mother and writer in a wild Vancouver household."); and there is a worthy and useful paperback library of Canadian, um, classics. Blue-chip Leacocks, some good Callaghans, and rather too many of our frontier-day unreadables indecently exhumed. In fact today the cultural heat is such that the shrewd downtown grocer who has survived supermarket competition must now live through another crisis: the spadebearded entrepreneur who wants to buy out the lease and convert the premises into an art gallery. Instead of Libby's soup and Kellogg's Super "K", pictures of

Libby's soup and Kellogg's Super "K". If when I was a student there was something shamefully un-Presbyterian in admitting you were a writer, today to merely let on that you're "creative" is to stand back and duck a shower of prizes and offers, and to enjoy a nice little side income in supplying radio and TV stations with your outspoken opinions on divorce, household pets, masturbation, and the Bomb (a shadow we live under).

—Hunting Tigers under Glass, "O Canada," pp. 15–16

"OUR PROBLEM IS SOLVED, darling," Sir Hyman said. "Mr. Berger will be joining us for dinner. He's also a Canadian. He met Lucy when he was a child."

That was hardly sufficient for Lady Olivia.

"He's at Balliol. A Rhodes Scholar. His father is a poet."

"Oh, how sweet," Lady Olivia said. "I didn't know they had any."

—Solomon Gursky Was Here, p. 192

AFTERWARDS BETTE INTRODUCED Atuk to Dr. Parks. "Doc Burt," she said, "has seven degrees. He's a doctor of philosophy, divinity, naturopathy, and goodness knows what else."

"I'm world-famous," Dr. Parks said, "all over Canada."

Yes, Atuk thought, for it seemed to him this was true of many people he had met in Toronto. What was their secret, he wondered.

—The Incomparable Atuk, p. 30

POOR MIRIAM. Her program's a clunker. Between playing records, she is obliged to read her listeners' letters aloud; once — to my ever-lasting glee — a letter that purported to come from a Mrs. Doreen Willis of Vancouver Island:

Dear Miriam,

I hope you don't mind my being so familiar, but out here on Vancouver Island we tend to think of you as family. So here goes.

Blush blush blush. Forty years ago today I was on the "yellow brick road" to Banff with Donald on our honeymoon. We drove a Plymouth Compact. It was blue, my favourite colour. I also like ochre, silver, and lilac. I don't mind canary yellow on some people, if you know what I mean. But I simply can't stand maroon. It was raining cats and coyotes. And then, what? A flat tire. I was fit to be tied. Donald, then in the early stages of multiple sclerosis, although we hardly suspected it at the time (I thought he was just too clumsy), wasn't able to fix it. And little me? Well I wasn't going to risk getting axle grease on my brand new two-piece polka-dot suit with semifitted top ending just below the waist. It was turquoise. Then along came a Good Samaritan in the nick of time to save our bacon. Whoops. I'm sure you don't eat it with your name, but no offense, eh? We were exhausted by the time we arrived at the Banff Springs Hotel. All the same, Donald insisted that we celebrate our safe arrival with a couple of Singapore Slings. The bartender had his radio on and Jan Peerce was singing "The Bluebird of Happiness." I tell you it gave me goose pimples. It fit our mood to a T. Today is our fortieth wedding anniversary and Donald, who has been confined to a wheelchair for years, is feeling blue (my favourite colour, natch). But I want you to know he still retains his sense of humour. I call him Shaky, which makes him giggle so hard, I then have to wipe his chin and blow his nose. Oh well, for better or for worse, isn't that what we pledged, although some wives I could name don't honour it.

Please play Jan Peerce's recording of "The Bluebird of Happiness" for Donald, as I know it will lift his spirits. Many thanks from a faithful listener.

Yours,
DOREEN WILLIS

Gotcha, I thought, pouring myself a big one, slipping into a soft-shoe shuffle. Then I sat down and began to scribble notes for another letter.

—*Barney's Version,* pp. 79–80

THE TRUTH IS CANADIAN WRITERS, curious about their real worth rather than their trading-stamp value, have traditionally packed their bags, sometimes defiantly, looking homeward only with scorn, which has hardly endeared them to those who, during difficult years, elected to stay home, fighting a lonely battle against bad taste and indifference, for a Canada Council, literate book pages, and a publishing industry with standards more than picayune.

—*Canadian Writing Today,* pp. 18–19

FINALLY I BECAME A SINNER. In the late sixties, I began to produce Canadian-financed films that were never exhibited anywhere for more than an embarrassing week, but which eventually earned me, and on occasion my backers, hundreds of thousands of dollars through a tax loophole since closed. Then I started to churn out Canadian-content TV series sufficiently shlocky to be syndicated in the U.S. and, in the case of our boffo *McIver of the RCMP* series, which is big on bonking scenes in canoes and igloos, in the U.K., and other countries as well.

When it was required of me, I could rumba as a latter-day patriot, sheltering in the Great Cham's last refuge of the scoundrel. Whenever a government minister, a free-marketeer responding to American pressure, threatened to dump the law that insisted on (and bankrolled to a yummy degree) so much Canadian-manufactured pollution on our airwaves, I did a quick change in the hypocrite's phone booth, slipping into my Captain Canada mode, and appeared before the committee. "We are defining Canada to Canadians," I told them. "We are this country's memory, its soul, its hypostasis, the last defense against our being overwhelmed by the egregious cultural imperialists to the south of us."

I digress.

—*Barney's Version,* p. 5

HAVING COMMISSIONED Graham Sutherland to paint her portrait, Helena Rubinstein was so upset by the unforgiving result that she absolutely refused to pay for it. Years later she met Lord Beaverbrook at a party. "I bought that Sutherland portrait of you," he said.

Helena was outraged. "But I told him it was to be destroyed. *What have you done with it?*" she demanded.

"It's on view in my museum in Fredericton, New Brunswick."

"Oh well," she said, relieved, "I suppose that amounts to the same thing."

—*Belling the Cat,* "Mr. Sam," p. 22

WHEN I WAS IN SEVENTH GRADE Mrs. Ogilvy once turned her dynamite bum to our class and wrote on the blackboard:

> CANADA IS —
> a. a dictatorship
> b. a post-colonial democracy
>   of limited culture
> c. a theocracy

None of the above answers apply. The truth is Canada is a cloud-cuckoo-land, an insufferably rich country governed by idiots, its self-made problems offering comic relief to the ills of the real world out there, where famine and racial strife and vandals in office are the unhappy rule. Buoyed by this thought, I hurried home, and had just poured myself a nightcap when the phone began to ring. It was Serge Lacroix. He had to see me urgently.

—*Barney's Version,* p. 386

Cauliflower ears. Soft, dim eyes. Scarred eyebrows. Pulpy nose. Swollen knuckles. And no wonder. Over the wasting years the New York mob had fed Maxie to Fritzie Zivic, Beau Jack, and the great Sugar Ray Robinson, among others.

PART III

THE JEWISH
AVENGER

The Holocaust is rarely altogether absent from Richler's work. His response often takes the form of a character who fights back against his oppressors. Some of Richler's avengers are more effective than others; a few are ambiguous. The Boy Wonder (The Apprenticeship of Duddy Kravitz) shows that Jews can be powerful — but he's a crook. The fictional cousin Joey (St. Urbain's Horseman), like the remembered, pseudonymous Jerry Greenfield (This Year in Jerusalem), is a failure who once seemed to embody a promise of triumph against the odds. Hy Rosen (Cocksure) is triumphant only in his own mind — but that, perhaps, is triumph enough.

For the most part, Richler's avenger is not the story's protagonist. One of the few exceptions may be Duddy Kravitz, but Duddy, of course, is not altogether admirable. The most ambiguous of all the avengers may be Solomon (Solomon Gursky Was Here). Solomon is not so much a character in the novel as a benign chimera. He embodies the ineffectual Moses Berger's fantastic wish for justice and retribution.

—J. W.

ONE BRIGHT, CLOUDLESS MORNING in July 1941, Noah, Gas, and Hershey arranged to meet on the balcony of Old Annie's candy store in Prévost, a village in the Laurentians, where their families had taken cottages for the summer. They were determined to climb the mountain behind the Nine Cottages to get to Lac Gandon, where the *goyim* were.

Hershey turned up first.

Old Annie, who was a tiny, grey-haired widow with black, mournful eyes, looked the boy up and down suspiciously. A first-aid kit and a scout knife were strapped to his belt. "What is," she asked, "a revolution?"

Hershey grimaced. "He who hears no evil, speaks no evil."

Old Annie's store was a squat sinking yellow shack all but covered with signs advertising Kik and Sweet Caporal cigarettes. She wasn't called Old Annie because she was sixty-two. Long ago, in Lithuania, the first three children born to her parents had not survived their infancy. So the village miracle-maker had suggested that if another child was born to them they should call her *alte* (old) instantly, and God would understand.

Gas arrived next. He had a BB gun and a package of crumbly egg and onion sandwiches.

"Knock, knock," he said.

"Who's there?" Hershey asked.

"Ago."

"Ago who?"

"Aw, go tell your mother she wants you."

Behind Old Annie's store was the scorched, spiky field that was used as a market. Early every Friday morning the French Canadian farmers arrived with poultry, vegetables, and fruit. They were a skeptical bunch, with hard, seamed faces, but the St. Urbain Street wives were more than a match for them and by late afternoon the farmers were drained and grateful to get away. The women, who were ruthless bargainers, spoke a mixture of French, English, and Yiddish with the farmers. "So *fiel*, Monsieur, for dis *kleine* chicken? *Vous* crazy?"

Pinky's Squealer saw the two boys sitting on the stoop, waiting for Noah. He approached them diffidently. "Where you goin'?" he asked.

"To China," Gas said.

When the Squealer's mother wanted him to go to the toilet she would step out on her balcony and yell, "Dollink, time to water the teapot." Pinky, who was the Squealer's cousin, was seventeen years old, and his proper name was Milton Fishman. He was rather pious and conducted services at Camp Machia. The Squealer was his informer.

"I've got a quarter," Pinky's Squealer said.

"Grease it well," Gas replied.

Habitually, those families who lived on Clark, St. Urbain, Rachel, and City Hall clubbed together and took cottages in Prévost for the summer. How they raised the money, what sacrifices they made, were comparatively unimportant — the children required sun. Prévost had an exceedingly small native population and most of the lopsided cottages were owned by French Canadians who lived in Shawbridge, just up the hill. The CPR railway station was in Shawbridge. Prévost, at the foot of the hill, was separated from Shawbridge by that bridge reputedly built by a man named Shaw. It was a crazy-quilt of clapboard shacks and cottages strewn over hills and fields and laced by bumpy dirt roads and an elaborate system of paths. The centre of the village was at the foot of the bridge. Here were Zimmerman's, Blatt's, The Riverside Inn, Stein the butcher, and — on the winding dirt road to the right — the synagogue and the beach. In 1941 Zimmerman and Blatt still ran

staunchly competitive general stores on opposite sides of the highway. Both stores were sprawling dumpy buildings badly in need of a
paint job and had dance halls and huge balconies — where you
could also dance — attached. But Zimmerman had a helper named
Zelda and that gave him the edge over Blatt. Zelda's signs were
posted all over Zimmerman's.

Over the fruit stall:

> AN ORANGE ISN'T A BASEBALL. DON'T
> HANDLE WHAT YOU DON'T WANT. THINK
> OF THE NEXT CUSTOMER.

Over the cash:

> IF YOU CAN GET IT CHEAPER BY THAT
> GANGSTER ACROSS THE HIGHWAY YOU CAN
> HAVE IT FOR NOTHING

However, if you could get it cheaper at Blatt's, Zelda always proved
that what you had bought was not as fresh or of a cheaper quality.

The beach was a field of spiky grass and tree stumps. Plump, middle-
aged ladies, their flesh boiled pink, spread out blankets and squatted
in their bras and bloomers, playing poker, smoking, and sipping
Cokes. The vacationing cutters and pressers seldom wore bathing
suits either. They didn't swim. They set up card tables and chairs and
played pinochle solemnly, sucking foul cigars and cursing the sun.
The children dashed in and out among them playing tag or tossing a
ball about. Boys staggered between sprawling sunbathers, lugging
pails packed with ice and shouting:

"Ice-cold drinks. Chawk-lit bahs. Cig'rettes!"

Occasionally, a woman, her wide-brimmed straw hat flapping as
she waddled from table to table, her smile as big as her aspirations,
gold teeth glittering, would intrude on the card players, asking —
nobody's forcing, mind you — if they would like to buy a raffle in aid
of the Mizrachi Fresh Air Fund or the JNF. Naked babies bawled.
Plums, peaches, watermelons were consumed, pits and peels

tossed indiscriminately on the grass. The slow yellow river was unfailingly condemned by the Health Board during the last three weeks of August, when the polio scare was at its height. But the children paid no attention. They shrieked with delight whenever one of their huge mothers descended into the water briefly to duck herself — once, twice — warn the children against swimming out too far — then, return, refreshed, to her poker game. The French Canadians were too shocked to complain, but the priests sometimes preached sermons about the indecency of the Jews. Mort Shub said, "Liss'n, it's their job. A priest's gotta make a living too."

At night most people crowded into the dance halls at Zimmerman's and Blatt's. The kids, like Noah, Gas, and Hershey, climbed up the windows and, peashooters in their mouths, took careful aim at the dancers' legs before firing. Fridays, the wives worked extremely hard cleaning and cooking for the Sabbath. Everybody got dressed up in the afternoon in anticipation of the arrival of the fathers, who were met in Shawbridge, most of them having arrived on the 6:15 excursion train. Then the procession through Shawbridge, down the hill and across the bridge, began; an event that always horrified the residents of the village. Who were these outlandish, cigar-chomping men, burdened with watermelons and Kik bottles, salamis and baskets of peaches, yelling at their children, whacking their wives' behinds and — worst of all — waving merrily at the sombre Scots who sat petrified on their balconies?

Noah showed up last.

"Pinky's Squealer wants to come with us," Gas said.

"Did you tell him where we're going?"

"Ixnay. You think I'm crazy?"

"He's got a quarter," Hershey said.

Pinky's Squealer showed Noah the quarter.

"All right," Noah said.

Old Annie, shaking her head sadly, watched the four boys start out across the fields. Noah led. Hershey, who came next, was Rabbi Druker's son; a scrawny boy with big brown eyes. His father had a small but devoted following. Hershey hung around the synagogue every evening and stopped old men on their way to prayers. "Give me a nickel and I'll give you a blessing." He didn't do too badly. "I'm holy as hell," he told Noah one evening.

Gas, trailing behind, was plump, fair-haired, and freckled.

The boys filed down the dirt road that led to the Nine Cottages, the sun beating against their brown bodies. They passed Kravitz's cottage, with its smelly outhouse, Becky Goldberg's place, and the shapeless shack that housed ten shapeless Cohens.

The tall grass at the foot of the mountain was stiff and yellow and made you itch. There were also mushy patches where the bull-rushes grew, but they avoided those. The sheltering trees cooled the boys, but they had a long climb ahead of them. The soft plump ground they tramped on was padded with pine cones, needles, and dead leaves. Sunlight filtered deviously among the birch and maple and fir trees and the mountain had a dark damp smell to it. There was the occasional cawing of crows, they saw two woodpeckers and, once, a hummingbird. They reached the top of the mountain about one o'clock and sat down on an open patch of ground to eat their lunch. Gas chased around after grasshoppers, storing them in an old mayonnaise jar that had two holes punched in the top. After they had finished their sandwiches they started out again, this time down the other side of the mountain. The foliage thickened and in their eagerness to get along quickly, they scratched their legs and arms in the bush, stumbling into the occasional ditch concealed by leaves and bruising their ankles against jagged stones. They heard voices in the distance. Noah, who had been given the BB gun, pulled back the catch. Gas scooped up a rock, Hershey unstrapped his scout knife. "We'll be late for *shabus*," Pinky's Squealer said. "Maybe we should go back?"

"Go ahead," Hershey said. "But watch out for snakes, eh?"

"I didn't say anything."

Voices, laughter too now, came splashing through the trees. The ground began to level off and, just ahead, they made out the beach. There were real canoes, a diving board, and lots of crazy-coloured umbrellas and deck chairs. The boys approached the beach cautiously, crouching in the bushes. Noah was amazed. The men were tall and slender and the women were awfully pretty, lying out in the sun there, just like that, not afraid of anything. There was no yelling or watermelon peels or women in bloomers. Everything was so clean. Beautiful, almost.

Gas was the first to notice the soft-drink stand. He turned to Pinky's Squealer. "You've got the quarter. Go get us Pepsis."

"Gas should go," Hershey said. "He's the least Jewish-looking of the gang. Look at his nose — Christ! They'll take him for a *goy* easy."

"You can have my quarter."

"Aw, go water your tea kettle," Gas said. "Maybe I don't look as Jewish as you or Noah, but they can always tell by pulling down your pants….'

They all giggled.

"It's not so funny," Hershey said. "That's how they found out about my uncle, who was killed in Russia."

"You're all chicken," Noah said. "I'm going. But I'm having my Coke right out there on the beach. If you want anything to drink you'll have to come too."

A convertible Ford pulled away and that revealed the sign to them. Gas noticed it first. Suddenly, he pointed. "Hey, look!"

THIS BEACH
IS
RESTRICTED
TO GENTILES

That changed everything. Noah, his excitement mounting, said they would hang around until evening and then, when the beach was deserted, steal the sign.

"Yeah, and walk back in the dark, eh?" Pinky's Squealer said. "It's Friday, you know. Ain't *your* paw coming?"

Gas and Hershey looked puzzled. Both of them had been forbidden to play with Noah by their mothers. Pinky's Squealer made sense, but if Noah intended to stay they would look cowardly if they left him behind. Noah certainly wanted to stay. Having his father up for the weekend usually meant two days of quarrelling.

"Aw, in a hundred years we'll all be dead," Gas said. Pinky's Squealer waited, kicking the stump of a tree petulantly. "If you come with me, Hershey, you can have my quarter."

"Watch out for snakes," Hershey said.

Pinky's Squealer ran off.

The afternoon dragged on slowly, but at last the sun lowered and a strong breeze was starting up. Only a few stragglers remained on the beach.

"Is a Gentile a Catholic and a Protestant too?" Hershey asked.

"Yeah," Noah said.

"But they're different," Hershey said, "aren't they?"

"Different," Gas said. "You know the difference between Hitler and Mussolini?"

Noah decided that as it was getting late they would have to risk it, stragglers and all. The few couples who remained were intent on each other and wouldn't notice them if they were cunning. Noah said that he and Gas should stroll out onto the beach, approaching the sign from different directions, nonchalantly. It didn't look as if it was stuck very solidly into the sand. Hershey was to holler if he saw anybody coming for them. He had stones and the BB gun.

So the two boys sauntered innocently out onto the beach. Noah whistled. Gas pretended to be searching for something. The wind kicked up gusts of sand and the sun, sinking still lower, was a blaze in the opposite hills. Suddenly, frantically, the two boys were yanking at the sign. Gas shook with laughter, tears rolling down his cheeks. Noah cursed. They heard, piercing the stillness, a high-pitched shout. "Look out!"

Gas let go, and ran off. Flying for the woods.

"Hurry!"

Noah persisted. A man, waving a canoe paddle, was running toward him. Noah gave one last, frenzied tug, and the sign broke free. The man was about twenty feet away now, wielding his paddle viciously. His eyes were wild. "You little son of a bitch!"

Noah swerved, racing for the bushes. A shower of pebbles bounced off his back. The paddle swooshed through the air behind him. But he was fast. Once in the bushes he scampered off, zigzagging into the mountain. He ran and ran and ran. Finally, clutching the sign in his hands, he tumbled down on the pine needles, his heart hammering.

Noah couldn't find Gas anywhere, but Hershey loomed up from behind a rock. Darkness fell quickly and they soon realized they were lost. Lost, and without a flashlight. Possibly, they were moving in circles. For all they knew they might come out of the woods again at Lac Gandon.

Noah and Hershey had stopped climbing; they had reached a level bit of ground and then all at once they heard many voices. Light beams shot through the darkness. Hastily, the boys concealed the sign under a mess of decaying leaves and climbed up the nearest tree — their pockets filled with stones. The voices and probing lights came nearer.

"Hershey!"

"Noah!"

"Boys!"

"HALLO!"

The boys began to quake with laughter. Every able-bodied man in Prévost must have been out on the mountain that night, armed with pitchforks, rakes, clubs, and baseball bats. Noah and Hershey had never thought they'd be grateful to Pinky's Squealer, but they were that Friday night. They slid down the tree and uncovered the sign and that was their night of glory in Prévost. Nothing was too good for them. Sunday morning Noah, Hershey, Mort Shub, and Gas planted the sign on their own beach. When the others came out to swim, they read:

THIS BEACH
IS
RESTRICTED
TO ~~GENTILES~~
LITVAKS

—*The Street*, pp. 62–69

MAX, IN FACT, delighted in telling tales about the legendary Boy Wonder. His favourite, a story that Duddy had heard over and over again, was the one about the streetcar transfer. Max loved to tell this tale, one he believed to be beautiful, to newcomers; and earlier that evening he had repeated it to MacDonald. Not just like that, mind you, because before he could begin Max required the right atmosphere. His customary chair next to the Coke cooler, a hot coffee with a supply of sugar cubes ready by his side, and a supporting body of old friends. Then, speaking slowly and evenly, he would begin, letting the story develop on its own, never allowing an interruption to nonplus him and not raising his voice until Baltimore.

"He was broke," Max began, "and he hadn't even made his name yet. He was just another bum at the time."

"And what is he now? The gangster."

"I'm warning you, MacDonald, if the Boy Wonder knocked off his mother, Max here is the guy who would find an excuse for him."

"I mean you could say that," Max continued. "We're like this, you know, and I'd say it to his face even. *The Boy Wonder was just another bum at the time.* Funny, isn't it? I mean his phone bill alone last year must have come to twenty Gs (he's got lines open to all the tracks and ballparks all day long, you know), but only ten years ago he would have had to sweat blood before he coulda raised a lousy fin."

"No wonder."

"How that goniff manages to keep out of jail beats me."

"It's simple," Debrofsky said, "the whole police force is on his payroll."

Max waited. He sucked a sugar cube. "Anyway, he's broke, like I said. So he walks up to the corner of Park and St. Joseph and hangs around the streetcar stop for a couple of hours, and do you know what?"

"He trips over a hundred dollar bill and breaks his leg."

"He's pulled in for milking pay phones. Or stealing milk bottles, maybe."

"All that time," Max said, "he's collecting streetcar transfers off the street and selling them, see. Nerve? *Nerve.* At three cents apiece he's up a quarter in two hours, and then what? He walks right in that door, MacDonald, right past where you're standing, and into the backroom. There, with only a quarter in his pocket, he sits in on the rummy game. Win? He's worked his stake up to ten bucks in no time. And what does he do next?"

"Buy a gun and shoot himself."

"I got it. He donates the ten spot to the Jewish National Fund."

Max smiled indulgently. He blew on his coffee. "Around the corner he goes to Moe's barbershop and plunk goes the whole ten spot on a filly named Miss Sparks running in the fifth at Belmont. On the nose, but. And you guessed it, MacDonald, Miss Sparks comes in and pays eleven to one. The Boy Wonder picks up his loot and goes to find himself a barbotte game. Now you or me, MacDonald, we'd take that hundred and ten fish and buy ourselves a hat, or a present for the wife maybe, and consider ourselves lucky. We mere mortals, we'd right away put some of it in the bank. Right? *Right*. But not the Boy Wonder. No, sir."

Max dropped a sugar cube onto his tongue and took some time sucking the goodness out of it.

"Picture him, MacDonald, a twenty-nine-year-old boy from St. Urbain Street and he's not even made his name yet. All night he spends with those low-lifes, men who would slit their mother's throat for a lousy nickel. Gangsters. Graduates of Saint Vincent de Paul. Anti-Semites, the lot. If he loses, OK, but if he wins — *If he wins*, MacDonald? Will they let that little St. Urbain Street punk, Jerry Dingleman, leave with all their money? He's up and he's down, and when he's up a lot the looks he gets around the table are not so nice." Max cleared his throat. "Another coffee, please, Eddy."

But Eddy had already poured it. For, at this point in the transfer story, Max always ordered coffee.

"Imagine him, MacDonald. It's morning. Dawn, I mean, like at the end of a film. The city is awakening. Little tots in their little beds are dreaming pretty little dreams. Men are getting out of bed and catching shit from their wives. The exercise boys are taking the horses out. Somewhere, in the Jewish General Hospital let's say, a baby is born, and in the Catholic Hospital — no offense, MacDonald — some poor misguided nun has just died of an abortion. Morning,

MacDonald, another day. And the Boy Wonder, his eyes ringed with black circles, steps out into God's sunlight — that was before his personal troubles, you know — and in his pocket, MacDonald, is almost one thousand de-is-ollers — and I should drop down dead if a word of this isn't true.

"But wait. That's not all. This is only the beginning. Because the Boy Wonder does not go home to sleep. No, sir. That morning he takes the train to Baltimore, see, and that's a tough horse town, you know, and they never heard of the Boy Wonder yet. He's only a St. Urbain Street boy, you know. I mean he wasn't born very far from where I live. Anyway, for six weeks there is no word. *Rien.* Not a postcard even. Imagine, MacDonald, try to visualize it. Has some dirty nigger killed him for his roll, God forbid? (There are lots of them in Baltimore, you know, and at night with those dim street lamps, you think you can even see those black bastards coming?) Is he a broken man, penniless again, wasting away in a hospital maybe? *The public ward.* Six weeks and not a word. Nothing. Expect the worst, I said to myself. Goodbye, old friend. *Au revoir.* Good night, sweet prince, as they say, something something something. Then one day, MacDonald, one fine day, back into town he comes, only not by foot and not by train and not by plane. He's driving a car a block long and sitting beside him is the greatest little piece you ever saw. Knockers? You've never seen such a pair. I mean just to look at that girl — And do you know what, MacDonald? He parks that bus right outside here and steps inside to have a smoked meat with the boys. By this time he owns his own stable already. So help me, MacDonald, in Baltimore he has eight horses running. OK; today it would be peanuts for an operator his size, but at the time, MacDonald, at the time. And from what? Streetcar transfers at three cents apiece. Streetcar transfers, that's all. I mean can you beat that?"

—*The Apprenticeship of Duddy Kravitz*, pp. 24–26

IT WAS SUGARMAN, albeit inadvertently, who lit the bomb. He told Joey that the windows in Jewish shops were being broken and swastikas had been painted on the pavement outside the *shul* on

Fairmount Street. French Canadian followers of Adrien Arcand were to blame.

"What are you going to do about it?" Joey asked.

What are we going to do? The children are forbidden to play softball on Fletcher's Field because of roaming gangs of French Canadian toughs.

The next afternoon Joey collected Arty, Duddy, Jake, Gas, and the rest of the boys and took them to play ball on Fletcher's Field. He accompanied them the following afternoon and the one after that. Now if the French Canadians got any ideas they sneaked one look at Joey, lolling on the grass behind the batter's cage, and faded away.

Duddy Kravitz, taking heart in Joey's presence, shouted obscenities in French after the retreating toughs. When the boys whirled around, Duddy, clutching his genitals, shouted, *"Votre soeur, combien?"*

One of the French Canadians hurled a stone.

"Yoshka in drerd arein," Duddy yelled.

Another stone bounced in the dirt. Duddy bent over, pulled down his trousers, and wiggled his pale narrow white ass in the air. "For Pope Pius," he hollered.

Unwillingly, the French Canadians started back. Joey rose, scooping up a bat, and took a few slices at an imaginary softball. The French Canadians dispersed.

Duddy, Jake, Arty, and the others brought glowing, exaggerated reports of the incident back to St. Urbain, but their parents were not pleased. There was already enough trouble. Street incidents caused by roaming gangs of truculent French Canadians were constantly increasing. Premier Duplessis's Union Nationale Party circulated a pamphlet that showed a coarse old Jew, nose long and misshapen as a carrot, retreating into the night with bags of gold. Laurent Barré, a minister in the Duplessis cabinet, told the legislature that his son, on entering the army, had been exposed to the insult of a medical examination by a Jewish doctor. "Infamous Jewish examiners," he said, "are regaling themselves on naked Canadian flesh." The next morning Uncle Abe, driving to his cottage in the mountains, was astonished to see *"À bas les Juifs"* painted on the highway. He met with other community leaders who contributed heavily to the Union Nationale election fund and they went to chat with a minister and were photographed together shaking hands and smiling benignly on the steps outside the Château Frontenac in Quebec City. The following day a junior minister issued a statement to the press. "Anti-Semitism," he said, "is grossly exaggerated. Speaking for myself, my accountant is a Jew and I always buy my cars from Sonny Fish."

Joey burst into the cigar stores, he visited the barber shops, exhorting the men, mocking them, asking them what they intended to do about such insults.

That was Wednesday. On Friday, a St. Urbain Street boy who had gone to the Palais d'Or dance hall to look over the *shiksas* made off with a girl whose husband was overseas with the Van Doos. The boy was beaten up and left bleeding on the sidewalk outside his house and the story was printed in all the newspapers. On Saturday morning Joey went from one cigar store to another, this time carrying the newspaper with him, upsetting the men, hectoring, goading, and in the evening a group of twelve embarrassed men, armed, it was reported, with baseball bats and lengths of lead pipe, set out in four cars for the Palais d'Or. French Canadian boys who came out with girls were separated from them and taken into the alley. When the police finally turned up the St. Urbain Street boys had already fled, leaving a French Canadian boy unconscious in the alley. The story made page one perhaps because the boy, who had not been involved in the previous brawl, happened to be a nephew of an advocate who was prominent in the St. Jean Baptiste Society. The boy was a student at the University of Montreal. The Palais d'Or was boarded up and the next night and the night after that police patrol cars cruised slowly up and down St. Urbain. Store owners and poolroom proprietors were fined for infractions of city bylaws that had not been enforced for years. Huberman, stopped for doing no more than thirty miles an hour, offered the traffic cop the traditional five-dollar bill with his license and found himself charged with attempting to bribe an officer. Leaders of the community sent a contrite letter to the French Canadian boy's family and another letter to the *Star*. No stone, the letter said, would be left unturned. A delegation, Uncle Abe among them, went to see the French Canadian advocate and promised that whoever had injured the boy would be uncovered by the community and turned over to the proper authorities for punishment.

On St. Urbain, stores shut down early and hardly anybody went out after dark. A special prayer was said at the Galicianer *shul*. People sat by their windows, waiting. The next morning, before anyone else in the house was up, Joey, who had been back home for all of five weeks, packed his bags and was gone again. Two days later, Jake remembered, they found Joey's fire-engine-red MG overturned in the woods off the highway. The rest was rumour.

Joey's car was discovered upended and gutted, burned out, alongside the road to New York, some ten miles out of town. Some said there had been two cars parked down the street from Joey's house all night and that six men had huddled there, smoking, passing a bottle, until Joey had emerged and they took off after him. Others argued, no, it was an accident. Not bloody likely, Jake thought, because one of Joey's suitcases had been found ripped open, the contents strewn in the woods. The lid had been torn off another suitcase and somebody had defecated inside. Among other items discovered in the vicinity there had been a photographic sheet with four studies of JESSE HOPE, exclusively represented by Nate Herman, Wiltshire Blvd., Hollywood. There was a profile and a full-face study, a photograph of Joey in boxing trunks and another showing him in a cowboy's outfit, drawing a gun menacingly.

Joey's wrecked MG was found on a Wednesday. The following Monday the cops visited Brotsky, the city councillor, as usual, for the weekly payoff, and there were no more surprise visits from Wartime Prices & Trade Board inspectors to neighbourhood stores and wholesalers. The case against Huberman, who had been arrested for speeding and charged with bribing an officer, was dropped for lack of sufficient evidence.

A month later Jenny quit the house on St. Urbain, whisking Hanna and Arty off to Toronto. Escaping, escaping. "From now on this family takes no more money from Uncle Abe," she proclaimed. "Sweet, fucking Uncle Abe."

— *St. Urbain's Horseman*, pp. 137–40

NEIGHING, THE STALLION REARS, obliging the Horseman to dig his stirrups in. Eventually he slows. Still in the highlands, emerging from the dense forest to scan the scrub below, he strains to find the unmarked road that winds into the jungle, between Puerto San Vincente and the border fortress of Carlos Antonio López.

In Frankfurt, the Horseman sits in the court presided over by Judge Hofmeyer.

A witness remembers Mengele.

"Exactly the way he stood there with his thumbs in his pistol belt. I also remember Dr. König, and to his credit I must say that he always got very drunk beforehand, as did Dr. Rohde. Mengele didn't; he didn't have to, he did it sober."

Dr. Mengele was concerned about the women's block.

"...The women often lapped up their food like dogs; the only source of water was right next to the latrine, and this thin stream also served to wash away the excrement. There the women stood and drank or tried to take a little water with them in some container while next to them their fellow sufferers sat on the latrines. And throughout it all the female guards hit them with clubs. And while this was going on the SS walked up and down and watched."

Bodies were gnawed by rats, as were unconscious women. The women were plagued by lice.

"Then Mengele came. He was the first one to rid the entire women's camp of lice. He simply had an entire block gassed. Then he disinfected the block."

Mengele's pitch, his most cherished place, was on the ramp with the Canada detail. The Canada men unloaded prison transports and collected the baggage of new arrivals. Watches, pocketbooks, blankets, jars of jam, sausages, bread, coats. These valuables were lugged to storehouses with the collective name Canada, so called because of the country's reputation as a land of immense riches.

"Mengele cannot have been there all the time."

"In my opinion, always. Night and day."

— *St. Urbain's Horseman*, pp. 177–78

The Warsaw Ghetto, 1943.

AFTER MY LECTURE my amiable host, Professor Zirker, took me to the museum, where we were shown the town's enviable collection of medieval manuscripts. Then we were led into another room, where the curator had laid out his Jewish artifacts on a long table especially for my perusal. As we browsed through early documents, I cynically concluded that they would come to an abrupt stop in 1933. But I had underestimated the curator. He led me to a poster proclaiming the Nürnberg laws of September 15, 1935, which deprived Jews of German citizenship and forbade marriages between Jews and Aryans. Next he showed me a folio of Jewish identity cards.

Photographs, fingerprints, basic information. "Please note," he said, "that this poor man is wearing his First World War medals, as if that was going to help him."

Finally we came to a stack of exercise book pages, lined sheets on which the names and addresses of Trier's Jewish population had been typed. A ruled line had been drawn in red ink through each name, followed by a policeman's notation. To begin with, "DESTINATION LODZ," a euphemism for Auschwitz, and then, simply, "DESTINATION UNKNOWN."

Noticing how flushed I had become, the curator said, "Some, you know, escaped to France."

"Some?"

"A few."

But for most of Trier's Jews there had been no gravestones, just a red line drawn through their names in a policeman's exercise book. That, and a final shower. Zyklon-B.

—*Belling the Cat*, "Germany 1978," pp. 122–23

Of the three Gursky brothers, Solomon alone is made of heroic stuff, as becomes clear in the story of how the family made its fortune.

SEPTEMBER 1916. Solomon, seventeen years old now, short for his age, wiry, his skin burnt nut-brown by the prairie sun, was perched on the corral fence behind the Queen Victoria Hotel with Bernard and Morrie. Plump Bernard, who parted his hair in the middle and already owned a three-piece grey serge suit and a homburg and spats, sucked on a caramel. Morrie, whittling away on a chunk of wood as usual, was apprehensive as Solomon had joined them on the fence for once, familiar as he was with Solomon's need to bring Bernard to the boil. Slapping at flies, squinting against the sun, the Gursky brothers were waiting for the sale to start. Aaron had bought a snorting, restive herd of wild mustangs from Hardy, overpaying again, and now hoped to sell to the farmers, most of whom were already in debt to him at the store. By this juncture the Gurskys had moved into town, living above

A. GURSKY & SONS
GENERAL MERCHANTS
Importers of Stable and Fancy
DRY GOODS
Sole Distributors of
DR. COLBY'S celebrated ANTI-COSTIVE
and TONIC PILLS, unequalled in the
Promotion of Regular Evacuation.

Cajoling, sweaty, Aaron bantered with the farmers at the corral, laughing too hard at their inane jokes. The farmers feigning indifference, most of them waiting for sundown when the jumpy Jew's prices would drop.

No sooner did Aaron cut a deal on a horse, realizing a small profit, than he would invite the buyer into the hotel bar for a ceremonial drink. The farmer would not order a beer like Aaron, but would spit on the sawdust-covered floor, wink at the bartender, and demand a double shot of the hard stuff, saying, "Both of my boys have already enlisted, but I suppose yours will be staying put."

Then a breathless Aaron would zip out to the corral again, counting the shiny rumps of the remaining horses, calculating likely losses in his head, mingling with the other farmers, thrusting gifts of coloured hair ribbons at their wives and children. Panicky at sundown, he would drop prices drastically.

Solomon prodded Bernard with his elbow. "Now that you're such a man of affairs, a student of correspondence courses, what do you make of all this?"

"Whatever I make of it is strictly my own business."

"Why can't we be like the three musketeers," Morrie asked, "all for one and one for all? The Gursky brothers."

"Well," Solomon said, "I'll tell you what I think. The bar's turning over a bigger profit than Paw is sucking up to that bunch of farmers.

What Paw ought to do is buy the hotel and sell drinks and let somebody else worry about the horses."

And then Solomon, terrifying Morrie, jumped down from the fence right into the flow of wild nervy horses in the corral. Solomon, Ephraim's anointed one.

Bernard didn't credit most of his brother's tales about his trek to the Polar Sea with their grandfather. But whatever had really happened out there, Solomon had returned blessed with a certain grace, an inner stillness. And watching him now, at ease with the wild mustangs, Bernard grasped that had he been the one to jump into the corral, probably stumbling in the dust, they would have smelled his fear and reared up on their hind legs, snorting, looking to take a chomp out of him. Bernard understood for the first time that he was a coarse, tubby little man with wet fishy eyes, and that he would have to scratch and bite and cheat to get what he wanted out of life, which was plenty, but that Solomon would sit, expecting the world to come to him, and he would be served. He watched Solomon crossing that corral, he watched choking on envy and hatred, and yet, for all that, he yearned for Solomon's approval. Then Solomon spoiled it by pausing to taunt him, calling back, "Follow me, Bernie, and I'll buy you a beer."

"Go straight to hell."

"Aw, you two," Morrie groaned. "Hey, you're crying."

"I am not. He's going to *shtupp* Minnie Pryzack now."

Minnie, comfortably ensconced in the Queen Victoria Hotel for years, was only seventeen when she first went west, working the first-class carriages on the train from Winnipeg to the coast and back again.

"He's going to *shtupp* Minnie and then he's going to join the poker game."

"They'd never let him play in the big autumn game. Besides, he's busted."

"I wasn't afraid of jumping into the corral, but then you would have had to come after and you could have been hurt. Is he really broke?"

"They cleaned him out last Thursday."

Aaron, sprawled at the kitchen table, smelling of manure, his ears and nose clogged with dust, his back aching, counted out his money twice, calculating that he had turned a profit of fifty-five dollars, provided two of the farmers honoured their notes.

Morrie stooped to remove his father's boots and then brought him a glass of lemon tea and a bowl of stewed prunes.

"Paw," Bernard said, "if you ask me, you work too hard for too little."

"You're a good boy," Aaron said. "Morrie too."

Rather than risk throwing everything into the pot in the heat of the game, Solomon gave Minnie his valise, as well as his railroad ticket out and five ten-dollar bills, which would see him through, if things turned out badly. Then he drifted through the kitchen of the Queen Victoria Hotel, climbed the back stairs to the third floor, and rapped three long, two short, and one long on the attic door.

McGraw shot the bolts. "You can't play. Not tonight."

Solomon didn't budge.

"It's different rules tonight, kid. You know that."

Not including Solomon, there were five of them gathered together for the big autumn game, the betting soaring so high it could only be risked once a year. McGraw, the owner of the hotel and the blacksmith's shop, a recent acquisition; George Kouri, the Lebanese, who had owned the five-and-ten-cent store and a shop that sold buggies and wagons; Ingram, Sifton's man, who dealt railroad land to the Slavs in their sheepskin coats; Charley Lin, who had owned the laundry and the butchershop, but since last autumn's big game only a couple of bedbug-ridden rooming houses; and Kozochar, the barber and fire chief. A side table was stacked with cold cuts, potato salad, and bottles of whiskey and vodka. There were two cots in an adjoining room, in case anybody needed to take a nap or wanted to send down for one of the girls, maybe changing his luck.

Last year's big game had ended acrimoniously after forty-eight hours, one of Charley Lin's rooming houses, the blacksmith's shop, two cow pastures, six heifers, three Polish whores and one Indian one and $4,500 changing hands. The men involved in the big game enjoyed the status it conferred on them by dint of the enormity of their winnings or losses. The game, a curse on the wives, had once been broken up by three of them marching on the tables. Since then it convened at a different place every year. The basement of Kouri's five-and-ten. The backroom in the fire station. And this year the attic of the Queen Victoria Hotel. Weeks before the men sat down to the table, the game was the subject of speculation in town, and was denounced from the pulpit by the Reverend Ezekiel Shipley, who blamed it all on the harlots of the town.

McGraw was adamant. "It just wouldn't be right to deal you in," he said.

McGraw had been against allowing Solomon into the weekly game in the first place. He was hardly a man of substance, like the rest of them, but merely a snooty kid. Besides McGraw liked Aaron, a dummy maybe, but an honest and hardworking Jew. Kouri had been indifferent, but Ingram was also opposed and Kozochar dead against it. "It would be like taking candy from a baby."

"His money's as good as yours or mine," Charley Lin said with appetite.

Ostensibly it was the need to teach Solomon a lesson that was his ticket of admission, because the men resented him without knowing exactly why. But there was another consideration. They wanted to impress him with their money and their moxie. That little son of a bitch.

His grandfather had been a squaw man, his father was a peddler, and, for all that, the boy, a mere seventeen-year-old, a squirt, a Jew, strode through the streets of town as if he were a prince-in-waiting, destined for great things. Unfailingly polite, considerate, it was difficult to fault him. If a fire broke out at four o'clock of a sub-zero morning, he was there at once to join the bucket brigade. When Miss Thomson was poorly, laid low with one of those feminine ailments, he took over the schoolhouse, enchanting the children. The Reverend Shipley, who could sniff evil in a year-old babe born to fornicate, sought out Solomon for discussions of the Holy Scripture. He was also more welcome on the reservation than any one of them, and could be gone with the Indians, God knows where, for ten days at a time. But there was something about him that riled the men and made them want to rub his nose in fresh dog shit.

Unlike pushy Bernard or Morrie (a really nice, polite kid), he didn't deign to serve in his father's store. But it was because he could be found there on occasion that the daughters were drawn to A. Gursky & Sons in swarms, blushing if he greeted them, the one he picked out for a buggy ride all but swooning on the spot. And, remarkably, the other young men in town, far from being jealous, vied for his favour, competing to recruit him as a hunting or drinking partner.

Once Solomon just happened to be passing in his buggy when McGraw's wagon was stuck in the mud. Immediately he jumped down and offered help. "No, no," McGraw protested, kneeling in the muck, his own shoulder to the wheel, "you'll only get dirty." Then McGraw turned pale, amazed at himself, because he would not have said such a thing to anybody else in town.

Solomon brought two hundred dollars to his first game, his poolroom earnings, and was promptly stripped of it. But he didn't sulk. He didn't complain. Instead he joked about it. "My initiation fee," he said.

So when he turned up again he was made welcome, the men digging deep for old hunting stories and gilding tales of past sexual triumphs, determined to prove to him that far from being a bunch of big-bellied hicks they were, if the truth were known, a band of hellraisers.

Solomon did reasonably well in his second game until he foolishly tried to bluff Kouri, showing three ladies, with what turned out to be no better than eights over deuces. He lost a third time and a fourth and now he was back, demanding a seat at the autumn game. McGraw didn't like it one bit. If they cleaned him out people would say they had taken advantage of a kid, but if he won it would be even more embarrassing.

"I must have dropped five hundred bucks at this table," Solomon said. "You owe me a chair."

"We don't owe you shit," Ingram said.

"No IOUs tonight. You want to sit down," McGraw said, sure that would be the end of it, "you got to show us at least a thousand dollars."

Solomon laid out his money on the table like bait immediately before Charley Lin.

"What can I get you to drink, kid?" Charley Lin asked.

Bernard brought his father a slice of honey cake. "Paw, I've got an idea."

Aaron, dazed by fatigue, itchy everywhere from horsefly bites, only half-listened.

"We could bring in a fiddler on Friday nights. Salt the pretzels more. Start a darts league. I know where we can get mugs with bottoms an inch thicker for the draft beer. Morrie could handle the cash register."

"And how would we raise the down payment?"

"McGraw buys his beer from Faulkner's. If we switched to Langham, signing a contract with them, they'd lend us some money. So would the bank."

"Sure. The bank."

"This isn't Russia, Paw."

"Neither is it Gan Eden."

Aaron, his money in hand, shuffled over to a corner of the kitchen, lifted a plank floorboard, dug out his strongbox, unlocked it, and howled and stumbled backward, a stricken man. Fanny, who had been tending to the pots simmering on the wood stove, was instantly by his side. "Aaron!"

His eyes had gone flat. All he could manage was a croak. "It's gone. The money."

"Some of that money's mine," Bernard yelled, seizing the box, turning it upside down and shaking it.

Out tumbled citizenship papers, a marriage license, birth certificates, but no cash and no deed to the general store.

"Should I go to the police?" Aaron asked in a failing voice.

"Only if you want to put your son in prison," Bernard said.

"How can you be sure it was him?" Morrie asked.

"I'll kill him for this," Bernard said. And he was off and running, pursued by Morrie. Bernard didn't stop before he stood red and panting before Boyd, the porcine clerk in the Queen Victoria Hotel. "Where's the fucken poker game?" he demanded.

Boyd, his smile bright with malevolence, pointed at the sign behind his desk: no cursing, no spitting, no games of chance allowed.

"Listen, you little shit, if you don't tell me where I can find Solomon I'm going to try every room in the hotel."

"You go right ahead, shorty, but there are some awful big guys in a number of them rooms, some of them entertaining company."

A tearful Morrie stepped between them. "Please, Mr. Boyd, we have to find Solomon."

"If I see him I'll tell him you're looking for him."

The Gurskys sat up all through the night waiting for Solomon to come home. Fanny moaning and Aaron seated in a chair with his hands folded, his eyes turned inward. "I'm too old to start over again," he said to nobody in particular.

It was dawn before Bernard slipped into the bedroom he shared with his two brothers and discovered that two of Solomon's drawers were empty and his valise was gone. Win or lose, he wasn't coming back.

"I've seen dead men look better than you do right now."

"Unfavourable winds," Solomon said to Minnie in the adjoining room. "How much did you bring?"

"Your fifty and the railway ticket and eight hundred of my own and my rings."

"What happens if I lose that too?"

"Then you must promise to marry me."

"Minnie," he said, inclined to be generous, "you must be thirty years old."

"Take it or leave it."

"It's blackmail," he said, scooping up the money.

"Now that's what I call a proposal."

It was time to open the store.

"What we should do," Bernard said, "is hire wagons and move all our stock somewhere safe, because tonight this place may no longer belong to us."

"He's a minor," Morrie said.

"Prick. If he signs over the deed and we don't honour his gambling debt, we're asking for a fire."

Bernard figured he wouldn't run away without saying goodbye to Lena Green Stockings, so he took the buggy and rode out to the reservation. Kids with scabs on their faces wrestling in the dirt, one of them with rickets. A drunk slumped against a tree trunk outside George Two Axe's store, scrawny chickens pecking at his vomit. Flies everywhere. Crows fluttering over the entrails of a dead dog, flying off with the ropey bits.

Bernard entered the tarpaper shack and was enraged to find it stocked with goods that could only have been swiped from A. Gursky & Sons, General Merchants. Tea. Sugar. An open ten-pound bag of flour on a high shelf. He found her out in the backyard, seated on a wicker chair with a broken seat, dozing.

"Lena!"

No answer.

"Lena, Solomon left in such a hurry he forgot to give me his new address."

When she finally raised her head, wizened as a walnut, he saw that she no longer had any teeth.

"It's important that I have it," Bernard said, pulling a bottle of rum out of his jacket pocket and waving it in front of her.

Lena smiled. "It's the boy with the two belly buttons," she said, remembering.

"Jesus Christ! Son of a bitch! Fuck! Everybody looks like that coming out of the swimming hole."

Her head began to slump again.

"Your shack is full of stolen goods. I could tell on you and then they'll come to lock you up."

Lena swatted a fly.

"Where's he going?"

"To see the world."

Passing through her shack again, Bernard paused to leave evidence of his passage, and then he went to see Minnie, taking the bar entrance to the hotel to avoid another encounter with Boyd. "I want you to give Solomon a message. Lena Green Stockings told me where he's planning to run to."

"How did you get that flour all over your suit?"

"Maybe my father won't go to the police, but I will. You tell him that."

Solomon came home three o'clock the next morning and went right to the kitchen sink, stooping to pump cold water over his head. He turned around just in time to see Bernard making a run at him, his arms outstretched, his fingers curled, ready to scratch. Solomon slapped him away and then went to his father and dropped the deed to the general store and a bundle of money tied with an elastic band onto his lap.

"Some of that money you stole was mine," Bernard said.

Emptying his pockets one by one, Solomon piled banknotes on the kitchen table, more money than the Gurskys had ever seen at one time.

"Big shot," Bernard said, "it's a good thing you were lucky for once."

Morrie went to make coffee and Bernard sat down to count the money.

"We are the new owners of the Queen Victoria Hotel and the blacksmith's shop on Prince Albert Street and a rooming house on Duke. The hotel comes with an eight-thousand-dollar mortgage, now our responsibility. Sell the rooming house. It's a fire trap. The blacksmith's shop is for André Clear Sky."

"I don't see any hotel deeds here," Bernard said.

Solomon reached into his jacket pocket and tossed the deeds on the table.

"You're a good boy," Aaron said.

"Like hell he is. He was planning to run away. Me, I stopped him."

Solomon waited until his mother had left the kitchen. "I want somebody to wake me up in time for the noon train. I'm going to Winnipeg. I'm joining the army. But please don't any of you say anything to Maw. I'll tell her myself."

Bernard stood apart, fulminating, as everybody fussed over Solomon at the train station. Minnie and the other whores, Lena, some farm girls whose names he didn't even know, a drunken McGraw, and Fanny Gursky awash in tears. Then Bernard ate lunch with his father. "I'm registering the hotel in my name, because I'm the eldest."

Wearing his homburg, his three-piece suit and spats, Bernard went to see the notary and then had a word with Morrie. "You know Boyd, the fat clerk at the hotel?"

"Yeah, sure."

"Go tell him he's fired. You're taking his place."

Next Bernard went to the hotel and arranged for a box of chocolates and a victrola to be sent to room twelve, and then he sailed into the bar and sat down at Minnie's table.

"If I invited you to sit here," she said, "remind me."

"You better learn to talk nice if you want to continue here. I'm boss now."

"It's Solomon's hotel."

"My kid brother left me in charge. Go to room twelve at once and wait for me there."

Minnie was waiting when Bernard entered the bedroom. "Help yourself to a chocolate," he said. "It's for you. The whole box. The largest on sale."

"Thank you."

"Do you read the funnies?"

"I look at the pictures," she said, blushing.

"My favourite is Krazy Kat, but I also like Abie Kabibble. How's the chocolate?"

"Very nice."

"It breaks my heart, but the army turned me down. Flat feet. I don't mind if you tell that to the other girls, but if you repeat anything else that happens here you will not be allowed into the bar again. Now tell me what you like better, waltz or ragtime?"

"Ragtime."

Sweaty, his hand trembling, Bernard nevertheless managed to set the record on the victrola: "Alexander's Ragtime Band."

"Are we going to dance first?" Minnie asked.

"Just you. Taking things off. But not your garter belt or stockings. And you mustn't look at me, not even a little peek," he said, reaching for a towel. But the record was finished before he was satisfied.

"What do I do now?" she asked.

He put on another record. "I Love My Wife, But, Oh, You Kid."

"Now you can get dressed and don't forget to take your chocolates."

"Would you like to do it, honey?"

"Don't honey me. I'm Mr. Gursky to you."

"Mr. Gursky."

"Do what?"

"Dress me."

"Shit, I know you can't read, but surely you know how to put your clothes on at your age."

"*Sorry.*"

"Well, hold on a minute. If I could do the brassiere I wouldn't say no."

"Oh, Mr. Gursky, chocolate makes my skin break out, but do I ever love Frenchy perfumes and scented soaps and anything made of silk."

Once she had gone, Bernard immediately washed his hands with soap and water, using a different towel. Then he curled up on the bed, hot with shame. Later he picked up the incriminating towel with two fingers and took it to room fourteen, which he knew was empty, and left it there. And he decided to punish himself for his indulgence. For the rest of the week, when he popped into Susy's Lunch to meet Morrie at four o'clock, as was his habit, he took his blueberry pie without ice cream.

—*Solomon Gursky Was Here,* pp. 350–61

Mortimer Griffin inadvertently offends Hyman Rosen, his colleague at work, and is not forgiven.

"Hello, dear! Kiss?"

"Up your ass."

"Oh, my. Bad day?"

"*Übersturmführer* Griffin sucked up to me again at the office.

Chicken-shit bastard," Hy said, slipping into a shuffle, his lightning left jab stopping just short of Diana's breasts, "think he doesn't know? One wrong move and I'll flatten him. *Like this,*" he said, his right hand suddenly flashing upward toward Diana's chin.

It was a feint. But Diana, taken by surprise, stupidly raised her guard, presenting Hy with a splendid opportunity to bury a right hook in her belly.

"Ooof," went Diana, staggering backward.

"Sucker," Hy hissed, following through with a hammering left to her kidney. A zig, a zag, and then a rat-tat-tat to her ears.

Finally, Diana flicked him off her. "Would you care for a drink before dinner, luv?" she asked warmly.

"I'm going out for dinner."

"Alone?"

Heh-heh. He didn't answer. Instead he shuffled backward, lunging, thrusting, shadowboxing his way into the bathroom. Hy stood on the bath stool, got his mouthpiece out of the medicine cabinet, and growled at his reflection in the mirror. Hyman Rosen, after all, was merely his goy-given name. Actually, he thought, baring his teeth at the mirror, I am Chaym ben Yussel, one of a great pugilistic line, which includes Black Aby, Cat's Meat Gadzee, Ikey Pig, Ugly Baruk Levy, Little Puss Abrahams, The Yokel Jew Sodicky and, above all, Daniel Mendoza. Mendoza! On January 9, 1788, Hy remembered, the great Mendoza, his ankle broken, fainted from pain, and his arch-enemy, the brutish Gentleman Dick Humphries, stood over him and shouted, "I have done the Jew!" The hell he had. For on May 6, 1789, Mendoza met Humphries again and reduced the braggardly goy to a bleeding pulp. *Grrr*, went Chaym ben Yussel. *Grrr*.

Oh, dear, Diana thought, recognizing the mood, Hy's Jewish-avenger mood. In such a state, he was inclined to rake the streets, searching for covert Jew-haters; testing people in bus queues, telling them to get fucked; charging after young couples coming out of espresso bars, cursing them in Yiddish; and spitting at old men out walking their dogs. All the same, it wasn't easy for Hy to provoke a fight. Most people had a too-well-developed sense of fair play to hit back at the crazed little man. If he persisted, they made sport of him.

But kicking, punching, his flow of obscenities unceasing, Hy was, on occasion, difficult to ignore, and once or twice he was badly mauled. *Grrr.*

— Cocksure, pp. 112–13

Richler's tribute to the fighter Maxie Berger is included, incongruously, in his book On Snooker.

IN THE THIRTIES AND FORTIES we counted football, golf, and tennis as strictly WASP as sliced white bread. We associated football with universities fastidious enough to have Jewish quotas, and golf and tennis with country clubs and resorts that wouldn't tolerate any Jews whatsoever. A down-and-dirty sport like boxing, on the other hand, belonged to tough kids out of Italian, black, Polish, Irish, and Jewish mean streets. Jack Solomons, one of ours, was the promoter with heft in London, and Joe "Yussel the Muscle" Jacobs called the shots in New York, where the great and near-great trained in Lou Stillman's gym. And welterweight champ Barney Ross, the son of a Talmudic scholar, gave us bragging rights.

In those days, boxing-beat hacks in Toronto had not yet been muzzled by political correctness. Describing a 1934 fight, one of them wrote: "For once, the Gentile barracking brigade will have to choose between the lesser of 'two evils,' when Sammy Luftspring and Dave Yack, a pair of Hebes, battle for supremacy at Frank Tenute's Elm Grove show at the Mutual Street Arena on Monday night." Not much later Lou Marsh, of the *Toronto Daily Star*, got to cover what was, as he put it, "an honest-to-Henry grudge fight between a Celt and a son of Moses," Sammy Luftspring versus Chick McCarthy. The good news was this promising "slugfest" had attracted an attendance of 6,000 — a record for Canada — "of which 5,795 talked turkey to the box office staff." Luftspring won a unanimous decision, but not before, wrote Marsh, "McCarthy opened the final round with a right-hander that made the aggressive little Jew boy lean like the Tower of Pisa."

A couple of days after Maxie Berger died, both the Toronto *Globe and Mail* and the *National Post* ran obituaries, noting that Maxie had briefly been world junior welterweight champion. Lacking the earlier verve of the *Star*, the tame *National Post* headline ran:

BOXER WAS LOVED
IN THE BRONX,
A STAR IN QUEBEC
Fought Five World Champions
He dressed well
and was popular
with women.

In common with other newspapers, the *National Post* featured a silly photograph of Maxie, obviously retrieved from an ancient Canadian Press file. It harked back to the days when newspaper photographers in a hurry could be counted on to honour their own code of clichés. Photographing a novelist, they had him hold his latest book to his chest. Snapping two politicians shaking hands, they enjoined them not to look at each other but to smile menacingly sincerely into the camera. Dispatched to shoot a photograph of a real estate developer who was launching a hospital building campaign with a $25,000 donation, they got the donor and recipient to pose together clutching a four-foot-long replica of the cheque. I used to drink with one of those photographers when I was a teenager writing for the now long-defunct *Montreal Herald*, filing for two cents a line. Late one afternoon he told me that he had been paid fifty bucks by Nat Sugarman, who was running for alderman again in our district, to attend his debate with Herb Feingold, who also coveted a job that came with advance real estate information that could be worth plenty. "Now listen to me," said Sugarman, "you don't load that fucking camera with film because I'm not paying for that. But every time I hold up my pencil like this — watch me, see, I'm now holding up my pencil — every time I do that, you leap out of your chair to go flash flash flash. But whatever that shit Feingold says, you never take his picture. Got it? Good."

The incongruous photograph of Maxie showed him assuming his ring stance, leading with his left. But he is standing in the corner of a room, wearing an open-necked sports shirt and trousers belted high, addressing a blank wall. His swept-back hair suggests that it was brilliantined or that he had just got out of a shower.

"Clean up good, Maxie, for Christ's sake. You know how long it is since they took your picture for the papers?"

Cauliflower ears. Soft, dim eyes. Scarred eyebrows. Pulpy nose. Swollen knuckles. And no wonder. Over the wasting years the New York mob had fed Maxie to Fritzie Zivic, Beau Jack, and the great Sugar Ray Robinson, among others. Maxie took on Sugar Ray in Madison Square Garden in 1942, and was knocked to the canvas twice before the referee stopped the fight. Maxie wanted to continue but the referee shouted at him, "Do you want to get killed?"

The son of immigrants out of a Polish *shtetl*, Maxie had an education

Boxer Maxie Berger, 1941.

limited to elementary school, after which he went to work as a gro-
cery delivery boy. He learned to box at the YMHA, on Mount Royal,
which was then in the heart of the city's working-class Jewish quarter.
He won a silver medal in the British Empire Games in the 1930s
before turning pro, fighting out of the Bronx. Married four times, on
his retirement he returned to Montreal and opened a custom-made
shirt business where the smart guys could acquire those ghastly
white-on-white shirts, inevitably worn with initialed cuff links and
what we used to call one-button-roll sports jackets, with outsize
padded shoulders.

I first encountered Maxie in the forties in the Laurentians, our
minor-league Catskills, at the Castle des Monts Hotel in Ste-Agathe.
A seething Maxie came roaring out of the hotel pursued by a hollering
wife. When we shot *The Apprenticeship of Duddy Kravitz* in 1974, I made
sure there was a small part for Maxie. The *National Post* obituary
writer noted that Maxie was "like a character in a Studs Terkel
novel," but Terkel never wrote a novel. The obviously nice man who
had written Maxie's obit also had it that "he became a stockbroker
in the early 1960s, profiting from the 1960s stock market boom."
Actually, he served as a factotum for a brokerage house. In those
days he would occasionally turn up in the Montreal Press Club, then
in the Mount Royal Hotel, and I would chat with him there, an
uncommonly gentle man who had taken too many punches to the
head in close to a hundred fights. He was out of it for the last ten
years of his life, a sufferer from dementia.

RIP, Maxie.

—On Snooker, pp. 89–93

---

*Mortimer Griffin quizzes the mysterious media mogul known only as
the Star Maker about the secret of his success.*

MORTIMER, REMEMBERING A CONVERSATION with Polly Morgan,
who knew absolutely everything about the cinema, said, "In those

early days, you made the Gasoline Alley films. Rather like the Andy Hardy series."

"Exactly. It was on our conscience."

"What was?"

"The WASPs. There we were, you see, a handful of kikes, dagos, and greaseballs, controlling the images Protestant America worshipped. We taught you that to be inarticulate, rather stupid in fact, like Gary Cooper, was manly. It was even manlier to avoid women. Our power was tremendous, you know. Prodigious. When Clark Gable turned up without a vest in *It Happened One Night* he practically killed the undershirt industry. We set the style in big tits. Etc., etc. But what I'm getting at is power, you know, has its responsibilities. Once a year we met to decide what we could do for the *goyim*. One year we gave them Andy Hardy and another Alice Faye or John Wayne. Anything to prop up the myths of the American heartland.... Well now, at the same time, to be honest, the stars we had under contract were beginning to give us trouble. This one was a queer, that one a nympho, and the next a shithead. Suddenly names we had made big — former waitresses and ditchdiggers — wanted script approval, if only to show they could read. Things were getting messy, Mortimer.

"I retreated to Las Vegas to ruminate. There was, I decided, nothing more vacuous, no shell emptier, than a movie actor. They speak the words writers put in their mouths. Any writer. If it's a woman and her legs are bad you shoot somebody else's legs for her. If she's got no tits you build her some, borrowing fat from her thighs. If she can't sing, you hire somebody to dub for her. If it's a man, somebody does his stunts for him. If he can't remember his lines you hold up an idiot card out of shot for him and do one line at a time, over and over again, maybe twenty-five times, until he gets it right. If he has no hair you stitch some on to him. If he's too short, you stretch him. You handle his women and money for him. You rewrite his past life for him.... Was I, the Star Maker, going to be dependent on the whims of such fleas? In a word, no.

"I returned to Hollywood and shared my thoughts with other studio heads and at long last they began to take a positive interest in my nonprofit science foundation. Mortimer, you should have seen my lab in those days! What a bunch of scientists I had! They came to me from the Vienna Radium Institute and Göttingen; from Rutherford's lab at Cambridge; from the University of Munich and Tokyo; from MIT and Princeton and Breslau. The cream of the cream. I read them Edward Gordon Craig's piece on the übermarionette. I brought in von Sternberg to tell them what he thought about actors. I told them about the contract troubles we were having with the stars and how we had to suppress the squalid details of their personal lives. Gentlemen, I said, each one of you here is a genius. You can have anything you want. Now get into that lab and don't come out again until you've made me a Star."

"What?" Mortimer asked.

"Easier said than done, as you can guess. Previously only God... But then with the other studios behind me at last, with a limitless budget, we set to work in earnest. The idea was to kill two birds with one stone. By manufacturing our own stars, no more than one model to a mould, we would be liberated from our contract troubles and so forth. By making our first star the prototype goy, we would be doing something uplifting for America.

"So Operation Goy-Boy began...."

— *Cocksure*, pp. 153–55

Duddy Kravitz takes a summer job as a waiter at Rubin's, a resort in the Laurentians.

WITH THE COMING OF JULY, the hottest and most gruelling month of the season, the waiters were soon too drained for midnight jaunts to Val Morin. They rose listlessly at seven to set their tables and squeeze fruit juices for breakfast, and once the last breakfast had been served, say ten-thirty, it was necessary to set the tables again for lunch. The brawls in the kitchen quickened and the competition for tips got fiercer. After lunch, if the boys had no cutlery to polish, they were usually off duty for two hours and all of them slept, either on the beach or in the darkened dormitory. Not Duddy, however. He hung around the card tables and picked up additional tips running errands for the players.

"There's nothing that little fiend wouldn't do for a dollar," Irwin told Linda, "and that's how I'm going to teach him a lesson. I've got it all figured out."

It was a long hot summer and soon a misplaced toothpaste tube or a borrowed towel was enough to set one boy violently against another. The dormitory over the dance hall had a corrugated tin roof and there were nights when it was too stuffy to sleep. Bernie Altman lost seven pounds and circles swelled under Donald Levitt's eyes, but Duddy showed no signs of fatigue. One afternoon, however, he felt faint, and instead of waiting on the card players he searched for a place to rest. He didn't dare go to the beach because he was a lousy swimmer and Irwin was certainly there, anyway, and he would ridicule his thin white body again, making the girls laugh. The garden was no use because he would surely be asked to fetch a handbag from a third-floor bedroom or search for a misplaced pair of sunglasses. So Duddy wandered round the back of the hotel and sat down on a rock. It was so different here from the beach or main entrance with its flower beds and multicoloured umbrellas and manicured lawns. Flies buzzed round a heap of garbage pails, and sheets and towels flapped on a dozen different lines that ran from the fire escapes to numerous poles. A group of chambermaids and kitchen helpers, permanent staff, sat on the fire escape. Dull, motionless, their eyelids heavy, they smoked in silence. Yvette waved, another girl smiled wearily, and Duddy waved back, but he didn't join them. He returned the next afternoon, however, and the afternoon after that, and each time he sat nearer to the drained, expressionless group on the fire escape. On Sunday afternoon he brought six bottles of ice-cold beer with him, laid them on the steps, shrugged his shoulders, and walked off to his rock again. Yvette went over to him.

"Is the beer for us?"

"Let's not make a fuss, eh? I got some big tips today, that's all."

"You're very nice. Thanks."

"Aw."

"Won't you join us?"

"I've got to get back," he said, "see you," and he hurried off, embarrassed, to the dormitory. He found Irwin going through his suitcase there.

"Hey!"

"Somebody stole my watch."

"Keep away from my stuff or you'll get this," Duddy said, making a fist. "You'll get this right in the kisser."

A couple of afternoons later Irwin rushed into the dormitory. "Do you know what Duddy told Linda this afternoon?" he asked the boys. "Some fantastic story about a brother Bradley who owns a ranch in Arizona."

"So?"

"I happen to know he only has one brother. He's in pre-med, I think."

"All right. He lied. Big deal."

"He's taking Linda out tonight," Irwin said in his liquid whisper.

"What?"

When Duddy entered the dormitory a half hour later, the boys watched apprehensively as he shaved and shined his shoes. Bernie Altman would have liked to warn him that something was up, but Irwin was there and it was impossible.

Duddy was pleased, but he felt jumpy too. He didn't know much about broads, though there had naturally been lots of rumours and reports. Of Flora Lubin, for instance, he had heard it said, "That one likes it the Greek way," but watching Flora walk down the street with her schoolbooks held to her breast Duddy couldn't imagine it. Neither could he credit another report, this one about Grepsy Segal's big sister, that, as A.D. put it, she jerks away for dear life every night. (A girl couldn't anyway, she didn't have a tool.)

Through the years Duddy had collected lots of injunctions about broads and the handling thereof. War Assets safes are not safe. Tell them anything but never put it in writing. "Talk, talk, talk, but no matter what they say there's only one thing they really want." Don't give your correct name and address unless it's really necessary. The hottest are redheads and the easiest single ones over twenty-seven. "A good thing is to start with tickling the back of the neck. That kills them. It's a scientific fact." Gin excites them. Horseback riding gives them hot pants too. Cherries are trouble, but married ones miss it something terrible. "Jewish girls like it just as much as *shiksas*. More, maybe. I know."

Sure, Duddy thought, sure, sure, maybe it was all on the legit, but applying it was another thing. A guy could get his face slapped, or worse.

There were various approaches, of course. He had learned some at the hotel. Paddy Schwartz, the bachelor who came to Rubin's every summer for a two-month stay, had a crack at all the goods under forty-five. "If nine say no," he told Duddy, "then maybe the tenth will be agreeable. The thing is to keep in there pitching." Paddy was tall and dark with greying curly hair, but Duddy was disheartened to discover that his private approaches were never nearly so dashing as his public style. After filling his filly of the night, that's what he called them, with drink, he'd say he had a bum ticker and had been given only six months to live. Then, his eyes filled with tears, he'd add that the filly was the most beautiful he had ever met, and was she going to send him to his maker without a night of love? Ed Planter, the furrier in 408, pursued the single ones, the office girls, but only after it had become clear to them that the vacation was ending with no marriage candidate around. He'd take them out, spending lavishly, and then back outside the single room at the hotel he'd say, "I had a little dream about you last night, honey. I dreamt that you were nice to me, very nice to me, and I made you a gift of a little fur jacket to keep you warm in winter here…and here…and here." Rubin confined himself to the chambermaids. "Why not?" he'd say. "To them it's nothing." But actually all he ever did was pinch them. He pinched hard.

Duddy knew that there were many techniques and he had had some experience himself. There had been that afternoon he had got Birdie Lyman's brassiere half off when the goddamn movie had suddenly ended, and once with a Belmont Park pick-up he'd had everything but. Still, he was scared.

"Yvette's got a real lust for you," Cuckoo told him one night. "Why don't you do something about it? You could bring her here if you wanted…."

"Aw. Yvette. Those are a dime a dozen."

But Linda was something else. Soft, curvy, and nifty enough for one of those snazzy fashion magazines, she seemed just about the most assured girl Duddy had ever met. She had been to Mexico and New York and sometimes she used words that made Duddy blush. Her cigarette holder, acquired on a trip to Europe, was made of real elephant tusk. At night in the recreation hall she seldom danced but usually sat at the bar joking with Irwin and Paddy and other favourites. Every afternoon she went riding and Duddy had often seen her starting down the dirt road to the stables, beating her whip against her boot. Linda was nineteen and the daughter of a hotel owner — she was maybe an inch and some taller than he was too — and Duddy couldn't understand why she wanted to go out with him. He'd been leading Thunder back to the stables when he had run into her.

"Day off today?"

"Yeah."

"Buy me a drink?"

"Wha'?"

"I'm thirsty."

"Sure. Sure thing."

He took her to the Laurentide Ice Cream Bar.

"No," she said. "A *drink*."

It was not even dark yet.

"Let's go to the Chalet," she said.

The bartender there greeted her warmly. Luckily Duddy had lots of money on him because she drank quickly. Not beer, either.

"Well, Duddy, how do you like shovelling food into the greedy mouths of the *nouveaux riches*?"

"Your father is a very decent man to work for," Duddy said earnestly. He couldn't understand why she looked so amused.

"Why?"

"Jeez. I dunno. I mean…"

"Did you know that he pinches all the chambermaids' little bums?"

"Maybe we oughta go?"

"No. Let's have another. Hey, Jerry. Two more on the rocks." Turning to Duddy again, she laughed. "You shouldn't let Irwin pick on you like that. You ought to talk back to him."

"I'm not scared. I keep quiet, but I've got my reasons."

"Is that so?"

There was that amused smile again. He didn't like it.

"Yeah."

"Like what?"

"Well," he said, feeling a little dizzy, "I don't really have to work as a waiter, you know. My father's in the transport business. But I'm making a study of the hotel business like."

"Shouldn't I warn my father that he's harbouring a future competitor in the dormitory?"

Duddy laughed. He was pleased. "Hey, have you ever read *God's Little Acre*?"

Duddy figured if she had, and admitted it, there might be something doing. But she didn't reply.

"I'm not much of a reader, really, but my Uncle Benjy has read millions of books. Hard-covered ones. My brother Lennie is gonna be a doctor."

"What are you going to be?"

Without thinking, he said, "I'm gonna get me some land one of these days. A man without land is nothing."

He told her about his brother Bradley and that the Boy Wonder, an intimate of his father's, was willing to back him in any line he chose.

"Why don't you take me dancing tonight?"

Duddy drank three cups of black coffee and took a swim to clear his head before he returned to the dormitory. Irwin, lying on the bed, made him nervous — Linda was supposed to be his girl — and Duddy couldn't understand why the others watched him so apprehensively while he dressed. Duddy took half an hour combing his hair into a pompadour with the help of lots of brilliantine. He selected from among his shirts a new one with red and black checks and the tie he chose was white with a black and blue pattern of golf balls and clubs. His green sports jacket had wide shoulders, a one-button roll, and brown checks. A crease had been sewn into his grey flannel trousers. He wore two-tone shoes.

Bernie Altman looked hard at Irwin and stopped Duddy as he was going out. "Listen," he said, "I'll lend you my suit if you like."

"Jeez, that's nice of you, Bernie. I'm going dancing tonight. But this is the first chance I've had to wear this jacket. A heavy date, you know. Thanks anyway."

Irwin choked his laughter with his pillow.

"Look, Duddy, I — Oh, what's the use? Have a good time."

Outside, Linda leaned on the horn of her father's station wagon. Duddy ran.

"You're a son of a bitch, Irwin. A real son of a bitch."

"Did I pick those clothes for him?"

"Why is she going out with Duddy?"

"Yeah, what have you two cooked up?" Donald asked.

Duddy and Linda drove to Hilltop Lodge, the resort with the best band, and ordered scotch on the rocks. Many of the bright young people there waved. Two or three raised their eyebrows when they saw that Linda was with Duddy. "We're engaged," Linda said. "He uses Ponds."

Duddy danced with her three or four times. She was OK on the slow ones, but when the band played something hot, a boogie-woogie, for instance, Duddy switched to his free-swinging FFHS Tea Dance style and all at once the floor was cleared and everyone stood around watching. At first this seemed to delight Linda, she laughed a lot, but the second time round she quit on Duddy in the middle of a dance. Once, during a slow number, he held her too close.

"Please," she said.

"This is called a 'Y' dance," Duddy said. But she didn't get the joke.

Linda invited three others to their table and Duddy ordered drinks for them. Melvin Lerner, a dentistry student, held hands with Jewel Freed. They were both working at Camp Forest Land. The other man was bearded and somewhat older than the others; he was thirty maybe. Peter Butler lived in Ste-Agathe all year round; he had built his own house on a secluded part of the lake.

"Peter's a painter," Linda said to Duddy.

"Inside or outside?"

"That's good," Peter said. "That's very good." He slapped his knees again and again.

Duddy looked puzzled.

"He's not joking," Linda said. "Peter's not a house painter, Duddy. He paints pictures. Peter is a nonfigurative painter."

"Like Norman Rockwell," Peter said, laughing some more.

"*Touché,*" Linda said, and she ordered another round of drinks.

"What do you do?" Melvin asked Duddy.

Mordecai Richler in 1997.

"He's making a study of the hotel business like," Linda said.

Peter and Linda danced two slow numbers together and when Duddy looked up again they were gone. An hour later Linda returned alone, her face flushed and bits of dead leaves stuck to her dress. "I need a drink," she said. "A big one."

"Maybe we oughta go. I've got to be up at seven tomorrow."

"One for the road."

So Duddy ordered another round. Maybe it was the liquor — he was certainly not used to it — but all at once it seemed to him that Linda had changed. Her voice softened and she began to ask him lots of questions about his plans for the future. She was not ridiculing him any more, he was sure of that, and he was no longer afraid of her. From time to time the room swayed around him and he was glad he wasn't the one who would have to drive home. But dizzy as he was he felt fine. He no longer heard all her remarks, however, because he was thinking that hotel owners' daughters had fallen for poor boys before and, given a shot at it, there were lots of improvements he could make at Rubin's. There was the *Laurentian Liner* too.

"Well, Duddy, are you game?"

The room rocked.

"Tell me if you don't want to. I won't be angry. Maybe Irwin would…"

"No, no. I'll do it."

"It'll give you a good start on your stake."

She helped him outside and into the station wagon. His head rolling and jerking loose each time they hit a bump, Duddy tried, he tried hard, to remember what he had agreed to. He had told some lies about himself and the Boy Wonder, they had talked about the gambling house he ran, and the conversation had come round to roulette. Duddy pretended to be an expert and Linda just happened to own a wheel. Then what? He told her he had already earned more than four hundred dollars in tips and Linda said that was plenty. Plenty? Plenty for him to act as banker for the roulette game they were going to run in the recreation hall beginning at one a.m. Sunday night. Wouldn't her father object? No, not if ten percent of each win went into a box for the Jewish National Fund. He couldn't lose — there was that too. She told him so. He might even come out a few hundred dollars ahead.

"Can you make it upstairs yourself?"

"Sure."

"Aren't you going to kiss Linda before you go?"

"Mm —"

That was Wednesday, and in the three days to go before the game Duddy began to fear for his money. "Sure you could win," Cuckoo said, "but you could lose too. If I were you I wouldn't do it." But if he was afraid for his money, neither did he want Linda to think that he'd welsh on a promise. She was so sweet to him these days. At night in the recreation hall she sometimes called him over to join her for a drink. Still, he thought, maybe I ought to speak to her. I work hard for my money and I need it. Then people began to stop him in the lobby or on the beach.

"I'll be there, kid," Paddy said.

Farber slapped him on the back and winked. "Count me in," he said.

Mr. Cohen stopped him outside the gym. "Is it OK if I bring along a couple of pals?"

The Boy Wonder, Duddy thought, would not chicken out in a situation like this. He would be cool. But Duddy couldn't sleep Friday night and he was ashamed to go and tell Cuckoo again that he was scared. He wouldn't want Linda or Irwin to know that, either. It was so nice, too. Suddenly people looking at him, smiling. He no longer had to go round to the back of the hotel to sit with the kitchen help and chambermaids for companionship. Aw, the hell, Duddy figured out that if the bank ever dropped below one hundred dollars he would stop the game, but he withdrew three hundred just in case. Linda took him aside on Saturday afternoon. "Maybe we'd better call it off," she said. "You might lose."

"You said I couldn't lose."

"I said, I said. How do I know?"

"I'm not calling it off. I can't. All those people. Jeez."

Cuckoo pleaded with him once more. "But what if you lose, Duddy?"

"Simple," Duddy said. "If I lose I drown myself. That's show biz."

On Sunday night the boys in Artie Bloom's band, who were in on the story, broke up early and everyone pretended to be going off to bed or somewhere else. The lights in the recreation hall were turned out and the front door was locked. Fifteen minutes later some of the lights were turned on again and a side door was opened. The players began to arrive. Duddy set up the table and announced the odds in a failing voice. He would pay thirty to one on a full number and the top bet allowed was fifty cents. That would pay fifteen dollars, one-fifty of which would go into the JNF box. Linda, who was helping him, began to sell change. Farber bought five dollars' worth and Mr. Cohen asked for ten. Once Duddy had counted forty players in the hall he asked for the door to be shut.

"Don't worry," Linda said. "The more players, the more money on the board, the better it is for the bank."

But Duddy insisted.

"I'll only take ten dollars' worth for a start," Irwin said.

Duddy looked sharply at Linda and it seemed to him that she was even more frightened than he was. "OK," he said. "Place your bets."

Duddy counted at least thirty dollars on the first run. Jeez, he thought. His hands shaky, he was just about to spin the wheel when a voice in the darkness shouted, "Nobody leave. This is a raid."

"Wha'?"

"My men have got the place surrounded. No funny stuff, please."

A spotlight was turned on and revealed Cuckoo Kaplan in a Keystone Cop costume. His nightstick was made of rubber and the height he shook it at made all the women laugh.

"You're a dirty pig, Cuckoo."

"Some cop."

Duddy shut his eyes and spun the wheel and number thirty-two came up. Nobody was on it. He paid off even money on two blacks, that's all.

"Come on, Cuckoo. Gimme a number. I'll place a bet for you. Quick."

Cuckoo took off his shoe, reached into an outlandishly patched sock, and pulled out a dollar bill. "Rubin just gave me an advance on next year's salary. He's crying in the kitchen right now."

"Cuckoo!"

"Put the works on number six for me, but I can't look."

After an hour of play Duddy was ahead more than two hundred dollars. "I'll tell you what," he said. "Lots of you seem to be losing. I'm no chiseller. From now on you can bet a dollar on a number if you want."

That's when Irwin changed another twenty-five dollars and sat down at the table and began to play in earnest. His bets seemed to follow no apparent pattern. On each spin of the wheel he placed a dollar on numbers fifteen, six, thirty-two, three, and twelve, and it was only the next morning when he looked closely at the wheel that Duddy realized these numbers ran together there. Irwin won; he didn't win on each spin, but whenever one of his numbers came up he collected thirty dollars and twice if his number repeated. Others, riding his streak of luck, began to bet with him, and once Duddy had to pay off three different people on number three.That cost him ninety dollars, not counting the side and corner bets.

"Don't worry," Irwin said. "David's father is in the transport business. He doesn't *really* have to work as a waiter."

Duddy turned to Linda, his look astonished.

"His brother Bradley is a big rancher in Arizona," Irwin said. "All David has to do is wire him for more money."

"It's getting late," Mrs. Farber said.

Ed Planter yawned and stretched.

"Don't go," Duddy said. "Not yet, please. Give me a chance to win some of my money back."

Farber saw that Duddy was extremely pale.

"Don't worry, kid," Mr. Cohen said. "Your luck will change."

But Duddy's luck didn't change, it got worse, and nobody at the table joked any more. The men could see that the boy's cheeks were burning hot, his eyes were red, and his shirt adhered to his back. When Duddy paid out on a number his hands shook.

Cuckoo pulled Irwin aside. "It's your wheel, you bastard. I found out."

"Really?"

"Do you know how hard that kid works for his money?"

Irwin tried to turn away, but Cuckoo seized him by the arm. "I'm going to speak to Rubin," he said. "First thing tomorrow morning I'm going to talk to him."

"Linda and I are going to be engaged," Irwin said. "Rubin is very pleased about that. I thought maybe you'd like to know."

"Come on," Duddy said. "Place your bets. Let's not waste time."

The men at the table were tired and wanted to go to bed, but they were also ashamed of winning so much money from a seventeen-year-old boy and they began to play recklessly, trying to lose. It was no use.

"We want to see you upstairs later, Irwin," Bernie Altman said.

On the next spin Duddy went broke and he had to close the game.

"That's show biz," Irwin said. "Right, Cuckoo?"

The men filed out without looking at Duddy, but Linda stayed on after the others had gone.

"Thanks," Duddy said. "Thanks a lot."

"How much did you lose?"

"Everything. Three hundred dollars." Duddy began to scream. "You said I couldn't lose. You told me it was impossible for me to lose."

"I'm sorry, Duddy. I had no idea that —"

"Aw, go to hell. Just go to hell please." He gave the wheel a shove, knocking it over, and rushed outside. Once on the beach he could no longer quell his stomach. Duddy was sick. He sat on a rock, holding his head in his hands, and he began to sob bitterly.

— *The Apprenticeship of Duddy Kravitz*, pp. 77–88

Moses Berger's quest for the missing Solomon Gursky has led him to compile research on the equally mysterious Sir Hyman Kaplansky.

A CEILING-TO-FLOOR BOOKCASE in the living room of Moses's cabin in the woods was crammed with books, newspaper and magazine clippings relating to the life of the elusive, obscenely rich Sir Hyman Kaplansky, as he then styled himself.

The index of the third volume of the celebrated diaries of a British MP with impeccable Bloomsbury bona fides revealed several entries for Sir Hyman Kaplansky.

May 17, 1944

Lunch at the Travellers with Gladwyn and Chips. We were joined by Hyman Kaplansky, his cultivated dandyish manner insufficient to conceal the ghetto greaser within. He allowed that he was frightened of the V.11s. I suggested that he ought to think of his loved ones on the battlefield who were at far greater risk than he was.

Hyman: "That wouldn't work for me at all, dear boy. I have no loved ones on the battlefield. They are all in firewatching right here. The buggers' battalions, don't you know?"

An earlier entry was dated September 12, 1941.

Dined at the Savoy with Ivor. When Hyman Kaplansky stopped at our table I told him how *triste* I felt about the martyred Jews of Poland and how after Eden had read his statement in the House we all stood up as a tribute.

"If my unfortunate brethren only knew it," he said, "I'm sure they would feel most obliged. Did the Speaker stand up as well?"

"Yes."

"How very moving."

The Jewish capacity for cynicism is really insufferable. Although I loathe anti-Semites, I do dislike Jews.

June 8, 1950

Lunch at the Reform Club. The beastly Sir Hyman is there with Guy and Tom Driberg. Driberg is carrying on about his favoured "cottages" in Soho.

"Why municipal vandals," he said, "should have thought it necessary to destroy so many of them I do not know. I suppose it is one expression of anti-homosexual prejudice. Yet no homo, cottage-cruising, ever prevented a hetero from merely having a whiz. While to do one's rounds of the cottages — the alley by the Astoria, the dog-leg lane opposite the Garrick Club, the one near the Ivy, the one off Wardour Street — provided homos, not all of whom are given to rougher sports, with healthy exercise."

June 7, 1951

Dinner at the Savoy. Sir Hyman Kaplansky at another table, entertaining some of the old Tots and Quots. Zuckerman, Bernal, and Haldane. Everybody is discussing the Burgess-Maclean affair. Sir Hyman says, "I know Guy to be a coward and a Bolshie and I'm not surprised he did a bunk."

The next entry for Sir Hyman dealt at length with that infamous dinner party in his Cumberland Terrace flat. A Passover *seder*, of all things, to which Sir Hyman — much to Lady Olivia's horror — had invited the MP and other noted anti-Semites. Among them, a couple of survivors of the Cliveden set, an unabashed admirer of Sir Oswald Mosley, a famous novelist, a celebrated actress, a West End impresario, a Polish count, and a rambunctious cabinet minister who was an adamant opponent of further Jewish settlement in troubled Palestine. Why did they come?

The novelist, arguably the most gifted of his time, wrote in his diary:

March 21, 1953

All in order for our trip to Menton. I am assured that the villa has been furnished to my taste, the servants will be adequate, and there will be no Americans to be seen. We travel in a filthy carriage to Dover and then board the boat. The usual drunken commercial travellers and this time a number of Jews, presumably tax evaders. This reminds Sybil that we are expected to dine at Sir Hyman Kaplansky's the evening after our return. The food and wine will be excellent. Certainly no problems with ration coupons in that quarter.

Another diary, this one kept by the actress, reminded her many admirers of exactly what she was wearing (an outfit especially created for her by Norman Hartnell) on the day the Bomb fell on Hiroshima. On another page she revealed for the first time that her only child lay dying in Charing Cross Hospital on the night theatrical tradition obliged her to open in *Peonies for Penelope*, a musical that ran for three years at the Haymarket in spite of the posh critics. An entry dated three days before Sir Hyman's dinner party described a lunch at the Ivy with the West End impresario, a noted sybarite.

April 12, 1953

Signs of the times. At one table a loud infestation of newly affluent proles. GI brides, Cockney accents. But I could hardly afford to eat here any more — if not for Hugh's kindness. Hugh is in a snit about the dinner party at Sir Hyman's.

"Will I be expected to put on one of those silly black beanies I've seen the men wear in Whitechapel?"

"Think of the caviar. He gets it from their embassy. Consider the endless bottles of Dom P. I am told there will be a whole baby lamb."

"Kosher, I daresay."

Hugh confessed how deeply he regretted casting Kitty rather than little me in *The Dancing Duchess*. Stuff and nonsense, I told him. I wouldn't hear a word against Kitty. She tries so hard.

Other diaries, memoirs, letter collections, and biographies of the period were rich in details of that disastrous night. There were contradictions, of course, each memoir writer laying claim to the evening's most memorable *bon mots*. Other discrepancies related to Lady Olivia, who had been born and raised an Anglican. Some charged that she had treacherously been a party to the insult, but others were equally certain that she was its true victim. Both groups agreed that the Polish count was her lover, but they split again on whether Sir Hyman condoned the relationship, was ignorant of it, or — just possibly — had planned the scandal to avenge himself on both of them. Whatever the case, there was no disputing the main thrust of events, only their interpretation.

Including Sir Hyman and Lady Olivia, there were thirteen at the refectory table, which made for much light-hearted bantering, the mood darkening only when Sir Hyman — insensitive or vindictive, depending on the witness — pointed out that that had been the precise number gathered at the most famous of all Passover noshes.

Every diary and memoir writer mentioned the table setting, describing it either as opulent or all too typically reeking of Levantine ostentation. The wine goblets and decanters were made of late-Georgian flint glass, their hue Waterford blue. The seventeenth-century candelabra were of a French design, with classic heads and overlapping scales and foliated strapwork. The heavy, ornate silver-ware was of the same period. Other artifacts were of Jewish origin. There was, for instance, a silver Passover condiment set, its style German Baroque, stamped with fruit and foliage. The *seder* tray itself, the platter on which the offending *matzohs* would lie, was made of pewter. It was eighteenth-century Dutch in origin, unusually large, engraved with Haggadah liturgies, artfully combining the pictorial and calligraphic.

An ebullient Sir Hyman welcomed his guests to the table with a prepared little speech that some would later condemn as grovelling and others, given the shocking turn of events, as a damned imperti-nence. In the first place, he said, he wished to say how grateful he was that everyone had accepted his invitation, because he knew how prejudiced they were against *some* of his kind. He hardly blamed them. Some of his kind, especially those sprung from Eastern Europe, were insufferably pushy and did in fact drive a hard bargain, and to prove his point he quoted some lines of T. S. Eliot:

> And the Jew squats on the window sill, the owner,
> Spawned in some estaminet of Antwerp,
> Blistered in Brussels, patched and peeled in London....

Such people, Sir Hyman said, embarrassed him and other gentlemen of Hebraic origin even more than they were an affront to decent Christians. In a lighter vein, Sir Hyman went on to say that he hoped his guests would find the rituals essential to the Passover feast a welcome little frisson. Each of them would find a little book at their place. It was called a Haggadah and they should think of it as a libretto. We should tell — that is to say, "hagged" — of our exodus from Egypt, not the last time the Jews did a midnight flit. The Haggadah — like the libretto of any musical in trouble in Boston or Manchester — was being constantly revised to keep pace with the latest Jewish bad patch. He had seen one, for instance, that included a child's drawing of the last *seder* held in Theresienstadt. The drawing, alas, was without any artistic merit, but — it could be argued — did have a certain maudlin charm. He had seen another one that made much of the fact that the Nazi all-out artillery attack on the grouchy Jews of the Warsaw ghetto had begun on the eve of Passover. A man who had survived that kerfuffle only to perish in a concentration camp later on had written, "We are faced with a Passover of hunger and poverty, without even 'the bread of affliction.' For eating and drinking there is neither *matzoh* nor wine. For prayer there are no synagogues or houses of study. Their doors are closed and darkness reigns in the dwelling places of Israel." However, Sir Hyman hastily pointed out, we have come here not to mourn but to be jolly. He beamed at Lady Olivia, who responded by jiggling a little bell. Servants refilled the champagne glasses at once.

Seder, Sir Hyman informed his captive audience, seemingly indifferent to their growing restiveness, literally means programme, which applies to the prescribed ceremonies of the Passover ritual. Raising the pewter *matzoh* platter, he proclaimed first in Hebrew and then in English: "This is the bread of affliction which our ancestors ate in the land of Egypt. Let all who are hungry come and eat."

"Hear, hear!"

"Goodo!"

It was now nine p.m., and though Sir Hyman's guests had begun to arrive as early as six, there had — much to their chagrin — been no hors d'oeuvres served. Not so much as a wizened olive or peanut or blade of celery. Stomachs were rumbling. Appetites were keen. Sensing his guests' impatience, Sir Hyman hurried through the reading of the Haggadah that necessarily preceded the feast, skipping page after page. Even so, he had to be aware of the shifting of chairs, the fidgeting that verged on the hostile, the raising of eyebrows, the dark looks. It did not help matters that each time the kitchen doors swung open the dining room was filled with the most tantalizing aromas. Steaming chicken broth. Lamb on the sizzle. Finally, at ten p.m., Sir Hyman nodded at an increasingly distressed Lady Olivia, who promptly jiggled her little bell.

Ah.

There were gasps of pleasure as a huge, wobbly, gleaming mound of beluga caviar was set down on the table. Next came an enormous platter of pleasingly moist smoked salmon. The salmon was followed by a silver salver heavy with baked carp and a surround of golden jelly. Everybody was set to pounce, but Sir Hyman, his smile gleeful, raised a restraining hand. "Wait, please. There is one more protocol of Zion, as it were, to be observed. Before indulging ourselves we are obliged to eat the bread of affliction. The *matzoh*."

"Let's get on with it, then."

"For God's sake, Hymie, I'm hungry enough to eat a horse."

"Hear, hear!"

Sir Hyman nodded and a servant removed the pewter *matzoh* platter, piled it high with the bread of affliction, and returned it to the table, covered with a magenta velvet cloth.

"What we have here," Sir Hyman said, "are not the tasteless, mass-produced *matzohs* you might expect to find on the tables of tradesmen in Swiss Cottage or Golders Green, their eyes on the main chance. These are the authentic *matzohs* of ancient and time-honoured tradition. They are called *matzoh shemurah*. Guarded *matzoh*. Baked behind locked doors, under conditions of the strictest security, according to a recipe first formulated in Babylon. Brought from there to Lyons in the year 1142, of the Christian era, and from there to York. These were made for me by a venerable Polish rabbi I know in Whitechapel."

"Come on, Hymie!"

"Let's get on with it."

"I'm starved!"

Sir Hyman yanked the magenta cloth free, and revealed was a stack of the most unappetizing-looking biscuits. Coarse, unevenly baked, flecked with rust spots, their surfaces bumpy with big brown blisters.

"Everybody take one, please," Sir Hyman said, "but, careful, they're hot."

Once everybody had a *matzoh* in hand, Sir Hyman stood up and offered a solemn benediction. "Blessed be God, who brings food out of the earth. Blessed be God, who made each *mitzvah* bring us holiness, and laid on us the eating of *matzoh*." Then he indicated that they were free to dig in at last.

The West End impresario, his eyes on the caviar, was the first to take a bite. Starchy, he thought. Bland. But then he felt a blister in the *matzoh* burst like a pustule and the next thing he knew a warm fluid was dribbling down his chin. He was about to wipe it away with his napkin when the actress, seated opposite him, took one look and let out a terrifying scream. "Oh, my poor Hugh," she cried. "Hugh, just look at you!"

But he was already sufficiently discomfited merely looking at her. A thick reddish substance was splattered over her panting ivory bosom.

"My God!" somebody wailed, dropping his leaky *matzoh shemurah*.

The fastidious Cynthia Cavendish cupped her hands to her mouth, desperate to spit out the warm red sticky stuff, then took a peek at it trickling between her fingers and subsided to the carpet in a dead faint.

Horace McEwen, smartly avoiding the sinking Cynthia, stared at his rust-smeared napkin, his lips trembling, and then stuck two fingers into his mouth, praying for loose teeth.

"It's blood, don't you know?"

"Bastard!"

"We're all covered in ritual blood!"

The Rt. Hon. Richard Cholmondeley knocked back his chair and, convinced that he was dying, began to bring up bile and what he also took for blood. "Tell Constance," he pleaded with nobody in particular, "that the photographs in the bottom left-hand drawer of my desk are not mine. Noddy gave them to me for safekeeping when he got back from Marrakech."

The cabinet minister's plump wife vomited all over his Moss Bros. dinner jacket before he could thrust her clear, sending her reeling backwards. "Now look what you've done," he said. "Just look."

The sodden novelist slid to the floor. Unfortunately he was clutching the antique Irish lace tablecloth at the time and, consequently, brought down some priceless wine goblets as well as the platter of smoked salmon with him. The impresario, with characteristic presence of mind, grabbed the other end of the tablecloth just in time to secure the sliding tureen of caviar. Torn between anger and appetite, he snatched a soup spoon and lunged at the caviar once, twice, three times before demanding his coat and hat. The Polish count, his face ashen, leaped up and challenged Sir Hyman to a duel.

Sir Hyman startled him by responding softly in fluent Polish. "Your father was a swindler and your mother was a whore and you, dear boy, are a ponce. Name the time and place."

Lady Olivia sat rocking her face in her hands, as her guests scattered, raging and cursing.

"You will pay dearly for this outrage, Hymie."

"You haven't heard the end of it!"

"Tell it not in Gath," Sir Hyman said, "publish it not in the streets of Askelon; lest the daughters of the Philistines rejoice...."

The last departing guest claimed to have heard a stricken Lady Olivia ask, "How could you humiliate me like this, Hymie?"

He purportedly replied, "There will be no more assignations with that squalid little Polack. Now let's eat the lamb before it's hopelessly overdone."

"I despise you," Lady Olivia shrieked, stamping her foot, and fleeing to her bedroom.

—*Solomon Gursky Was Here,* pp. 502–10

Jerusalem

While Richler as a youth repudiated the religious orthodoxy of his family, he embraced a socialist — liberal, progressive — form of Zionism. Sometimes, as boys do, he imagined himself as a Jewish Avenger fighting the Arabs. In later years, he reaffirmed this commitment by visiting Israel, and by writing articles and a book about those visits. In his novels he sometimes satirized Jewish fundraising events and activities. Barney Panofsky (Barney's Version), for example, uses his voluntary position with the United Jewish Appeal as a kind of social camouflage. Richler's nonfiction recollection of the boy who introduced him to militant Zionism, and what became of him, is a sober reflection on what sometimes becomes of youthful ideals.

Mr. Yalofsky taught Richler in the parochial school in Montreal.

MR. YALOFSKY WAS A DEVOUT JEW — unlike most of our Hebrew teachers at the Talmud Torah, who had to pay lip service to religious practices in deference to "certain families out of the Stone Age." But our Hebrew teachers were staunch Zionists. One of them, Mr. Weingarten, had come to us in 1941 all the way out of Russian-occupied Poland, through Siberian exile, a hike into Manchuria, then Japan, and by timely freighter to Vancouver. At recess, we ridiculed his broken, heavily accented English.

In arts and crafts class, we built a huge relief map representing a chunk of the Galilee, claiming it for our people:

El yivneh ha-Galil,
An´u nivneh ha-Galil....

God will rebuild Galilee,
We shall rebuild Galilee,
We are off to Galilee,
We will rebuild Galilee....

We erected a balsa-wood watchtower and instant stockade, establishing a kibbutz, populating it with Plasticine *chalutzim* (pioneers) and livestock made of pipe cleaners.

The swamps were being drained, we were told, and the desert reclaimed to yield melons, grapefruit, oranges, figs, dates, and tomatoes. We were taught about our heroes, and none loomed larger than the champion of Tel Hai, Joseph Trumpeldor, in whose memory that settlement set the statue of a lion.

Trumpeldor, who lost his left arm during a perilous mission in the Russo-Japanese War, rose to become one of the few Jewish officers in the army of the Czar. He made *aliyah* in 1912, and worked for a time at Degania, on Lake Kinneret, Israel's first kibbutz. In the Great War he fought again, this time for the British at Gallipoli, leading the Zion

Mule Corps — 650 Jewish muleteers and 750 mules. This corps was the precursor of the Jewish Legion, made up of East End Londoners, American and Canadian volunteers, and members of the Yishuv, who had enlisted in three battalions of the Royal Fusiliers (the 38th, 39th, and 40th) and joined General Allenby's campaign to wrest Palestine from the Turks. Trumpeldor did not serve in the Legion but left for Russia during the revolution, and put together a group of young Jews pledged to make *aliyah*. He was back in Palestine in 1920, at a time when the Arabs, reacting to increased Jewish immigration, were attacking such settlements as Tel Hai in the Galilee. During the raid on Tel Hai, he was shot in the stomach. He ordered a comrade to stuff his protruding intestines back into his belly and bind the wound. Then he carried on directing the defense of the settlement. Trumpeldor died on a stretcher on his way to neighbouring Kfar Giladi. His last words, according to legend, were "It is good to die for our country."

Many an afternoon when my parents and elder brother were out, I would crawl on the floor all the way from the kitchen to the front door, propelling myself with my good arm, shoving my Red Ryder air rifle ahead of me, even as I dodged Arab bullets. Eventually the trail of blood from my abdominal wound would attract the attention of one of the many gorgeous nurses who revered me, but I would wave her off, saying, "It's nothing, just a flesh wound. Look after the other *chaverim* first."

—*This Year in Jerusalem*, pp. 13–15

I JOINED HABONIM — the youth group of a Zionist political party, rooted in socialist doctrine — shortly after my bar mitzvah, during my first year at Baron Byng High School. I had been recruited by a Room 41 classmate whom I shall call Jerry Greenfeld.

Jerry seemed blessed. Only a few months older than I was, he already had to shave every day. Rubbing his jaw as he shot out of school late in the afternoon, bound for an hour or two of snooker at the Mount Royal Billiards Academy, he would wink and say, "Four o'clock shadow," and I would burn with envy. School days he usually

The Labour Zionist Centre, Montreal, early 1950s.

wore a sharkskin windbreaker with JERRY embossed in gold letters across his broad back and a hockey-team crest over his heart. Jerry appeared effortlessly gifted in all those pursuits in which I longed, unavailingly, to shine. He had fought in the Golden Gloves for the YMHA, eliminated in a semifinal bout against an Irish boy out of Griffintown only because, he explained, the referee was an obvious anti-Semite. He was a high scorer on our school basketball team. He also pitched for a baseball team that actually wore uniforms — the North End Maccabees, sponsored by a local scrap dealer. At the occasional late-afternoon "tea dance" in our school gym, Jerry, his manner breezy, could entice pretty girls in grade ten, maybe three years older than he was, to jitterbug with him. His mother had died when he was six years old and his father didn't care what time he came home. Saturday nights he would strut down St. Urbain Street, wearing a one-button roll jacket, and trousers rakishly pegged, if not quite zoot. If he condescended to stop at the corner of Fairmount

Street, immediately outside Wilensky's store, where we used to hang out, he might grant us a peek at the condom he kept in his wallet. "Just in case," he'd say.

One day Jerry approached me in the schoolyard and asked, "Can you help me out this Saturday aft?"

"Sure. How?"

"You own a baseball mitt?"

"Sure."

Starting that Saturday afternoon, Jerry allowed me to catch for him in the lane behind our cold-water flat as he worked on his fast-ball, low and just nibbling the outside of the plate, which he assumed would one day attract the attention of Labish "Lefty" Mandelcorn. Labish had survived a season playing left field for a Class C team in the Carolinas, and had a photograph of himself and several other players chatting with Connie Mack. If not for his asthma, he would have made the majors. Never without his pencil, its end chewed out, a spiral notebook, and his wrinkled brown bag of sunflower seeds, he now claimed to be a local scout for the Brooklyn Dodgers, parent team of our Montreal Royals of the Triple A International League. It was on his recommendation, he said, that two indigenous French Canadian infielders, Roland Gladu and Stan Bréard, had been signed by the Royals. But I had my suspicions. He often dropped the name "Branch," and I had read in Dink Carroll's column in the Montreal *Gazette* that everybody, even Leo Durocher, called the Dodgers' general manager "Mr. Rickey."

Following one Saturday afternoon workout, Jerry bounced a mock punch off my shoulder, as was his habit now, and asked, "What are you doing tonight?"

"Fff-all."

"Let's go to supper at Dinty Moore's."

That was not a neighbourhood delicatessen but a real restaurant. Downtown. Beyond the pale. "Are you kidding?" I asked.

Jerry paid for our corned beef and cabbage, and apple pie and ice cream, with American dollars. Real money. He left the waitress a big tip and told her she was a looker. And then, swearing me to secrecy, he revealed that his father had been married once before, and that he had a stepbrother who was flying a P-38 with the U.S. Fifth Air Force in the Pacific *right now*, and already had five Japs to his credit. Gary sent Jerry a few bucks from time to time, and when the war was over he was going to fetch him and the two of them would settle in Palestine.

"Why does it have to be such a secret? Gary, I mean."

"Hey, I've already blabbed too much. Why don't you come to Habonim with me on Friday night? If you like it, maybe you'll join."

So Jerry, chewing on a matchstick, picked me up after supper on Friday and then we went to collect two other *chaverim* (comrades), whom I shall call Hershey Bloom and Myer Plotnik. Hershey, six foot even then, was a member of our high-school student council executive, an admirer of John Gunther's books and of movies with social content (*Watch on the Rhine, The Corn Is Green*), an awfully serious boy with puffy red cheeks and a weakness for chocolate éclairs, his big belly bulging out of his trousers. His father had died of a heart attack at the age of thirty-seven and Hershey was convinced that he was destined to do the same, which added to his aura of importance in our eyes. "It's in my genes," he often said.

A meeting of the youth wing of the Labour Zionist Organization in the late 1940s.

Myer, with his tight curly black hair and quick laughter and bouncy carefree walk, radiated goodwill and was popular with the girls, who warmed to his nonthreatening nature. His father was a barber whose favourite routine depended on having a new customer in his chair, the man's face swaddled in hot wet towels. Then Mr. Plotnik would sharpen his straight razor on the strop and ask, "Hey, you ever seen *Sweeney Todd*?"

"Who?"

Gleefully lathering the man's face, he would tell him about it. "You know, that play about the *meshuggener* barber who used to slit men's throats. Some people say it was based on a true-life story. Anyways..."

Mr. Plotnik's specialty for teenagers was the pompadour, and for an additional twenty-five cents he would also squeeze out unwanted blackheads with a special tool.

Slouching toward Habonim meetings with Jerry, Hershey, and Myer, the four of us puffing on Sweet Caps, became a Friday night

ritual that continued unbroken through almost four years of high school, by which time Jerry had to quit Habonim in disgrace. Our rambling, three-story meeting house was in the heart of Montreal's old working-class Jewish quarter, on Jeanne Mance Street, which we used to mispronounce Jean Mance, provoking exasperated laughter from French Canadians.

—*This Year in Jerusalem,* pp. 4–7

ON IMPULSE, I went down to the Black Watch Armory on Bleury Street one afternoon. Claiming to be eighteen years old, I enlisted in the Reserve Army. It appealed to my sense of irony to have the Black Watch train me to fight the British — the British, who were now beyond the pale, so far as I was concerned.

Wednesday nights I turned up in uniform at the armory, where I learned to field-strip and reassemble a machine gun and drink beer out of a bottle. In order to prove his manhood, Isaac Babel, riding with the Red Cavalry, had to wring a goose's neck. All that my new battalion mates required of me, in the sleazy bar we frequented after an evening in the armory, was that, following their example, I should fart resoundingly at the table. They were a good, hard-working bunch: middle-aged men, mostly, who worked in the Angus machine shops or at Pratt-Whitney or on one construction site or another. One evening, Gord, the battalion clown, who had been raised on a farm in the Eastern Townships, explained how his father had avoided military service in the Great War. "Mister Man," he said, "before going in for his medical, he injected milk into his cock, and they turned him down because they thought the drip meant he had the syph or something for sure."

Another evening, Gord told us that his brother-in-law, who had worked in a bobbin mill in the Townships, had died two days earlier, aged forty-three. "He was driving my sister to St. Louis, where we got cousins, and he and Sally put up at one of them roadside little hotels on the way, and a burglar came in through the window after they went to sleep and Reg saw him, shot bolt upright in bed, and died of a heart attack on the spot."

"Why, that's terrible, Gord."

"Aw," Gord said, "Reg always did have a yellow streak down his back."

The men relished their evening out, striding downtown in their uniforms, hoping, even as I did, that girls would mistake them for veterans who had been to hell and back again.

— *This Year in Jerusalem,* pp. 26–27

I COULDN'T SLEEP, so thrilled was I to be in Israel. Eretz Yisrael. Even the tourist office handout, *A Visitor's Guide to Israel,* had a characteristic warmth to it. "Let's hope not, but should you require medical attention such services are easily obtainable...." All my life I seem to have been heading for, and postponing, my trip to Israel. In 1936, when I was five years old, my maternal grandfather, a Hasidic rabbi, bought land in Holy Jerusalem. He intended for all of us to immigrate. He died, we didn't go. When I was in high school I joined Habonim, the Labour Zionist youth movement. On Friday evenings we listened to impassioned speeches about soil redemption, we saw movies glorifying life on the kibbutz, and danced the hora until our bodies ached. Early Sunday mornings we were out ringing doorbells for the Jewish National Fund, shaking tin boxes under uprooted sleepy faces, righteously demanding quarters, dimes, and nickels to help reclaim our desert in Eretz. Our choir sung stirring songs at fundraising rallies. In the summertime we went to a camp in a mosquito-ridden Laurentian valley, heard more speakers, studied Hebrew and, in the absence of Arabs, watched out for fishy-looking French Canadians.

When fighting broke out in Israel, following the Proclamation of Independence on May 14, 1948, I lied about my age and joined the Canadian Reserve Army, thinking how rich it would be to have

Richler at Masada, Israel, 1992.

Canada train me to fight the British in Eretz, but in the end I decided to finish high school instead.

If I could put what I felt about Israel into one image I would say the news photo of Ben-Gurion, taken on his arrival in Canada. It shows that grumpy knot of a Polish Jew reviewing an honour guard of Canadian Grenadier Guards. The Guards are standing rigidly at attention; Ben-Gurion's tangle of white hair hardly comes up to their chests. I have held on to that photograph because of the immense satisfaction it gives me.

—*Hunting Tigers under Glass,* "This Year in Jerusalem," pp. 132–33

So I DECIDED TO INFILTRATE the Jewish establishment, set on qualifying as a pillar or at least a cornice. For openers, I volunteered to work as a fundraiser for United Jewish Appeal, which explains how late one afternoon I actually found myself sitting in the office of a suspicious but hot-to-trot clothing manufacturer. Certainly I had come to the right place. A Man-of-the-Year plaque hung on the wall behind tubby, good-natured Irv Nussbaum's desk. So did a pair of bronzed baby shoes. There was an inscribed photograph of Golda Meir. In another photograph Irv was shown presenting a Doctor of Letters scroll to Mr. Bernard Gursky on behalf of the Friends of the Ben-Gurion University of the Negev. A model of an eighteen-foot yacht that Irv maintained in Florida was mounted on a pedestal: the good ship *Queen Esther,* after Irv's wife, not the biblical Miss Persia. And photographs of Irv's obnoxious children were here, there, and everywhere. "You're kind of young for this," said Irv. "Usually our fundraisers are, well, you know, more mature men."

"A guy can't be too young to want to do his bit for Israel."

"Care for a drink?"

"A Coke would be nice. Or a soda water."

"How about a scotch?"

"Darn it. It's too early in the day for me, but you go right ahead, please."

Irv grinned. Obviously, contrary to reports, I wasn't a boozer. I had passed a test. So now I submitted to a crash course of dos and don'ts.

"I'm going to trust you with just a few cards to begin with," said Irv. "But listen up. Rules of the game. You must never visit your target in his office, where he is king shit and you're just another *shmuck* looking for a handout. If you run into him in the synagogue, you can butter him up with Israel's needs, but it's no good putting the touch on him there. Bad taste. Money-changers in the temple. Use the phone to schedule a meeting, but the time of day you get together is of the utmost importance. Breakfasts are out, because maybe his wife wouldn't let him bang her last night, or he didn't sleep because of heartburn. The ideal time is lunch. Pick a small restaurant. Tables far apart. Some place you don't have to shout. Make it eyeball to eyeball. Shit. We've got a problem this year. There's been a decline in the number of anti-Semitic outrages."

"Yeah. Isn't that a shame," I said.

"Don't get me wrong. I'm against anti-Semitism. But every time some asshole daubs a swastika on a synagogue wall or knocks over a stone in one of our cemeteries, our guys get so nervous they phone me with pledges. So, things being how they are this year, what you've got to do is slam-dunk your target about the Holocaust. Shove Auschwitz at him. Buchenwald. War criminals thriving in Canada to this day. Tell him, 'Can you be sure it won't happen again, even here, and then where will you go?' Israel is your insurance policy, you say.

"We will provide you with the inside info on your target's annual income, and if he starts to cry, saying he's had a bad year, you say bullshit and read him numbers. Not the numbers on his tax returns. The real numbers. You tell him now that we've got that fucker Nasser to contend with, his pledge has to be bigger this year. And if he turns out to be a hard nut, a *kvetcher*, you slip in that everybody at Elmridge, or whatever country club he belongs to, will know exactly how much he pledged, and that his order books could suffer if he turns out a piker. Hey, I understand you've gone into television production. You need help with casting, Irv's your man."

—*Barney's Version*, pp. 188–90

SIFTING THROUGH MY NOTEBOOKS in the bar of the Dan Hotel that evening, I was suddenly overcome by homesickness for my nearly empty, unspeakably rich, sinfully misgoverned country. Suffering from a surfeit of Israel's seemingly insoluble dilemmas, I longed for the familiar nursery-school name-calling between English and French — *our* two founding races, so to speak — the progeny, not of Sarah and Hagar, but of dispossessed Highland sheep farmers and peasants out of Brittany and Normandy. I yearned for some Canadian homebrew farce rather than the daily death toll of Arab and Jew.

October 25. Five IDF soldiers were killed, and three seriously wounded, in a Hizbullah roadside bomb attack against an IDF convoy inside the eastern sector of the security zone in south Lebanon. And Arab workers, waiting to enter Israel from Gaza at the Erez checkpoint, rioted, heaving rocks. Three buses were partially burned, fifteen Arabs were injured, and a daylong commercial strike was declared in Gaza.

Outside the Old City in Jerusalem, near the Jaffa Gate.

October 27. Attacks by Palestinian gunmen with grenades in Jenin, and another attack by knife- and ax-wielders in Gaza wounded two Israelis. A Gazan in Khan Yunis, and another in Gaza City, were both shot dead by other Palestinians, apparently for cooperating with the authorities. A Katyusha rocket fired into Kiryat Shmona killed fourteen-year-old Vadim Shuchman, whose family had emigrated from Russia two years earlier. A neighbour, also a new Russian immigrant, told a *Post* reporter, "I never thought that in the Jewish State we would need to hide like mice. We have a strong army and we should bombard the terrorists with at least a hundred shells for every one of their Katyusha rockets."

All at once, I was fed up with the tensions that have long been Israel's daily bread. I resented the need to stiffen every time an Arab came striding toward me. I was weary of the West Bank's loopy, God-crazed *yeshiva buchers* toting Uzis on the streets of Jerusalem and Tel Aviv. Ironically, the American-bred *olim* among them, playing latter-day gunslingers, actually owed more to their TV heritage of *Maverick* and *Rawhide* than they did to the teachings of Hillel, the great sage of the Second Temple period, or Rabbi Akiva ben Joseph (c. 50–137 A.D.), the legendary biblical scholar. I also didn't want to encounter any more appealing boys and girls in uniform, lugging submachine guns rather than briefcases stuffed with textbooks.

I was raised to proffer apologies because my ostensibly boring country was so short of history, but now, after five weeks in a land choked by the clinging vines of its past, a victim of its contrary mythologies, I considered the watery soup of my Canadian provenance a blessing. After travelling through the Rockies, Rupert Brooke had complained that he missed "the voices of the dead." Me, I was grateful at last for their absence.

— *This Year in Jerusalem,* pp. 236 38

I LIED.

When somebody called from Whitehorse, in 1984, to say that Jerry Greenfeld had died of a heart attack and would I come to the funeral, I protested that I hadn't seen or heard from him in forty years. But late one summer afternoon in 1981, just as I was settling in for a nap on the sofa, Jerry phoned. "Mordy, you old turkey you, how goes the battle?"

"Jerry?"

"Yowza."

"Where are you calling from?"

"Wilensky's. Where else? I had to have me a 'Special,' if only for old times' sake. But I could like hop into a taxi and be at your place in fifteen minutes."

I told him that I was just about to leave for the Montreal Press Club, and asked him to meet me there for drinks.

Jerry's hair, steel-grey now, was brushcut. He wore horn-rimmed glasses and had cultivated a handlebar mustache. He didn't, as I had anticipated, bounce a mock punch off my shoulder. Instead, we shook hands, Jerry squeezing hard. "Jeez, you've got palms soft as a baby's ass," he said, "and that's some gut you've got there."

Jerry was still trim, broad-shouldered as ever, with the natural grace of an athlete. His sharkskin windbreaker had been displaced by a biker's studded black leather jacket, zippers everywhere. His jacket squeaked when he reached for his drink — a boilermaker. Leaning across our table to clink glasses, he said, "*Skol. L'chaim.* It's good to see you, old *chaver* of mine."

"It's good to see you too. I should have brought my mitt."

"You remember those days?"

"Damn right I do."

He had been demobilized five years earlier, he said, and now lived in Edmonton with his second wife, Marylou, a real beaut. "Built? You better believe it," Jerry said. He hung out with Wayne Gretzky, Mark Messier, Paul Coffey, and the rest of the Oilers. Peachy guys. But they never went out boozing the night before a game. "We're going to win the Stanley Cup next year, you bet your sweet ass we are!"

"What do you do in Edmonton?"

"I've got me a garage and body shop, four guys on my payroll, not one of them a frog, because I won't put up with their shit."

"They don't like putting up with ours either, and would you mind lowering your voice, please?"

"Don't tell me you're scared of that bunch."

"No, but a number of my frog friends just happen to be sitting at the bar right now."

"Roger. Got the message. Hey, it's a good place to bring up children."

"Edmonton?"

"Yeah, and it's only an hour into real mountains, not the worn-out little hills you've got here."

"How many children have you got?"

"Two left at home. Marylou's and mine. I love them. But I had to kick out the eldest, Bruce, from my first marriage, after he came home one night with an earring in his left ear," said Jerry, wetting his little finger and passing it over his eyebrows. "Hey, am I upsetting you?"

"No."

"You got some of *them* sitting at the bar too?"

I laughed and ordered another round.

"Maybe you think I phoned because I want to borrow money?"

"No. Honestly."

"I own three cars, two of them vintage. A '64 Mustang and an MG TD, both worth plenty if I wanted to sell, which I don't need to. You heard of Peter Pocklington?"

"Yes. Certainly."

"I handle his cars, and any time I feel like taking in a game, I phone him, and I sit with Peter and his wife. We've gone fishing together on the Great Slave Lake."

"Why did you join the army, Jerry?"

"What do you do in Edmonton? How many kids you got? Why did you join the army? Is this like some kind of interview?"

"No."

"No. Yes. Haven't *you* got anything to say?"

"Sure."

"Go ahead, then. I'm listening."

"How about another round?"

"I thought you'd never ask. Hey, I read a hundred and four books last year, two a week, most of them in hard covers. What do you think of Follett, *The Key to Rebecca*?"

"Sorry, but I haven't read it."

"What if I wanted to write up my experiences in life, all the crazy characters I met in Germany and elsewhere, the hard knocks I took, the broads I've had, the funny things my kids say, would you be willing to give it a gander if I sent it to you? I mean, like with your connections I could get a publisher and maybe even a movie sale."

"I saw Myer in London."

"Don't look now, Millicent, but he's changing the subject on me."

"He manages a group called The Highlanders. He's doing awfully well."

"Big fucking deal, The Highlanders. A zillion Chinese never heard of them. Hey, let's face it, we were such a bunch of little pricks back then. Dancing the hora at Camp Kvutza. Watching all those boring documentaries. Pretending we were going to make *aliyah* one day. Aw."

"Ezra made *aliyah*. So did Sol and Fayge Cohen."

"Let me tell you something, old friend, I've been around, and Canada's the greatest country in the world, and I'm proud to have served in its armed forces overseas, on the Western world's front line against the Communist menace, with the greatest bunch of guys you could ever meet, real friends," he said, his eyes shiny, the drink getting to him, "*loyal*, not the sort to turn on you, taking you for a crook."

"Are you going to look up Hershey while you're here?" I asked, fishing.

"What for? So he can give me a tour of his Westmount mansion again, letting me see his collection of first editions that cost him a small fortune? Or some fuckin' plaque saying he's Man of the Century for what he gave to UJA? Or show me photographs of the cottage he keeps in Vermont, just in case he has to pull out of Montreal, P.Q., or Piss Quick, as we used to say? Well, let me tell you something, if it comes to independence or sovereignty association or whatever they're calling it this week, it's guys like me you'll come crying to, and I'll have to re-enlist to protect you, and you can tell those friends of yours at the bar to go shit in their hats if they don't like it. Oh, big bloody successes, you, Myer, Hershey. Always sticking it to me. Rolling in *mezuma*. Well, there are more important things than money, let me tell you. Maybe I never finished high school, but at night Marylou and I listen to symphonic music together. I've got my pride, you know I can remember when I had all the girls and the three of you were glad to be seen with me after what I did in a basketball game against Montreal High or Westmount. Remember Rifka Seligman?"

"Sure I do."

"I happen to know you took her out umpteen times and never got to first base with her, but she used to like nothing better than licking my dick, kiddo. Friday nights. After our meetings. So, looking for a trip down memory lane, I phone her last Friday night, she's married to Manny Fishbein, a doctor yet, and a maid answers and says, it's the Sabbath, the Fishbeins don't take phone calls. Is there any message? Tell her Jerry Greenfeld called, and I leave a number. But she never calls back. I'm bad news, eh? Do they cash cheques here?"

"Only for members."

"Shit. This should be my round, but I got to the bank too late."

"Don't worry. I'll get it," I said, ordering.

"I want to know what Hershey told you about the time I stayed with him."

"He never mentioned it."

"Bullshit."

"Okay, okay. He says he put you up, and you were gone early the next morning, and so was a pearl necklace belonging to his wife, and a few other things."

"Well, I've got to hand it to him," he said, shaking his head, chuckling.

"It isn't true?"

"*Emmes* is what you want, you got it. The truth. It must have been back in the Swinging Sixties, I was in a jam, just in from Calgary, I'd had too much to drink and I got mugged. I asked Hershey, that old *chaver* of mine, could he put me up for the night. He hemmed, he hawed. But he had to say yes, didn't he," said Jerry, leaning closer, "because of what he knew I knew and didn't want his stuck-up wife to hear. Hanna Rosen, I knew her before her nose job. Boy, what a pair! I don't mean hers. I mean them. Hershey and Hanna. He grudgingly pours me a drink. 'This isn't ordinary scotch, I'd like you to know. It's a single malt.' Glen *tuchis-lecker* or whatever. 'Twenty-one years old.' And she quickly slips a coaster under my glass, I might leave a watermark on her antique table, for two cents I'd piss all over it. Sure, I'm allowed to sleep there, but before I'm shown to a tiny bedroom, just enough room for me and their laundry, he makes a big ceremony of locking his liquor cabinet and the glass bookcase with his precious first editions. Tell me, what is this first editions horseshit? Isn't the story exactly word for word in a second or third edition of a book?"

"You're absolutely right, but people also fork out thousands for old baseball cards or movie posters. Collectors are a special breed."

"I didn't steal anything, but I was so angry that before I split I took her pearl necklace, broke the strand, and scattered the pearls on the floor. And yes, I also grabbed a sterling silver tray, got out my Swiss Army knife, scratched FUCK YOU into it, and dumped it on their lawn. Don't you understand anything? He used me to put in a whacking big insurance claim. He probably came out a few thousand bucks ahead on my overnight visit. Couldn't you countersign a cheque for me and get them to cash it?"

"Forget it. I'll order you another drink," I said, signalling the bartender.

"What about you?"

"I think I'll pass on this round."

"Ha ha. So much for your rep as a boozer. You can't even keep up with your old *chaver*."

"Okay, I'll have another one as well," I said.

"Only two weeks ago, Marylou put it to me. Either you give up drinking, she said, or I'm leaving. Hey, I said, I'm sure going to miss you."

"Oh."

"Do you only laugh at your own jokes?"

"Tell me what you meant by, Hershey knew what you knew and didn't want his wife to hear."

"Ixnay. I'm not the kind to say anything behind Hershey's back." His eyes charged with rancour, Jerry simulated an inner struggle. He stroked his handlebar mustache. He chewed his lip. "All right, then tell me something, you have such a good memory. Friday nights we all went to Habonim together. Affirmative or negative?"

"Yes. So?"

"If nobody answered the front doorbell, because my father was out or snoozing maybe, and I was playing records in the backroom, how did you guys get in?"

"We climbed over the front balcony and in through the living-room window."

"What I can never forgive Hershey is that he made me suspect my beloved father of having stolen our money. My father, may he rest in peace, who had to bring me up without the help of a wife."

"But you detested your father."

Jerry, bracing himself against the table, slid back in his chair. "You can say anything you like about me," he said, "but insult my father's memory and I'll have to flatten you right here."

"My God, are you really trying to tell me that Hershey broke into your place and took the money?"

"Negative. I said no such thing. I just explained how he could have got into my bedroom."

"But any of us could have got in that way. Me included."

"Elementary, my dear Watson. Only you never would have had the guts."

"Why would Hershey have done such a thing?"

"Question, why? Answer, because he had assumed that Rifka was going to make him host at her Sweet Sixteen party, he had already paid for her corsage in advance, the prick, but it was me she picked."

"So he stole the money we had collected for Israel?"

"Knowing that I would get the blame."

"You're crazy, Jerry."

"Like a fox."

"How do you know it was Hershey?"

"I know it in here," he said, tapping his forehead. Then all at once he began to cough. Beads of sweat slid down his forehead. "Excuse me," he said, unzipping a breast pocket, fishing out a little aspirin tin, and swallowing an oblong coloured pill with his drink.

"What's that?" I asked.

"Digitalis. For my angina. I was discharged from the army because of my bum ticker. The medics give me two years to live. So this is my last trip ever to good old Montreal, Piss Quick. One for the road, eh?"

"Jerry, I don't believe Hershey stole the money. You never had a stepbrother fighting the Japs in the Pacific. Rifka Seligman never gave you a blowjob. You don't know Wayne Gretzky and you can't phone Peter Pocklington for hockey tickets. And I'm willing to bet those pills you're popping are either vitamins or tranquilizers. There's nothing wrong with your heart. In fact, you look to be in great shape. But you are also the world's greatest bullshit artist."

"You finished?"

"Yeah," I said, laughing.

"I don't believe the second one is mine," he said, beginning to sniffle. "What am I supposed to do?"

"What are you talking about now?"

"Little Darlene. The youngest. She doesn't look like me. Marylou works at a club. She's an exotic dancer."

"A stripper?"

"Slip her ten bucks, and she'll dance on your table and pick up a silver dollar with her coozy. You can buy them at the bar. The silver dollars."

"Oh my God, Jerry, what are you going to do?"

"Look," he said. And he stood up and turned his trouser pockets inside out to show me that they were empty. "I'm not going back to her. I'm heading for North of Sixty. I've got my plane tickets for tomorrow and the offer of a good job in Yellowknife."

"What about your garage?"

"Never mind. That's my business. But I've spent my last buck and I've got nowhere to sleep tonight," he said, smiling at me, waiting.

I lit a cigarillo, taking my time.

"Yeah, I thought as much," he said. "You would never put me up. I'm contaminated."

I pulled money out of my pocket and counted it. "I've got two hundred and twelve bucks here. Take it."

"But like it's a loan," he said.

"Sure thing."

"Boy, I'll bet you're pleased to humiliate me like this. I made your day, eh?"

"Oh, calm down, Jerry. Have one more drink."

"Not with you I won't," he said, getting out of his chair, stumbling. "You know how many times you looked at your watch since I sat down with you?"

"No."

"Eight. I counted. So thanks for the loan and up yours," he said, moving unsteadily toward the door.

—*This Year in Jerusalem,* pp. 262–71

Although some in the PQ insist that the
term "Québécois" embraces all those who
live in the province, that concept, to
my mind, is a public-relations fib.
A chimera.

PART IV

LIFE IS FUNDAMENTALLY ABSURD

Richler was a wonderful writer of farce. And the times in which he lived provided him with an embarrassment of material to fashion into comic prose. He satirized everything from modern parenting and the sexual revolution to television and the film business. These were easy targets, and no other writer skewered them with such joyful savagery.

Jewish themes, however, were tougher topics for satire. His portrait of Duddy Kravitz as a Jew "on the make," for example, earned him the wrath of some members of the Jewish community who viewed Richler as a "self-hating Jew" — or worse.

— J. W.

"I was Barney Panofsky when I was writing it, but not before and not after.… But I share Barney's notion that life is fundamentally absurd and nobody understands anybody else, but you make the best of it."

— Michael Posner, *The Last Honest Man,* p. 303

At Waterloo Air Terminal Norman spotted the balloon at once. It had moved a little to the right, but outside of that there was no change.

Norman sat down beside a square, chubby American, who was reading *Look*, and told him the story of the balloon.

"A damn shame," the man said, studying the trapped balloon.

"How do you think they'll get it down?"

"A ladder would do the trick."

"Maybe," Norman said, "they'll just leave it there."

The square, chubby man returned to Norman Vincent Peale's column.

"Aren't you interested?" Norman asked.

"Sure thing."

"Did you notice the balloon before I sat down to tell you about it?

"Nope."

"What do you think they ought to do about it?"

"I don't want to sound unneighbourly, but frankly speaking, son, I've got bigger worries."

"That's not the point."

"Look," the man said, "why not be a good fellow and let me read my magazine in peace?"

Norman rose and walked out of the air terminal.

—*A Choice of Enemies*, pp. 184–85

Mortimer Griffin's wife Joyce is a thoroughly modern mother.

"Now come on, Doug. Enough is enough," she called out.

But he absolutely refused to get out of the bath. "Can't I play just a little bit longer?" he pleaded.

The water, Joyce saw, was up to his chin. Plastic boats floated in the tub. So did a beach ball.

"Have you any idea why you want to stay longer in the tub —"

"Because it's jolly good fun."

" — *with the water up to your chin?*"

"Because it's jolly good fun."

"No. That's only the superficial reason. The real reason is because it makes you feel secure. Like," Joyce said, puffing out her stomach, "you were still floating in the waters inside me."

Doug's hand flashed out to pull the plug.

"Don't twitch."

"I'm not twitching."

"If you remember the picture book I showed you —"

"Y-y-y-es I do! Honestly!"

"The bag you floated in is called the membrane and you fed off a placenta." Suddenly Joyce bared her teeth. "See?"

"What?" he asked, shivering.

"The fillings. The decay."

"Yes."

"While you were growing inside me, you took the best part of my calcium."

"I'm sorry."

"You mustn't be. It's a natural thing. Neither should you apologize for feeling very, very safe in deep warm water. Many grown men feel the same way."

"Daddy too?"

"Daddy more than many. It's called a retreat to Mother's womb."

"I see," Doug said, drying himself.

"You're so lucky, Doug. I was brought up on lies, you know. My father — and he was a doctor, you know — told me that the stork had brought me."

Doug managed a deprecating laugh.

"He never told me I came out of my mother's vagina, just like you came out of mine. I had to learn about orgasms all by myself."

"He told you lots of lies, didn't he?"

"Too many," she said, following him into his bedroom.

'Remember the lie about Christmas?"

"Which one?"

"How he used to buy you smashing presents with money taken from poor patients and then pretend that Santa Claus had come down the chimney with them? How you and your brothers used to crawl out of bed at dawn to see what Santa had brought…and your father would be sitting there, waiting for you, drinking White Russian vodka and smoking non-union cigarettes?"

"Yes."

"Could you tell me that lie tonight? With all the details?"

"Not again. We're going to read another chapter from our book instead."

The bedtime book was *Hiroshima*. An illustrated edition. They had already finished reading Hilberg's *The Destruction of the European Jews*. Both volumes had become mandatory once Joyce had discovered that Doug had a cowboy gun hidden under his pillow. She wanted him to understand clearly where gunplay led to.

"Well now," Joyce said, shutting the book at last, "that's enough for tonight. Good night, Doug."

"Where's Daddy?"

"Lecturing. He'll be home late. Good night."

"Good night, Mother."

Two hours later Joyce was startled to see Doug standing at

the door of her bedroom. He was red-eyed and shivering.

"What is it now?" Joyce asked.

"I had a scary dream."

Joyce slipped into her dressing gown, got out of bed, and turned off the television. Meanwhile, Doug slid into her bed.

"And what, may I ask, do you think you're doing?"

"Could I just lie here with you for a minute?" Doug asked, his teeth chattering.

"Only if you fully face up to why you want to lie in bed with me."

"It's because I'm scared, Mother."

"Balls. It's because you desire to make physical love to me. You wish to supplant your father."

"I do not!"

"But it's perfectly natural, Doug. All sons are secretly in love with their mothers. I just want you to be truthful with me, as I am with you. Now, why do you want to get into bed with me...when your father's out?"

Doug looked at the floor.

"A straight question deserves a straight answer, don't you think?"

"Yes, Mother."

"Well, then?"

"I think," Doug said, leaping off the bed as soon as she sat down beside him, "I'll go back to my own room now."

"That's being a very mature boy, Doug. I'm proud of you."

"Why?"

"Because this way you will suffer no psychological damage. When you're a grownup you'll never need an analyst. Like I did. Good night, Doug."

"Good night, Mother."

Doug had only just gone back to his room when Mortimer came in.

"Well, well," Joyce said snidely, "Malcolm Muggeridge returns."

"What's eating you?"

"Doug's had another nightmare. Mortimer, why must they show those dreadful canned American TV shows here? The violence does children irreparable harm, I think."

—*Cocksure*, pp. 91–94

Mordecai Richler in 1980.

Solomon's daughter Lucy does the right thing.

IN THE MORNING she hurried to a gallery on New Bond Street to buy Moses a Hogarth etching he had once admired and, in another shop, a first edition of Sir John Franklin's *Narrative of a Journey to the Shores of the Polar Sea*. She fired Edna the same afternoon.

"But I thought you adored her," Moses said.

"I did. I do. But haven't you read about the bus boycott in Montgomery, Alabama, you *schmuck*? Everybody's talking about that Martin Luther King now. I found out people are saying it's just typical of Miss Moneybags to have a black maid. I had to let her go."

"I hope you told her why."

"She's so thick, that one, she'd never understand."

—*Solomon Gursky Was Here,* p. 204

WE NEED MORE GENTILE NOVELISTS, they should be encouraged, if only as an antidote to Gore Vidal, John Rechy, and Hubert Selby Jr. For it would be sad indeed if non-Christian readers, already sufficiently prejudiced against the majority, were left with the impression that "among them" there was only homosexual love. Or that their writers, from Sinclair Lewis, through John O'Hara, to Terry Southern, had nothing nice to say about the white American *goy* who, after all, yielded to the world Ike Eisenhower, vinyl, the hero sandwich, Norman Rockwell, the deep-freeze, John Wayne, Red Skelton, baggies, and *The Reader's Digest*, among other things.

—*Shovelling Trouble*, "Porky's Plaint," pp. 112–13

Duddy Kravitz hires an arty English director, Peter John Friar, to make a film of Mr. Cohen's son's bar mitzvah.

DUDDY DIDN'T SAY A WORD all through the screening, but afterwards he was sick to his stomach.

"It's not that bad," Yvette said. "Things could be done to it."

"You think we'd be making a mistake?" Duddy said. "Jeez. I could sell Mr. Cohen a dead horse easier than this pile of —"

"If you so much as cut it by one single frame," Mr. Friar said, "then my name goes off the film."

Duddy began to laugh. So did Yvette.

"Timothy suggested we try it at Cannes."

"Jeez," Duddy said. "Everyone's going to be there. But everyone. The invitations are all out."

Duddy took to his bed for two days. He refused to see anyone.

"I'm so worried," Yvette said.

Mr. Friar kissed her hand. "You have a Renaissance profile," he said.

"He won't even answer the phone. Oh, Mr. Friar, please!" she said, removing his hand.

"If there were only world enough and time, my love…"

"I'm going to try his number once more," Yvette said.

But Duddy was out. On the third day he had decided that he could no longer put off seeing Mr. Cohen. He went to his house this time. "Ah," Mr. Cohen said, "the producer is here."

"Have you got the movie with you?" Bernie asked.

Mrs. Cohen poured him a glass of plum brandy. "If you don't mind," she said, "there are a few more names I'd like to add to the guest list."

"I've got some bad news for you. I'm cancelling the screening. Tomorrow morning my secretary will call everyone to tell them the show's off."

"Aw, gee whiz."

"Is it that bad?" Mr. Cohen asked.

"It's great. We're going to enter it in the Cannes Festival."

"I don't understand," Mrs. Cohen said.

"You won't like it. It's what we call *avant-garde*."

"Watch it," Mr. Cohen said. "This is where he begins to lie. Right before your eyes the price is going up."

Duddy smiled at Mrs. Cohen. "I suppose what you expected was an ordinary movie with shots of all the relatives and friends…well, you know what I mean. But Mr. Friar is an artist. His creation is something else entirely."

"Can't we see it, Maw?"

"Aren't you taking a lot for granted, young man? Don't you think my husband and I can appreciate artistic quality when we see it?"

"Don't fall into his trap," Mr. Cohen said.

Duddy turned to Mr. Cohen. "I'll let you in on a secret," he said. He told him that Mr. Friar had been a big director, but he had had to leave Hollywood because of the witch hunt. That was the only reason why he was in Montreal fiddling with small films. He wanted to make his name and get in on the ground floor of the Canadian film industry, so to speak. Turning to Mrs. Cohen, he added, "Please don't repeat this, but if not for Senator McCarthy I wouldn't have been able to hire a man as big as Friar for less than five thousand dollars. Not that he isn't costing me plenty as it is."

Mr. Cohen started to say something, but his wife glared at him. She smiled at Duddy. "But why can't we see the movie? I don't understand."

"It's different. It's shocking."

"Oh, really now!"

"Mr. Friar has produced a small screen gem in the tradition of *Citizen Kane* and Franju's *Sang des Bêtes*."

"How can we cancel all the invitations at this late date? We insist on seeing it."

Duddy hesitated. He stared reflectively at the floor. "All right," he said, "but don't say I didn't warn you first."

Mr. Cohen laughed. "Don't believe a word he says, Gertie. It's good. It must be very good. Otherwise he wouldn't be here talking it down. But listen here, Kravitz, not a penny more than I promised. Wow! What a liar!"

Duddy gulped down his plum brandy. "I'm not selling," he said. "That's something else. You can see it, but..."

"Hey," Mr. Cohen said, "hey there. Are you getting tough with an old friend?"

"I want it, Daddy. I want the movie! Gee whiz, Maw."

"You outsmarted yourself, Mr. Cohen. You wouldn't give me an advance or put anything in writing."

"Sam, what's the boy saying?"

"You gave me your word, Kravitz. A gentleman doesn't go back on his word."

Bernie began to cry.

"You can't blame him, Mrs. Cohen. He didn't want to take too big a chance on a young boy just starting out."

"All right," Mr. Cohen said hoarsely, "just how much do you want for the film?"

"Money isn't the question."

"Such a liar! My God, never in my life — Will you stop crying, please. Take him out of here, Gertie."

"I'm not going."

"Well, Kravitz, I'm waiting to hear your price. Gangster!"

Duddy hesitated.

"Please," Mrs. Cohen said.

"I can't sell outright. I'd still want to enter it in the festival."

"Of course," Mrs. Cohen said warmly.

"We can't talk here," Mr. Cohen said. "Come up to my bedroom."

But Duddy wouldn't budge. "For fifteen hundred dollars," he said, "I'll give you an excellent colour print. But you'd have to sign away all rights to a percentage of the profits on Canadian theatre distribution."

"What's that? Come again, please?"

"We're going to distribute it as a short to Canadian theatres."

"Gee whiz."

"For twenty-five hundred dollars in all I'll make you a silent partner. I'd cut you in for twenty percent of the net theatre profits. My lawyers could draw up the agreement. But remember, it's a gamble. This is an art film, not one of those crassly commercial items."

"Would my husband's name appear anywhere?"

"We could list him in the credits as a co-producer with Dudley Kane Enterprises."

Mr. Cohen smiled for the first time. "A boy from the boys," he said, "that's what you are."

"Maybe you'd like to think it over first."

"Sam."

"All right. OK, I'll write him a cheque right now." Mr. Cohen looked at Duddy and laughed. "Look at him. He's shaking."

— *The Apprenticeship of Duddy Kravitz*, pp. 148–51

Richler reports on a visit to the Cannes Film Festival.

SOMETHING ELSE: The producer, who cheats gleefully, is gleefully swindled in turn by most distributors. In a typical deal, a distributor will buy a film for, say, Brazil, signing a cheque for $10,000 against a guaranteed further $40,000 to come out of receipts. No sooner has he issued the cheque than he phones his bank and stops payment on it. Then, still on the line to Brazil, he hustles various cinema chains, trying to unload the film he has just purchased. If he succeeds, making a profit, he will ultimately let his cheque go through; if not, not. But the seller knows, without a doubt, that he will never see his further $40,000. "Then why does he insist on it?" I ask Harry Saltzman.

"Because when he returns to his backers, and they shout, why did you sell so cheap, what's ten thousand for Brazil, he says, yes, but look, there's another forty to come. He takes his contract to the bank and uses the forty for collateral. They'll advance him more money against it to finance his next film. And the secret of this business is to have a new film going on the floor before your last disaster has been released. That way you can go on for years."

Such convoluted dealings are especially demanding of the fledgling filmmaker, but some make it, among them the young Canadian director of *Cannibal Girls* ("They eat men!"), which he sold before the festival was done. Buck Dane, it's true, walked out, disgusted, after twenty minutes'

Samuel Z. Arkoff, king of the low-budget cult movie.

viewing, but he returned another day with Samuel Z. Arkoff, who bought American distribution rights.

"Let me tell you," Dane said, "that kid is something. He sat with Arkoff, an old pro, the boy's only twenty-six years old, he talked grosses, percentages, cooperative advertising, never giving an inch. Those things you don't learn at school in Toronto. His film is awful, but he'll go far. You wait and see."

— Notes on an Endangered Species and Others,
"Notes on an Endangered Species," pp. 106–07

BETTE DOLAN WAS CANADA'S DARLING.

She was not the biggest TV star in the country, our only beauty queen or foremost swimmer; neither was she the first Canadian girl to make a film. But Bette Dolan, while in the same tradition as such diverse Canadian talents as, say, Deanna Durbin, Marilyn Bell, Barbara Ann Scott, and Joyce Davidson, surpassed all of them in appeal. Bette Dolan was a legendary figure. A Canadian heroine.

Bette's beginnings were humble. She came from a small town in southern Ontario, the neighbourly sort of place where retired people live. Her fierce father, Gord Dolan, was a body-building enthusiast, a devotee of the teachings of Doc Burt Parks. Once Mr. Best Developed Biceps of Eastern Canada, he still retained the title of Mr. Niagara Fruit Belt Sr. His wife, May, was a long thin woman with a severe mouth. Formerly a schoolteacher, she was still active in the church choir. The Dolans would have ended their days predictably; he, enjoying an afternoon of manly gossip in the barbers and his sessions in the gym; and she, planning the next meeting of the Supper-of-the-Month Club, if only their surprisingly lovely daughter had not lifted them out of decent obscurity with one superhuman stroke.

Bette Dolan was the first woman to swim Lake Ontario in less than twenty hours.

As if that weren't sufficiently remarkable, she was only eighteen at the time, an amateur, and she beat three others, all professionals, while she was at it: an American, an Egyptian, and a celebrated Australian marathon swimmer. The American and the Egyptian woman gave up early on and even the much-heralded Australian was pulled out of the lake and rushed to the hospital after only fourteen hours in the black icy water. But the incredibly young, luscious, then-unknown Canadian girl, coached by her own father, swam on and on and on. True, she had sobbed, puked, and pleaded to be pulled out of the water, but, the very first time that happened, Gord Dolan, ever watchful in the launch ahead, spurred his daughter on by holding up a blackboard on which he had written:

DADDY DON'T LIKE QUITTERS

The young girl's effort in the face of seemingly invincible odds caught the imagination of Toronto as nothing had before. It's true the much-admired Marilyn Bell had already swum the lake, but it had taken *her* twenty hours and fifty-one minutes, and it was much as if her accomplishment, remarkable as it was, redoubled interest in Bette Dolan's attempt to better it. Anyway, the fact is that by six o'clock in the morning a crowd, maybe the largest, certainly the most enthusiastic, ever known in the history of Toronto, had gathered on the opposite shore to wait for Bette. They lit bonfires and sang hymns and cheered each half mile gained by the girl. Television technicians set up searchlights and cameras. Motorcycle policemen and finally an ambulance arrived.

Back in Toronto, as morning came and radio and television newscasters spoke feverishly of twelve-foot waves, some people prayed, others hastily organized office pools or phoned their bookies, and still more leaped into their cars and added to the largest known traffic jam in Toronto's history. Sunny Jim Woodcock, the People's Prayer for Mayor, spoke on Station CKTO. "I told you when I was elected that I would put Toronto on the map. Bette Dolan is setting an example here for youth all over the free world. *More power to your elbows, kid!*" The *Standard*, never a newspaper to be caught off the mark, printed two sets of their late-morning edition. One with the headline, SHE MAKES IT! WOW!, the other, TOUGH LUCK, SWEETHEART!

On the launch, Gord Dolan watched anxiously, he prayed, kissed his rabbit's foot, and spat twice over his left shoulder, as his daughter struggled against the oncoming waves.

"Please pull me in," she called. "Please... I can't make it...."

He scrawled something hurriedly on the blackboard and held it up for Bette to see again.

THE OTHER BROADS HAVE QUIT.
PARK AVE. SWIMWEAR OFFERS $2,500 IF YOU FINISH.
DON'T DROWN NOW. DADDY

But Bette had already been in the lake for sixteen hours. The plucky girl had come thirty-four miles. Thrashing about groggily, her eyes glazed, she began to weep. "...can't feel my legs any more... can't...think...going to drown...."

"All right," Dolan said, gesturing his girl toward the launch, "we'll pull you in now, kid."

But as Bette, making an enormous effort, swam to within inches of the launch, Gord Dolan pulled ahead a few more yards.

"Come on, honey. Come to Daddy."

Again she started for the launch and again Gord Dolan pulled away. "You see," he shouted to her. "You can do it."

(When Gord Dolan spoke on television several weeks later, after accepting the Canadian-Father-of-the-Year Award, he said, "That was the psychology-bit. I've made a study of people, you know.")

Initially, the prize money being offered was five thousand dollars, but once the last of the foreign competitors pulled out, as soon as it became obvious that Toronto had taken the surviving Canadian youngster to its heart and, what's more, that she was on the brink of collapse, Buck Twentyman made a phone call. Minutes later a helicopter idled over Gord Dolan's battered launch, a uniformed man descended a rope ladder, and Dolan was able to chalk up on his board:

TWENTYMAN HISSELF OFFERS
TEN MORE GRAND — IF YOU MAKE IT.
DADDY IS MIGHTY PROUD. GO, BABY.

When Bette Dolan finally stumbled ashore at seven p.m., after nineteen hours and forty-two minutes in the lake, she was greeted by a frenzied crowd. Newsreel cameramen, reporters, advertising agents, some who had prayed and others who had won bets at long odds, swarmed around her. Souvenir-crazed teenagers pulled eels off Bette's thighs and back. The youngster collapsed and was carried off to a waiting ambulance. When she woke the next afternoon it was to discover that her life had been irredeemably altered. Bette Dolan was a national heroine.

—*The Incomparable Atuk,* pp. 12–16

Lucy underwrites a stage production of The Diary of Anne Frank *to showcase her acting skills.*

SIR HYMAN KAPLANSKY came to the opening night. So did some producers, directors, and a surprising number of performers at liberty. Some had come out of curiosity, others because they were pursuing Lucy's production company for outlandish deals; there was also a Bushmill claque, but still more were there in a perverse spirit of fun, anticipating the worst. Bushmill played the mushy Dutch condiments dealer, Otto Frank, as if he had wandered into the doomed attic out of a Tory garden fête. The other performers were competent at best. But Lucy was intolerable. A natural mimic, but clearly no actress, she played her scenes like an over-wrought Shirley Temple with a disconcertingly gay Peter Van Daan. When that didn't work, she switched to the Elizabeth Taylor of *National Velvet.*

Moses wandered into the theatre dangerously drunk, but determined to behave himself. Unfortunately the excruciatingly banal play outlasted his resolution. Nodding off briefly in the first act he was confronted by Shloime Bishinsky in his mind's eye. "What I'm trying to say, forgive me, is that such princes in America are entitled to their mansions, a Rolls-Royce, chinchilla coats, yachts, young cuties out of burlesque shows. But a poet they should never be able to afford." *Or a theatre. Or an audience.* "It has to do with what? Human dignity. The dead. The sanctity of the word."

They were being noisy up there on stage, which wakened him to the troubling sight of an attic and its denizens trebling themselves. Poor Bushmill, emoting about something or other, now had six weak chins stacked one on top of another and maybe twenty-two eyes. Moses shook his head, he pinched himself, and the stage swam into focus again. Damn. It was that maudlin Hanukkah scene, overripe with obvious irony, wherein the pathetic Mr. Frank Bushmill seated with the others at the attic table — all of them hiding from the Gestapo — praises the Lord, Ruler of the Universe, who has wrought wonderful deliverances for our fathers in days of old. There were no *latkes*, but insufferably adorable Anne (the bottom of her bra stuffed with Kleenex) came to the table armed with touchingly conceived pressies. A crossword-puzzle book for her sister. "It isn't new. It's one that you've done. But I rubbed it all out and if you wait a little and forget, you can do it all over again." There was some hair shampoo for the horny Mrs. Van Daan. "I took all the odds and ends of soap and mixed them with the last of my toilet water." Two fags for Van Daan's oafish husband. "Pim found some old pipe tobacco in the pocket lining of his coat...and we made them...or rather Pim did."

Once more the images on stage throbbed, trebling themselves. Moses squinted. He made fists, driving his fingernails into the palms of his hands. And there were four Anne/Lucys, each one of them out of tune, rising to sing:

> Oh, Hanukkah, Oh, Hanukkah.
> The sweet celebration.

Suddenly there was a crash from below the attic. The Green Police? The Gestapo? Everybody on stage froze. Straining to hear. For a few seconds there was a total silence and then something in Moses short-circuited. Not rising, but propelled out of his seat, he hollered, "Look in the attic! She's hiding in the attic!"

—*Solomon Gursky Was Here*, pp. 207–08

Richler's unconventional view of the effects of McCarthy's blacklist, first expressed in the 1960s, reappears much later in Barney's Version.

THIS ERA OF TREACLY, brother-loving films, in which so many of the good guys were Jews or Negroes and nearly all the shits were WASPs, broke up with the coming of McCarthyism. Ultimately Senator McCarthy — so despicable in his time, seen to be such a buffoon in retrospect — may come to be appreciated as the most effective of cultural brooms. He did more than *Cahiers du Cinema* or *Sight & Sound* to clean the liberal hacks as well as some talented men out of Hollywood.

—*Hunting Tigers under Glass,* "Writing for the Movies," p. 89

WHICH WAS WHEN a seemingly comatose Boogie suddenly shifted gears, going into overdrive. "When the witch hunt is over," he said, "and everybody is embarrassed, as they were after the Palmer Raids, McCarthy may yet be appreciated with hindsight as the most effective film critic ever. Never mind Agee. The senator certainly cleaned out the stables."

Hymie would never have taken that from me, but, coming from Boogie, he decided to let it fly. It was amazing. Here was Hymie, an accomplished and reasonably affluent man, a successful film director, and there was Boogie, poor, unknown, a struggling writer, his publications limited to a couple of little magazines. But it was an intimidated Hymie who was determined to win Boogie's approval. Boogie had that effect on people. I wasn't the only one who needed his blessing.

"My problem," Boogie continued, "is that I have some respect for the Hollywood Ten as people, but not as writers of even the second rank. *Je m'excuse.* The third rank. Much as I abhor Evelyn Waugh's politics, I would rather read one of his novels any day than sit through any of their mawkish films again."

"You're such a kidder, Boogie," said a subdued Hymie.

"'The best lack all conviction,'" said Boogie, "'while the worst / Are full of passionate intensity.' So said Mr. Yeats."

—*Barney's Version,* pp. 37–38

I HAD RUN INTO HIM a couple of days earlier in the Polo Lounge, where he told me he was making a documentary about the Hollywood blacklist. In a mood to bullshit, I had bragged about all the blacklisted types I had met through Hymie in London in 1961, and I agreed to be interviewed in the hope that Mike might see it. No, because I liked the idea of being asked to pontificate.

Seated under the hot lights, squinting, simulating deep thought, I said, "Senator McCarthy was an unprincipled drunk. A clown. True enough, but now that the witch hunt is long past, I do believe he can be seen, with hindsight, as the most perspicacious and influential film critic ever. Never mind Agee." Then, remembering to pause for effect, I dropped my sandbag. "He certainly cleaned out the stables, as it were."

"I dare say," said the Beeb's presenter, "I've never heard it put quite like that before."

Seemingly groping for words, obviously troubled, I hesitated before I ventured, "My problem is I had considerable respect for The Hollywood Ten as people, but not as writers of even the second rank. That driven bunch invested so much integrity in their foolish, guilt-ridden politics that they had none left for their work. Tell me, did Franz Kafka need a swimming pool?"

That won me a tight little laugh.

"I don't like saying it, but for the BBC, *veritas*. The truth is, much as I detested Evelyn Waugh's politics, I would happily take one of his novels to bed rather than watch a rerun of one of their sentimental, knee-jerk liberal films on late-night TV."

Gabble, gabble, gabble. Then, pausing to light my first Montecristo of the day, pulling on it, removing my reading glasses, I looked directly into the camera, and said, "Let me leave you with a couple of pertinent lines from W. B. Yeats. 'The best lack all conviction, while the worst / Are full of passionate intensity.' So it was, I fear, in those days."

My shtick done, the grateful producer thanked me for my original thoughts. "Super stuff," he said.

—Barney's Version, pp. 241–42

"OLD ONE." ATUK LOATHED addressing him like that, but ever since his father had figured in that prize-winning National Film Board short he had insisted on it. "Old One," Atuk continued, "I have found the girl I want to marry."

"Is she a nice Eskimo girl?"

Atuk scratched the back of his neck.

"Speak no more. Atuk, my son, I remember when your eyes were deep and true as the blue spring sea. I recall when your soul was pure and white as the noon iceberg. This is no more. Today —"

"For Christ's sake, will you cut out that crazy talk. You sound like you were auditioning for Disney again or something."

"If not for the fact that I was taller than John Mills —"

"All right. I'm not saying you shouldn't have had the part. But —"

"I do not wish to hear of marriage with a non-Eskimo girl."

"You know something, Old One. You're a bigot. You've never overcome your igloo mentality."

"I'm proud of my heritage."

"So am I. Only I refuse to be imprisoned by it."

"Tell me, Atuk. What would you do about the children?"

He didn't reply.

"How would it be for me to sit your little half-breed on my lap and he wouldn't be able to speak an Eskimo word?"

"We've discussed the question of children. We intend to give them a modern-type education."

"Ha! But will his friends at school let him forget he is an Eskimo? Atuk, Atuk, harken to me."

"Won't you even meet the girl? I love her."

"Shall I go to their home? To be stared at? An Eskimo. Would I feel relaxed there, Atuk? I'd have to wash and eat with cutlery. Do they know the joys of smoked deer meat? Minced seal pancakes? No. I'd be expected to eat condemned foods. Like filet mignon."

"So you'd make a few adjustments. A big deal."

The Old One gave Atuk a savage look. He sighed deeply. "It all begins with taking a bath. It seems a little compromise, I know. But one day you take a bath and the next you have turned your back on your own people. Now I suppose," he added contemptuously, "it is nothing for you to eat fish that has been cooked?"

"There are other problems besides the Eskimo problem, Old One. I am a man who just happens to be an Eskimo."

"You can stand there and tell me that when you know as I do

that before the great ice sheet drew back this land was ours from sea to sea."

"Let's face the facts. We're never getting the land back."

"Atuk, you have a good Eskimo head on your shoulders. Think. They believe in pills and *artificially* frozen foods. How could you ever feel at home in such a background?"

"I'm not marrying a background. I'm marrying the girl I love."

"Ignak is right. An Eskimo who lives away from his land is no Eskimo."

"Ignak is an Eskimo fascist. OK. Don't say it. It all starts with taking a bath."

"Go, marry. But you have not got your father's blessing."

"She's a fine girl, Old One. Very fat and oily. Stinky too. Like one of ours. Won't you even meet her?"

"Tell me, what would she say, for instance, if you wanted to hunt next Saturday?"

"Well, as a matter of fact, Saturday wouldn't do. It's their day of rest."

The Old One looked baffled.

"You see, their God...em, created the world in six days," Atuk said in a faltering voice, "and on the seventh day, Saturday, he rested."

"Oh," the Old One said, slapping his knee, "it's one of those one-God religions, is it?"

"*So what?*"

"Through all the ages, from the time of the great ice sheet, what has held our people together? Speak!"

"Our belief in plenty of gods."

"We are the chosen pagans, my son. We have a message for the world."

"You live in the past, Old One. The ice is never coming back. Our people will never again hunt the white bear in the Bay of San Francisco or run dogsled races in Miami."

"It is written that —"

"I don't care what's written."

"No. You think it's poetry, that's all. Good reading." The Old One paused for breath. "What would she say, Atuk, if you wanted to eat smoked caribou? Remember the caribou sandwiches after the hunt at Benny's? With blubber on the side?"

Atuk grinned.

"Well, what would she say?"

"Deer is out. It's unclean."

"What?"

"You see, in this particular branch of one-God religions —"

"What is it called?"

"It's called the Jews. The Hebrews."

"Are they Jews or Hebrews?"

"It depends on their income. The poor ones are Jews."

"Jews, Christians, Hebrews. I'm not concerned with nuances. They're all white. Atuk, it's hard to be an Eskimo. I told you so long ago. But you must hold your head high. Why, in this country when it comes to culture what is there besides the Eskimo? Our sculpture is acclaimed the world over. Our poetry too. And one day we shall rise again and claim the land that is rightly ours…from sea to sea, as it is written…."

Atuk lowered his head.

"Return with me to Baffin Bay. Tonight."

"No. Never. What is there for me at the Bay? Disney shoots about one picture every two years and the Film Board pays nigger wages. Shall I be like Kupi? Can you see me building a block of igloos with inferior ice and soaking my tribe for it? I'm going to marry the girl and settle here."

"You think you've been accepted, don't you? Ha!" The Old One grinned spitefully. "Tell me, Atuk, will you be obliged to use the missionary position?"

"That's none of your goddamn business!"

"For the rest of your life —" he gasped, shaking with laughter. "For — the miss —" Again, it was too much. "The miss — missionary position."

Laughter came from the hall too. The giggling of girls.

"Oh, that's rich! What fun! The miss —"

Everyone but Ignak scattered when Atuk opened the door.

"Assimilationist!"

Atuk pushed him aside.

"But you will be getting what you deserve very soon," Ignak called after him, "or haven't you seen today's headlines?"

Atuk poured himself a stiff drink. Afterwards he didn't bathe, even though it was the tenth day of the month and he had promised himself, as a matter of personal discipline, to bathe at least once a month. She will have to take me as I am, he thought. An Eskimo. No more missionary position.

—*The Incomparable Atuk,* pp. 83–88

Bernard Gursky, on his seventy-fifth birthday, is feted for his many achievements and contributions to the Jewish community.

IN THE EVENING there was a banquet in the ballroom of the Ritz-Carlton Hotel, suitably bedecked for the occasion with Canadian, Québécois (this, in the name of prudence) and Israeli flags. Red roses, flown in from Grasse, festooned every table. There were one-ounce bottles of perfume for the ladies, from a house recently acquired by Gursky, and slim gold cigarette lighters for the men, that were manufactured by yet another Gursky enterprise. Ice sculptures of Gursky-endowed university buildings and hospitals and museums and concert halls, set on side tables everywhere, testified to Mr. Bernard's largesse.

The centrepiece on each table was a papier-mâché doll of Mr. Bernard, wearing a glittering crown at a jaunty angle. King Bernard. The figure, mounted on a charger, held a lance, banners flowing from it. Each banner broadcast another accomplishment of Mr. Bernard: a directorship, a medal, an award, an honorary degree. Lionel Gursky announced, "If you will be kind enough to turn over your plates, you will find that one plate at each table has a crown stuck on its underside. Whoever has the crown has won the right to take home the figure of Mr. Bernard at their table."

Everybody, absolutely everybody, who counted in the monied, if not the larger, Jewish community was there. The ladies perfumed, their hair sculpted and lacquered, their eyes shadowed green or silvery, outsize rings riding their fingers; the ladies were breathlessly there, triumphantly there, glittering in gowns of écru silk *façonné* or shimmering cyclamen satin or purple chiffon, acquired and tactfully altered for them by the Holt Renfrew boutique. The men were harnessed in velvet dinner jackets, wine-coloured or midnight blue or murky green, buttoned punishingly tight; they wore ruffled shirts, edged in black, like condolence cards, ornate satin cummerbunds and twinkly buckled Gucci shoes.

Their antidote for ungrateful children — unwanted polyps — was plaques, plaques, and more plaques, which they awarded one another at testimonial dinners once, sometimes twice, a month in this very ballroom. At ease in the Ritz-Carlton they took turns declaring each other governors of universities in Haifa or Jerusalem or Man of the Year for State of Israel Bonds. Their worthiness certified by hiring an after-dinner speaker to flatter them for a ten-thousand-dollar fee, the speaker coming out of New York, New York; either a former secretary of state, a TV star whose series hadn't been renewed or a senator in need. But tonight wasn't make-believe. This was the real thing. This, after all, was Mr. Bernard, *their* Mr. Bernard no matter how large his international importance, and they were there to bask in his aura. A pleasure immeasurably sweetened by the knowledge that some people whom they could mention by name if they wanted to, some cherished friends they would be sure to phone tomorrow if only to establish that *they* had been there, some so-called *knackers* had been excluded, adjudged unsuitable.

Bliss.

So now they applauded, they cheered, they banged forks against wine glasses as tributes to the great man proliferated, and Mr. Bernard himself sat there inexplicably charged with unease, grinding his dentures.

The Israeli ambassador, delivered from Ottawa in a Gursky jet, presented Mr. Bernard with a Bible, encased in a cover of hammered gold, the flyleaf signed by Golda. There was a bronze plaque testifying that even more forests paid for by Mr. Bernard had been planted in Israel. Zion, soon to be Gursky green from shore to shore. There was a medal from Bolivia, where Mr. Bernard had copper interests, but an OBE, ardently pursued for the occasion on Mr. Bernard's instructions, had been denied him, just as he had failed in the past to procure a seat in the senate.

One of Mr. Bernard's most cherished charities was remembered: The Hospital of Hope, which cared for children with terminal diseases.

An official of the Canadian Football League passed Mr. Bernard a ball, a memento of last year's Grey Cup game, that had been auto-graphed by all the players on the winning team, and then one of the team's most celebrated players, a behemoth who peddled Crofter's Best in the off season, wheeled a paraplegic child to the head table. Mr. Bernard, visibly moved, presented the ball to the boy as well as a cheque for five hundred thousand dollars. Three hundred guests leaped to their feet and cheered. The boy, his speech rehearsed for days, began to jerk and twist, spittle flying from him. He gulped and began again, unavailingly. As he started in on a third attempt to speak, Mr. Bernard cut him off with an avuncular smile. "Who needs another speech," he said. "It's what's in your heart that counts with me, little fellow." And *sotto voce*, he told the player, "Wheel him out of here, for Christ's sake. People are beginning to feel shitty."

And hungry too.

Once dinner was done, the lights were dimmed for the ultimate surprise, the specially commissioned birthday film. Mr. Bernard, increasingly tense, his lower lip trembling, yanked out a handkerchief to hide his tears. And in his mind's eye he saw Solomon jumping off that corral fence again, right into the flow of wild mustangs, only some of them green-broke. *Follow me, Bernie, and I'll buy you a beer.*

"Oh my sweetie-pie," Libby said, patting his hand, "I'm so glad you're enjoying yourself. The best is yet to come."

Ignoring her, Mr. Bernard turned on Lionel. "What were you doing in Yellowknife?" he demanded.

"Somebody has to check out the oil-lease properties from time to time, don't you think?"

"There are no discos in Yellowknife. You went there to see Henry to try to buy his shares. Then you flew to London to try to sweet-talk Lucy out of hers."

"Vanessa and I took the jet to London to take in Wimbledon."

"It's too late to lie. I know now. I know sure as I'm sitting here what you've been up to," he said, and his cheeks bleeding red, he reached out to snatch Lionel's hand, thrusting it into his mouth and biting down on his fingers as hard as he could. Lionel, groaning, finally wrenched his throbbing hand free, tucking it under his armpit…and the lights were extinguished and the film began.

Jimmy Durante, one of Mr. Bernard's favourite entertainers, stood before a concert piano, raised a glass of champagne to the old man, a Gursky brand, and then settled down to croak and play "Happy Birthday, Mr. Bernard" followed by a medley of his most famous ditties.

The Schnozz's impudent image yielded to that of the Chief Rabbi of Israel, who stood before the Wailing Wall and pronounced a blessing in Hebrew. His voice was soon superimposed over a montage of selected Gursky history, beginning with a shot of the sod hut on the prairie (now a museum, a Gursky shrine), the sod hut where Mr. Bernard had been born, and then dissolving to a shot of the first distillery, the St. Jerome distillery, Mr. Bernard and Mr. Morrie posing in the foreground, only the merry bright-eyed figure of the other brother, Solomon Gursky, air-brushed out of the picture, as it was out of all the others.

Next Golda offered a tribute.

Then Harvey Schwartz's wife Becky was discovered in a golden kaftan seated at her Louis XIV *bureau-plat* of deal veneered with ebony and boulle marquetry. She turned to the audience, her smile demure, and began to read a tribute she had composed for the occasion, even as the camera tracked in on a prominently displayed copy of her book, a collection of columns about family life first published in the *Canadian Jewish Review: Hugs, Pain, and Chocolate Chip Cookies*.

Jan Peerce proposed a toast to Mr. Bernard and then sang "The Bluebird of Happiness."

Zero Mostel raised a laugh extolling the virtues of Gursky blends, even as he staggered about a stage feigning drunkenness, singing, "If I Were a Rich Man."

A harpist played the theme song from *Love Story* as Mr. Bernard and Libby were seen strolling hand-in-hand through the streets of Old Jerusalem. The famous star of many a biblical blockbuster sat in the garden of his Coldwater Canyon home and recited Mr. Bernard's favourite stanzas from Longfellow.

Then there was a slow dissolve to the wine-dark sea. The custom-built one-hundred-and-ten-foot-long Gursky yacht was seen cruising the Greek isles as a voice that sounded like Ben Cartwright's began to recite:

> The barge she sat in, like a burnish'd throne,
> Burn'd on the water. The poop was beaten gold;
> Purple the sails, and so perfumed that
> The winds were love-sick with them; the oars were silver,
> Which to the tune of flutes kept stroke, and made
> The water which they beat to follow faster,
> As amorous of their strokes.

The camera eye tracked past a snoozing Mr. Bernard to reveal a sixty-five-year-old Libby, lounging on deck in a flower-print halter and pedal pushers, attended by black stewards in white linen jackets.

> …For her own person,
> It beggar'd all description. She did lie
> In her pavilion, cloth-of-gold tissues,
> O'erpicturing that Venus where we see
> The fancy outwork nature.

Laughing, her belly rocking with delight, Libby fed caviar with chopped onion and Coca-Cola to one grandchild, chopped liver on crackers to another.

> …On each side her
> Stood pretty dimpled boys, like smiling Cupids,

With divers-colour'd fans, whose wind did seem
To glow the delicate cheeks which they did cool,
And what they undid did.

The image of Libby cavorting with her grandchildren yielded to a longer shot of the yacht at sunset as another voice declaimed, "From William Shakespeare, the Bard of Avon."

Finally the children of a kibbutz in the Negev, photographed from a helicopter, stood in a pattern in the Bernard Gursky Park and spelled *l'chaim*, the apostrophe raising a bottle of Masada Blanc, a Gursky brand, to Mr. Bernard.

The film done, a spotlight illuminated Mr. Bernard, seemingly crushed by such acclaim, swimming in tears, a sodden handkerchief clenched between his dentures. Everybody was enormously moved, especially Libby, who now rose into the light to sing their song to him:

Bei mir bist du schön,
Please let me explain,
Bei mir bist du schön,
Means that you're grand....
I could sing Bernie, Bernie,
Even say "voonderbar."
Each language only helps me tell you
How grand you are....

There wasn't, Libby would remember, a dry eye in the house, the rest of her song lost in applause, soaring applause as Mr. Bernard leaped to his feet, knocking back his chair, and fled the ballroom.

"He's just an old softie at heart, you know."

"Don't you just want to hug him?"

The truth was Mr. Bernard had to piss again, he had to piss something terrible, there was such a burning inside him, and when it came out it was, to his astonishment, red as Big Sur burgundy, another Gursky brand. A week later they began to cut and a tearful Kathleen O'Brien lighted the first of many candles at the Cathedral of Mary, Queen of the World. Mr. Morrie, responding to a summons, visited his brother at home for the first time in twenty years.

"So," Mr. Bernard said.

"So."

"Look at Barney now. I was right about him all along. I want you to admit it."

"I admit it."

"No resentments?"

"No."

"How's Ida?"

"She'd like to come to pay her respects."

"Tell her to bring Charna with her. I don't mind."

"Charna's dead."

"Oh shit, I forgot. Did I go to the funeral?"

"Yes."

"I'm glad."

"Bernie, I've got something to say, but please don't shout at me."

"Try me, you little prick."

"You must make provision for Miss O."

"A big brown envelope. It's in the office safe."

They cut and pared Mr. Bernard a week later, pronouncing him fit, but Mr. Bernard knew better. He sent for Harvey Schwartz. "I want my lawyers here at nine sharp tomorrow morning. All of them."

Later the same afternoon Mr. Bernard saw Miss O'Brien.

"I'm going to die, Miss O."

"Would you like me to do your weenie now?"

"I wouldn't say no."

— *Solomon Gursky Was Here,* pp. 119–25

RORY PEEL THREW HIS ARMS UP IN THE AIR, exasperated. "Fellas, fellas," he said, "he's no ordinary Eskimo. Atuk would be an asset to our club."

"For the last time," Bernstein said, "we're not prejudiced here. His being an Eskimo has nothing to do with it one way or another. It's that he's a *goy*."

"But —"

"Rory, look at it this way. Personally, I have nothing against the *goys*. But if you let even a few of them in, the next thing you know their kids and our kids are playing together at the pool. They go out on a date. What's one date, you say. Yeah, sure. *Then one night your daughter comes home and she wants to marry one.*"

—*The Incomparable Atuk*, p. 150

Oh Quebec!

Few aspects of life were more annoyingly absurd, in Richler's view, than Quebec politics. His pronouncements on the subject, and especially his condemnation of the racialist strain in Quebec nationalism, provoked enormous controversy in his native province. When he wrote an article on Quebec for The New Yorker *in the fall of 1991, which had the effect of exposing the separatists to international ridicule, the controversy became especially intense. But, for all his delight in the absurd excesses of, say, Quebec's language police, Richler's essays on politics were thoroughly researched and intelligently thought out.*

René Lévesque, leader of the Parti Québécois, 1984.

THE TRUTH IS, Quebec hasn't been quite the same ever since the separatist Parti Québécois, led by Lévesque, surprised themselves more than anybody, riding into power in the election of November 15, 1976. The PQ charged into office riding a protest vote. The preceding Liberal government of Robert Bourassa had already alienated English-speaking voters, especially immigrants, with a tough language bill of its own, Bill 22, an ill-advised attempt to outflank the PQ. Bourassa called an unnecessary election, thinking that he could defeat the PQ one more time; Lévesque would then retire, and the party would be diminished as a serious threat. He was wrong on all counts. The PQ, which was elected with 41 percent of the popular vote, winning 70 seats out of a possible 110, displaced a government that had come to be held in contempt by most Quebecers, separatist or not. Shrewdly, the PQ chose not to run on its traditional independence platform in 1976, though it was always there, the sustaining floor of their political structure. Instead, they seized the day, promising an electorate weary of strikes, corruption, and ineptitude *un vrai gouvernement* to be followed by a referendum before any move toward independence.

Immediately, Montreal became the centre of the battleground, still lacking sufficient sympathy in those days only because President Carter had failed to stand at the psychological wall that divided the English from the French — say, St. Denis Street — and proclaim, "*Moi aussi, je suis Montréalais.*"

Even so, we had never walked so tall. Pollsters tested our temperature on the hour, and there was hardly a taxi driver or bartender who had not had his in-depth views sought out by hungover foreign correspondents on the fly, fresh from Belfast, en route to Beirut. Suddenly, we were a real trouble spot. Edge City.

Here, we didn't sneak into print by seizing a hundred pounds of heroin, worth untold millions on the street. Or by grabbing a cache of cocaine landed by glider in a remote cow pasture. When the incomparable Quebec police pounced, it was the stuff that deserved to make headlines the world over. One night a friend phoned me from Beverly Hills to say he had read in the *Los Angeles Times* that the police had seized 15,000 Dunkin' Donut bags in Montreal. Hard put to contain his laughter, he asked me if it was true.

"Damn right it is," I said.

"Why?"

"Because they weren't bilingual."

—*Home Sweet Home,* "Language (and Other) Problems," pp. 230–32

I WAS NOT THE FIRSt Québécois who had lectured at Trier. I had been preceded by the then Quebec minister of cultural development and retribution, Camille Laurin, who had told the students that in all of North America only the Québécois maintained a European cultural link. I noted that the library of Québécois literature Laurin had provided for the university included no work by Hugh MacLennan, Irving Layton, Mavis Gallant, Leonard Cohen, or me. In the new Quebec, as visualized by Laurin, there would obviously be only *ein Volk, eine Kultur*.

—*Belling the Cat,* "Germany 1978," p. 122

AMONG THE REGULARS AT DINK'S these days there are a few divorcées, a number of journalists, including the *Gazette* columnist Zack Keeler, a couple of bores to be avoided, some lawyers, a marooned New Zealander, and a likeable gay hairdresser. Our star turn and my best friend there is a lawyer, who usually claims his bar stool at noon and doesn't surrender it until seven, when we yield Dink's to ear-splitting rock music and the young, there to make out.

John Hughes-McNoughton, born into Westmount affluence, misplaced his moral compass years ago. His thin hair dyed brown, he is a tall, scrawny, stoop-shouldered man, his blue eyes radiating scorn. John was a brilliant criminal lawyer until he was undone by two costly alimony settlements and a deadly mixture of booze and irreverence. Defending a notorious swindler-cum-lounge-lizard some years back, a man charged with sexual assault on a woman he had picked up in the Esquire Show Bar, John made the mistake of going out to a long liquid lunch at Delmo's before returning to the courtroom to deliver his summing up. Floating into the well of the court, slurring his words, he said, "Ladies and gentlemen of the jury, it is now my duty to make an impassioned speech in defense of my client. Then you will benefit from the judge's unbiased summary of the evidence you have heard here. And following that, ladies and gentlemen of the jury, you, in your wisdom, will pronounce on whether you find my client innocent or guilty. But, honouring Juvenal, who once wrote *probitas laudatur et alget*, which I won't insult you by translating, let me admit that I am far too drunk to make a speech. In all my years in court, I have yet to come across an unbiased judge. And you, ladies and gentlemen of the jury, are incapable of deciding whether my client is innocent or not." Then he sat down.

In 1989, John addressed public meetings in support of a quirky new Anglophone protest party that would elect four members to our so-called National Assembly in Quebec City. He also published corrosive op-ed pieces here and there ridiculing the province's loopy language laws, which ordained, among other foolish things, that henceforth English, or even bilingual, commercial signs would be *verboten*, an affront to the *visage linguistique* of *la belle province*. In those contentious days even Dink's suffered a visit from an inspector (or tongue trooper, as we called them) from the Commission de Protection de la Langue Française. This latter-day, pot-bellied *patriote* in a Hawaiian shirt and Bermuda shorts was saddened to discover a banner suspended from the bar that read:

ALLONS-Y EXPOS
GO FOR IT, EXPOS

His manner beyond reproach, the inspector allowed that the sentiment was admirable but, unfortunately, the sign was illegal, because the English lettering was the same size as the French, whereas the law clearly stated that the French must be twice the size of the English. It was past three p.m. when the inspector pronounced and a well-oiled John was already into his shouting mode. "When you can send in an inspector who is twice the size of us Anglophones," he hollered, "we'll take down the sign. Until then, it remains in place."

"Are you *le patron?*"

"*Fiche le camp. Espèce d'imbécile.*"

Six months later John was in the news. He had failed to pay his provincial income tax for the past six years. An oversight. So he summoned reporters to Dink's. "I am being persecuted," he said, "because I am an Anglophone, a spokesman for my people who have been denied their constitutional rights. Rest assured I will not be intimidated or silenced. And I will survive. For, as Terence put it, *fortis fortuna adiuvat.* That's spelt T, E, R, E, N, C, E, gentlemen."

"But have you paid your taxes or not?" asked a reporter from *Le Devoir*.

"I refuse to countenance hostile questions put to me by politically motivated reporters from the Francophone press."

Riding a surfeit of vodka and cranberry juice, his preferred tipple, John could be truly obnoxious, his favourite foil the harmless gay hairdresser he shouts at, denouncing him as a bowel-troweller or worse, infuriating Betty, our incomparable barmaid, as well as everybody else in the bar. Betty, born to her job, sees to it that nobody who is not a certified member of our group is ever seated at our end of the horseshoe-shaped bar. She fields unwanted phone calls with panache. If, for instance, Nate Gold's wife calls, she will look directly at Nate for a sign, even as she calls out, "Is Nate Gold here?" She cashes cheques for Zack Keeler, among others, and hides them until she is assured they will not be returned NSF. When drink has rendered John too much to bear, she will take him gently by the arm, and say, "Your taxi is here."

"But I didn't order a..."

"Yes, you did. Didn't he, Zack?"

—*Barney's Version,* pp. 82–84

Jacques Parizeau.

HAPPY DAYS AHEAD. According to today's *Gazette,* Mayor André Auger of St. Lin (pop. 6,000) is pushing through a new bylaw to properly reward French Canadian fertility. Under his innovative scheme, which will do zilch for TV ratings but keep a lot of couples busy elsewhere, a family will now receive $500 for having a third child, $600 for a fourth, $700 for a fifth, and so on. "I am a Quebec national-ist," Auger said. "I believe Quebec should repopulate itself *itself.*"

Quebec's birthrate, once legendary, is now among the lowest in the Western world, and this has got jolly Jacques Parizeau, the new leader of the separatist Parti Québécois, thinking deep and dirty. He is concerned lest French Canadians, failing in their conjugal obligations, wake up one morning to find themselves a minority in their own homeland. And so, if elected, Parizeau will stand up for more fruitful fucking, sponsoring a baby-bonus program. Well, okay. Very nice. But like most proposed PQ measures this one does not go nearly far enough. Obviously something will have to be done about randy Jews (I speak as an unapologetic father of five), horny WASPs and what the PQ charmingly calls neo-Quebecers, that is to say Greeks, Italians, and Portuguese, all notoriously sex-crazed. In order for the bonus to do its work, I think it should apply only to bona fide Québécois, and that the rest of us should be fined rather than rewarded for not being more careful between the sheets.

—*Broadsides,* "Journals," p. 252

ALTHOUGH SOME IN THE PQ insist that the term "Québécois" embraces all those who live in the province, that concept, to my mind, is a public-relations fib. A chimera. Going back to René Lévesque, never mind the Abbé Groulx, there has been too much damning evidence to the contrary. When René Lévesque appointed Robert Boyd head of Hydro-Quebec, he hastily pointed out that in spite of his Anglo-sounding name Boyd was a bona fide Québécois, that is to say, of *pure laine* origin. More recently, the ineffable Pierre Bourgault warned that there would be trouble in store for non-Francophones if their vote deprived "real" Quebecers of independence, a sentiment endorsed by the former Tory cabinet minister Marcel Masse. Then, in February 1995, Bloc Québécois MP Philippe Paré accused "immigrants" of getting in the way. "Couldn't they, if they don't want to contribute to the Quebec solution, avoid putting on the brakes by voting against us?" Another Bloc backbencher, Gilbert Fillion, declared, "Who's to say that at some point two years from now, they won't wind up in Toronto, these people?" And Bloc MP Suzanne Tremblay snarled at Joyce Napier, a Montreal-born reporter, that, judging by her accent, she probably wasn't "a Québécois at the start."

The truth is, the goodwill of pure-of-heart separatists notwithstanding, their movement is essentially xenophobic, and an independent Quebec would not be a healthy environment for non-Francophones.

Immigrants to this country, whether Norman peasants, dispossessed Scots, Irish fleeing the potato famine, *shtetl* Jews, poor Ukrainians, Greeks, Italians, Chinese, Koreans, or Portuguese, came to these shores to escape tribalism and discrimination. Our grandparents or great-grandparents, wherever they came from, were mostly dirt poor. If anybody's blood in this country is blue, it's not owing to their progenitors but is a consequence of the climate. And that includes the *pure laine.* Together we eventually forged a civil society where everybody was equal, at least in their democratic rights. But now, after all these years, tribal conflict is threatening to undo us; and, to the amazement of people in less fortunate lands, this incomparably rich, still nearly empty country, everybody's second chance, may soon self-destruct, splitting into two acrimonious parts. And if that happens, there will certainly be another mass exodus from Montreal, and the only ethnics left in town, "getting in the way," will be the poor and the elderly.

Three or four years from now, when Bouchard, adding up his humiliation points, pronounces it time for Referendum III, the separatists could win by default. Since the first referendum, in 1980, at least 150,000 of *les autres* have quit the province, and over the next few years another 50,000 unwelcome anglophones and ethnics, maybe even more, could easily vote with their feet. The PQ's policy of genteel, nonviolent ethnic cleansing may yet win them a country with a depleted but uniform population, where the only surviving English-language sign would read For Sale.

—*Belling the Cat,* "From the Ottawa Monkey House...
to Referendum," pp. 329–30

A POLL, TAKEN EARLY IN 1983, revealed that if an election was held immediately the PQ would lose badly, even though confronted by a Liberal Party led by an interim leader. Six years after the PQ originally came to power, only 19 percent of Quebecers said they would vote for them again.

"No independence," Pierre Bourgault wrote in the *Gazette,* "no social democracy, no dream. I am angry — and very sad."

But René Lévesque, just possibly on his way out, had already achieved something like *de facto* separation for Quebec. Repressive language laws, once in the statute books, were unlikely to be revoked even by a Liberal government, terrified of being labelled the running dogs of the English-speaking minority. Head offices, once uprooted, will never return to Montreal. The young, having set themselves up in Toronto or the West, will be coming back only for funerals. English-speaking Quebecers will continue to quit the province. The most ambitious of the new immigrants will naturally want their children educated into the North American mainstream (that is to say, in English), so they will settle elsewhere in Canada. Montreal, once the most sophisticated and enjoyable city in the country, a charming place, was dying, its mood querulous, its future decidedly more provincial than cosmopolitan.

—*Home Sweet Home,* "Language (and Other)
Problems," p. 264

EARLY IN MAY Claude Ryan, who had once complained in *Le Devoir* that what the Liberal Party suffered from was a lack of *le leadership,* delivered the latest refinement of Bill 178. It introduced his "two-for-one" rule on indoor bilingual signs, which meant that French signs had to be twice as large or twice as numerous as English ones. His ruling, which would affect some 100,000 Quebec businesses with four or fewer employees, had to be complied with by December 1990. It was, Ryan insisted, the simplest possible application of the markedly predominant principle. Variations on the theme, he said, would be dealt with individually. If, for instance, a store's French signs were neon green and the English ones plain beige, but there weren't twice as many French signs as English ones, an inspector from the language commission would file a detailed report, and the commissioners would eventually decide whether French signs had a "much greater impact."

Of course, Ryan's interpretation of the law, which could involve bringing in colour charts as well as the expert testimony of interior decorators, was immediately attacked by Québécois language zealots and outraged Anglophones.

The president of the St. Jean Baptiste Society said, "The message to Quebecers is that now we have two languages in the province and one is somehow bigger than the other so we should feel secure." And the new president of Alliance Quebec denounced Bill 178 as a colossal absurdity. "It is incredible," he said, "that people of a sup-posedly reasonable degree of intelligence should have spent three seconds dealing with this kind of issue." But he doubted that the law was vulnerable to a court challenge. "Frankly," he said, "it's too silly to dignify by contesting it."

At Woody's Pub, it was ordained that the law, as set forth by Ryan, did not go far enough, and we immediately formed something called the Twice As Much Society. The society, it was decided, would lobby for an amendment to Bill 178 that would call for French to be spoken twice as loud as English inside and outside. Inspectors from the language commission would be armed with sound meters to detect Anglophones who spoke above a whisper, sending offenders to the slammer. A Francophone hockey player scoring a goal for le Club de hockey canadien would have to be cheered twice as loud as a minority group teammate. A member of the collectivity, ordering a meal in a restaurant, would have to be served a double portion, and so forth and so on. We also drafted a letter to Premier Bourassa demanding that his fertility payola be made available only to *Québécois de vieille souche*, lest garlicky Allophones, driven by avarice, take to polluting the province with racially impure families of a dozen kids or more.

Then, awash on another round of drinks, we tried to imagine how English would be impoverished if, in order to oblige linguistic zealots, it was shorn of all its French words. One of our number, a middle-aged clothing manufacturer, started things off by recalling how in his first year of puberty the very sight of the word "brassiere," never mind a photograph of a girl actually modelling one — just the word itself — was sufficient to propel him into the bathroom to run cold water over his head. Next we tried to improvise a story, which ordinarily could lean on gallicisms here and there, but now had to make do with Anglo-Saxon substitutes. It began:

"Clarissa and I got together for a head-to-head later that morning. Ah, but how attractive she appeared, seated on her long chair, wearing a linen article from her woman's wardrobe, through which I could just catch a glimpse of her mammary-gland hanger. We had filtered coffee and crescents for breakfast. Then she asked me if we could also have dinner together.

'Of course I could manage it,' I replied. 'Excellent,' she said, 'because I have heard of a public eating place that happily does not specialize in the new kitchen. In fact, the cook has studied at the school of the blue rope.'"

—*Oh Canada! Oh Quebec!*, pp. 56–58

TODAY THERE ARE probably more French Canadians and Jews rooted in the mansions of Upper Westmount than there are Scots Presbyterian bankers, which suits me just fine, incidentally. And not one of these bankers enjoys anything like the clout of an executive of the Caisse de dépôt et placement du Québec, a.k.a. *La Machine à milliards*, with an estimated bundle of thirty-five billion bucks to play with. And if the banker is still being chauffeur-driven each morning, it is surely to his French lessons and only later to his office on the street that has long since been born again as rue Saint-Jacques. And your average habitant, though certainly not rich, is doing very nicely these days, thanks to a federally imposed milk quota that entitles Quebec's farmers to produce 48 percent of Canada's industrial milk, needed for the production of yogurt, cheese, and other products. Something else. That legendary bastion of WASP privilege, the Ritz-Carlton Hotel, is now managed by French Canadians, and any day of the week you will hear more French than English being spoken in the bar, which is as it should be.

—*Oh Canada! Oh Quebec,* pp. 71–72

RENÉ LÉVESQUE RESIGNED from the leadership of the PQ in 1985, and two years later he was dead of a heart attack. Unfortunately, I never had an opportunity to talk to him again. In this country, where we are served by so many resoundingly mediocre politicians, he was a happy exception to a depressing rule. Charismatic, vulnerable, a leader without whom the separatists would have remained trapped within the fringe RIN (Rassemblement pour l'indépendance nationale), he nevertheless did not merit his reputation for honesty.

My enduring feeling about René Lévesque is that if he had chosen to hang me, even as he tightened the rope round my neck, he would have complained about how humiliating it was for him to spring the trapdoor. And then, once I was swinging in the wind, he would blame my ghost for having obliged him to murder, thereby imposing a guilt trip on a sweet, self-effacing, downtrodden Francophone.

—*Oh Canada! Oh Quebec!,* p. 132

LYING IN THE DARK, fulminating, I recited aloud the number I was to call if I had a heart attack.

"You have reached the Montreal General Hospital. If you have a touch-tone phone, and you know the extension you want, please press that number now. If not, press number seventeen for service in the language of *les maudits anglais,* or number twelve for service *en français,* the glorious language of our oppressed collectivity."

Twenty-one for emergency ambulance service.

"You have reached the emergency ambulance service. Please hold and an operator will come to your assistance as soon as our strip-poker game is over. Have a nice day."

While I waited, the automatic tape would play Mozart's *Requiem.*

—*Barney's Version,* p. 11

I only got to see the great Richard twice.
Saving money earned collecting bills for a
neighbourhood butcher on Sunday mornings, my
friends and I bought standing-room tickets for
the millionaires' section. And then, flinging
our winter caps ahead of us, we vaulted
barriers, eventually working our way down to
ice level.

PART V

THE SPORTING LIFE

While no athlete, Richler gave himself to spectator sports — especially baseball (the Expos) and hockey (the Canadiens) — with wholehearted enthusiasm. Magazine assignments provided him with the opportunity to get close to the players and yielded memorable portraits of, among others, the redoubtable Gordie Howe. An encounter with bodybuilders was transferred almost word for word onto the pages of The Incomparable Atuk, *and interviews with wrestlers gave him material for the first of the Jacob Two-Two children's books. Later he became a fly fisherman and indulged an old passion for snooker, originally nurtured on The Main.*

— J. W.

IN AN OTHERWISE GENEROUS REVIEW of my most recent novel, *Barney's Version*, that appeared in the London *Spectator*, Francis King had one caveat. Noting the sharpness of protagonist Barney Panofsky's intelligence and the breadth of his culture, he doubted that he could also be a sports nut. "Would such a man, obsessed with ice hockey, be able to pronounce with such authority on topics as diverse as the descriptive passages in the novels of P. D. James, *Pygmalion* as play, musical, and film, the pornography published by Maurice Girodias's Olympic Press and Dr. Johnson's *The Vanity of Human Wishes?* — rather strains credulity."

But North American literary men in general, and the Jewish writers among them in particular, have always been obsessed by sports. We acquire the enthusiasm as kids and carry it with us into middle age and beyond, adjudging it far more enjoyable than lots of other baggage we still lug around. Arguably, we settled for writing, a sissy's game, because we couldn't "float like a butterfly and sting like a bee," pitch a curveball, catch, deke, score a touchdown.

— *On Snooker,* pp. 167–68

THERE ARE TIMES WHEN my obsession with time-wasting sports irritates the hell out of me. After my restorative afternoon snooze every day in London, I habitually venture out to pick up an *International Herald Tribune* at a newsstand on Sloane Square, and then I stroll over to the Crescent, that most agreeable of little bar/restaurants on the Fulham Road. I order an espresso and the Macallan and settle into the *Trib*, turning first to the sports pages to ponder the baseball or hockey scores, depending on the season. Okay, these are enthusiasms I was infected with as an innocent child and adolescent, long before I began to suffer from gravitas. But why do I also have to check out the standings in the latest golf tournament?

When Northrop Frye discovered that my friend Robert Weaver golfed, he was appalled. "I had no idea you indulged in executive sports, Bob," he said.

I've never golfed. To this day I don't know the difference between a birdie and a bogey. And yet — and yet — for reasons that I can't fathom, I worry about Phil Mickelson and the Canadian Mike Weir. I was truly pleased when another Canadian golfer, Ms. Lori Kane, finally won a tournament.

— On Snooker, p. 83

LOOK AT IT THIS WAY: if [snooker player John] Higgins could make a maximum, or David Cone pitch a perfect baseball game, then just maybe, against all odds, a flawless novel was possible. I can't speak for other writers, but I always start out pledged to a dream of perfection, a novel that will be free of clunky sentences or passages forced in the hothouse, but it's never the case. Each novel is a failure of sorts. No matter how many drafts I go through, there will always be compromises here and there, pages that will make me wince when I read them years later. But if Higgins could achieve perfection, maybe, next time out, I could too.

— On Snooker, p. 86

ON WEEKDAY AFTERNOONS [at Delorimier Downs] kids were admitted free into the left-field bleachers, and by the third inning the more intrepid had worked their way down as far as the first-base line. Ziggy, Yossel, and I would sit out there in the sun, cracking peanuts, nudging each other if a ball struck the Miss Sweet Caporal sign hitting the young lady you know where. Another diversion was a porthole in the outfield wall. If a batter hit a ball through it, he was entitled to a two-year supply of Pal Blades.

Sunday afternoons the Royals usually attracted capacity crowds, but come the Little World Series, fans also lined up on the roof of the adjoining Grover Knit-to-Fit Building, and temporary stands were set up and roped off in centre field. Ziggy, who used to sit out there, liked to boast, "If I get hit on the head, it's a ground-rule home run."

—*Dispatches from the Sporting Life,* "From Gladu, through Kitman, to the Victoire Historique and After," p. 222

IN 1945, THE ROYALS acquired one of ours, their first Jewish player, Kermit Kitman, a William and Mary scholarship boy. Our loyalty to the team redoubled. Kitman was a centre fielder. On opening day, a story in *La Presse* declared, *"Trois des meilleurs portecouleurs de Montréal depuis l'ouverture de la saison ont été ses joueurs de champ: Gladu, Kitman et Yeager. Kitman a exécuté un catch sensationnel encore hier après-midi sur le long coup de Torres à la 8e manche. On les verra tous trois à l'oeuvre cet après-midi contre le Jersey-City lors du programme double de la 'Victoire' au stade de la rue Delorimier."*

In his very first at-bat in that opening game against the Skeeters, Kitman belted a homer, something he would not manage again until August. Alas, in the later innings he also got doubled off second. After the game, when he ventured into a barbershop at the corner of St. Catherine and St. Urbain, a man in another chair studied him intently. "Aren't you Kermit Kitman?" he asked.

"Yeah," he allowed, grinning, remembering his homer.

"You son of a bitch, you got doubled off second. It cost me five hundred bucks."

—*Dispatches from the Sporting Life,* "From Gladu, through Kitman, to the Victoire Historique and After," p. 223

IT WAS SPORT THAT FIRST enabled me, as a child, to grasp that the adult world was suspect. Tainted by lies and betrayals. This insight came about when I discovered that our home baseball team, the

Triple A Montreal Royals, which I was enjoined to cheer for, was in fact made up of strangers, hired hands, most of them American Southerners who were long gone once the season was over and had never been tested by a punishing Montreal winter. Only during the darkest days of the Second World War when deprivation was the unhappy rule, coffee and sugar and gasoline all rationed, American comic books temporarily unavailable, one-armed Pete Gray toiling in the Toronto Maple Leafs outfield — only then did French Canadian players off the local sandlots briefly play for the Royals: Stan Bréard at *arrêt-court*, Roland Galdu at *troisième bu*, and Jean-Pierre Roy as *lanceur*. A few years later my bunch could root for a Jewish player, outfielder Kermit Kitman, who eventually married a Montreal girl and settled here, ending up in the schmata trade. Lead-off hitter for the Royals, only twenty-two years old, but a college boy, rare in baseball in those days, he was paid somewhat better than most: $650 monthly for six months of the year, a bonanza enriched by $13 a day meal money on the road. Kitman told me, "As a Jewish boy, I could eat on that money and maybe even save a little in those days. The Gentile players had enough left over for beer and cigarettes." If the Royals went all the way, winning the Little World Series, he would earn another $1,800.

My disenchantment with the baseball Royals, counterfeit home-towners, didn't matter as soon as I discovered that I could give my unqualified love to the Montreal Canadiens, *Nos Glorieux*, then a team unique in sport because most of its star performers were Quebeckers born and bred, many of whom had to drive beer trucks or take construction jobs in summer in order to make ends meet. I speak of the incomparable Richard brothers, Maurice and Henri; goalie Jacques Plante, who knitted between periods; and Doug Harvey, universally acknowledged as the outstanding defenseman of his time, who never was paid more than $15,000 a season, and in his last boozy days earned his beer money sharpening skates in his brother's sports shop, for kids who had no idea who he was.

— *Dispatches from the Sporting Life*,
"Writers and Sports," pp. 96–98

Baseball great Jackie Robinson, 1946.

WHEN I WAS A BOY in Montreal, during the Second World War, my parents feared Adolf Hitler and his seemingly invulnerable panzers beyond all things, but my old bunch, somewhat more savvy, was in far greater terror of Mr. Branch Rickey. Let me explain. In those days our hearts belonged to the late, great Montreal Royals of the old International League. In 1939, the Royals signed a contract with Mr.

Rickey — the baseball intellectual who built the legendary Brooklyn teams — making the club the Dodgers' number-one farm team. Five years later, our club was sold outright to the Dodgers. This meant that come the dog days of August, the imperial Mr. Rickey could descend on our colony and harvest its best players to bolster the Dodgers' perennial pennant drive. Gone, gone were Duke Snider, Jackie Robinson, Roy Campanella, Ralph Branca, Don Newcombe, and Carl Furillo just when we needed them most. My romance with baseball, still unrequited, goes back that far.

Since then, of course, there have been many changes in the game, some of them heartening but most of them diminishing. Among the most heartening changes I naturally count the coming of major league baseball in the shape of those suddenly traditional bridesmaids, our very own Expos, to Montreal in 1969. Mind you, if once we lost our most gifted players to the majors, now that we are in the biggies ourselves we can't even sign them. Take young Pete Incaviglia, for instance. He was the Expos' number-one college-draft choice in 1985, but, obviously having majored in geography rather than haute cuisine, he didn't want to come this far north. He was lost to the balmier climes of Texas, where in early July he was hitting .266, with thirteen home runs and forty-two RBIs (and I hope suffering heartburn on a daily diet of greasy ribs and twice-warmed-over chili).

— *Dispatches from the Sporting Life,*
"You Know Me, Ring," pp. 85–86

MY PROBLEM WITH MONTREAL BASEBALL is compounded by the fact that in a climate where we are fortunate to reap seven weeks of summer, maybe six, the game is played on a zippered carpet in a concrete container that resembles nothing so much as an outsize toilet bowl — a toilet bowl the cost of which would humble even a Pentagon procurement agent. The ugly Olympic Stadium, more properly known in Montreal as the Big Owe, cost $650 million to build in 1976, *more than the combined cost of all the domed stadiums constructed in North America up to that time.* And this price doesn't include the parking facilities, which set taxpayers back another $70 million. Nor did it take into account the so-called retractable roof, finally put in place in 1988, its reported cost another $80 million. A roof that retracted only erratically come 1989 and already leaked in several places.

—*Dispatches from the Sporting Life,* "From Satchel, through Hank Greenberg, to El Divino Loco," pp. 124–25

AH, THE BIG OWE. The largest, coldest slab of poured concrete in Canada. In a city where we endure seven long months of winter, and spring comes and goes in an afternoon, it is Drapeau's triumph to have provided us with a partially roofed over six-hundred-and-fifty-million-dollar stadium, where the sun seldom shines on the fans.

The Olympic Stadium in Montreal.

Tim Burke, one of the liveliest sportswriters in town, once said to me, "You know, there are lots of summer afternoons when I feel like taking in a ball game, but I think, hell, who wants to sit out there in the dark."

—*Dispatches from the Sporting Life,* "From Gladu, through Kitman, to the Victoire Historique and After," pp. 212–13

SUMMER.

Drifting through Soho in the early evening, Jake stopped at the Nosh Bar for a sustaining salt beef sandwich. He had only managed one squirting mouthful and a glance at the unit trust quotations in the *Standard* (S&P Capital was steady, but Pan Australian had dipped again) when he was distracted by a bulging-bellied American in a Dacron suit. The American's wife, unsuccessfully shoehorned into a miniskirt, clutched a *London A to Z* to her bosom. The American opened a fat credit-card-filled wallet, briefly exposing an international medical passport which listed his blood type; he extracted a pound note and slapped it into the waiter's hand. "I suppose," he said, winking, "I get twenty-four shillings change for this?"

The waiter shot him a sour look.

"Tell your boss," the American continued, unperturbed, "that I'm a Galicianer, just like him."

"Oh, Morty," his wife said, bubbling.

And the juicy salt beef sandwich turned to leather in Jake's mouth. It's here again, he realized, heart sinking, the season.

Come summer, American and Canadian show-business plenipotentiaries domiciled in London had more than the usual hardships to contend with. The usual hardships being the income tax tangle, scheming and incompetent natives, uppity *au pairs* or nannies, wives overspending at the bazaar (Harrods, Fortnum's, Asprey's), choosing suitable prep schools for the kids, doing without real pastrami and pickled tomatoes, fighting decorators and smog, and of course keeping warm. But come summer, tourist liners and jets began to disgorge demanding hordes of relatives and friends of friends, long (and best) forgotten schoolmates and army buddies, on London, thereby transmogrifying the telephone, charmingly inefficient all winter, into an instrument of terror. For there was not a stranger who phoned and did not exude warmth and expect help in procuring theatre tickets and a night on the town ("What we're really dying for is a pub crawl. The swinging pubs. Waddiya say, old chap?") or an invitation to dinner at home. ("Well, Yankel, did you tell the Queen your Uncle Labish was coming? Did she bake a cake?")

The tourist season's dialogue, the observations, the complaints, was a recurring hazard to be endured. You agreed, oh how many times you agreed, the taxis were cute, the bobbies polite, and the pace slower than New York or, in Jake's case, Montreal. "People still know how to enjoy life here. I can see that." Yes. On the other hand, you've got to admit...the bowler hats are a scream, hotel service is lousy, there's nowhere you can get a suit pressed in a hurry, the British have snobby British accents and hate all Americans. Jealousy. "Look at it this way, it isn't home." Yes, a thousand times yes. All the same, everybody was glad to have made the trip, it was expensive but broadening, the world was getting smaller all the time, a global village, only next time they wouldn't try to squeeze so many countries into twenty-one days. "Mind you, the American Express was very, very nice everywhere. No complaints in that department."

Summer was charged with menace, with schnorrers and green-horns from the New Country. So how glorious, how utterly delightful, it was for the hardcore showbiz expatriates (those who weren't in Juan-les-Pins or Dubrovnik) to come together on a Sunday morning for a sweet and soothing game of softball, just as the Raj of another dynasty had used to meet on the cricket pitch in Malabar.

Sunday-morning softball on Hampstead Heath in summer was unquestionably the fun thing to do. It was a ritual.

Manny Gordon tooled in all the way from Richmond, stowing a fielder's mitt and a thermos of martinis in the boot, clapping a sporty tweed cap over his bald head and strapping himself and his starlet of the night before into his Aston-Martin at nine a.m. C. Bernard Farber started out from Ham Common, picking up Al Levine, Bob Cohen, Jimmy Grief, and Myer Gross outside Mary Quant's on the King's Road. Moey Hanover had once startled the staff at the Connaught by tripping down the stairs on a Sunday morning, wearing a peak cap and T-shirt and blue jeans, carrying his personal Babe Ruth bat in one hand and a softball in the other. Another Sunday Ziggy Alter had flown in from Rome, just for the sake of a restorative nine innings.

Frankie Demaine drove in from Marlow-on-Thames in his Maserati. Lou Caplan, Morty Calman, and Cy Levi usually brought their wives and children. Monty Talman, ever mindful of his latest twenty-one-year-old girlfriend, always cycled to the Heath from St. John's Wood. Wearing a maroon track suit, he usually lapped the field eight or nine times before anyone else turned up.

Jake generally strolled to the Heath, his tattered fielder's mitt and three enervating bagels filled with smoked salmon concealed under the *Observer* in his shopping bag. Some Sundays, like this one, possibly his last for a while, Nancy brought the kids along to watch.

The starting lineup on Sunday, June 28, 1963, was:

AL LEVINE'S TEAM	LOU CAPLAN'S BUNCH
Manny Gordon, ss.	Bob Cohen, 3b.
C. Bernard Farber, 2b.	Myer Gross, ss.
Jimmy Grief, 3b.	Frankie Demaine, lf.
Al Levine, cf.	Morty Calman, rf.
Monty Talman, 1b.	Cy Levi, 2b.
Ziggy Alter, lf.	Moey Hanover, c.
Jack Monroe, rf.	Johnny Roper, cf.
Sean Fielding, c.	Jason Storm, 1b.
Alfie Roberts, p.	Lou Caplan, p.

Jake, like five or six others who had arrived late and hungover (or who were unusually inept players), was a sub. A utility fielder, Jake sat on the bench with Lou Caplan's Bunch. It was a fine, all but cloudless morning, but looking around Jake felt there were too many wives, children, and kibitzers about. Even more ominous, the Filmmakers' First Wives Club or, as Ziggy Alter put it, the Alimony Gallery, was forming, seemingly relaxed but actually fulminating, on the grass behind home plate.

First Al Levine's Team and then Lou Caplan's Bunch, both sides made up mostly of men in their forties, trotted out, sunken bellies quaking, discs suddenly tender, hemorrhoids smarting, to take a turn at fielding and batting practice.

Nate Sugarman, once a classy shortstop, but since his coronary the regular umpire, bit into a digitalis pill, strode onto the field, and called, "Play ball!"

"Let's go, boychick."

"We need a hit," Monty Talman, the producer, hollered.

"*You* certainly do," Bob Cohen, who only yesterday had winced through a rough cut of Talman's latest fiasco, shouted back snidely from the opposite bench.

Manny, hunched over the plate cat-like, trying to look menacing, was knotted with more than his usual fill of anxiety. If he struck out, his own team would not be too upset because it was early in the game, but Lou Caplan, pitching for the first time since his Mexican divorce, would be grateful, and flattering Lou was a good idea because he was rumoured to be ready to go with a three-picture deal for Twentieth; and Manny had not been asked to direct a big-budget film since *Chase. Ball one, inside.* If, Manny thought, I hit a single I will be obliged to pass the time of day with that stomach-turning queen Jason Storm, 1b., who was in London to make a TV pilot film for Ziggy Alter. *Strike one, called.* He had never hit a homer, so that was out, but if come a miracle he connected for a triple, what then? He would be stuck on third sack with Bob Cohen, strictly second featuresville, a born loser, and Manny didn't want to be seen with Bob, even for an inning, especially with so many producers and agents about. K-NACK! *Goddammit, it's a hit! A double, for Chrissake!*

As the players on Al Levine's bench rose to a man, shouting encouragement —

"Go, man. Go."

"Shake the lead out, Manny. Run!"

— Manny, conscious only of Lou Caplan glaring at him ("It's not my fault, Lou"), scampered past first base and took myopic, round-shouldered aim on second, wondering should he say something shitty to Cy Levi, 2b., who he suspected was responsible for getting his name on the blacklist years ago.

Next man up to the plate, C. Bernie Farber, who had signed to write Lou Caplan's first picture for Twentieth, struck out gracefully, which brought up Jimmy Grief. Jimmy swung on the first pitch, lifting it high and foul, and Moey Hanover, c., called for it, feeling guilty because next Saturday Jimmy was flying to Rome and Moey had already arranged to have lunch with Jimmy's wife on Sunday. Moey made the catch, which brought up Al Levine, who homered, bringing in Manny Gordon ahead of him. Monty Talman grounded out to Gross, ss., retiring the side.

Al Levine's Team, first inning: two hits, no errors, two runs.

Leading off for Lou Caplan's Bunch, Bob Cohen smashed a burner to centre for a single and Myer Gross fanned, bringing up Frankie Demaine and sending all the outfielders back, back, back. Frankie whacked the third pitch long and high, an easy fly had Al Levine been playing him deep left instead of inside right, where he was able to flirt hopefully with Manny Gordon's starlet, who was sprawled on the grass there in the shortest of possible Pucci prints. Al Levine was the only man on either team who always played wearing shorts — shorts revealing an elastic bandage which began at his left kneecap and ran almost as low as the ankle.

"Oh, you poor darling," the starlet said, making a face at Levine's knee.

Levine, sucking in his stomach, replied, "Spain," as if he were tossing the girl a rare coin.

"Don't tell me," she squealed. "The beach at Torremolinos. Ugh!"

"No, no," Levine protested. "The civil war, for Chrissake. Shrapnel. Defense of Madrid."

Demaine's fly fell for a homer, driving in a panting Bob Cohen.

Lou Caplan's Bunch, first inning: one hit, one error, two runs.

Neither side scored in the next two innings, which were noteworthy only because Moey Hanover's game began to slip badly. In the second Moey muffed an easy pop fly and actually let C. Bernie Farber, still weak on his legs after a cleansing, all but foodless, week at Forest Mere Hydro, steal a base on him. The problem was clearly Sean Fielding, the young RADA graduate whom Columbia had put under contract because, in profile, he looked like Peter O'Toole. The game had only just started when Moey Hanover's wife, Lilian, had ambled over to Al Levine's bench and stretched herself out on the grass, an offering, beside Fielding, and the two of them had been giggling together and nudging each other ever since, which was making Moey nervy. Moey, however, had not spent his young manhood at a yeshiva to no avail. Not only had he plundered the Old Testament for most of his winning *Rawhide* and *Bonanza* plots, but now that his Lilian was obviously in heat again, his hard-bought Jewish education, which his father had always assured him was priceless, served him splendidly once more. Moey remembered his *David ha' Melech: And it came to pass in the morning, that David wrote a letter to Joab, and sent it by the hand of Uriah. And he wrote in the letter, saying, Set Uriah in the forefront of the hottest battle, and retire ye from him, that he may be smitten, and die.*

Amen.

Lou Caplan yielded two successive hits in the third and Moey Hanover took off his catcher's mask, called for time, and strode to the mound, rubbing the ball in his hands.

"I'm all right," Lou said. "Don't worry. I'm going to settle down now."

"It's not that. Listen, when do you start shooting in Rome?"

"Three weeks tomorrow. You heard something bad?"

"No."

"You're a friend now, remember. No secrets."

"No. It's just that I've had second thoughts about Sean Fielding. I think he's very exciting. He's got lots of appeal. He'd be a natural to play Domingo."

As the two men began to whisper together, players on Al Levine's bench hollered, "Let's go, gang."

"Come on. Break it up, Moey."

Moey returned to the plate, satisfied that Fielding was as good as in Rome already. May he'll do his own stunts, he thought.

"Play ball," Nate Sugarman called.

Alfie Roberts, the director, ordinarily expected soft pitches from Lou, as he did the same for him, but today he wasn't so sure, because on Wednesday his agent had sent him one of Lou's properties to read and — Lou's first pitch made Alfie hit the dirt. That settles it, he thought, my agent already told him it doesn't grab me. Alfie struck out as quickly as he could. Better be put down for a rally-stopper than suffer a head fracture.

Which brought up Manny Gordon again, with one out and runners on first and third. Manny dribbled into a double play, retiring the side.

Multicoloured kites bounced in the skies over the Heath. Lovers strolled on the tow paths and locked together on the grass. Old people sat on benches, sucking in the sun. Nannies passed, wheeling toddlers with titles. The odd baffled Englishman stopped to watch the Americans at play.

"Are they air force chaps?"

"Filmmakers, actually. It's their version of rounders."

"Whatever is that enormous thing that woman is slicing?"

"Salami."

"*On the Heath?*"

"Afraid so. One Sunday they actually set up a bloody folding table, right over there, with cold cuts and herrings and mounds of black bread and a whole bloody side of smoked salmon. *Scotch. Ten and six a quarter, don't you know?*"

"On the Heath?"

"Champagne *in paper cups*. Mumm's. One of them had won some sort of award."

Going into the bottom of the fifth, Al Levine's Team led 6–3, and Tom Hunt came in to play second base for Lou Caplan's Bunch. Hunt, a Negro actor, was in town shooting *Othello X* for Bob Cohen.

Moey Hanover lifted a lazy fly into left field, which Ziggy Alter trapped rolling over and over on the grass until – just before getting up – he was well placed to look up Natalie Calman's skirt. Something he saw there so unnerved him that he dropped the ball, turning pale and allowing Hanover to pull up safely at second.

Johnny Roper walked. Which brought up Jason Storm, to the delight of a pride of British fairies who stood with their dogs on the first-base line, squealing and jumping. Jason poked a bouncer through the infield and floated to second, obliging the fairies and their dogs to move up a base.

With two out and the score tied 7–7 in the bottom half of the sixth, Alfie Roberts was unwillingly retired and a new pitcher came in for Al Levine's Team. It was Gordie Kaufman, a writer blacklisted for years, who now divided his time between Madrid and Rome, asking a hundred thousand dollars a spectacular. Gordie came in to pitch with the go-ahead run on third and Tom Hunt stepping up to the plate for the first time. Big black Tom Hunt, who had once played semi-pro ball in Florida, was a militant. If he homered, Hunt felt he would be put down for another buck nigger, good at games, but if he struck out, which would call for rather more acting skill than was required of him on the set of *Othello X*, what then? He would enable a bunch of fat, foxy, sexually worried Jews to feel big, goysy. Screw them, Hunt thought.

Gordie Kaufman had his problems too. His stunning villa on Mallorca was run by Spanish servants, his two boys were boarding at a reputable British public school, and Gordie himself was president, sole stockholder, and the only employee of a company that was a plaque in Liechtenstein. And yet — and yet — Gordie still subscribed to the *Nation*; he filled his Roman slaves with anti-apartheid dialogue and sagacious Talmudic sayings; and whenever the left-wing *pushke* was passed around he came through with a nice cheque. I must bear down on Hunt, Gordie thought, because if he touches me for even a scratch single I'll come off a patronizing ofay. If he homers, God forbid, I'm a shitty liberal. And so with the count 3 and 2, and a walk, the typical social-democrat's compromise, seemingly the easiest way out for both men, Gordie gritted his teeth, his proud Trotskyite past getting the best of him, and threw a fastball right at Hunt, bouncing it off his head. Hunt threw away his bat and started for the mound, fist clenched, but not so fast that players from both sides couldn't rush in to separate the two men, both of whom felt vindicated, proud, because they had triumphed over impersonal racial prejudice to hit each other as individuals on a fun Sunday on Hampstead Heath.

Come the crucial seventh, the Filmmakers' First Wives Club grew restive, no longer content to belittle their former husbands from afar, and moved in on the baselines and benches, undermining confidence with their heckling. When Myer Gross, for instance, came to bat with two men on base and his teammates shouted, "Go, man. Go," one familiar grating voice floated out over the others. "Hit, Myer. Make your son proud of you, *just this once.*"

What a reproach the first wives were. How steadfast! How unchanging! Still Waiting For Lefty after all these years. Today maybe hair had greyed and chins doubled, necks had gone pruney, breasts drooped, and stomachs dropped, but let no man say these crones had aged in spirit. Where once they had petitioned for the Scotsboro Boys, broken with their families over mixed marriages, sent their boyfriends off to defend Madrid, split with old comrades over the Stalin-Hitler Pact, fought for Henry Wallace, demonstrated for the Rosenbergs, and never, never yielded to McCarthy...today they clapped hands at China Friendship Clubs, petitioned for others to keep hands off Cuba and Vietnam, and made their sons chopped liver sandwiches and sent them off to march to Aldermaston.

The wives, alimonied but abandoned, had known the early struggling years with their husbands, the self-doubts, the humiliations, the rejections, the cold-water flats, and the blacklist, but they had always remained loyal. They hadn't altered, their husbands had.

Each marriage had shattered in the eye of its own self-made hurricane, but essentially the men felt, as Ziggy Alter had once put it so succinctly at the poker table, "Right, wrong, don't be silly, it's really a question of who wants to grow old with Anna Pauker when there are so many juicy little things we can now afford."

So there they were, out on the grass chasing fly balls on a Sunday morning, short men, overpaid and unprincipled, all well within the coronary and lung cancer belt, allowing themselves to look ridiculous in the hope of pleasing their new young wives and girlfriends. There was Ziggy Alter, who had once written a play "with content" for the Group Theater. Here was Al Levine, who used to throw marbles under horses' legs at demonstrations and now raced two horses of his own at Epsom. On the pitcher's mound stood Gordie Kaufman, who had once carried a banner that read *No Pasarán* through the streets of Manhattan and now employed a man especially to keep Spaniards off the beach at his villa on Mallorca.

And sweating under a catcher's mask there was Moey Hanover, who had studied at a yeshiva, stood up to the committee, and was now on a sabbatical from Desilu.

Usually the husbands were able to avoid their used-up wives. They didn't see them in the gaming rooms at the White Elephant or in the Mirabelle or Les Ambassadeurs. But come Brecht to Shaftesbury Avenue and without looking up from the second row centre they could feel them squatting in their cotton bloomers in the second balcony, burning holes in their necks.

And count on them to turn up on a Sunday morning in summer on Hampstead Heath just to ruin a game of fun baseball. Even homering, as Al Levine did, was no answer to the drones.

"It's nice for him, I suppose," a voice behind Levine on the bench observed, "that on the playing field, with an audience, if you know what I mean, he actually appears virile."

The game dragged on. In the eighth inning Jack Monroe had to retire to his Mercedes-Benz for his insulin injection and Jake Hersh, until now an embarrassed sub, finally trotted onto the field. Hersh, thirty-three, one-time relief pitcher for Room 41, Fletcher's Field High (2–7), moved into right field, mindful of his disc condition and hoping he would not be called on to make a tricksy catch. He assumed a loose-limbed stance on the grass, waving at his wife, grinning at his children, when without warning a sizzling line drive came right at him. Jake, startled, did the only sensible thing: he ducked. Outraged shouts and moans from the bench reminded Jake where he was, in a softball game, and he started after the ball.

"Fishfingers."

"*Putz!*"

Runners on first and third started for home as Jake, breathless, finally caught up with the ball. It had rolled to a stop under a bench where a nanny sat watching over an elegant perambulator.

"Excuse me," Jake said.

"Americans," the nurse said.

"I'm a Canadian," Jake protested automatically, fishing the ball out from under the bench.

Three runs scored. Jake caught a glimpse of Nancy, unable to contain her laughter. The children looked ashamed of him.

In the ninth inning with the score tied again, 11–11, Sol Peters, another sub, stepped cautiously to the plate for Lou Caplan's Bunch. The go-ahead run was on second and there was only one out. Gordie Kaufman, trying to prevent a bunt, threw right at him and Sol, forgetting he was wearing his contact lenses, held the bat in front of him to protect his glasses. The ball hit the bat and rebounded for a perfectly laid down bunt.

"Run, you shmock."

"Go, man."

Sol, terrified, ran, carrying the bat with him.

Monty Talman phoned home.

"Who won?" his wife asked.

"We did. 13–12. But that's not the point. We had lots of fun."

"How many you bringing back for lunch?"

"Eight."

"*Eight?*"

"I couldn't get out of inviting Johnny Roper. He knows Jack Monroe is coming."

"I see."

"A little warning. Don't, for Chrissake, ask Cy how Marsha is. They're separating. And I'm afraid Manny Gordon is coming with a girl. I want you to be nice to her."

"*Anything else?*"

If Gershon phones from Rome while the guys are there please remember I'm taking the call upstairs. And please don't start collecting glasses and ashtrays at four o'clock. It's embarrassing. Bloody Jake Hersh is coming and it's just the sort of incident he'd pick on and joke about for months."

"I never coll —"

"All right, all right. Oh, shit, something else. Tom Hunt is coming."

"The actor?"

"Yeah. Now listen, he's very touchy, so will you please put away

Sheila's doll."

"Sheila's doll?"

"If she comes in carrying that bloody golliwog I'll die. Hide it. Burn it. Hunt gets script approval these days, you know."

"All right, dear."

"See you soon."

— St Urbain's Horseman, pp. 238–49

"YOU'LL FIND THIS IS A GOOD STORY FOR YOU," he said. "A real Canadian success story."

The party at the other end of the line was Ben Weider, president of the International Federation of Body Builders, who was sponsoring the Official Combination Contests to Select Mr. America and Mr. Universe at the Monument National Theatre, in Montreal, in 1960. The competition, according to advance publicity, was going to be the "Greatest Physical Culture Contest ever organized anyplace in the World!"

"I've been to eighty-four countries in the last six years," Weider told me, "including Red China. But I'm not a communist, you know."

Weider was a man of many offices. He was, with his brother Joe, the Trainer of Champions, with outlets in cities as far-flung as Tokyo, Rio de Janeiro, and Vienna. He was president and director of Weider Food Supplements (makers of Super Protein 90 and Energex) and the Weider Barbell Company, and managing editor of *Mr. America* and *Muscle Builder,* among other magazines. He was the author of such books as *MANGEZ BIEN et restez svelte* and *JEUNE toute sa vie.* In one of his many inspirational articles, "The Man Who Began Again," he wrote, "True sportsmen always cheer for the under-dog…for the guy who has come up from down under — the hard way," and that's certainly how Ben Weider had risen to eminence as manufacturer, publisher, author, editor, world traveller, and number one purveyor of muscle-building equipment and correspondence courses in North America.

Weider was only thirty-six years old. His brother Joe, who ran the American end of their various enterprises out of Union City, New Jersey, was thirty-nine. They had both been brought up in Montreal's

St. Urbain Street area during the thirties. Skinny, underdeveloped boys, they first took to body development as a form of self-improvement. Then, in 1939, they began to write and publish a mimeographed magazine that would tell others how they could become he-men. To begin with, the magazine had a circulation of five hundred copies. Enthusiasts started to write in to ask where they could get the necessary equipment to train themselves. And so, from their modest offices on Colonial Street, the Weiders began to supply the desired equipment and correspondence courses until, Ben Weider said, they became the acknowledged leaders in the field. *Muscle Builder* and *Mr. America*, no longer mimeographed, now appeared monthly in ten languages with, Weider claimed, a total circulation of a million copies.

In May 1960, Ben Weider moved into his own building on Bates Road, from which he overlooked his widespread empire in the comfort of a most luxurious office. For inspiration, perhaps, there hung behind Weider's desk a painting of a resolute Napoleon, sword drawn, mounted atop a bucking stallion. It was here, amid trophies, diplomas, and the odd bottle of Quick-Wate (Say Goodbye to Skinny Weakness), that we had our first chat.

"Why don't you send me a chapter from your next novel," Weider offered, "and we could shove it into *Muscle Builder* or *Mr. America*. It ought to win you a lot of new readers."

Yes, possibly. But, alas, I had to let on, I had never been considered A BIG HITTER by the muscle-building set.

Weider looked at me severely.

Later, once I had read some of his correspondence courses, I realized that he had probably spotted my inferiority complex. I was not thinking BIG, *positive* thoughts. "DON'T BE ENVIOUS OF SOMEONE ELSE'S SUCCESS," brother Joe advised people who felt inferior. "MAYBE SOMEONE ELSE ENVIES YOU! They are bald...*you have a head full of hair*. They are fat...*you are building a he-man body*."

Weider was a soft-spoken, courteous, ever-smiling man ("YOUR TEETH," Joe wrote, "ARE THE JEWELS OF YOUR FACE") with a high-pitched voice. A conservative dresser, he had surely grasped, just as Joe advised in BE POPULAR, SELF-CONFIDENT, AND A

HE-MAN, that it was necessary to MAKE YOUR FIRST IMPRESSION A GOOD ONE! Why? Because, as Joe said, *your packaging is your appearance.* Another thing was that Ben had chosen his hairstyle wisely. *It fitted his face!* He was not the sort of birdbrain Joe complained about who wore his hair in, say, a Flat-Top Crew Cut, just because "it's what everybody else is wearing now."

Weider, married in 1959, had recently become a father. His boy, he told me, weighed ten pounds eleven ounces at birth. *He was also twenty-three inches long!*

"CONGRATULATIONS!!!" I said, grasping his hand *firmly*. And, even as we parted, I made a note to remember his name, for…"people like to be called by name…. You can make yourself a real *somebody* by being known as the one man who never forgets names."

At home, I had time to read only one of Weider's correspondence lessons before going to bed. My choice was *Secrets of a Healthy Sex Life*.

Choosing the right girl, brother Joe wrote, was vitally important. "*Is she sports-minded?*" he asks. "Would she frown on you having your own home gym? DOES SHE LIKE WORKING OUT WITH YOU?"

Weider also suggested that young couples should pray together, use a good deodorant and positive thinking, and keep their weight *normalized*. He offered sensible advice to young husbands. "Wear clean pyjamas each night…and be sure that you have a variety of patterns in pyjamas. You would not expect her to retire in a torn nightgown with cold cream daubed over her face…hence you should make yourself as attractive as she."

All in all, *Secrets* gave me plenty of food for thought. It seemed a good idea to absorb its message before plunging into other, more advanced lessons, like *How to Get the Most Out of People*, although this particular pamphlet looked most intriguing. The illustration on the cover showed an assured, smiling young man grasping piles of dollar bills, coins, and money bags. I was keen to learn from him how to use people, but one BIG, *positive* thought was enough for one day. So, putting the lessons aside, I turned to *Muscle Builder*. There I read that Chuck Sipes, a recent Mr. America champion, had built his TERRIFIC muscles by using the Weider Concentration Principle.

Contestants in the 1950 Mr. Universe competition in London.

introduce Dr. Tilney. "The doctor," he said, "has travelled all over the world and is one of the most famous editors and writers in it."

"Well, then," Dr. Tilney said, "I'm sure all you washed-out, weak, worn-out, suffering, sickly men want to renew your youth and delay that trip to the underground bungalow."

A body builder came out and struck a classic pose.

Dr. Tilncy beamed at us. "We have assembled here some of the finest examples of manhood in the world. We are building a new race of muscular marvels, greater than the Greek gods. We're doing it scientifically."

Mr. Ireland assumed a heroic pose.

"You too," Dr. Tilney told us, "can develop a physique like Bill Cook's and overcome constipation, hernia, hardening of the arteries, diarrhea, heart disease, tuberculosis, rheumatism, and so forth."

We were introduced to Ed Theriault and his eight-year-old son, who demonstrated the Weider Chest Expander.

"This man here," the doctor said, "is the strongest short man in the world. He can do it — so can you! And look at this boy here. Isn't he sensational? Body building is one of the finest means of overcoming delinquency. If the kid's in the gym he's not in the poolroom. Why, I'm sure none of you want your boy to grow up a skinny runt — puny! You want him to be a real Weider he-man!"

Some other men came out to demonstrate weightlifting.

"And just look at the fine equipment, Weider equipment," the doctor said. "Guaranteed to last a lifetime. No parts to break. Isn't it something? And I have news for you. Eaton's is going to make this beautiful equipment available to you on their wonderful convenient time-payment plan. Isn't that something?"

Ben Weider applauded.

"You men out there," the doctor said, "want to have the bodies the Creator meant you to have, don't you?"

Mr. Scotland Sr. asked if he could say a few words.

"Sure."

"I just wanted to tell you," he said, "that I'm glad to be in your city, it's a wonderful opportunity, and I think body building is marvellous."

"Isn't that sensational?" Dr. Tilney said.

Chuck Sipes, the former Mr. America, came out and bent some enormous nails. He asked for a hotwater bottle and blew it up and exploded it just like a child's balloon.

"He's demonstrating wonderful lung power," Dr. Tilney said.

Chuck said he'd like to tear a telephone book for us.

"You'll notice," the doctor said, "that he's starting on the real tough end, the bound end of the book."

Chuck pulled, he grimaced, he grunted, he pulled again.

"A lot of you folks have heard body builders are musclebound. Well, you just watch Chuck here demonstrate…"

Chuck couldn't tear the book. He apologized, explaining that his hands were still greasy from having rubbed so much olive oil on his chest before posing for us.

"See you on Sunday at the Monument National," Dr. Tilney said.

The crowd began to disperse. I went home to study Weider's magazines and correspondence courses and to read up on Dr. Tilney, in anticipation of the grand contest on Sunday.

—*Dispatches from the Sporting Life,*
"A Real Canadian Success Story," pp. 43–50

THERE WERE, I'D SAY, only about four thousand fans at the Forum for the occasion. Many of the older men still wore their working clothes. The teenagers, however, favoured black leather jackets, their names implanted with steel studs on the back. The most engaging of the preliminary performers was Tiger Tomasso, an uncouth villain who not only eye-gouged and kicked below the belt but also bit into his opponent's shoulder when aroused.

Before the main bout, a precautionary net was tied around the ring. This was necessary because Kowalski, a strapping six feet seven, is, all the same, a most bashful performer, given to fleeing the ring when the going gets rough. Not only that. Struck the slightest blow, he tends to whine and even plead for mercy from his opponent. Even so, the wily Pole made short work of the golden-haired Nature Boy and won the coveted championship belt. This was a popular win with all us non-Anglo Saxons.

The next afternoon, back in the modest offices of Canadian Athletic Promotions, Kowalski told me, "I indulge in lots of histrionics in the ring. I shout, I snarl, I jump up and down like a madman. Am I mad? I earn more than $50,000 a year."

Kowalski told me that he used to work on the Ford assembly line in Windsor for $50 a week. He was paid more than that for his first wrestling match in Detroit and quickly realized that he was in the wrong business. A top performer in 1960, Kowalski wrestled three times a week, usually for a percentage of the gate, and lived with his brother and sister-in-law in a house he had recently bought in Montreal. He was thirty-three years old and expected to be able to go on wrestling until he reached his mid-forties. Meanwhile, against that retirement day, Kowalski had been investing his money in securities.

"I've built up a personality," he said, "a product, and that's what I sell. Ted Williams is no different. Why do you think he spat at the crowd that day? It's showmanship. Everything is showmanship today. Richard Nixon has his act and I have mine." Kowalski bent over and showed me a scar on his head. "Last week in Chicago," he said, "after I'd won a match, my opponent hit me over the head with a chair. You think he wanted to hurt me? He wanted to make an impression, that's all."

Norman Olson, who had joined us earlier, now began to stir anxiously. "You're forgetting that wrestling takes a lot of natural ability," he said.

"Sure," Kowalski said.

"You've got to keep in shape."

"The most dangerous thing," Kowalski said, "are those crazy kids. They come to the matches with clothespin guns and sometimes they shoot rusty nails at us. Once one got embedded in my side." Kowalski also pointed out that young performers, taking part in their first big match, are also a threat. "They're so nervous," he said, "they might do something wrong."

I asked Kowalski if there was any animosity among wrestlers.

"No," he said.

"Tell him about the night here when you ripped off Yukon Eric's ear," Olson said gleefully.

"Well," Kowalski said, "one of my specialties is to climb up on the ropes and jump up and down on my opponent. One night Eric slipped aside, trying to avoid me, and I landed on his ear, ripping it off. He was very upset and he fled to his dressing room. Before long the dressing room was full of reporters and relatives and fans. Finally Eric looked up and asked for his ear. He'd forgotten it in the ring. The referee had picked it up, put it in his pocket, and by this time was showing it to all his friends at the other end of the Forum. When they got it back from him it was too late to sew it on again."

—*Dispatches from the Sporting Life,* "Eddie Quinn," pp. 133–35

TURNED TO THE Montreal *Gazette* sport pages first, a lifelong habit. No joy. The fumblebum Canadiens, no longer *nos glorieux*, had disgraced themselves again, losing 5–1 to — wait for it — The Mighty Ducks of California. Toe Blake must be spinning in his grave. In his day only one of this inept bunch of millionaires could have played in the NHL, never mind suiting up for the once-legendary *Club de hockey canadien*. They don't have one guy willing to stand in front of the net, lest he take a hit. Oh for the days when Larry Robinson would feed a long lead pass to Guy Lafleur, lifting us out of our seats chanting, "Guy! Guy! Guy!" as he went flying in all alone on the nets. *He shoots, he scores.*

—*Barney's Version,* p. 51

1943–44. COUSINS AND OLDER BROTHERS were overseas, battling through Normandy or Italy, and each day's *Star* brought a casualty list. Others, blessed with a nice little heart murmur, stayed home, making more money than they had ever dreamed of, moving into Outremont. But most of us still lingered on St. Urbain Street, and we seldom got to see a hockey game. Our parents were not disposed to treat us, for the very understandable reason that it wouldn't help us to become doctors. Besides, looked at closely, come playoff time it was always our pea-soups, which is what we used to call French Canadians in those days, against their — that is to say, Toronto's — English-speaking roughnecks. What did it have to do with us? Plenty, plenty. For, much to our parents' dismay, we talked hockey incessantly and played whenever we could. Not on skates, which we also couldn't afford, but out on the streets with proper sticks and a puck or, failing that, a piece of coal. Saturday nights we huddled around the radio, playing blackjack for dimes and nickels, our eyes on the cards, our ears on the score. And the man who scored most often was Maurice Richard, once, memorably, with an opposing defenseman

The Rocket scores, 1953.

riding his back, and another time, in a playoff game against Toronto, putting the puck in the net five times. Then, in 1944–45, Richard accomplished what no other player had done before, scoring fifty goals in a fifty-game season.

I only got to see the great Richard twice. Saving money earned collecting bills for a neighbourhood butcher on Sunday mornings, my friends and I bought standing-room tickets for the millionaires' section. And then, flinging our winter caps ahead of us, we vaulted barriers, eventually working our way down to ice level. Each time we jumped a barrier, hearts thumping, we tossed our caps ahead of us, because if an officious usher grabbed us by the scruff of the neck, as often happened, we could plead, teary-eyed, that some oaf had tossed our cap down and we were only descending to retrieve it.

—*Home Sweet Home,* "The Fall of the Montreal Canadiens," pp. 189–90

I CAN REMEMBER EXACTLY where I was on VE-Day, on the day John F. Kennedy was shot, and when the first man landed on the moon. If I can't recall what I was doing on the day Stalin died, I do remember that a journalist I know was in the elevator of the *Montreal Star* building the morning after. Ascending, she turned to a neighbour and said, "Stalin died."

The elevator operator overheard. "Oh my God, that's terrible," he said. "Which floor did he work on?"

The point I'm trying to make is that on days that shook the world, or my world, at any rate, I was never on the spot until the night of September 2, 1972, when Team Canada tested our belief in God, the free-enterprise system, and the virility of the Canadian male by taking on the Russians at the Montreal Forum in the first of an eight-game series. A series, Tim Burke wrote in the *Gazette*, that the Canadian public viewed as something of a political Armageddon. Going into the contest we were more than overconfident — with pity our hearts were laden. The pathetic Russian players had to lug their own equipment. Their skates were shoddy. The players themselves had names appropriate to a plumbing firm working out of Winnipeg's North End, but otherwise unpronounceable: Vasiliev, Liapkin, Maltsev, Mikhailov, Kharmalov, Yakushev, and, oh yes, Tretiak. Everybody but John Robertson, then with the *Montreal Star*, predicted that our champions would win all the games handily or, at worst, might drop a game in Russia. A matter of *noblesse oblige*. Robertson called for the USSR to win the series six games to two. On the other hand, Alan Eagleson, one of the organizers of the series, ventured, "Anything less than an unblemished sweep of the Russians would bring shame down on the heads of the players and the national pride."

After Ypres, following Dieppe, Team Canada and our very own belated St. Crispin's Day. Brad, Rod, Guy, Yvan, Frank, and Serge, once more unto the breach, once more for Canada and the NHL.

> From this day to the ending of the world,
> But we in it shall be remember'd;
> We few, we happy few, we band of brothers...

We were only thirty seconds into the fray at the Forum when Phil Esposito scored. Some six minutes later, Paul Henderson, taking a pass from Bobby Clarke, scored again. But the final count, as we all know, was Communism 7, Free Enterprise 3. And our players were booed more than once in the Forum, ostensibly for taking cheap shots at the Russians as they flew past but actually for depriving us of one of our most cherished illusions. We already knew that our politicians lied and that our bodies would be betrayed by age, but we had not suspected that our hockey players were anything but the very best. If Team Canada finally won the series, Paul Henderson scoring one of hockey's most dramatic goals at 19:26 of the third period in the last game in Moscow, the moral victory clearly belonged to Russia. After the series, nothing was ever the same again in Canada. Beer didn't taste as good. The Rockies seemed smaller, the northern lights dimmer. Our last-minute win came more in the nature of a relief than a triumph.

After the storm, a drizzle. Which is to say, the endless NHL season that followed was tainted, revealed as a parochial affair, and the Stanley Cup itself, once our Holy Grail, seemed suddenly a chalice of questionable distinction. So, alas, it remains. For the Russians continue to be the dominant force in real hockey, international hockey, with the Czechs and Swedes not far behind.

But when I was a boy, and the Russians were still learning how to skate, the major league was right here. And furthermore, the most dashing and aesthetically pleasing team to watch, in the old vintage six-team league, was our own unrivalled Montreal Canadiens. *Les Canadiens sont là!*

—*Dispatches from the Sporting Life,*
"The Fall of the Montreal Canadiens," pp. 246–48

CLEARLY, HE CAME FROM GOOD STOCK. Interviewed on television in 1979, his eighty-seven-year-old father was asked, "How do you feel?"

"I feel fine."

"At what time in life does a man lose his sexual desires?"

"You'll have to ask somebody older than I am."

His son was only five when he acquired his first pair of skates. He repeated the third grade, more intent on his wrist shot than reading, developing it out there in the subzero wheat fields, shooting frozen horse buns against the barn door. When he was a mere fourteen-year-old, working in summer on a Saskatoon construction site with his father's crew, both his strength and determination were already celebrated. He could pick up ninety-pound cement bags in either hand, heaving them easily. Preparing for what he knew lay ahead, he sat at the kitchen table night after night, practising his autograph.

Gordie Howe was born in Floral, Saskatchewan, in 1928, a child of prairie penury, and his hockey career spanned thirty-two seasons in five decades. The stuff of legend.

Gordie.

For as long as I have been a hockey fan, Mr. Elbows has been out there, skating, his stride seemingly effortless. The big guy with the ginger-ale-bottle shoulders. I didn't always admire him. But as he grew older and hockey players apparently younger, many of them younger than my oldest son, he became an especial pleasure. My God, only three years older than me, and still out there chasing pucks. For middle-aged Canadians, there was hope. In a world of constant and often bewildering change, there was one shining certitude. Come October, the man for whom time had stopped would be out there, not taking dirt from anybody.

Gordie, Gordie, the old fart's champion.

—Dispatches from the Sporting Life, "Gordie," pp. 167–68

UNLIKE THE ROCKET, Bobby Hull, Bobby Orr, and Guy Lafleur, Howe always lacked one dimension. He couldn't lift fans out of their seats, hearts thumping, charged with expectation, merely by taking a pass and streaking down the ice. The most capable all-round player the game may have known was possibly deficient in only one thing — star quality. But my oh my, he certainly could get things done. In the one-time rivalry between Detroit and Montreal, two games linger in the mind — but first a few words from Mr.

Elbows himself on just how bright that rivalry burned during those halcyon years.

"Hockey's different today, isn't it? The animosity is gone. *I mean, we didn't play golf with referees and linesmen.* Why, in the old days with the Red Wings, I remember once we and the Canadiens were travelling to a game in Detroit on the same train. We were starving, but their car was between ours and the diner, and there was no way we were going to walk through there. We waited until the train stopped in London and we walked around the Canadiens' car to eat."

Gordie Howe scored his thousandth goal at age 49.

Going into a game in Detroit against the Canadiens, on October 27, 1963, Howe had 543 goals, one short of the retired Rocket's then-record of 544. The aroused Canadiens, determined not to allow Howe to score a landmark goal against them, designated Henri Richard his brother's recordkeeper, setting his line against Howe's again and again. But in the third period Howe, who had failed to score in three previous games, made his second shot of the night a good one. He deflected a goalmouth pass past Gump Worsley to tie the record. Howe, then thirty-five, did not score again for two weeks, until the Canadiens came to town once more. Again they put everything into stopping Howe. But in the second period, *with Montreal on the power play,* Detroit's Billy McNeil sailed down the ice with the puck, Howe trailing. As they swept in on the Canadiens' net, Howe took the puck and flipped a fifteen-foot shot past Charlie Hodge, breaking the Rocket's record, one he would later improve on by 127 NHL goals.

Item: In 1960, there was a reporter sufficiently brash to ask Howe when he planned to retire. Blinking, as is his habit, he replied, "I don't want to retire, because you stay retired for an awfully long time."

Twenty years later, on June 4, 1980, Howe stepped up to the podium at the Hartford Hilton and reluctantly announced his retirement. "I think I have another half year in me, but it's always nice to keep something in reserve." The one record he was terribly proud of, he added, "is the longevity record."

Thirty-two years.

And just possibly we were unfair to him for most of those years. True, he eventually became an institution. Certainly he won all the glittering prizes. But true veneration always eluded Howe. Even in his glory days he generated more respect, sometimes even grudging at that, than real excitement. Outside of the West, where he ruled supreme, he was generally regarded as the ultimate pro (say, like his good friend of the Detroit years, Tiger outfielder Al Kaline), but not a player possessed. Like the Rocket.

In good writing, Hemingway once ventured, only the tip of the iceberg shows. Put another way, authentic art doesn't advertise. Possibly that was the trouble with Gordie on ice. During his vintage years, you seldom noticed the flash of elbows, only the debris they left behind. He never seemed *that* fast, but somehow he got there first. He didn't wind up to shoot, like so many of today's golfers, but next time the goalie dared to peek, the puck was behind him.

With hindsight, I'm prepared to allow that Gordie may not only have been a better all-round player than the Rocket but maybe the more complete artist as well. The problem could have been the fans, myself included, who not only wanted art to be done but wanted to see it being done. We also required it to look hard, not all just in a day's work.

—*Dispatches from the Sporting Life,* "Gordie," pp. 172–74

Edmontonians were not pleased by the following incidental description of their city.

IF CANADA WERE NOT A COUNTRY, however fragmented, but instead a house, Vancouver would be the solarium-cum-playroom, an afterthought of affluence; Toronto, the counting room, where money makes for the most glee; Montreal, the salon; and Edmonton, the boiler room. There is hardly a tree to be seen downtown, nothing to delight the eye on Jasper Avenue. On thirty-below-zero nights, grim religious zealots loom on street corners, speaking in tongues, and intrepid hookers in miniskirts rap on the windows of cars that have stopped for traffic. There isn't a first-class restaurant anywhere in town. For all that, Edmontonians are a truly admirable lot. They have not only endured great hardships in the past but also continue to suffer an abominable climate as well as isolation from the cities of light. And to some degree, like other Westerners, they thrive on resentments against the grasping, self-satisfied East, which has exploited their natural resources for years, taking their oil and gas at cut prices to subsidize inefficient Ontario and Quebec industries.

Insults, injuries.

For as long as Edmontonians can remember, the biggies were elsewhere. Though they had contributed many fine hockey players to the game, they could only hear about their feats on radio or later see them on television. Hockey was *their* game, damn it, *their* national sport, but New York, Chicago, Detroit, and Boston were in the NHL long before the league's governors adjudged Edmonton not so much worthy as potentially profitable. But in 1984, Canada's hockey shrines were either in decline, as was then the case in Montreal, or in total disrepute, as in Toronto. In those glory days, if Easterners wanted to see the best player in the game more than twice a season, if they wanted to catch a dynasty in the making, why, then, they had to pack their fat coats and fur-lined boots and head for Edmonton, home of the Stanley Cup champions and the Great Gretzky himself.

—*Dispatches from the Sporting Life,* "Gretzky in Eighty-five," pp. 108–09

Barney Panofsky is the fictional character whose passion for hockey,
combined with his more obviously admirable cultural attainments,
struck one reviewer as unbelievable.

ACTUALLY, I HAVE MADE IT MY BUSINESS to find work for
Solange in just about everything done by Totally Unnecessary
Productions Ltd., going back to the seventies. Sixty-something
years old now, still nervously thin, she persists in dressing like an
ingenue but otherwise is the most admirable of women. Her husband, a gifted set designer, was taken out by a massive heart attack
in his early thirties, and Solange has brought up, and seen to the
education of, her daughter, the indomitable Chantal, my personal
assistant. Saturday nights, providing the new, improved, no-talent,
chickenshit Canadiens are in town, each one a multimillionaire,
Solange and I eat an early dinner at Pauzé's, and then repair to the
Forum, where once *nos glorieux* were just about invincible. My God, I
remember when all they had to do was to leap over the boards in
those red-and-white sweaters and the visiting team was a goner.
Those, those were the days. Fire-wagon hockey. Soft but accurate
passes. Fast-as-lightning wrist shots. Defencemen who could hit.
And no ear-piercing rock music played at 10,000 decibels while a
face-off was held up for a TV commercial.

Anyway, it now seems that my traditional if increasingly exas-
perating Saturday night out with Solange is threatened. I'm told I
behaved like a hooligan again last Saturday night, embarrassing
her. My alleged offence happened during the third period. The effete
Canadiens, already down 4–1 to the Ottawa Senators, for Chrissake,
were on their so-called power play, scrambly, a minute gone and yet
to manage a shot on the nets. Savage, that idiot, passed to an open
wing, enabling a slo-mo Ottawa defenceman, a journeyman who
would have been lucky to make the QSHL in the old days, to ice the
puck. Turgeon collected it, glided to centre ice, and golfed it into
the corner, Damphouse and Savage scrambling after, throwing up
snow just short of the mêlée. "Goddamn that Turgeon," I hollered,

"with his contract, he's earning something like a hundred thousand a goal. Béliveau was never paid more than fifty thousand dollars* for the whole season and he wasn't afraid to carry the puck over the blue line."

"Yes, I know," said Solange, rolling her eyes. "And Doug Harvey never made more than fifteen a year here."

"I told you that. You didn't know it."

"I'm not denying you told me that, I don't know how many times. Now will you please be quiet and stop making an exhibition of yourself."

"Look at that! Nobody parked in front of the net, because he might have to take an elbow. We'll be lucky if Ottawa doesn't score another short-handed goal. Shit! Fuck!"

"Barney, please."

"They ought to trade Koivu for another Finnish midget," I said, joining in the chorus of boos.

A no-name Senator hopped out of the penalty box, gathered in the puck, skated in all alone on our petrified goalie, who naturally went down too soon, and lifted one over his blocker arm. Five–one Ottawa. Disgusted fans began to cheer the visitors. Programs were thrown on the ice. I yanked off my rubbers and aimed them at Turgeon.

"Barney, control yourself."

"Shettup."

"I beg your pardon?"

"How am I supposed to concentrate on the game with your non-stop chattering?"

— *Barney's Version,* pp. 121–23

ONCE JIM HAD ANCHORED at their first drop, out of sight of the others, Moses started out with a Silver Doctor, went to a Green Highlander, and then a Muddler without getting anything to rise. Things were no better on the second drop. On the third drop they saw a big salmon roll and another leap, maybe thirty feet out. Moses laid

* In 1970–71, his last season with the Canadiens, Béliveau was actually paid $100,000.

every fly he could think of over their heads, but they weren't taking. Then there came a hollering and a squealing from the Fence Pool. "It's probably only a grilse they got," Jim said.

A half hour passed and then the deer flies came out and it began to drizzle. Covering the far fast water, stripping his line quickly, Moses got his strike. A big fish, maybe thirty pounds, taking so hard Moses didn't even have to set the hook, his rod already bent double. Immediately the line screeched and the fish shot downriver, taking most of Moses's backing before it paused and he started to reel in the slack. Jim lifted anchor and began to paddle gently toward shore, his net within reach. The fish came close enough to look at the canoe and raced downriver again, breaking water about fifty feet out. Flipping in the air. Dancing on its tail.

"Hey there, Moses. Hey there."

The fish struck for the bottom and Moses imagined it down there, outraged, rubbing its throbbing jaw against the gravel, trying to dislodge the hook. It couldn't, obviously, so it gave in to bad temper, flying out of the boiling water once more, shaking its angry head, diving, then resting deep, maybe pondering tactics. After Moses had played the fish for another twenty minutes, he heard and then saw the others in their canoes returning from their pools. Approaching Vince's Hole, Gilles and Len both cut their outboards back sharply, as courtesy required, but not Armand, whom Barney had instructed to actually accelerate into the opposite bank before killing his engine. Frank Zappa bounced over the water at God knows how many decibels. Cursing, Moses reeled the fish in close. It was lying on its side on the surface now, panting desperately, but good for one more run. Moses vacillated only briefly before leading the exhausted fish toward the net. And that's when Mary Lou stood up to take pictures, her flash attachment exploding again and again. Distracted, Moses didn't notice his line tangling round the butt of his rod. The fish bolted, running his line taut and jerking free of the hook. Moses's rod sprung upright, his line going slack.

"Well now," Barney said, "like the old hands say: it's more difficult than you think."

—Solomon Gursky Was Here, pp. 274–75

A couple of days later I met Sipes at the Mount Royal Studio, where he had come to train for the approaching contest.

"Been in weightlifting a long time?" I asked.

"Yeah."

"Like it?"

"Yeah."

"Enjoying your stay in Montreal?"

"Yeah."

Sipes managed a gym in Sacramento, California. He told me that when he started lifting weights eight years ago he had been just another puny guy of some 165 pounds, but now he weighed in at 204. I wished him luck in the contest and went on to chat with Mr. Ireland, Mr. Bombay, and Mr. Hercules of India, all fine fellows. But the man who made the greatest impression on me was Mr. Scotland Sr., otherwise known as R. G. Smith, of the electricity board in Edinburgh. Smith, who was to become my friend, had come to Montreal both to visit his children and to enter the contest — not that he had the slightest chance of winning. Smith was fifty-four years old. He had begun to practice body building at forty-seven.

The body builders' exhibition was held on Eaton's fourth floor on the Friday night before the contest. There was a good turnout. Some three to four hundred people, I'd say. An associate of Weider's introduced me to Dr. Frederick Tilney, who had flown in from Florida to be one of the contest judges. "Dr. Tilney," the man said, "has seven degrees."

The doctor, a sturdily built man in his mid-sixties, looked surprisingly young for his years.

"Can you tell me," I asked, "at what colleges you got your degrees?"

"What's the difference what college? A college is a college. Some college graduates end up digging ditches. It's what you make of yourself that counts in this world."

"What exactly do you do, Doctor?"

"Oh, I lecture on health and success and that sort of stuff."

Suddenly Ben Weider was upon us. "Sorry to interrupt your interview," he said, "but the show must go on."

A young French-Canadian body builder mounted the platform to

CHANNEL-SURFING one summer evening in our cottage in the Eastern Townships, only a couple of weeks before I would finally get together with Thorburn in Toronto, I caught a snooker trick-shot exhibition on a sports channel. Willie Thorne attempted to enliven his performance with a tired line of patter and Thorburn, next man up, earned only sporadic laughter with his equally banal repertoire of knee-slappers. The contest was tiresome, even embarrassing. The truth is, most champions past their prime are strangers to dignity. I once saw Jack Dempsey referee a wrestling match in the Montreal Forum, threatening Gorgeous George with a theatrical fist for fighting dirty, the wrestler obligingly falling to his knees, pleading for mercy. Plangent Joe Louis lived long enough to serve as a greeter in a Piccadilly nightclub. Maurice "The Rocket" Richard used to do Grecian Formula hair-colour commercials on TV. Where is Joe DiMaggio now that we need him, Paul Simon asked in that famous song, and when he finally met DiMaggio, the baffled ballplayer responded, "I haven't disappeared. I'm doing Mr. Coffee commercials." Multimillionaire Wayne Gretzky, still a young man, will do TV promos for just about any product that will have him, except, so far, Tampax. So clap hands for Ted Williams and Sandy Koufax and Jean Béliveau, who have never been seen peddling.

— *On Snooker*, pp. 104–05

The flip side of this cultural refinement is
that the brothel, or cat-house, will yield
to the library as the forbidden place where
sinners meet to tryst (unzipping or lowering
panties, to converse grammatically) under
constant threat of closure by the antiliteracy
squad. And the new social disease will be
intelligence. Remember, you read it here first.

PART VI

I'M GIVEN TO WRITING LOVE STORIES

Speaking of the fictional character Barney Panofsky (Barney's Version), Richler once explained that he was "given to writing love stories," and it's true: There is a romantic strain running through Richler's fiction. This tendency is offset by humour, and by the frank acknowledgment of the power of sex untainted by love. But there is also a biographical arc to these expressions: the younger Richler is more apt to dwell on raw desire; the more mature writer expatiates on the rewards of matrimony.

Richler is not Barney. Richler, however, did lead a Bohemian life in the 1950s. He first lived with, and then married, Cathy Boudreau in London, in 1954. The marriage came unstuck when he fell in love with Florence Wood, a model, actress, and the wife of a friend. Both couples separated from their first spouses, and Mordecai and Florence were married in Montreal in 1960. It was, by all accounts, an extraordinarily strong and happy union.

— J. W.

"WELL, YEAH. RIGHT. You know what these days are?"

"Cold."

"No, no. Anybody knows that. If you're Jewish, but."

"Colder."

"Oh, very funny. Ha ha."

"What then, Daddy?"

"These are the Days of Awe. Tomorrow is Rosh Hashonna, our new year, and like a week later it's Yom Kippur, when if you shit on anybody during the year you got a legal right to repent. And God forgives you. We're going to the synagogue in the morning, you know."

"Aw, Daddy."

"Aw, Daddy, nothing. We're going for once. It's only proper, Josh. We're Hebes, you and me, and don't you forget it."

Joshua and his father were sitting together in the backyard. On a clammy October morning in 1946, the sky a shimmering blue, the swirling leaves already slick with frost. His father had asked him to help put up the double windows. But once Joshua had followed him into the rotting grey shed to help sort them out, he produced a quart of Labatt's ale and two glasses and invited him to continue out into the yard. They settled down together on a squishy old sofa, long abandoned, bleeding stuffing where it had once been slashed with razors or where the rats had gnawed into it.

"How old are you now?"

"Fifteen."

"Already? Well, yeah. Right. It's certainly time we talked."

"About what?" Joshua asked.

Reuben shot him his most solemn look. "About fucking, and the Jewish tradition."

"In that order?"

"Don't get smart with me or I'll land you a good one."

"Aw, Daddy, you never hit me once."

"Well, I shoulda, maybe. You shouldn't be talking about quitting school, it's a shame."

His father was fidgety, embarrassed, and in his hand, Joshua saw, he now held a Bible. The real thing. The King James Version. His copy had markers sticking out here, there, and everywhere.

"Hey, Daddy, don't tell me you've been reading *that*."

"Why not?" he replied, indignant.

Joshua slapped his cheek and whistled.

"Listen here," his father said, "let's not get excited. There's no need for you to lose your temper. Tell me, you really want to be a newspaperman, or is it just that, you know, like you once thought you'd be a ballplayer?"

"Well, yeah. I dunno. A sportswriter, maybe."

"Sportswriters are drunks. They're bums, every one of them," Reuben said, remembering old grievances.

"I could be different, but."

"Let me tell you something," his father said, brandishing his Bible with enthusiasm, "this thing here is just filled with book titles and savvy sayings. I mean, I used to think, you were a writer you had to make things up out of your own head, but you'd be surprised how many of their titles and sayings were swiped out of this one here, and there's plenty left, so you could do a lot worse than —"

"Why don't we talk about fucking first?"

"What did you have in mind?"

"Me? Nothing. You're the one who brought it up."

"Yeah, well. Right. You know how it's done?"

"Yeah."

"*You do?*"

"You're goddamn right I do."

"Have you done it with anybody yet?"

"No."

"OK, that's it."

"What do you mean, *that's it*?"

"If you know how, eventually you'll get some. It figures. What more do you want me to say?"

"Don't I get any useful instructions?"

"*We're not going to talk dirty out here, you understand?*"

"Don't shout at me. I didn't bring up the subject."

"You don't do it the night before a fight, it drains you, that's what Al Weill always used to say."

"I'm not going to be a fighter."

"Look, there are more important things in the world than fucking." His father cracked his knuckles. "I shoulda seen that you had a stricter upbringing."

"How do I get some?"

"I'm not a pimp, for Chrissake." His father topped up their glasses with more Labatt's. "You see all those pimples you got on your face?"

"Yeah. So?"

"Don't worry. They're going to clear up. You'll be left with little holes in your cheeks here and there, but what the hell."

"You mean fucking drains you, but it's good for pimples?"

"Goddamn it, Josh, I don't know how we got into this!"

"You started it."

Lowering his voice to a whisper, his father said, "You are invited into a lady's boudoir, well, if you're a gentleman the first thing you do is take off your hat."

"Is that how you get it going?"

"You fold your trousers neat, see, and you're wearing clean socks, that's important, and if you got your wallet with you, you keep it under your pillow. You got that?"

Joshua nodded.

"And I want you to be wearing fresh underwear. No skid marks. But even so you wash up good first, if only as an example to her, because sometimes they can be real smelly down there."

"Down where?"

"*We're not going to talk dirty.*"

"You said 'down there,' not me."

"I want to teach you about the etiquette of the matter, not the actual doing of it."

"Some help."

"All right. OK. You know what it is?" he asked, blushing a little as he thrust a three-pack of Sheiks at him.

"Yeah," Joshua said, smirking.

"As soon as your dick gets stiff, you roll one on. Don't forget that."

"And then what?"

"Why don't you read a book on the subject and leave me alone?"

"You're my father, but."

"Yeah, right. Well afterwards —"

"Afterwards?"

"Yeah, afterwards, you remember to wash up, using soap and hot water. But if, say, a couple of weeks later it hurts you to piss or it's coming out the wrong colour you go right to the doctor, you don't wait. Got that?"

"Right."

"Well, that's it. Good luck."

"Aw, come on, Daddy."

Grudgingly, his father came to a decision. He dipped into his inside jacket pocket and unfolded a sheet obviously torn from a medical book. "I've been to the library on your behalf," he said, shoving the page at him. "That's what it looks like close up."

"What?"

"Her *thing*, that's what! The snatch."

Joshua groaned; it looked so uninviting.

"You must understand," his father said with some tenderness, "that this is merely a scientific diagram. A map, like."

"Uh huh."

"Look, if I showed you a relief map of the Rockies, in black and white, you think you'd be impressed?"

His father had once fought in Calgary. Another time at a smoker in the Banff Springs Hotel. He adored the mountains.

"Well," Joshua began.

"You see this little thing right here?"

He nodded.

"You diddle it with your finger, they really like it, they begin to purr."

"No shit?"

"You'd be surprised," he said, grinning fondly. "But afterwards," he added, turning solemn again, "you wash your hands with soap and hot water before you touch your face."

"There seems to be an awful lot of washing up involved, Daddy."

"You can't be too careful these days." Then he sighed, relieved, and turned to the Bible. "How many commandments are there?"

"Ten."

"Yeah, well. Right, right. Now, can you recite them to me?"

"Aw, come on, Daddy."

"But you could the batting order of the Royals. Or the Dodgers. With the averages."

"Yeah."

"We've got to have these educational talks more often, or you'll grow up a jerk like me."

"I don't think you're a jerk," Joshua said, appalled.

"Well, yeah," his father said, pleased, "but what do you know?"

"I'd certainly like to know more about fucking."

"Well, it's a big subject and it's best to pace yourself, taking it round by round. I mean, we've made a good start, right?"

"Right."

—Joshua Then and Now, pp. 65–68

THE TRUTH IS, I hadn't joined Habonim in the first place because of an overwhelming commitment to Zion. I had done it to spite my grandfather. I was also flattered by Jerry Greenfeld's attention. There was another consideration: I longed to meet girls who could stay out after ten o'clock at night. And according to the disapproving gossip I had overheard in the Young Israel Synagogue, the girls in the movement, especially those who were allowed to sleep over at our Camp Kvutza, where there was no adult supervision, practiced "free love." Mind you, in those days this promise of sexual whoopee translated into no more than some necking, within vigorously defended territorial limits, usually on the front porch at night, after the overhead light bulb had been loosened, but with couples still leaping apart abruptly when footsteps were heard or a car turned the corner — and even this much certainly never on a first date. A date often meant taking in a double feature at the Rialto, and a good indicator that your girl might be in the mood for a bit of monkey business was that she agreed to seats in the last row of the balcony. Unfortunately the *chaverta* who came to tolerate my kisses wore braces on her teeth, which pinched my lips.

— *This Year in Jerusalem,* p. 31

JENNY, WHO WEPT for Abelard and Héloïse, lent him *Nana,* and kept *The Shropshire Lad,* a gift from Kenny, under her pillow, was, to Jake's mind, altogether too rare a creature for St. Urbain. So on those evenings when he would contrive to cycle up and down outside Laurel Knitwear at closing time, he would be heartsick to see her emerge, looking as coarse as the other factory girls, her face drawn, sullen, her forehead greasy, until she saw him and would laugh, delighted, allowing him to cycle home beside her.

"Well, well," she'd say, yanking his hair, "picking up girls outside a factory. What would your Uncle Abe say?"

"Aw."

One evening she announced he could be her date; she would take him to the movies next Saturday afternoon.

"On *shabus?*" he whispered.

"You think you'll be struck by lightning?"

"I'm not even scared."

Instead of starting out together they met furtively on a street corner and did not go to a downtown movie, where they might run into neighbours, but to a movie in an unfamiliar *goyische* district. Afterwards Jenny took him to a soda bar and lectured him about Emily Dickinson and Kenneth Patchen. They agreed to meet again the following Saturday. Jenny, amused with herself, dressed up

for these occasions, but out of consideration for Jake she never, after the first time, wore high heels or her hair in an upsweep, so that Jake, straining (and, though she didn't know it, with wads of newspaper stuffed under his socks), seemed almost as tall as she was.

On the first Saturday they did no more than hold hands stickily, but just as the main feature came on the second time out Jenny lifted Jake's arm over her shoulders and snuggled up against him. It was the same the next Saturday and the one after that. Then, one Saturday afternoon, as Jake put his arm around her his hand fell accidentally over her breast, dangling, the little finger barely grazing the softness there. He froze, not bold enough to go further but not willing to retreat either, until Jenny whispered impatiently, "It's all right. Honestly, it isn't a crime," and Jake, swallowing hard, squeezed her breast with such sudden and pent-up savagery that she had to grit her teeth to save herself from crying out in pain. Then Jenny took his hand and showed him how and he began to stroke and squeeze her gently and as soon as he seemed less frantic, Jenny (Oh my God, he thought) unbuttoned her dress, unsnapped her bra, and stroking his hand reassuringly led it over her bare breast and amazingly stiff nipple. Time passed achingly, deliriously slow, until, sweating with fresh alarm, he felt her hand undoing his fly buttons, groping inside, freeing him, and then caressing him and pulling him briefly, too briefly, before he shot off, humiliated, into her hand. "I'm sorry," he whispered, but Jenny shushed him and reached into her purse for a handkerchief and wiped them both. Afterwards they went to a soda shop. Jenny lit a corktipped cigarette. "Want one?" she asked, her eyes taunting him.

"Sure," he said, but the cigarette made him cough.

"Do you pull off at night? Like Arty. With pictures?'

"*You crazy?*"

"I thought so," she said, her smile venomous as she reached for her coat.

"You going?"

"Yes. And no more movies. Come back when you're old enough."

Old enough. How they longed to be old enough, Jake remembered.

In the afternoons they studied for their bar mitzvahs at the Young Israel Synagogue and at night they locked the door to Arty's room, dropped their trousers to their ankles, and studied themselves for bush growth. Pathetic, miserable little hairs, wouldn't they ever proliferate? Duddy Kravitz taught them how to encourage hair growth by shaving, a sometimes stinging process. "One slip of the razor, you shmock, and you'll grow up a hairdresser. Like Gordie Shapiro." Duddy also told them how Japanese girls were able to diddle themselves in hammocks. Of course Duddy was the bushiest, with the longest, most menacingly veined, thickest cock of all. He won so regularly when they masturbated against the clock, first to come picks up all the quarters, that before long they would not compete unless he accepted a sixty-second handicap.

—*St. Urbain's Horseman,* pp. 143–45

CLARA WAS TERRIFIED OF FIRE. "We live on the fifth floor," she said. "We wouldn't have a chance." Unexpected knocks on our hotel-room door made her freeze, so friends learned to announce themselves first. "It's Leo," or "It's the Boogieman. Put all your valuables into a bag and pass them through the door." Rich food made her vomit. She suffered from insomnia. But, given sufficient wine, she would sleep, a mixed blessing because that prompted nightmares from which she would waken trembling. She didn't trust strangers and was even more suspicious of friends. She was allergic to shellfish, eggs, animal fur, dust, and anybody indifferent to her presence. Her periods brought on headaches, cramps, nausea, and vile temper. She endured lengthy attacks of eczema. She kept a plugged earthenware jug under our window, a bellarmino, filled with her own urine and fingernail clippings, to throw back evil spells. She feared cats. Heights scared her. Thunder petrified her. She was frightened of water, snakes, spiders, and other people.

Reader, I married her.

Given that I was a horny twenty-three-year-old at the time, it wasn't because Clara was such a sexual wildcat. Our romance, such as it was, was not enriched by abandon between the sheets. Clara, the compulsive flirt and dirty talker, turned out to be as prudish with me, in any event, as the mother she professed to abhor, denying me what she denigrated as my "thirty seconds of friction" time and again. Or enduring them. Or did her utmost to stifle any joy we might have salvaged out of our increasingly rare and frustrating couplings. After all these years, it's her admonitions that I remember.

"I want you to scrub it with soap and hot water first, and then don't you dare come inside me."

She condescended to fellate me once, and was immediately sick to her stomach in the sink. Humiliated, I dressed in silence, quit the room, and tramped along the quais as far as the Place de la Bastille and back again. On my return, I discovered that she had packed a suitcase and was sitting on the bed, hunched over, shivering, in spite of wearing layers of her shawls. "I would have been gone before you got back," she said, "but I'm going to need money for another room somewhere."

Why didn't I let her go, while I could still have managed it with impunity? Why did I take her in my arms, rocking her even as she sobbed, undressing her, easing her into bed, stroking her until she slipped her thumb into her mouth and began to breathe evenly?

I sat by her bedside for the remainder of the night, chain-smoking, reading that novel about the Golem of Prague, by what's-his-name, Kafka's friend, and early in the morning I went to the market to fetch her an orange, a croissant, and a yogurt for breakfast.

"You're the only man who ever peeled an orange for me," she said, already working on the first line of the poem that is now in so many anthologies. "You're not going to throw me out, are you?" she asked in her little girl's Mother-may-I-take-a-step voice.

"No."

"You still love your crazy Clara, don't you?"

"I honestly don't know."

Exhausted as I was, why didn't I give her money right then, and help her move into another hotel?

My problem is, I am unable to get to the bottom of things. I don't mind not understanding other people's motives, not any more, but why don't I understand why *I* do things?

In the days that followed, Clara couldn't have been more contrite, docile, ostensibly loving, encouraging me in bed, her simulated ardour betrayed by her tense, unyielding body. "That was good. So wonderful," she'd say. "I needed you inside me."

Like fuck she did. But, arguably, I needed her. Don't underestimate the nursing sister longing to leap out of somebody even as cantankerous as I am. Looking after Clara made me feel noble. Mother Teresa Panofsky. Dr. Barney Schweitzer.

Scribbling away here and now at my rolltop desk at two in the morning in twenty-below-zero Montreal, pulling on a Montecristo, trying to impose sense on my incomprehensible past, unable to pardon my sins by claiming youth and innocence, I can still summon up in my mind's eye those moments with Clara that I cherish to this day. She was an inspired tease, and could make me laugh at myself, a gift not to be underestimated. I loved our moments of shared tranquillity. Me, lying on our bed in that box of a hotel room, pretending to read, but actually watching Clara at her work table. Fidgety, neurotic Clara totally at ease. Concentrating. Rapt. Her face cleansed of its often-disfiguring turbulence. I was inordinately proud of the high esteem others, more knowledgeable than I, had for her drawings and published poems. I anticipated a future as her guardian. I would provide her with the wherewithal to get on with her work, liberated from mundane concerns. I would take her back to America and build her a studio in the countryside with northern light and a fire escape. I would protect her from thunder, snakes, animal fur, and evil spells. Eventually, I would bask in her fame, playing a dutiful Leonard to her inspired Virginia. But, in our case, I would be ever watchful, safeguarding her against a mad walk into the water, her pockets weighed down with rocks. Yossel Pinsky, the Holocaust survivor who would become my partner, had met Clara a couple of times, and was skeptical. "You're not a nice man any more than I am," he said, "so why try? She's a *meshugena*. Ditch her before it's too late."

But it was already too late.

"I suppose you want me to have an abortion," she said.

"Hold on a minute," I said. "Let me think." I'm twenty-three years old, is what I thought. Christ Almighty. "I'm going out for a walk. I won't be long."

She was sick again in the sink while I was out and, on my return, she was dozing. Three o'clock in the afternoon and Clara, the insomniac, was in a deep sleep. I cleaned up as best I could and an hour passed before she got out of bed. "So there you are," she said. "My hero."

"I could speak to Yossel. He would find us somebody."

"Or he could manage it himself with a coat-hanger. Only I've already decided I'm going to have the baby. With you or without you."

"If you're going to have the baby, I suppose I should marry you."

"Some proposal."

"I'm only mentioning it as a possibility."

Clara curtsied. "Why, thank you, Prince Charmingbaum," she said, and then she hurried out of our room and down the stairs.

Boogie was adamant. "What do you mean, it's your responsibility?"

"Well, it is, isn't it?"

"You're crazier than she is. Make her have an abortion."

That evening I searched for Clara everywhere, and finally found her seated alone at La Coupole. I leaned over and kissed her on the forehead. "I've decided to marry you," I said.

"Gee whiz. Wow. Don't I even get to say yes or no?"

"We could consult your I Ching, if you like."

"My parents won't come. They would be mortified. *Mrs.* Panofsky. Sounds like a furrier's wife. Or maybe the owner of a clothing store. Everything wholesale."

I found us a fifth-floor apartment on the rue Notre-Dame-des-Champs, converted from four *chambres de bonne*, and we were married at the *mairie* in the Sixième. The bride wore a cloche hat, a ridiculous veil, an ankle-length black wool dress, and a white ostrich-feather boa. Asked if she would take me as her lawfully wedded husband, a stoned Clara winked at the official, and said, "I've got a bun in the oven. What would you do?" Boogie and Yossel were both in attendance and there were gifts. A bottle of Dom Perignon, four ounces of hashish implanted in knitted blue booties from Boogie; a set of six Hotel George V sheets and bath towels from Yossel; a signed sketch and a dozen diapers from Leo; and an autographed copy of *Merlin*, featuring his first published story, from Terry McIver.

Making the arrangements for the wedding, I finally got a peek at Clara's passport, and was startled to discover the name on it was Charnofsky. "Don't worry," she said. "You caught yourself a blueblood *shiksa*. But when I was nineteen I ran off with him and we were married in Mexico. My art teacher. Charnofsky. It only lasted three months, but it cost me my trust fund. My father disinherited me."

Once we moved into our apartment, Clara began to stay up into the early-morning hours, scribbling in her notebooks or concentrating on her nightmarish ink drawings. Then she slept in until two or three in the afternoon, slipped out of our apartment, and was not seen again until evening, when she would join our table at the Mabillon or Café Select, her manner delinquent.

"As a matter of interest, Mrs. Panofsky, where were you all afternoon?"

"I don't remember. Walking, I suppose." And then, digging into her voluminous skirts, she would say, "I brought you a gift," and would hand me a tin of *pâté de foie gras*, a pair of socks, and, on one occasion, a sterling silver cigarette lighter. "If it's a boy," she said, "I'm going to call him Ariel."

"Now that comes trippingly off the tongue," said Boogie. "Ariel Panofsky."

"I vote for Othello," said Leo, his smile sly.

"Fuck you, Leo," said Clara, her eyes hot, suffering one of her unaccountable but increasingly frequent mood changes. Then she turned on me. "Maybe Shylock would be most appropriate, all things considered?"

Surprisingly, once Clara was over her morning sickness, playing house together turned out to be fun. We shopped for kitchenware and bought a crib. Clara made a mobile to hang over it and painted rabbits and chipmunks and owls on the walls of our nursery. I did the cooking, of course. Spaghetti bolognese, *the pasta strained with a colander*. Chopped chicken-liver salad. And, my *pièce de resistance*, breaded veal chops garnished with potato latkes and apple sauce.

Boogie, Leo with one or another of his girls, and Yossel often came to dinner, and once even Terry McIver, but Clara refused to tolerate Cedric, who had failed to appear at our wedding. "Why not?" I asked.

"Never mind. I just don't want him here."

She also objected to Yossel.

"He has a bad aura. He doesn't like me. And I want to know what you two are up to."

So I settled her on the sofa and brought her a glass of wine. "I've got to go to Canada," I said.

"*What?*"

"I'll only be gone for three weeks. A month at most. Yossel will bring you money every week."

"You're not coming back."

"Clara, don't start."

"Why Canada?"

"Yossel and I are going into the cheese-export business together."

"You're joking. The cheese business. It's too embarrassing. Clara, you were married in Paris, weren't you? Yes. To a writer or a painter? No, a cheese fucking salesman."

"It's money."

"You would think of that. I'll go crazy all alone here. I want you to get me a padlock for the door. What if there's a fire?"

"Or an earthquake?"

"Maybe you'll do so well with the cheese that you'll send for me in Canada and we could join a golf club, if they have them there yet, and invite people in to play bridge. Or mah jongg. I'm not becoming a member of any synagogue ladies fucking auxiliary and Ariel's not going to be circumcised. I won't allow it."

I managed to register a company in Montreal, open an office, and hire an old school friend, Arnie Rosenbaum, to run it, all within three febrile weeks. And Clara grew accustomed, even seemed to look forward to, my flying to Montreal every six weeks, providing I returned laden with jars of peanut butter, some Oreos, and at least two dozen packs of Lowney's Glosette Raisins. It was during my absences that she wrote, and illustrated with ink drawings, most of *The Virago's Verse Book*, now in its twenty-eighth printing.

It includes the poem dedicated to "Barnabus P." That touching tribute which begins,

> he peeled my orange and more often me,
> Calibanovitch,
> my keeper.

I was in Montreal, hustling, and Clara was into her seventh month, when Boogie tracked me down in my room at the Mount Royal Hotel early one morning.

"I think you had better answer it," said Abigail, the wife of my old school friend who managed our Montreal office.

"Yes."

Boogie said, "You better grab the first flight back."

I landed at oh whatever in the hell that airport was called before it became de Gaulle* at seven a.m. the following morning, and made right for The American Hospital. "I'm here to see Mrs. Panofsky."

"Are you a relative?"

"Her husband."

A young intern, contemplating his clipboard, looked up and regarded me with sudden interest.

"Dr. Mallory would like to have a word with you first," said the receptionist.

I took an instant dislike to Dr. Mallory, a portly man with a fringe of grey hair who radiated self-regard and had obviously never treated a patient worthy of his skills. He invited me to sit down and told me that the baby had been stillborn, but Mrs. Panofsky, a healthy young woman, would certainly be able to bear other children. His smile facetious, he added, "Of course I'm telling you this because I take it you are the father."

He seemed to wait on my response.

"Yes."

"In that case," said Dr. Mallory, flipping his colourful braces, his riposte obviously rehearsed, "you must be an albino."

Taking in the news, my heart thudding, I delivered Dr. Mallory what

---

* Charles de Gaulle airport never existed under any other name. The airport referred to is doubtless Le Bourget.

I hoped was my most menacing look. "I'll catch up with you later."

I found Clara in a maternity ward with seven other women, several of whom were nursing newly born babes. She must have lost a good deal of blood. Pale as chalk she was. "Every four hours," she said, "they attach clamps to my nipples and squeeze out the milk like I was a cow. Have you seen Dr. Mallory?"

"Yes."

"'You people,' he said to me. 'You people.' Brandishing that poor, wizened dead thing at me as if it had slid out of a sewer."

"He told me I could take you home tomorrow morning," I said, surprised at how steady my voice was. "I'll come by early."

"I didn't trick you. I swear, Barney. I was sure the baby was yours."

"How in the hell could you be so sure?"

"It was just once and we were both stoned."

"Clara, we seem to have an attentive audience here. I'll come for you tomorrow morning."

"I won't be here."

Dr. Mallory was not in his office. But two first-class airplane tickets to Venice and a confirmation slip for reservations at the Gritti Palace sat on his desk. I copied the number of the hotel reservation slip, hurried over to the nearest Bureau de Poste, and booked a call to the Gritti Palace. "This is Dr. Vincent Mallory speaking. I wish to cancel tomorrow night's reservations."

There was a pause while the desk clerk flipped through his file. "For the entire five days?" he asked.

"Yes."

"In that case, I'm afraid you will lose your deposit, sir."

"Why you cheap little mafioso, that doesn't surprise me," I said, and hung up.

Boogie, my inspiration, would be proud of me. That master prankster had played far worse tricks on people, I thought, beginning to wander aimlessly. Raging. Murder in my heart. I ended up, God knows how, in a café on the rue Scribe, where I ordered a double "Johnnie Walkair." Lighting one Gauloise off another, I was surprised to discover Terry McIver ensconced at a table in the rear of the café with an overdressed older woman who was wearing too much makeup. Take it from me, his "pleasingly pretty" Héloise was squat, a dumpling, puffy-faced, with more than a hint of moustache. Catching my eye, equally startled, Terry withdrew her multi-ringed hand from his knee, whispered something to her, and ambled over to my table. "She's Marie-Claire's boring aunt," he said, sighing.

"Marie-Claire's affectionate aunt, I'd say."

"Oh, she's in such a state," he whispered. "Her Pekinese was run over this morning. Imagine. You look awful. Anything wrong?"

"Everything's wrong, but I'd rather not go into it. You're not fucking that old bag?"

"Damn you," he hissed. "She understands English. She's Marie-Claire's aunt."

"Okay. Right. Now beat it, McIver."

But he did not leave without a parting shot. "And in future," he said, "I'd take it as a kindness if you didn't follow me."

McIver and "Marie-Claire's aunt" quit the café without finishing their drinks and drove off not in an Austin-Healey but in a less-than-new Ford Escort.** Liar, liar, liar, that McIver.

I ordered another double Johnny Walkair and then went in search of Cedric. I found him in his favourite café, the one frequented by the *Paris Review* crowd as well as Richard Wright, the Café le Tournon, high on the rue Tournon. "Cedric, old buddy of mine, we've got to talk," I said, taking his arm, and starting to propel him out of the café.

"We can talk right here," he said, yanking his arm free, and directing me to a table in the corner.

"Let me buy you a drink," I said.

He ordered a *vin rouge* and I asked for a scotch. "You know," I said, "years ago my daddy once told me that the worst thing that could happen to a man is to lose a child. What do you think, man?"

"You've got something to say to me, spit it out, man."

"Yes. Quite right. But I'm afraid it's bad news, Cedric. You lost a son yesterday. My wife's. And I am here to offer condolences."

"Shit."

"Yeah."

** The Ford Escort didn't go into production in England until January 1968.

"I had no idea."

"That makes two of us."

"What if it wasn't mine either?"

"Now there's an intriguing thought."

"I'm sorry, Barney."

"Me too."

"Now do you mind if I ask you a question?"

"Shoot."

"Why in the hell did you marry Clara in the first place?"

"Because she was pregnant and I thought it was my duty to my unborn child. My turn now."

"Go ahead."

"Were you screwing her after as well as before? We were married, I mean."

"What did she say?"

"I'm asking you."

"Shit."

"I thought we were friends."

"What's that got to do with it?"

Then I heard myself saying, "That's where I draw the line. Fooling around with the wife of a friend. I could never do that."

He ordered another round and this time I insisted that we click glasses. "After all," I said, "this is an occasion, don't you think?"

"What are you going to do about Clara now?"

"How about I turn her over to you, Daddy-o?"

"Nancy wouldn't dig that. Three in a bed. Not my scene. But I do thank you for the offer."

"It was sincerely meant."

"I appreciate that."

"Actually, I think it was awfully white of me to make such an offer."

"Hey, Barney, baby, you don't want to mess with a bad nigger like me. I might pull a shiv on you."

"Hadn't thought of that. Let's have another drink instead."

When the *patronne* brought over our glasses, I stood up unsteadily and raised mine. "To Mrs. Panofsky," I said, "with gratitude for the pleasure she has given both of us."

"Sit down before you fall down."

"Good idea." Then I began to shake. Swallowing the boulder rising in my gorge, I said, "I honestly don't know what to do now, Cedric. Maybe I should hit you."

"Goddamn it, Barney, I hate to tell you this, but I wasn't the only one."

"Oh."

"Didn't you know that much?"

"No."

"She's insatiable."

"Not with me she wasn't."

"Maybe we ought to order a couple of coffees, then you can hit me if it will make you feel better."

"I need another scotch."

"Okay. Now listen to your Uncle Remus. You're only twenty-three years old and she's a nutcase. Shake her loose. Divorce her."

"You ought to see her. She's lost lots of blood. She looks awful."

"So do you."

"I'm afraid of what she might do to herself."

"Clara's a lot tougher than you think."

"Was it you who made those scratches on her back?"

"What?"

"Somebody else then."

"It's over. *Finito*. Give her a week to get her shit together and then tell her."

"Cedric," I said, breaking into a sweat, "everything's spinning. I'm going to be sick. Get me into the john. Quick."

—*Barney's Version,* pp. 110–21

DUDDY LOOKED CLOSELY AT YVETTE. "We need a couch in here," he said hoarsely. "We oughta have a couch." He let Mr. Friar's number ring and ring. There was no answer. "He's probably asleep. Stop looking so worried, please. He needed money for film or something, that's all." Duddy hung up and told Yvette that he wanted her to find him an apartment downtown. "I also want you to get me subscriptions to

Mordecai Richler and his wife, Florence.

Fortune, Time, Life, and — There's another one, but I forget. We also ought to get some stills to hang on the walls. The bigger the better… Come here a minute," he said, taking her hand and guiding it. "Some flagpole, eh? A regular Rock of Gibraltar."

Yvette wanted to wait, but Duddy insisted, and they made love on the carpet.

"I don't get it," Duddy said. "Imagine guys getting married and tying themselves down to one single broad for a whole lifetime when there's just so much stuff around."

"People fall in love," Yvette said. "It happens."

"Planes crash too," Duddy said. "Listen, I've got an important letter to write. We'll eat soon. OK?"

— *The Apprenticeship of Duddy Kravitz,* p. 191

WHEN NANCY HAD FIRST MET JAKE, at one of Luke's parties, she had asked him, "Are you a writer?" swallowing the too.

"No," he had replied, affronted, "I'm the director."

Which was awfully conceited, yes, but preferable to how he had recently come to identify himself.

"I'm a director. Not the kind you send for — the type you use if he's in town."

1959 it was, following Luke's Royal Court triumph and while Jake was teetering in limbo, drinking prodigiously as he awaited the opportunity to direct his first film.

On arrival at Luke's party, only a day after she had flown into London, Nancy, thrust into a roomful of jabbering strangers, was instantly aware of a dark, slouching, curly-haired man watching her. Unevenly shaven, his tie loosened, his shirt riding out of his baggy trousers, Jacob Hersh hovered on the edge of whatever group she joined. Scrutinizing the tilt and fullness of her breasts, appraising the curve of her bottom, and searching for a flaw in the turn of her ankle. When she sat on the sofa, crossing her long legs, in animated conversation with an actor, she was not altogether surprised to catch him sinking to the floor opposite, drink in hand, edging lower and lower. Shamelessly seeking out her stocking tops. Infuriated, flushing, Nancy briefly considered hiking her dress, shedding her panties, and flinging them in his mournful face. Instead she drew her legs closer to her, tugging at her dress. It wasn't, she grasped, so much that he was a dirty little man as that he probably felt she was inaccessible to him and was therefore determined to find fault with her. Being a singularly lovely girl, she was in fact used to the type, having suffered considerably at their hands at university. And Jake, more than anything, reminded her of those insufferably bright boys on campus, self-declared intellectuals, usually Jewish, charged with bombast and abominable poetry in lowercase letters, who were aroused by her presence, and yet were too gauche (and terrified) to speak out and actually ask for a date. Instead they sat at the table next to her in the student union, aggressively calling attention to themselves. Speculating loudly on what they took to be her icy manner. Or they slid belligerently into the seat next to her at lectures, trying to bedazzle with their questions. They also ridiculed her to girls less happily endowed, wreaking vengeance for a rejection they anticipated, but were too cowardly to risk, and bandied suggestions about her secret sexual life sufficiently coarse to make her cry. No matter that she took immense pains not to be provocative, swimming in sloppy joe sweaters, sensible skirts, and flat shoes. Going out of her way to discourage boys the other girls coveted. For this only proved that Nancy Croft was remote; splendidly made, yes, but glacier-like.

Drink in hand, Jake trailed after her everywhere, always on the rim of her group. If she so much as ventured an observation on London, or remarked on a play she had seen, he didn't comment, but smirked condescendingly, as if to say, idiot. If she was trapped into conversation with a bore, he condemned her with his eyes for tolerating him, raising his eyebrows, as if to say, only a dolt would have time for him. Loping after her from room to room, he twice made forays into her group. On the first occasion, as a man, whispering in her ear, made her laugh, he barged in, gratuitously rude, and when that failed to demolish him, inquired pointedly after the man's wife and children. On the other occasion, adjudging her too responsive to the flirtations of a man more handsome, taller, he actually plucked him by the sleeve and called him aside on one pretext or another. Jacob Hersh would not let her out of sight, even to refill his glass, until she was safely in conversation with a homosexual, when he would lurch off grinning widely.

Finally, Nancy thrust her empty glass at him. "Would you mind getting me a drink?"

"Who? Me?"

"Yes. You."

"WehaventmetmynamesJacobHersh."

It was then she asked him, Are you a writer, swallowing the too, and he replied, no, I'm the director, which allowed her a chance to smile.

Vengefully, he countered, "Don't tell me you're an actress?"

"No."

Redeeming her glass, she turned her back on him to chat with somebody else, responding with exaggerated warmth. Then, as she could sense his eyes raking her back, lingering on her bottom, she resisted her first impulse, which was to wiggle it at him, and slid away, her back against the wall, a man between them, so that Jake could not see and judge any of her. And as the man proved a bore, yet another competitor among so many jousting egos, she excused herself abruptly and went to fetch her coat.

"Would you call me a taxi, please, Luke."

Fumbling hands helped her into her coat. "I've got a car," Jake insisted.

"I think I'll walk. I could do with some fresh air."

"Me too," Jake chipped in cheerily and, without waiting for an invitation, he followed her.

Not a word was said until they started down Haverstock Hill together, Nancy's black hair flowing, her pale oval face bemused.

"What a beautiful girl you are," Jake allowed angrily.

"Thank you."

"Well, it's not the first time you've heard it," he muttered, shrugging.

"No. It isn't."

"But it's the first time you heard it from me," he hollered, waving a finger in her face, "and I don't say it to everybody. Like Shapiro. That glib prick."

"Who's he?"

"The one who was licking the wax out of your ears."

"Oh, him," she exclaimed with simulated warmth.

"Are you living in London or just visiting?"

"It depends on whether or not I'll like it."

"You'll like it," he assured her.

"It's settled, then?"

"Are you being sarcastic now?"

"I'd have to find a job."

"Maybe I can help. What do you do?"

"Strip at parties."

"Seriously, what do you do?"

"What's the difference?"

"You're not, for Chrissake, a social worker?"

"Why are you looking for reasons to dismiss me?"

"Or, God help us, a child psychologist?"

"Guess again."

"You rich?"

"My father's a shoe salesman."

"Attention must be paid."

"Oh, but you are a funny fellow!"

Which brought them to the front door of her flat on Arkwright Road. As she drove the key into the door, he lingered.

"All right. You can come in for a nightcap," she said, "if you promise not to be awkward."

He nodded, acquiescing, but she didn't care for his smile.

"So long as it's crystal clear," she said, "that I'm not inviting you into my bed."

While she fetched the drinks, she could see him, through the kitchen hatch, lifting up magazines, like a judge sifting evidence. Two years' detention for reading *Vogue*. Six months in solitary for *Elle*. *The Ladies' Home Journal*, off with her head. Next he stooped to scan the bookshelves, probing for bad or modish taste, and snickering with delight to find evidence of both. Enjoying herself, she did not protest that she had sublet the flat. Then Jake stumbled on *The Collected Stories of Isaac Babel* lying on the coffee table and seized it, taken aback. "Are you reading this?" he demanded accusingly.

"No. I hoped I'd be able to bring you back here and I left it out to impress you. Do you recommend it?"

Jake retreated, narrowing his eyes. His manner softened. "I'm sorry," he said.

"You've been judging me all night. What right have you?"

"None. Come to dinner with me tomorrow night."

But she already had tickets for *Hedda Gabler*.

"It's a terrible production," Jake exploded. "An abortion. That bastard couldn't direct traffic," and he carried on to denounce Binky Beaumont, the Royal Court Theatre, Donald Albery, J. Arthur Rank, Granada, and the BBC. Until finally, she said: "I'm very, very tired. I only arrived yesterday, you know."

Leaping up, Jake emptied his glass. "I didn't make a pass, because you said — Maybe I should try. Maybe you didn't really mean it."

"I mean it. Honestly."

But he attempted to kiss her anyway. She did not respond. "OK, OK, you meant it. Can I pick you up at the theatre and take you to dinner after the play?"

"I'm going with someone."

"You are. Who?"

"Is it your affair?"

"You're not ashamed, are you?"

And so she told him who.

"Him. Oh my God," he exclaimed, clapping a hand to his forehead, "you poor child. He's a hopeless prick."

"Like Shapiro?"

"Worse. He's one of the biggest phonies in town. He'll call you darling and send back the wine and flatter the hell out of you. Why are you going out with him?"

"If you don't mind —"

"What about Thursday night?"

"Luke's taking me out."

Which seemed, quite abruptly, to crush him. He didn't protest. He wasn't rude. He turned to go.

"I'm free Friday night," she said.

"All right. Friday night."

But, on Thursday, only ten minutes before Luke was to arrive, Nancy's phone rang.

"I'm in my bedroom," Luke said, "and I've got to talk quickly. Jake Hersh is here. Remember him?"

"Yes, indeed."

"He came by to invite me to dinner. It's awkward. He's in a truculent mood. I told him I had a date, but he said we could both come. Would you mind, terribly?"

Within minutes, Jake sat beaming on her sofa. Luke, agitated, was flicking his thumbnail against his teeth. Nancy poured drinks.

"I'll get the ice," Jake said, jumping up. "Don't you bother, Nancy. I know where it is."

"I will get the ice," Nancy said evenly.

"My God, I hope I'm not intruding."

But, once at Chez Luba, it was Nancy who began to feel curiously redundant. As the two friends vied for her approval, flicking stories off each other like beach boys with towels, ostensibly in fun, but stinging each time, she was, at once, immensely entertained but hardly ever allowed to get a word in herself. Luke told amusing anecdotes about the actors in his play, evoking her laughter, Jake's bile.

"Tell her about the New York producer," Jake said, glaring over the rim of his wine glass. "You know, and the girl who was there especially for you to —"

"Jake never betrays a confidence," Luke interrupted.

Then Jake told her about the time he had directed a play, for Granada TV, and one of the leading actors had died of a heart attack during transmission, and how from there on in he had had to improvise with his cameras.

Luke invited her to spend an afternoon watching them shoot at Pinewood Studios and Jake asked her to see a television play from the control booth.

On and on they volleyed, slamming at each other, and Nancy, exhausted, was grateful when it was finally time to go, Jake seizing the bill.

"We'll take a taxi," Luke said, taking Nancy's arm.

But Jake, betting on Luke's stinginess overriding all, said, "No, I'll drive you. It's on my way home."

Jake held the front door of his car open for Nancy, but she slid gracefully into the back seat, close to Luke. Bitch, whore.

"Who shall I drop off first?" Jake sang out.

"We're going to Nancy's place."

She didn't invite Jake in for a nightcap when he braked hard outside her front door. "Shall I wait for you here?" he asked Luke.

"Good night," he said, whacking the door shut, "and thanks for dinner."

Ungrateful bastard. Second-rate talent. Jake swung around the block, waiting out a red light and obliged to make a short detour to avoid a one-way stream, before he pulled up on the other side of the road and doused his lights to wait. *Adonoi, Adonoi*, Jake prayed, let this be her time of month. Make her bleed. *Not that he'd mind, the filthy goy bastard.*

A half hour passed. The living room lights went off and the bedroom curtains were drawn.

— Oooo, she moans, oooo, your hands are driving me crazy. Please come inside me now.

Trembling with excitement, Jake lit one cigarette off another.
— But why are you still small?
Heh heh. Jake laughed out loud, slapping his knee. Second-rate talent, a miser, and can't get it up, either.

— Let me eat you, then.
Oh, no. Don't, Nancy. He's got trench mouth.

An hour. The bedroom lights out. Come to think of it, Jake decided, she's not that bright. Or beautiful. Her teeth are uneven.

Two hours. And Jake, loathing her, enraged with himself for sitting there in the dark like a moonstruck teenager, reflected, if I die before I wake, and the Lord my soul does take, I will be buried without ever having directed Olivier, had a black girl, seen Jerusalem, delivered my speech turning down the Academy Award, tried heroin, fought for a cause, owned a cabin cruiser, had a son, been a prime minister, given up smoking, met Mao, had a homosexual experience, made a film of the Benye Krick stories, rejected a knighthood, had two ravishing girls in my bed at the same time, killed a Nazi, brought Hanna to London, sailed first class on the *Île de France*, cast Lauren Bacall in a thriller, met Evelyn Waugh, read Proust, come four times in a night (do they, really?), or had a season of my films presented at the National Film Theatre.

At your age, Orson Welles was famous. Dostoevski had written *Crime and Punishment*. Mozart had done his best work. Shelley, dead.

It was never my wish
To be Sir Bysshe

Ineffably depressed, Jake started the car and drove off.

— *St. Urbain's Horseman,* pp. 54–61

Barney, on the rebound from Clara, finds himself unhappily married to The Second Mrs. Panofsky.

I PROVED TO BE such an adroit fundraiser that Irv invited me to his twenty-fifth-wedding-anniversary party, a dinner dance for the quality held in private rooms at Ruby Foo's, black tie, everybody there except me good for a minimum twenty-thousand-dollars-a-year UJA bite, never mind the bond drive, and other community appeals for vigorish. And that's where I met the virago who would become my second wife. Damn damn damn. Here I am, sixty-seven years old, a shrinking man with a cock that trickles, and I still don't know how to account for my second marriage, which now sets me back ten thousand dollars a month before adjustments for inflation, and to think that her father, that pompous old bore, once feared *me* as the fortune hunter. Looking back, in search of anything that would justify my idiocy, pardon my sins, I must say I was not the real me in those days but an impersonator. Pretending to be the go-getter Clara had damned. Guilt-ridden. Drinking alone in the early-morning hours, fearful of sleep, which was invaded by visions of Clara in her coffin. The coffin, as ordained by Jewish law, was made of pine, holes drilled into it, so that the worms might fatten on that too-young corpse as soon as possible. Six feet under. Her breasts rotting. "...you'll be able to entertain guys at the United Jewish Appeal dinner with stories about the days you lived with the outrageous Clara." Bingeing on respectability, I was now determined to prove to Clara's ghost that I could play the nice middle-class Jewish boy better than she had ever dreamed. Hey, I used to stand back, observing myself, as it were, sometimes tempted to burst into applause in celebration of my own hypocrisy. There was the night, for instance, when I was still caught up in the lightning one-month courtship of the time-bomb who would become The Second Mrs. Panofsky, taking her to dinner at the Ritz, drinking far too much as she continued to yammer about how she would do up my Hampstead respectability trap with the help of an interior decorator she knew. "Will you be able to drive me home," she asked, "...in your condition?"

"Why," I said, bussing her on the cheek, and improvising on a script that could only have been produced by Totally Unnecessary Productions Ltd., "I could never forgive myself if you were hurt in an accident, because of my 'condition.' You're far too precious to me. We'll leave my car here and take a taxi."

"Oh, Barney," she gushed.

I shouldn't have written "'Oh, Barney,' she gushed." That was rotten of me. A lie. The truth is I was an emotional cripple when I met her, drunk more often than not, punishing myself for doing things that went against my nature, but The Second Mrs. Panofsky had sufficient vitality for the two of us, and a comedic flair, or sparkle, all her own. Like that old whore Hymie Mintzbaum of blessed memory, she possessed that quality I most admire in other people — an appetite for life. No, more. In those days a determination to devour all matters cultural, even as she could now wolf her way through the counter in the Brown Derby without pause. The Second Mrs. Panofsky didn't read for pleasure, but to keep up. Sunday mornings she sat down to *The New York Times Book Review*, as though to an exam that had been set for her, noting only those books likely to be discussed at dinner parties, ordering them promptly, and careering through them at breakneck speed: *Dr. Zhivago*, *The Affluent Society*, *The Assistant*, *By Love Possessed*. The deadliest sin, so far as she was concerned, was time-wasting, and I was accused of it again and again, squandering hours on nobodys encountered in bars. Shooting the breeze with superannuated hockey players, boozy sports columnists, and small-time conmen.

On a three-day junket to New York we stayed at the Algonquin, booked into separate bedrooms, which I insisted on, eager to play by what I took to be the rules. I could have happily passed that interlude wandering aimlessly, drifting in and out of bookshops and bars, but she was locked into a schedule that would have required a fortnight for a normal person to fill. Plays to be monitored afternoon and evening: *Two for the Seesaw*, *Sunrise at Campobello*, *The World*

of Suzie Wong, The Entertainer. Between times her checklist included forced marches to out-of-the-way craft shops and jewellery designers recommended by *Vogue.* Footsore, she was still among the first through the doors of Bergdorf Goodman when it opened in the morning, hurrying on to Saks, and those places on Canal Street, known only to the *cognoscenti,* where Givenchy's new "bag" dresses could be bought on the cheap. Flying down to New York, she wore an old outfit that could be dumped into her hotel-room wastepaper basket as soon as she acquired her first new one. Then, on the morning of our scheduled flight home, she tore up incriminating sales receipts, retaining only those that obliging salesladies had fabricated for her, say a bill for $39.99 for a $150 sweater. Boarding the plane, she wore only God knows how many sets of underwear, and one blouse over another, and then she clowned her passage past the Montreal customs inspector, flirting with him *en français.*

Yes, The Second Mrs. Panofsky was an exemplar of that much-maligned phenomenon, the Jewish-American Princess, but she succeeded in fanning my then-dying embers into something resembling life. When we met she had already served a season on a kibbutz and graduated from McGill, majoring in psychology, and was working with disturbed children at the Jewish General Hospital. They adored her. She made them laugh. The Second Mrs. Panofsky was not a bad person. Had she not fallen into my hands but instead married a real, rather than a pretend, straight arrow, she would be a model wife and mother today. She would not be an embittered, grossly overweight hag, given to diddling with New Age crystals and consulting trance-channellers. Miriam once said to me, Krishna was licensed to destroy, but not you, Barney. Okay, okay. The truth, then.

"You're far too precious to me," I gushed. "We'll leave my car here and take a taxi."

"Oh, Barney," she said, "are you ever full of shit tonight."

—*Barney's Version,* pp. 190–93

Jake's ardent courtship of Nancy is both guileful and awkward.

STEALTHILY, PRETENDING all the while there had been no change in their relationship — admitting, in principle, she was free to see other men — he began to move into her flat by calculated inches. One night he came with fresh asparagus from Harrods, a thoughtful gift, and the next he arrived with steaks as well — and a teak salad bowl — and a machine for grinding coffee, beans — and when she protested heatedly that they would either eat what she could afford or he could visit after dinner, he seemed so hurt, even ill-used, that she surpassed herself in bed, flattering the bejesus out of him, and this he took as license, on the weekend, to turn up with a carful of groceries and liquor, cartons of his favourite food and drink.

To begin with, he lingered in her bed until three in the morning and then, because she insisted on her independence, which meant separate flats, he rose groggily, overcome with self-pity, to drive off in the cold and flop on his own bed. But having once been allowed to stay overnight, it seemed no more than sensible to keep a toothbrush at her place, his shaving things, clean shirts, and underwear. And, come to think of it, scripts he had to read, his bedside lamp, the morning papers *he* wanted, and matzohs which he munched absently in bed. Her bed. Phone calls began to come for him at the flat. Indignantly, she took messages. Like his secretary. Or mistress. *But you are his mistress now, aren't you, Nancy, dear, and your day doesn't truly begin until he comes through the door. You sleep better with him beside you.* Which only heightened her self-disgust. For why should she be dependent on another for her happiness? Who knows if he could be trusted? If she hadn't already begun to pall on him? Then one morning, scratching himself on her sheets, he was foolish enough to wonder aloud, "Why don't we stop kidding ourselves and move in together?"

Which made her spring out of bed, "No, no, no. This is my place," and hastily stack his things in the middle of the living room. His shirts. His underwear. His coffee-grinding machine. His scripts.

His bedside lamp. His jar of pickled herring. He disappeared into the bathroom, taking a suspiciously long time to collect the rest of his stuff, and then with an, oh well, if that's the way you want it, scooped up his things, a salami riding the top of the heap. She stood by the window, tears sliding down her face, as she watched him descend the outside stairs, chin dug into his mound of possessions, his bedside lamp cord trailing after him, the plug bouncing on the steps.

Typically childish, he didn't phone the next morning, and she wept copiously, humiliated because she didn't dare leave the flat in the afternoon, just in case he did phone. He didn't come by in the evening, either, and she was incensed. Suddenly, the flat seemed empty. Without excitement or promise. Such was her rage at what she had to admit was her dependence that when he did condescend to phone the next morning, she informed him, with all the frostiness she could muster, that no, sorry, she had a date tonight.

Nancy bathed and oiled and powdered herself, she put on the garter belt that had made him whoop, beating the pillow for joy, and the bra with the clasp he couldn't solve. She slithered into her dress, undoing the top two buttons, then doing them up again contritely, feeling wretched, fearful she couldn't yield to another man. *And why not? She was hers to give, wasn't she?* So she defiantly opened her medicine cabinet to make sure — just in case, as it were — that she was not without vaginal jelly. She was still searching for the tube and her cap, incredulous that he would actually have the gall, cursing him, when the doorbell rang and, running to answer it, she undid first two, then three, buttons of her dress, blushing at her own boldness.

Tall, tanned, solicitous Derek Burton, the literary agent who had phoned her every morning for a week, wore a Westminster Old Boy's tie, carried a furled umbrella, and did not instantly sink to the sofa, kicking off his shoes, but remained standing until she had sat down, and lit her cigarette with a slender lighter he kept in a chamois pouch, and raised his glass to say, cheers. He didn't have to be asked how she looked, grudgingly pronouncing her all right, and taking it as an invitation to send his hand flying up her skirts, but immediately volunteered that she looked absolutely fantastic. Outside, he opened his umbrella, and held it over her. Derek drove an Austin-Healey with a leather steering wheel and what seemed, at first glance, like six headlights and a dozen badges riding the grille. There were no apple cores in the ashtray. Or stale bagels in the glove compartment. Instead, there were scented face tissues mounted in a suede container. There was also a coin dispenser, cleverly concealed, filled with sixpences for parking meters. As well as a small, elegant flashlight and a leatherbound logbook. Once at the restaurant, Derek tucked the car into the smallest imaginable space, managing it brilliantly, without cursing the car ahead of him, or behind, in Yiddish. Then she waited as he fixed a complicated burglar-proof lock to the steering column. Jake would absolutely hate him, she thought, which made her smile most enticingly and say, "How well you drive."

"One does try," he allowed, and he asked if she had ever competed in a car rally.

Alas, no.

Could she read maps, then?

No.

A pity, that, because he had hoped they might compete together.

Somehow or other, mostly by encouraging him to tell her about his military service in Nigeria, they struggled through dinner without too many embarrassing silences, but she was hard put to conceal her boredom, and would certainly not have invited him into her flat for a drink had she not espied a familiar car parked across the road, the lights out.

Fortunately, Derek was easily managed and when, breathing quickly, his cheeks flushed, he did lunge at her, squeezing her breasts like klaxons, murmuring all the while that she was super, a smashing girl, the phone began to ring. Ring and ring.

"Shouldn't one answer it?" he asked.

"Would you mind taking it, please?"

He did. Listened, blanched. And hung up.

"Don't let it worry you," Nancy said. "It's a local pervert. He usually gives me a tinkle at this hour."

Which was when he began to pull insistently at her dress, his expectations seemingly fired by the phone call, and, pleading fatigue, she handed him his umbrella and saw him out. Once he had driven off, she crossed the street, swinging her hips, and stopped in front of Jake's car to hike her dress and adjust her garter.

Sliding out of the car, he shrugged, shame-faced.

"Ooo," Nancy exclaimed, "I never dreamed it would be you. I was hoping to turn over a quick fiver."

"All right," he said. "All right," and he trailed after her into the flat, contemplating the dents in the sofa.

"Come," she said, opening the bedroom door, "don't you want to see if the sheets are mussed?"

"OK," he protested, "OK," but he did peer into the bedroom.

"Bastard. What did you say to him on the phone?"

"I don't know what you're talking about," he said, fleeing into the bathroom, and emerging to demand, "Have fun?"

"Super fun. Would you care for a drink?"

But he was already pouring himself one.

"I have been invited for a weekend in the country," she announced, curtsying. "With the Burtons. The Berks. Burtons, don't you know?"

"Well now, I never suspected you of social climbing."

"And can you give me one good reason, Jacob Hersh, why I shouldn't go?"

"Go," he said.

"Oh. Oh. Go to hell! And what if we were to marry and I was to bore you after ten years. What then? Would you trade me in for a younger model, like your fine friends?" His film friends.

"I love you. You could never bore me."

"How can you be sure?"

"Oh, Nancy, please!"

"You can't know. How can you know? And maybe you'd bore me after ten years?"

"I've got it. Let's get a divorce right now."

She had to laugh.

"Look here, if we continued to anticipate, without venturing, we can suck all the pleasure out of it."

"Yes. I know. May I have a drink too, please?"

Instead, he kissed her and, undoing her buttons, led her to the bed, where suddenly she didn't respond, explaining she couldn't, not tonight, because her equipment had mysteriously disappeared.

"How could that be?" Jake asked, his voice quivering.

"You tell me."

"Maybe if you looked again...."

"Oh, Jake. Darling Jake. I suppose I will have to marry you."

"When?"

"Tomorrow, if you like."

"Christ Almighty!"

—*St. Urbain's Horseman*, pp. 216–20

JAKE WAS WAKENED by the phone before nine the next morning.

"So, shmock, your big friend finally gets a play on in London, why don't you direct it?"

"Who in the hell is this?"

"Can you use a smoked brisket? Direct from Levitt's."

"Duddy, what are you doing in London?"

"Launching a star. I've got to speak to you."

"All right, then. What are you doing right now?"

"Masturbating. And you?"

Within the hour, Duddy was at Jake's flat insisting that he read the play he had brought with him — read it immediately — before they talk — and Jake's protests were unavailing. Grudgingly, he retired to his bedroom and when he emerged, having skimmed through the play, Duddy leaped up from the sofa. "So, big expert, what do you think?"

"I hope you're not putting any money into it. It's a disaster."

"Atta boy. I'll buy that dream," Duddy said, and then he unburdened himself.

He and Marlene Tyler, née Malke Tannebaum, showstopper of the Mount Carmel Temple's production of *My Fair Zeyda*, and occasionally seen on CBC-TV, were wed, or as the rabbi put it, joined hands for nuptial flight, within two months of their first meeting. Something of a showbiz celebrity by this time, often seen around Toronto with local lovelies, Duddy was interviewed by the *Telegram*. "When it comes to wedlock," he said, "there was never any doubt in my mind that I would marry one of our own brethren. I've seen too many mixed marriages. It just can't work." And Marlene said, "It may sound silly, but we won't have milk after meat in our house for hygienic reasons germane to our faith."

The house Duddy built in Forest Hill, the letter K woven into the aluminum storm door, antique coach lamps riding either side, double garage doors electronically controlled, was sumptuously furnished for Marlene Tyler, the girl of his dreams, pink and white, like a nursery. But he had assumed that after their marriage, she would give up stage and television, as she was only an adequate performer and could see for herself that they were rich and there was no need. After the lonely years of struggle and bachelorhood, gulping meals in restaurants and sleeping with *shiksas*, he had yearned for home-cooked meals, an orderly home life, and screwing on demand. "Like on drippy Saturday afternoons after you come home loaded from a bar mitzvah *kiddush*. Or like on Saturday night after the hockey game and there's only Juliette on TV. I even had a TV set put in the bedroom with remote control, so that we could watch from the bed and get in the mood before they picked the three stars. Foreplay, that's the word I want."

Duddy had anticipated nights on the town together, marvellous dinner parties, and, in the fullness of time, children. A son. "After all, what's the struggle for? It's a hard world, you know, everybody in business is rotten to the core." Somebody who would not know his early hardships, but would have a first-class education. The Harvard Business School. And ease the pressure on him at Dudley Kane Enterprises, because who could you trust if not your own? Nobody. "But instead, damn it, I was fool enough, for a wedding gift, to buy the Toronto rights on an off-Broadway musical. I backed the production on the condition that Marlene would star in it. Well, you know she wasn't absolutely awful. Some reviewers liked her. And next thing I know she's beginning to get work here and there. TV variety shows, theatre reviews, dances. And one, two, three, I'm a bachelor again. Only worse. Dinner at home? Sure, why not? The maid defrosts a TV dinner for me in the oven. Or I eat out and spend the night playing poker with pals. And then what? Me, I'm too tired to stand. I drive down to the theatre or TV studios to pick her up. She's standing outside in her furs, giggling with the rest of the cast. Most of them are fags, all right, but the others? Who knows what they do in the dressing rooms? You haven't met Marlene yet. *Oy*. For a Jewish girl she likes it, let me tell you. Now I'm a man of some sexual experience, you know. Not to brag, I'm well-hung. It's a big one. Masturbating helps, can you beat that? I mean, remember on St. Urbain we were told it would give us pimples or stunt growth? Bullshit. Scientifically speaking, what's a cock? Tissue and veins. You pull it, it stretches. You don't use it, it shrivels. Where was I? Oh, I've had a hundred and ninety-two girls, not counting Marlene, and more than one has pleaded for me to stop. Enough, Kravitz, you insatiable monster. Big Dick, one of the girls used to call me. Nice, huh? I liked that. Big Dick Kravitz. The girls tell me I'm a very virile guy and I don't come quick as a sneeze either, like lots of *shmecks* today. Or need to be spanked, no shit, you'd be shocked what some *goyim* go in for. Those girls are expensive but an education, the things they can tell you. Would you believe that in Toronto, Ontario, there is a genius of a broker sitting on Bay Street who forks out a hundred dollars every Friday night to have a girl stand on him in her high heels, that's all she's wearing, and pee all over him? Goddammit, Jake, that bastard is one broker in a thousand, he's one of the greats. I'd get into high heels and piss on him for nothing every day and twice on Saturday if only he'd handle my portfolio. Anyway, in Marlene I met my match. She can take it and come back for more, pumping away for dear life. So what goes on there at rehearsal, they're always grabbing each other in those dance numbers, hands everywhere, and everybody in tights and getting worked up? She's a good Jewish girl, it's true, but the way I look at it they're only human. So I pick her up at midnight, I'm pooped, let me tell you, and I have to be at the office at eight thirty or they'll steal me blind. And she, she's rarin' to go. Let's have a drink at the Celebrity Club, don't be an old square, she says to me, and all the fags trail along with us, giggling like high school girls. And who pays each time? Daddy Warbucks, you can count on it. They're all squealing with laughter at jokes I don't get, I'm half asleep in my chair, and when we finally get home, she wants to eat. Who can wake up the maid? She'd leave us. So me, *me*, I make her scrambled eggs. I'm sleepwalking and what does she say, thank you, darling? No. She says you never talk to me, you sit there like a lump. Yawning in my face. It's two o'clock, I say, I'm all talked out, what do you want from me? You can sleep in until noon. Me, I'm out at eight. And quiet. I mustn't wake her, poor thing."

So Duddy went on to explain, he had made a deal with Marlene. He agreed to bring her to London, where he had some business to transact in any case, and try to get the play produced. He would let her do it, with the proviso that if it failed she would renounce the theatre and have a child. "So," Duddy asked, "do you think anybody would be crazy enough to put it on here?"

"No. In Toronto, maybe. Who wrote it, incidentally?"

The author's name had been xxx'd over on the title page.

"Doug Fraser."

"Oh, my God, I should have known as much."

"Geez, I didn't realize the time," Duddy said, leaping up. "Would you have dinner with us tonight. I promised Marlene…."

"Not tonight. I'm busy. Tomorrow, if you like."

"Done. Oh, one thing. If Marlene asks, we had lunch together today. Dig?"

"Look here, Big Dick, I thought you were in love with her."

"Sure I am. But she's bound to be unfaithful to me sooner or later. It's in the cards. Why should I be the one to look like a fool? This way I get my licks in first. Tomorrow at seven. Right?"

— *St. Urbain's Horseman,* pp. 208–11

MORTIMER AND JOYCE were at the breakfast table when the doorbell rang.

"Ziggy! It's Ziggy!" Mortimer embraced his old friend. "Goddamn it, Ziggy, but I'm glad to see you. If only you knew how glad!"

"Um, sure," Ziggy said, disengaging himself, glancing apprehensively at Joyce over Mortimer's shoulder, wondering what manner of reception she would give him. "Look, man, I've only got French bread on me. Like there's this taxi waiting…."

Mortimer hurried outside to settle with the taxi driver.

"Coffee?" Joyce asked noncommittally.

"You're looking very well," Ziggy said.

Which was when Joyce realized that she was still wearing her chiffon negligée. "Oh, dear," she said, her cheeks reddening. "Excuse me a minute."

Joyce returned buttoned up to the throat in her brown velvet dressing gown, hand in hand with Doug. Ziggy grinned at the boy. "Remember your Uncle Ziggy, kiddo?"

"Y-y-yes."

Mortimer poured Ziggy a vodka-on-the-rocks and explained, "This is terrible, Ziggy, but I must go to the office this morning. There's something I simply must straighten out. Look, don't go out, will you? I'll hurry back."

Ziggy nodded graciously. Joyce poured him another coffee.

"What's bugging Mortimer? I've never seen him look so lousy."

"I don't want to talk about it," Joyce said, pushing her chair back from the table and fleeing to the kitchen.

Oi, Ziggy thought, oi, as he heard sobs coming from the bedroom. He finished his coffee and poured himself another cup. There was no household money in the coffee tin. Or the sugar canister. Suddenly Doug stood before him, beaming.

"Daddy's got a popsie," Doug said.

"Mortimer! No shit?"

"Quite," Doug said, getting into his coat. "I think it's rather super, don't you?"

"You cutting out, kid?"

"I thought perhaps you'd like to speak to Mother alone."

"I see."

"I won't be back until three. I haven't got a key so I'll have to ring, actually."

"You're a swinger, kid. *Ciao.*"

"*Ciao.*"

Ziggy rubbed his jaw pensively. He slipped a hand under his armpit, withdrew it, and smelled. Foo! He reached for the kitchen towel, wet it, and wiped under both armpits. He found the cutlery drawer, took out a paring knife, and methodically cleaned his finger-nails. Then Ziggy went into the hall, studied himself in the mirror, and ruffled his hair. He started for the bedroom, where she was still sobbing fitfully. Wait! Ziggy lowered his hand into his underwear, took a good grab, and had a whiff of his fingers. Pig! He went back for the kitchen towel.

"May I come in?" he asked in his tippy-toe voice.

Naturally she didn't answer. So Ziggy turned the door handle softly and sat down beside her on the bed, where she lay face down. "Joyce?" He began to stroke her tenderly, from top to bottom. "Stop crying, Joyce." He raked her more slowly now, lingering where it was warmest. "I hope you're not contemplating the bitchy thing, the obvious thing...."

"What?" Joyce turned over sharply, arching away from his hand, the five fevered fingers. "You bastard," she said.

Ziggy nodded, emphatically agreeing. "You're the only one," he said, "who has always been able to see right through me."

"Oh, you're rotten," she said, as he reached for the top button of her dressing gown. "Mortimer looks up to you. There's nobody he admires more."

"Yes, yes. And who could blame you, poor kid, if you wanted to get even with him."

—Cocksure, pp. 141–43

Barney attempts to use The Second Mrs. Panofsky's infidelity with an old friend to his own advantage — as grounds for divorce.

"You screwed my wife, you son of a bitch."

"I think we should have a drink before we get into this."

"I haven't even had breakfast yet."

"It's too early to eat," he said, pouring both of us stiff ones.

"How could you do this to me?"

"I did it to her, not you. And if you had phoned before leaving

Montreal, this embarrassing business could have been avoided. I think I'll go for a swim."

"Not yet, you won't. So it's my fault, is it?"

"In a manner of speaking, yes. You've been shirking your conjugal duties. She said it was seven months since you last made love to her."

"She told you that?"

"Cheers," he said.

"Cheers."

"She came into my room with a tray," he said, pouring us another drink, "and sat down on my bed in that short nightie. Now it was already awfully humid, so I could hardly blame her, but I suspected there was a message in there somewhere. A subtext. *Skoal.*"

"*Skoal.*"

"I laid my book aside. John Marquand's *Sincerely, Willis Wayde.* Now there's a novelist who is sadly underrated. Anyway, following a forced exchange of niceties (Hot, isn't it? I've heard so much about you. It's so good of you to put up with me in my condition, et cetera et cetera), and an awkward silence or two — I'd really like to go for a swim. May I borrow your snorkel and flippers?"

"Goddamn it, Boogie."

He poured us another drink and we both lit up Montecristos. "I guess we're going to have to fix our own lunch today," he said. "*A votre santé.*"

"Sure. Now get on with it, please."

"And then, unbidden as it were, she began to tell me about the problems you two were having, hoping for some good advice. You preferred the barroom companionship of losers to home most evenings, and on the rare occasions you deigned to come straight home from the office, you didn't talk to her but read a book at the table. Or *The Hockey News*, whatever that is. If she had other couples in to dinner, old friends of hers, you ambushed them. If they were of the right, you argued that it was the Soviets who had won World War II, and that one day Stalin would be recognized as the man of the century. But if they were of the left, you claimed there was scientific evidence to prove blacks were of inferior intelligence and too highly sexed; and you praised Nixon. Whenever you joined her parents for a

Sabbath dinner, you whistled at the table, an offense to her mother. She married you over the objections of her father, a distinguished intellectual, and then what? You neglect her in bed and she discovers that you are keeping a mistress in Toronto. Say, I happen to know there are some devilled eggs in the fridge. What do you think?"

So we moved to the kitchen table, taking the bottle and our glasses with us. "*L'chaim*," he said.

"*L'chaim*."

"I must say, she is given to verbosity. In full flow, there was no stopping her, and I fear my mind had begun to drift. But the next thing I knew, she leaned over to remove my tray and I caught a glimpse of her pleasing bosom. She sat down on my bed again, and began to sniffle, and I felt obliged to take her in my arms to comfort her, and still she didn't stop her prattling. I began to stroke her here and then there, and her protests, a kind of cooing, struck me as an invitation. 'You mustn't.' 'We ought to stop right now.' 'Oh please, not there.' And then, pretending that she wasn't returning my caresses, she started in on a dream she had had the previous night, even as she voluntarily raised her arms so that I could ease her out of her nightie, and, man, I figured the only way to shut her up was to fuck her, and that's how it happened. I think this bottle is empty."

—*Barney's Version,* pp. 294–96

THEN SUDDENLY, it was November 4, 1956, and Joshua stood in Trafalgar Square, along with thousands of others, come to hear Nye Bevan speak, and, in his case, possibly, just possibly, catch a glimpse of Pauline.

Any way you looked at it, it was a black Sunday. At breakfast Joshua read in the *Observer* that a high American government official had said, "There are people inside the National Security Council who have already urged that we use tactical atomic weapons...to help Hungary.... If the Hungarians are still fighting on Wednesday, we will be closer to war than we have been since August 1939."

Three-thirty in the afternoon, as Joshua stood in front of Canada House, in Trafalgar Square, Russian tanks had already encircled

Budapest, an Anglo-French invasion fleet had set sail from Cyprus, pipelines in Iraq and Syria were aflame, and Israeli troops had routed the Egyptian army in Sinai.

Thousands had been drawn to the meeting organized by the Labour Party and the Trades Union Congress. Pauline simply had to be amongst them, but where, and how to find her?

People filled the square, they filled the streets bordering the square, and they spilled over the steps of the National Gallery and St. Martin-in-the-Fields. It was the largest demonstration since the war and many who had come to protest were astonishingly young. They had, it's true, a special interest. Many had already been called up. Others were expecting to be called up soon.

The audacious Nye Bevan was at his corrosive best. While the pigeons of Trafalgar Square, temporarily homeless, swooped and complained above, he said, "If Eden is sincere in what he is saying — and he may be — then he is too stupid to be prime minister. He is either a knave or a fool. In both capacities, we don't want him."

"Eden must go!" the crowd roared back. "Eden must go!"

A perplexed Tory to Joshua's right countered with, "Yes, but who's going to replace him?"

Once Bevan had finished, the aroused crowd churned about hopelessly for a moment or two, private arguments flaring up here and there, and then, suddenly, spontaneously, it knit into a marching group. A toothy girl in a green cashmere twin set turned to her escort. "I say," she said, "they're actually going to march on Downing Street."

March on Downing Street they did, thousands upon thousands of them, bringing traffic to a dead stop, waving banners and shouting, "Eden must go! Eden must go!"

And there she was. Unmistakably. Pauline, Pauline. And, oh my God, she was wearing her tempting two-part partygoer for Yves-tide, with its whisper of silk ruffles.

To hell with Hungary! Fuck Suez! Oh my darling, my love, but beside her bobbed the ineffable Colin, beet-faced, hollering, "Eden must go!"

And you too, you little prick!

Bobbies, many of them young, apple-cheeked boys, stood about ten feet apart all the way down Whitehall, even as Joshua, possessed of an insane will, bulled his way through the crowd, hopping up and down for a glimpse of honey-coloured hair, listening for the whisper of silk ruffles above the din.

Pauline, Pauline.

At first the bobbies didn't interfere, but when the demonstrators reached Downing Street, out charged the mounted police. "Shame," the crowd chanted. "Shame!"

A long, pallid, black-bowlered man banged his furled umbrella on the pavement again and again. "Well done, the police," he shouted. "Well done, the police."

Joshua came up behind her and she turned, just for an instant, and smiled before she turned away again, driving her back shamelessly into him.

Heaven.

And he knew, he could swear, she was also wearing her Bali "Self-Expression" Seamless Front Closure Contour Bra, and time and patience would reveal what more.

"Eden must go!" cried a crazed, unknowing Colin.

His arms slid around her waist, her honey-coloured hair was driven into his face, and he began to tug her back and away.

The crowd surged forward, trying to breach Downing Street, the mounted police pushed them back again, then the crowd heaved again; and Joshua was dizzy with Pauline's perfume.

"Stop pulling. Patience," she said. "We've got to wait for Colin."

"He's just been arrested," Joshua said.

"Where?"

"I saw."

"You didn't."

"It's the pokey for him tonight. He'll be absolutely thrilled."

"You're lying," she said gaily, not taking her hand from his, falling against him again, laughing.

Joshua kissed Pauline on the mouth for the very first time.

"Marry me," he said.

"You're crazy."

"Marry me, marry me."

"But I've already got a husband."

"Of sorts."

"Joshua!"

"I'll take care of him. I come from a family of gangsters."

"Oh, I'll bet," she said.

When they finally quit Whitehall around six o'clock, the traffic had started to move once more and the pigeons were in possession of Trafalgar Square again. The next morning in bed they read in the *Daily Mail* that even while they had been heaving and chanting, Sir Anthony Eden had been sitting in session at Number 10 with leading cabinet ministers. The *Mail* observed that the demonstrators' ranks had included "large numbers of coloured men, some accompanied by white women. There were also Greeks, Cypriots, Indians, Pakistanis — many of them waving communist publications...."

Once more, a spiffy Canadian contingent had been overlooked.

— *Joshua Then and Now,* pp. 215–18

Miriam, the third Mrs. Panofsky, now also separated from him, finds him losing the battle with Alzheimer's.

MIRIAM ARRIVED THE NEXT MORNING, and the two of them went to lunch at the Ritz, where the maître d' didn't help matters, saying, "Why, I haven't seen you two together here for years. Just like old times, isn't it?"

Later Miriam told Saul: "I could see that the menu baffled him, and he asked me to order for both of us. But, to begin with, he was lighthearted. Even playful. I'm looking forward to games of hide-and-go-seek, and spin-the-bottle, with the other loonybins in whatever hospital I end up in. Maybe they'll have tricycles for us. Bubble gum. Triple-scoop ice creams. Stop it, I said. He ordered champagne, but what he actually said to the waiter was bring us a bottle of, you know, with the bubbles, what we used to have here, and the waiter laughed, thinking he was trying to be witty, and I was so insulted for him. When my husband, I wanted to say, intends to be witty, he is witty.

"Wouldn't it have been grand, Barney said, if I had agreed to fly to Paris with him on his wedding night. We recalled the good times, our salad days, and he promised not to be sick as he had been at our first lunch together. Although come to think of it, he said, it would make for a certain symmetry, wouldn't it? But this needn't be our last lunch together, I said. We can be friends now. No, we can't, he said. It has to be everything or nothing. I had to get up twice to go to the ladies' room for fear of breaking down at the table. I watched him pop I don't know how many different-coloured pills, but he drank his champagne. He reached for my hand under the table, and told me I was still the most beautiful woman he had ever seen, and that he had once dared to hope that we would die simultaneously, in our nineties, like Philemon and Baucis, and that beneficent Zeus would turn us into two trees, whose branches would fondle each other in winter, our leaves intermingling in the spring.

"Then, I don't know, maybe he shouldn't have had the champagne. He began to mispronounce words. He had trouble dealing with his cutlery. Selecting a spoon when it was a fork he needed. Picking up a knife by the blade rather than the handle. An embarrassing change came over him, possibly prompted by frustration. His face darkened. Lowering his voice, he motioned me closer, and said Solange was forging cheques. She was swindling him. He was fearful she might force him to sign a will she had fabricated. She was a nymphomaniac who once yanked his apartment doorman into the elevator with her and raised her dress to show him she wasn't wearing panties. The bill came and I could see that he was unable to add it up. Just sign it, I said, which made him laugh. Okay, he said, but I doubt they'll recognize my new signature. Hey, I still remember some things, he said. I once brought her here with her mother, and that old bitch said, 'My husband always tips twelve and a half percent.'

"Then his manner altered yet again. He was tender. Loving. Barney at his most adorable. And I realized that he had forgotten that I had ever left him, and obviously assumed we would now go home together, and maybe take in a movie tonight. Or read in bed, our legs tangled together. Or catch a late flight to New York, the way he used to pull surprises out of a hat. Oh, in those days he was so much fun, so unpredictable, so loving, and I thought what if I didn't return to Toronto, and did go home with him? That's when I went to the phone and called Solange and asked her to come at once. I got back to the table and he wasn't there. Oh my God, where is he, I asked the waiter. Men's room, he said. I waited outside the men's room, and when he came out, shuffling, his smile goofy, I saw that his fly was still unzipped and his trousers were wet."

—Barney's Version, pp. 408–09

Hot Stuff

There's love, and then there's...what sometimes passes for love. As a writer who helped break down the barriers to free expression in the 1950s and 1960s, Richler was called upon by newspaper and magazine editors to comment on aspects of the Sexual Revolution. Such assignments, including reviews of books like Rachel Swift's How to Have an Orgasm...as Often You Want, *and Desmond Morris's* Intimate Behaviour, *provided Richler with the opportunity to riff on the comic possibilities of unbridled desire, and with further material for his fiction.*

Barney Larkin (not to be confused with Barney Panofsky in Barney's Version) *considers purchasing sex in a Spanish brothel.*

A FOG OF CIGARETTE FUMES drifted about the anteroom. The sweaty walls seemed to shed faded wallpaper like dead skin. Seated atop a high stool, plump Rosita presided over a counter on which were piled orderly stacks of chips. Had Rosita been born a man or of a good family she might have been a tycoon or a politician; as it was, she was sole owner of the *casa.* She twirled the faceless, dirty, copper coins in her hands. Dependent on their size they merited; *uno vez,* *dos veces,* the whole night. She was dressed in a black gown. She had about her the air of the smug showman assured of an unending season and the universality of her attractions. She was human though, Rosita. She had loved, she had suffered. Was there no justice? With all her loot, all her gold, where was she admitted? And ha! she could tell them! she was no worse, not one bit worse, than any of them! And *madre mía* she knew them all. They all came dribbling through her door, their lust-hungry tongues hanging and their eyes popping — so cheap they couldn't talk to a girl without pinching, squeezing, feeling, pawing…crawling for their copper chips, begging for their quickies or their nights of splendour. And they were all the same — the anarchists and the bankers…the jerk-off Jesuits and the ac/dc nuns raiding the collection plate for the one-a-month hallelujah go with *pequeña Pepita mía!*…the workers cheating on their bread money because ah the charms of Pilar! And the pot-bellied bastards! the giggling men-children, saving it up like misers, careful not to lift anything heavy and following a special diet, still good for only one huff-and-puff throw. And she, Rosita (if not for her they would be walking the streets, going for months without a decent examination), not worthy of them?! Oh, the stories she could tell.

Giddy with anger Rosita fingered a copper coin that was worth a full night of uninterrupted lovemaking. She smiled at Barney — properly respectful, properly reserved. Only her lips contradicted her superficial amicability. They were bitter, twisted, knowing.

"Hell, she's a real businessman, you know. No funny stuff. I can tell that by just looking at her."

"Yes. She is very shrewd."

"Look — em — frankly, I mean. Do you think any of them are sick? I've got a wife and…"

"They are clean."

"Swell."

"Come into the parlour with me."

The parlour was painted pink. It was a huge, unfurnished room. Wooden benches lined the drab walls. The other end of the room led into a long hallway and the bedrooms. Eight or nine men, their faces distorted in various stages of sexual anticipation, lingered restlessly on the benches. They laughed too loudly at each other's jokes, they slapped each other too heartily on the back. An old, pot-bellied man was seated apart from them. His skin was jaundiced, wrinkled. He brought the girls their pails of hot water and towels when they drifted into the bedrooms with their lovers. Beside him, on the bench, lay a basket of sweets. Now and then he shuffled about the room, insulting and cursing the men until they condescended to buy their girl a candy. He picked idly at his nose and sneaked glances at Pilar because her breasts were showing. Pilar despised him. But there were some things the other men would not do.

"Sweetheart," a young soldier said in a falsetto voice, "how much to do a little job for me?"

All the men on the bench giggled.

The old man spat over his shoulder. "What a soldier! How much do you earn a month, boy? Is it enough to spend fifteen minutes with Pilar? Or do you think you could last that long?"

"Old pimp! Is it true that the girls play games with you after the house closes down?"

"You talk as if you feel at home here, boy. Perhaps your mother works here?"

"Say that again!"

"Perhaps your mother works here? Or perhaps she only drops in to bring your sister sandwiches?"

Two of the other men got up and pushed the soldier back on the bench.

"Don't be a fool!"

"He's just a filthy old bastard!"

The old man roared with laughter.

The girls, dressed in kimonos or black underwear or sheer gowns, gossiped noisily in a corner of the room. They sat around like stuffed animals, absently scratching their thighs. Their faces were dull and their bodies weary, legs and arms as impersonal as empty stockings. They were neither sad nor forlorn — just empty, like dead souls. None was older than thirty or younger than fourteen. Some of them had been dancers, others had played bit parts in music halls. Occasionally one of the girls would break away from the group and spring onto one of the young men's laps, kissing and fiddling with him. This failing to encourage him she would soon abandon him, slapping him playfully in parting. Soon another girl came along — blonde following brunette, fat following lean, young following old — until the aroused men were forced into selecting a partner. Amid laughter they would make their way to the bedroom.

"They are very young here," Luís said.

"I like the one in the black slit skirt. Hell, she looks like the goods all right!"

"Shall I call her over?"

Barney hesitated. "You're sure they're okay, huh? No clap or anything?"

"I am certain."

"How many times do you think they get it every night?"

"I don't know. It depends."

"There must be at least thirty of them here, huh?"

"Yes."

"She must really clean up!"

"We call her the Queen."

"Why?"

"It's difficult to explain."

"I'll bet it is. This is no place for a queen!"

The girls were gathered around Lolita. She was new, from Cadiz. She had first gone into a brothel in Seville, five years ago, when she had been fourteen. That year, among the tourists in town for Holy Week, there had been a phenomenal demand for virgins. An enterprising pimp had picked her up in the slums of Cadiz and offered her five hundred pesetas to come to Seville. What a girl she had been then! Such a body! (She showed the others a photo.) Now she was weary — always as if she had just finished running a race. She no longer excited men — *Qué lástima, Lolita!* You make love like a dead woman. Isn't my money as good as the next man's? And now she was only able to attract clients by permitting the perversions that had horrified her four years ago. And even then she was only an extra girl, working small towns that lacked for amusements during the off season.

Spread out on her lap was an album, cheap blurred snaps of the Photomaton variety. Each tawdry photo represented one of her lovers, lovers of a night and sometimes lovers of a month. In her whining, frightened voice she was telling the girls about Ramón. Yes, she agreed with Carmen, he hadn't been as handsome as López or as generous as René, but he had been really funny. And if Jaime had been free and easy with his money hadn't he been the one who had infected her? Yes…(slowly, nostalgically, she flipped over the page). Ah, here was Jorge! He came every night for six weeks. Look, the Norwegian! And Julian, who had paid extra so that he might beat her with a belt. But, the Norwegian. Arne, I think, was his name….

Suddenly Valentina kicked up her leg and the album went flying through the air. Photos scattered in all directions, flipping and twisting, slowly spiralling downwards.

Lolita gasped. She turned pale. "Why did you do that? You didn't have to do that."

Pilar snickered. The others remained silent. Valentina was chieftain among the girls. Also, she was Francisco's mistress. It was Francisco who arranged those appointments for the afternoon and those lovely weekends in the country. It was Francisco who journeyed to Palma for hashish. If one offended Valentina one was liable to be cut off for a week.

"Silly bitch!" Valentina said. "What do we care for your pictures? If you are going to work here you will have to learn not be proud. Understand?"

Lolita got down on her hands and knees and began to gather up the photos.

A few of the girls laughed grimly.

"Do you think they get any fun out of it?" Barney asked.

"It's just a job."

"You know it's okay with a whore if you know what I mean. You can horse around a bit. With your wife it's a different story. I mean a guy feels kind of dirty. Don't you think so?"

"Yes."

A dark girl caught Barney's eye and smiled at him beneath drooping eyelids. Smiling still, she ran her hands down her kimono. She fondled herself not in joy or with a sense of wonder, but as if she understood, as if everyone understood. Slowly she walked towards him.

She sat down beside him, her kimono hanging open.

"*Cómo se llama su amigo?*" she asked Luís.

"*No capishe!*" Barney said.

"She wants to know your name."

"My name is Jones…Henry Jones."

"*Él se llama Enríque.*"

"*Quién es?*"

"*Es un tonto Americano.*"

"What's going on? What did she say?"

"She says you are very handsome."

'Tell her she's okay."

"*Él dice que tu es muy guapa.*"

"*Tío! Claro.*"

Long locks of hair fell down to her shoulders and gathered in silken tangles on her black kimono. The richer black of her hair glistened on the shabby robe like strands of ebony. She sat down on Barney's lap and kissed him. Barney laughed.

"Hey! She's really the goods." Barney kissed her and he was careful not to touch her lips. "Me come. Me you boom-boom!'"

She laughed, tickling him under the chin.

"Ask her how much."

Across the room Pilar found herself a lover. The old man, the guardian of the pails and towels, was dozing. The couple crept up on him silently and careful not to awaken him. Then, just as they were upon him, Pilar turned her plump behind on him and broke wind. The old man awakened with a start.

"Ask her how much!"

— *The Acrobats*, pp. 101–06

CUT THE CAKE ANY WAY YOU LIKE. Modern life is empty, experience is meaningless, sex deadening, but when we lined up for *Blow-Up* we knew, in our hearts, exactly what we hoped to see. A tit show. Not only that. In the scene where the anti-hero romps with two nude girls on his studio floor, there was supposed to be a crotch shot, pubic hairs that would not titillate but were indicative of our spiritual malaise, the sick times we live in, etc. etc. etc.

In these heady, permissive times, the movies have it all over your adult sex novel. The four-letter words, all spelled the same, soon pall on us, not so the breasts and private parts of stars and starlets, especially when we can ogle in the name of art, with no guilt attached, as there would be coming out into the sun after an afternoon at the nudies.

The fact is a number of so-called serious film directors have been able to con the censor, getting away with a good deal of windy talk on the subject of sex as a profound comment on our Godless time, when it is merely salacious. Not that I'm against nudity in films; it gives me a charge. Why, I am even grateful that the orgy scene has become as integral a part of so many adult films (*La Dolce Vita*, *Darling*, *The Loved One*) as freckled kids and dogs with wagging tails were to Walt Disney. What I do object to is the hot stuff going by another name.

Sydney Lumet, for instance, was able to argue successfully for a bare-breasted shot of a coloured prostitute in his ponderous, prosaic *The Pawnbroker*, claiming high purpose and, incidentally, acquiring a lot of useful publicity. Most likely, Lumet believed the shot necessary to the film, just as he obviously considered it powerful stuff to show a nude, sexy Jewish wife waiting for her SS man on her concentration camp bed. If so, he is a man of integrity who suffers, alas, from a failure of taste and imagination.

In any event, I would give a lot to sit with Jack Valenti and his bunch, or the Catholic Legion of Decency, as they deliberate — loftily, I'm sure — on whose breasts are edifying, whose lascivious. On their curious, decidedly prudish scale of values, I rather imagine Ingrid Bergman's breasts are the cleanest, whereas Raquel Welch's big boobs would come at the bottom of the scale, the very nipples being dirty-minded.

Raquel Welch in London, 1970.

—*Hunting Tigers under Glass,*
"Writing for the Movies," pp. 95–96

WHEREVER BETTE WENT she was instantly recognized. Ordinary people felt better just for having seen her. But if Canada loved Bette Dolan it was also true that she so loved the country that she felt it would be unfair, sort of favouritism, for her to give herself to any one man. So although many, including cabinet ministers, actors, millionaires, and playboys, had tried, Bette remained, in her mother's words, a clean girl. Until, that is, she met Atuk.

Bette first met Atuk at the party for him at the Park Plaza Hotel and saw him again at another party a couple of months later. Atuk was enthralled and promptly asked if he could meet Bette again. To his amazement, she said yes. Actually, Bette was more grateful than he knew, because by this time nobody bothered to ask her for a date any more. Bette made dinner for Atuk at her apartment. Carrot juice, followed by herb soup and raw horse steak with boiled wild rice. Atuk, thoughtful as ever, had scraped together some money and brought along a bottle of gin. Bette, lithe and relaxed in her leotards, told Atuk about her father and how his life had been changed by the teachings of Doc Burt Parks. She sensed Atuk felt depressed, maybe even defeated by Toronto, and tried her best to encourage him. "You'll be a success here yet," she said.

"I don't know. It is so difficult."

"But success doesn't depend on the *size* of your brain," she assured him.

Atuk hastily added some gin to the carrot juice.

"Dr. Parks has always said," Bette continued, too absorbed to protest, "that if you want to succeed you must always shoot for the bull's-eye."

Atuk promised to try.

"You're as good as the next fellow. You simply must believe that, Atuk. You see, the most successful men have the same eyes, brain, arms, and legs as you have."

"I drink now. You too."

"'I'll bet,' she said, narrowing her eyes, "that you envy some people."

"Many, many people."

"*But still more people envy you.*"

"Do they?"

"Sure. Some are bald — you have a head full of hair. Some are blind — you can see. *Everybody envies somebody else.* You must learn to have faith in yourself."

Soon they were sipping gin and carrot juice together nightly and Bette continued to do her utmost to fill Atuk with confidence.

"Why go to so much trouble?" he once asked her.

"Because I have to help people. That's me." Her long, powerful, Lloyd-insured legs curled under her on the sofa, a lock of blonde hair falling over her forehead, Bette smiled and said, "Do you realize you're just about the only male who has never — never tried the funny stuff with me?"

"Don't you admire me for it?" he asked hopefully.

"Yes. Certainly I do." She got down on the floor and began a lightning series of chin-ups. A sure sign she was troubled. "But don't you love me?" She rolled over on her back, supporting her buttocks with her hands and revolving her legs swiftly. "Everybody loves Bette Dolan," she insisted.

"And so do I. Oh, so do I!"

So Atuk told her his dreadful secret. "I lack confidence," he said, "because I am unable to make love. All that stands between me and hitting the bull's-eye is a woman who can…well, encourage me over the hump." He lowered his head. "I need help, Miss Dolan."

A plea for help was something Bette Dolan had never taken lightly. She sprang to her feet, bouncing upright. Her lovely face filled with determination. After a long and solemn pause, she said, "I will help you, Atuk."

"Would you? Honest?"

To prove it she stepped right up to him, her eyes squeezed shut against anticipated distaste, and kissed him on the mouth. "It's the very first time for me," she said.

"I'm so afraid," Atuk said, his voice quavering, "of failing."

Bette kissed him again, forcing his mouth open. When she was done, Atuk cleared his throat and poured himself a rather strong gin and carrot juice.

"Aren't you even…don't you feel…?"

"It's no use," he said.

Bette pulled him down to the rug with her and led his hand to her breast. "This should be very stimulating for you," she said. She kissed him even more passionately, rolled over on him, tried a couple of other sure-fire things, and then pulled back to look at him quizzically.

"Well," he said, "I do feel a certain…"

"Good."

"I think my pulse-beat *has* quickened."

"That's progress, isn't it?"

But it seemed to Atuk there was a sour edge to her voice now.

"That's all for tonight," she said.

At the door, however, she suddenly clung to him. "I hope you realize," she said, "that no man has ever even held me in his arms before. I couldn't, you see. Because I belong to the nation. Like Jasper Park or Niagara Falls."

"I do understand."

"I'm trying to help, that's all."

She had Atuk back early the next afternoon for a lecture.

"I think your trouble may be mental," she said.

"Very likely. Many times the Old One has said —"

"Well," she interrupted, taking a deep breath, "the first thing you must understand is that every human being from the beginning of time has possessed sex organs and was produced as a result of sexual intercourse. Does that shock you?"

Atuk whistled.

"I thought it would. You must learn to think of your sex organ," she said, drawing a sketch on the blackboard, "as being just as common as your hands, your heart, or your pectoral muscles. If you analyze the penis as you analyze the function of any other part of your body you will find that it's made up of essentially the same kind of materials."

"I'm going to love it in Toronto," Atuk said.

"What?"

"Nothing," he said, hastily pouring himself another gin and carrot juice.

"Then, to quote Dr. Parks, if you analyze the sex act itself in the same clear-thinking way, you will see that this simple function is no more mysterious or filthy than eating, breathing, or urinating."

After the lecture Bette shed her smock and was revealed in the most provocative silk pajamas. Her work clothes, she called them offhandedly, and she at once engaged Atuk in a series of practical exercises: therapy. Soon there were lectures every afternoon and by the end of the first week there was rather less time spent at the blackboard and more at therapy. She was, Atuk thought, very inventive for a novice. Usually, she was also the acme of patience. A model teacher. Though there were times when the therapy became so real for her that the final, inevitable disappointment made her petulant.

"I want you," she ultimately said, "to go for broke today."

"You mean shoot for the bull's-eye?"

"Yes," she said, exasperated. "I'm not enjoying this, you know. I'm only trying to help. But I'm getting discouraged. You must try to help yourself, you know."

"I couldn't. I…"

Bette sprang up and caught him in a judo hold. "You shoot for the bull's-eye, goddam it," she said, "or I'll…"

So Atuk finally made love to Bette.

Afterwards Bette lay so still, she seemed so remote, that Atuk wondered if she suspected that she had been seduced.

But Bette had been lifted into a hitherto unsuspected sphere. It had never occurred to her before that lovemaking could be anything but nasty. Filthy. Like her father belting her mother into submission in the next room. How utterly wonderful, she thought, that indulging in the funny stuff could be such a generous and Christian thing to do. There was truth, after all, in her mother's saying, time and again, that there was no joy greater than helping others.

Atuk spiked his carrot juice with more gin.

"I think," Bette said, her voice jarringly submissive, "that you ought to try again, sweetheart."

And so Canada's Darling, the unobtainable Bette Dolan, became Atuk's grateful mistress, and Atuk was soon reconciled to phone calls at all hours of the day or night.

"You must come over immediately," she'd say. "I feel the need to help you."

So at a quarter to eight Atuk started out of the rooming house, jumped a bus, and hurried over to Bette's place.

Perhaps it was because he was so lonely, maybe he drank too many gin and carrot juices, but that evening Atuk confessed to Bette what he had done on the tundra.

Bette was certainly horrified by the nature of his crime, but she said, "The case is closed. You have nothing to worry about, darling."

"I didn't mean any harm. What did I know of such things?"

"Of course, of course," she said, pulling him to her again.

"You must promise never to repeat what I have told you," Atuk said, suddenly realizing that he had revealed his most dreadful secret. "You must swear it, Bette."

"I swear it. Now come here."

—*The Incomparable Atuk,* pp. 18–24

RACHEL SWIFT is the pseudonym of "an average woman in her thirties" who, having finally had her first orgasm during sex, decided to publish a step-by-step self-help book for others who were missing out. Practise control, she advocates. Prepare yourself by becoming proficient at masturbation. "Your own hands," she writes, "are the most useful tool...[because] they are warm as well as uniquely sensitive." But she also recommends rolled-up socks, or the arm of a teddy bear, which is soft *and* firm.

Once, she writes, while she was staying in a hotel room in Bali, "the waiter knocked on the door with a dish of exotic fruit. Feeling horny, I sized up the man — and decided his bananas looked more appetizing than he did. When he had shut the door, I unpeeled a not-too-ripe banana and used it to great effect."

My considered advice is that if you are invited to Ms. Swift's home for dinner, turn down the fruit salad.

—*Belling the Cat,* "Supersex," p. 87

BUT THEN THE FEMALE FORM, as [zoologist Desmond] Morris sees it, can be fairly said to bristle with genital substitutes, the mouth being by far the most important of these, as it "transmits a great deal of pseudo-genital signalling during amorous encounters." Morris then alludes to the unique development of everted lips in our species, and goes on to say that their fleshy pink surfaces have developed as a labial mimic at the biological, rather than purely cultural, level. "Like the true labia they become redder and more swollen with sexual arousal, and like them they surround a centrally placed orifice."

Yes, quite, but the implications are unnerving. For, if we allow that evolution is a continuing process (as witness the astonishing percentile leap of genital-shaped female navels), encouraged not only by modern photographers but novelists as well, and then take into account the contemporary novelist's propensity for describing fellatio, it seems possible that the labia, compensating, will eventually emerge as a mouth mimic. One day women, like egg timers, will be the same rightside up as upside down. What I'm suggesting is that not in our time, certainly, but when our great-grandchildren pass from self-intimacy (head scratching, leg-crossing, masturbation) to the joys of full-scale pair-bonding, they may encounter true serendipity, that is to say, a laughing labia, or possibly one that can even tell stories. In a word, a pseudo-mouth substitute.

— *Notes on an Endangered Species and Others,*
"Intimate Behaviour," pp. 159–60

BOOGIE WROTE:

Mankind, manifestly imperfect, is still riding the evolutionary cycle. In the far future, if only for the sake of convenience, the genitals of both men and women will rise to where our heads are now, and our increasingly redundant noggins will sink to where our genitals once rested. This will enable young and old to lock into each other without tiresome romantic foreplay or the inevitable struggle with buttons or zippers. They will be able to "only connect," as Forster advised, while waiting for a traffic light to change, or lining up before the supermarket cashier, or on a synagogue bench or church pew. "Fucking," or the more genteel "lovemaking," will be known as "a header," as in, "Walking down Fifth Avenue, I sniffed this fetching chick, and threw her a header."

The flip side of this cultural refinement is that the brothel, or cat-house, will yield to the library as the forbidden place where sinners meet to tryst (unzipping or lowering panties, to converse grammatically) under constant threat of closure by the antiliteracy squad. And the new social disease will be intelligence. Remember, you read it here first.

— *Barney's Version,* p. 186

MOSES TURNED THE MERCEDES onto a narrow bumpy track and eased it down a steep incline, tucking it among the trees where it could not be seen from either the road or the river. Then he led Darlene to where he had laid out the quilted blanket.

"Oh, you're such a *dreadful* man," she squealed, setting down her camera.

Moses lifted the vodka bottle out of the ice bucket, dipped in for some ice cubes, and poured her a long one. He sat down and watched enviously, his heart aching, as she gulped it. Then she contrived to tumble into his lap, the glass rolling away, her drink spilling on the blanket. He was still mourning the lost liquor as she squirmed out of her jeans and he slid her jersey over her head. He began to fondle and kiss her breasts.

"Oh boy, do I ever go for *that*," she said, swaying from side to side, her pentangle clipping him in the nose as she jiggled her breasts and cooed, "You never guessed, didja?"

"How Lyndon was lost in the mail?"

"*Nooo!* How I had them made as a fortieth-birthday surprise for Barney."

"Your breasts?"

"They're implants, you silly."

A troubled Moses retreated from her, unwrapped a Montecristo and lighted it with a shaky hand. "Did he pick the size?"

"He didn't *exactly*, but hint hint, he did show me pictures from magazines of the kind of tits that turned him on. I'm such an airhead. Nothing could happen. I knew *that*, the doctor assured me, but for the first few months I wouldn't let anybody squeeze too hard and I didn't dare sit close to the fireplace at the ski lodge, because I was scared they might — Well, you know. *The heat.*"

Moses inhaled deeply, wishing that he were somewhere else, somewhere alone. Sensing that he had begun to drift, a pouting Darlene got him out of his shirt and began to probe between his legs, fishing for him. "There isn't a manual I haven't read," she said. "Talk as dirty as you want. Order me to do things."

She bit his ear. Moses yelped and bit right back.

"Hey, there! Hold your horses. *Woa!*" she said, thrusting him from her with surprising strength.

"What's wrong?"

"It's my fault. I shoulda told you right off that there's to be no scratching or biting or even hard pinching, honey, because he checks me out for bruises every night." She had him out of his trousers now, but stopped abruptly short of descending on him, her face clouding. "How many times can you come at your age, honey? I should know that before I risk spoiling any multiples for me."

Possibly, he thought, back in Chapel Hill, where they were very big in furniture, she did door-to-door surveys.

"Are you still there?" Reaching down to root out his testicles, she discovered, to her consternation, that he only had one. "Holy Toledo," she said, a shopper short-changed.

"What did you expect? A cluster?"

"FAR OUT!" she exclaimed, running her tongue from his groin to his throat like he was an envelope to be sealed.

But now her camera had become painfully lodged in his back. Moses pried it free. "What did you bring this for?" he asked, holding it up.

"Silly. I brought it along because I thought you'd surely want to take some pussy pictures for a souvenir to remember me by. Look!"

Leaping up, she turned her back to him and bent over to clasp her knees, ass riding high, and then she hooked one finger through her black bikini panties, tugging at them. Shifting to an upright position, her back still turned to him, she shot him an over-the-shoulder naughty wink, licked her lips and then popped her thumb into her mouth, fellating it. He was reminded of the Goldberg Brothers Auto Parts calendar stapled to the wall in the Texaco station on Laurier Street. Unable to help himself, Moses shook with appreciative laughter. "Oh, Darlene, you are perfection. Honestly."

"Then why aren't you snapping any pictures?" She struck another Playmate pose, this one obliging her to at least partially dress. "Go ahead and shoot the whole roll, but please remember to take it with you."

Only then did she notice that he was also dressed.

For her, he hoped, it would not be passion frustrated or, God help us, unrequited love so much as gym class cancelled for today.

"Maybe it's better this way," she said, "our being, well you know, platonic friends...but I did think we had come here to fuck our brains out and I never did it with a *real* highbrow before."

"Maybe we should start thinking about getting back."

"Not yet. Jim Boyd says you can make a salmon dance on its tail. Show me," she said, her eyes taunting. "Show me."

"Okay, but it will be strictly catch-and-release."

"Like me," she said, startling him.

— *Solomon Gursky Was Here,* pp. 285–87

THE BAR WAS ROCKING with chattering men and women wearing name tags, educators gathered from all ends of the continent to ponder WHITHER THE GLOBAL VILLAGE? But, as Moses started into his fourth double scotch, most of them had dispersed, only a handful of dedicated drinkers surviving. Then a lady came flying into the room, out of breath, obviously too late for the party. She snuggled into the stool immediately beside Moses and ordered a vodka on the rocks. "Prosit," she said.

MY NAME IS CINDY DUTKOWSKI wore a snug woollen dress and carried an enormous shoulder bag. Fierce she was, black hair unruly, petite, forty maybe. She taught Communications 101 at Maryland U. "Say, do my eyes deceive me, or didn't I see you in Washington last week, rapping with Sam Burns at the Sans Souci?"

"You're mistaken."

"I'll bet you're also a media personality and I should know your name."

"Sorry about that."

"If you tell me your name, I won't bite."

"Moses Berger," he said, signing his bar bill and starting to slide off his stool. She shoved him back.

"Hey, you're really shy. It's a form of arrogance, you know. It also protects you against rejections in highly charged social encounters. I was a psych major." Hers, she said, was an open marriage, which allowed both partners a lifestyle enabling them to explore their full sexual potential.

"That must be awfully convenient for you."

"Oh come on. Do I have to spell it out? I'm interested if you are."

MY NAME IS CINDY DUTKOWSKI scooped up her enormous shoulder bag and they went up to his room, not hers, because she was sharing with a real square, she said, a lady from Montana who undressed in the bathroom. "I'm willing to act out your favourite fantasy, so long as it isn't too kinky."

"The usual," an intimidated Moses said, "will suit me fine."

In that case, she had a menu of her own. "I'm going to be your laid-back, but secretly horny high school teacher and you are the nerdy little teenager. I've asked you to report to my office after classes, pretending that we have to go over your latest assignment, but actually because I caught you peeking up my skirt when I sat on your desk this morning and it really turned me on. Now you go wait out in the hall and don't knock on my office door until I call out 'ready.' You dig?"

"I'm not sure exactly how you want me to behave."

"Well, you know. You don't know from nothing. Like Canadian will do."

"Gotcha," he said, slipping out of the room, tiptoeing over to the elevator bank, and then grabbing a taxi at the front door of the hotel. "Take me to a bar where they don't play loud music."

—*Solomon Gursky Was Here,* pp. 325–26

Even when I was a boy his admonitions were few.
"Don't embarrass me. Don't get into trouble."
I embarrassed him. I got into trouble.

PART VII

IT WAS A QUESTION OF SURVIVAL

While the portraits of parents and family members in Richler's essays, stories, and fiction are, in some measure, based on his own experience, the novels are unreliable as autobiography. It may be noted, however, that Richler's fictional mothers (like Joshua's mother, the aspiring stripper, in Joshua Then and Now*) are often distant and self-involved, as his own mother was. And his fictional fathers (like Issy Panofsky, the cop, in* Barney's Version*) are passive but also roguish and charming.*

Richler's escape to Europe when he was young was certainly an escape from family, among other things. What is striking is the familial affection that survived the early emotional battering and the later interpolation of distance. Richler's fondness for the (real) failed fighter Maxie Berger bears some similarity to the tenderness with which he portrays a variety of male characters — from Duddy's Uncle Benjy (The Apprenticeship of Duddy Kravitz) *to Noah's grandfather Melech* (Son of a Smaller Hero)*, and his own singularly unassertive father.*

— J. W.

I WAS VERY CLOSE TO MY MOTHER for a certain period and then she became insufferable, and I ended up very close to my father. He was a very shy, very timid, modest, not incredibly bright man, who had a very hard life. She was driving me crazy. She would turn up unannounced at seven in the morning. And she was very paranoid. She turned up one day at lunchtime — I was sitting in the garden reading the paper, very hungover — and reproached me because I wasn't using her as a babysitter. I wasn't using her as a babysitter because the kids couldn't stand her. And I'd been sending her money for years too. In Europe it was easy because I'd bring her over once a year and it was two weeks, and it was all right, we got through it. But when we were here, she wanted to move in, and I thought, "I won't be able to live here." So it was a question of survival, and I chose mine. It must have been 1974. The sour truth is that when she said "I don't want to see you," I was kind of relieved. It was very selfish. She was a ball of anger and it kept her alive into her nineties. I could have behaved better, but I didn't.

—Michael Posner, The Last Honest Man, pp. 181–82

AFTER WEEKS OF CAROUSING ON IBIZA, taking in the cockfights with Juanito and his cronies, staggering out of Rosita's at dawn, Joshua certainly couldn't claim to be paddling his own canoe through the storms of temptation. There was simply no stroke, stroke, stroke. The truth was, he had to admit, he was not so much interested in writing as in being a writer. Somebody well-known. But his twenty-first birthday had come and gone and he was not yet famous. He not only embraced unclean women, but gorged himself on forbidden foods: *gambas, calamares,* spider crab. Only eight years after his bar mitzvah, whorehouse orgies.

Gehenna beckoned.

But to be fair to himself, his bar mitzvah, he recalled, had not exactly got him off to an auspicious start if he was meant to mature into an observant Jew.

"Don't worry, kiddo," his mother had said. "You're going to have a party. Oh boy, are you ever going to have a party!" In the morning, she had actually roused herself to make him breakfast and, charged with enthusiasm, she said, "Make me a list."

"Of what?"

"The boys you want for your party."

"Forget it," he said.

"I'm going to be a good mother from now on, Josh. No more fucking with Ryan." And then, looking at him quizzically, she added, "Something tells me it upsets you."

"I don't want a party."

"Why not?"

"What would we do?"

"Well, we won't play pin-the-tail-on-the-donkey or Parcheesi. It's going to be a surprise."

When he came home from school he found his mother on her knees, scrubbing the floors. The beds had been made, the dishes washed. The garbage was ready to be carted out. "You have an appointment with Mandelcorn for six o'clock. He's going to teach you all the mumbo-jumbo you need for the synagogue. If he asks if we eat kosher here, you say yes," and once more she demanded a list of boys.

A week before his bar mitzvah she decorated the hall with crêpe paper and Chinese lanterns. Streamers ran from wall to wall in the living room. Balloons hung from every light fixture.

Gifts began to arrive. Uncle Harvey sent phylacteries, a silver wine goblet, and $25 in war savings certificates. Euclid delivered

Ed Ryan's peace offering — a sharkskin windbreaker, THE CHAMP embossed on the back, the pockets stuffed with silver dollars. Colucci sent books: a biography of Marconi, an illustrated history of the Jewish people, and a collection of Winston Churchill's speeches. There was also a case of V.O. in a box tied with a ribbon.

Saturday morning, in the synagogue, Joshua stumbled through the blessings he was obliged to pronounce, older members of the congregation shaking their heads, amazed that anyone, even a gangster's boy, could be so ignorant. And what about the mother? A Leventhal girl. Her eyelashes false, her cheeks rouged. Reeking of perfume.

No sooner did they get home than his mother wiggled out of her dress, buttoned on a housecoat, and, consulting her newly acquired cookbook, set to work in the kitchen. Louis Armstrong belted out "The Saints Go Marching In" as her marble cake was mixed and then slapped into the oven. She poured what looked like a half-bottle of kirsch into her fruit salad. Onions flew in all directions as, bolstered with Dewar's, she started in on the chopped liver. Meatballs, varying a good deal in size, were pitched into a pan and then stacked on a platter like cannonballs. Her sponge cake failed to rise, her cheese pie obstinately refused to set. Boiled chicken pieces, churning in fat, bounced back from her probing fork again and again. Burnt edges had to be scraped off her chocolate chip cookies.

Of the twenty boys Joshua had invited to his party the following afternoon, only twelve turned up — the others, he gathered, having been forbidden to attend. Seymour Kaplan was there, of course, so were Morty Zipper, Mickey Stein, Bernie Zucker, Bobby Gross, Max Birenbaum, Yossel Kugelman, his cousin Sheldon, and, to his surprise, Eli Seligson and Izzy Singer. They were all combed and shined, wearing their High Holiday suits, but Joshua could see at once that they were ill at ease. Most of them did not know what to expect. Neither did Joshua, decidedly apprehensive, as his mother had been into the Dewar's again since shortly after breakfast, her mood menacingly cheerful.

The boys had been gathered in the living room for only half an hour, increasingly fidgety, when it became obvious to them that there was not going to be a movie or whatever. In fact, it seemed like there was going to be absolutely nothing to do.

"Who would like to play Information, Please?" his mother called out cheerily.

Groans and moans.

"What about sardines?"

"Hey, we're not kids any more," Mickey admonished her.

"Good. That's what I thought. All right, Josh. Draw the blinds."

Oh boy, a movie after all.

But Joshua knew different, because she was already screwing in the red light bulb that throbbed on and off.

"Maw, you can't."

"That's what they said to the Wright Brothers."

"They wouldn't understand."

"Shettup and put on the record."

"Maw, please."

"Do as I ask. Come on, Josh."

So he put on "Snake Hips."

"Now don't anybody move," his mother said, running off.

The baffled boys sat on the floor, as instructed. Even as they were becoming restless, there was a rap on the door and Joshua started playing "Snake Hips" again. Then the door opened enough to allow a long black-stockinged leg ending in a spike-heeled shoe to come slithering through. It was withdrawn just as swiftly, as if bitten, making the startled boys wonder if it had been an apparition. Then it came creeping through again. The leg, seemingly disembodied, was now being caressed by a feathery pink fan. Higher, higher. The spike-heeled shoe slipped off to reveal toenails painted green. The leg rubbed longingly against the doorknob. It slid away, rose again. With maddening slowness the door opened to throbbing drums, a pulsating red light, and in glided Joshua's mother, her eyes saying peekaboo behind feathery fans. Silver stars had been pasted to her legs. She wore a see-through scarlet blouse and a black skirt slit to her thighs.

"I've got to go home," Izzy Singer called out, petrified, diving for his coat and fleeing the house.

"Snake Hips" started yet again and, with a wicked wink of a loosening false eyelash, Mrs. Shapiro turned her back to the boys. Hands on her knees, she gyrated her upturned ass at them. She straightened up, unzipping her skirt, wiggling out of it. Next she peeled off her blouse, letting it float to the floor. Then she whirled around to confront the boys in mock horror. Her ruby-red lips forming an enormous outraged *O*, arms folded saucily over her breasts, legs squeezed together. Frozen there, reduced to panties, belt, and stockings, she suddenly hissed at Joshua: "Now."

"What?"

"*Now, I said.*"

Remembering, Joshua slipped two fingers into his mouth to whistle, he stamped his feet, and the boys quickly followed suit.

Now those wanton fans, with a will of their own, began to stroke her, allowing the briefest of peeks at the perkiest breasts on any mother on the street.

Tears rolled down Eli Seligson's cheeks. Sheldon was drenched in sweat. But the others simply squatted there, stunned, some with their mouths open, as, responding to the beat of the drums, she began to bump and grind to a finale.

And, suddenly, the record was done. Mrs. Shapiro slipped into her housecoat, switched on the lights, lit a Pall Mall, retrieved her Dewar's and a splash from a table, and sat down on a stool to chat with her audience. "Did you like it?" she asked.

A flushed Seymour leaped up to applaud.

"I'm turning pro, you know. I'm going to be playing at the Roxy here."

Holy shit, Joshua thought.

"Now I want everybody who got a hard-on watching my act to be a good boy and put up his hand."

Seymour's hand shot up.

"Oh, come on, boys, I couldn't have been that lousy."

Three more hands were raised, then two more.

"Joshua doesn't count, because I'm his mother and it wouldn't be according to Hoyle."

—Joshua Then and Now, pp. 144–48

1951 IT WAS AND JAKE, who had been studying at McGill for three years, had decided not to register for the autumn term, beginning tomorrow. New York, New York, was his heart's desire. If only, he thought, lying on his bed, smoking, I can raise the fare. And money to keep me for a month.

His mother entered his room without knocking. "You should tell your father what you've decided to do. He's so bloated. I saw him on the street, he looks like a frog now. I wouldn't say a word against him, after all, he's your father, you hear? *Where are you going suddenly?*"

Compulsively, without design, he drifted all the way down to St. Urbain Street, entering Tansky's Cigar & Soda to phone his father, who had lived in a room nearby, ever since his parents had finally divorced four years earlier. Mr. Hersh came to fetch him in his battered Chevy, the back seat, as ever, buried in samples. Stationery supplies, ballpoint pens, calendars, blotters. Another inclement Montreal winter had eaten into the body work since Jake had last seen him. The car was rusty and rotting. "How are you, Daddy?"

Issy Hersh looked at his son and groaned. "*Oy veh.*"

Jake wore a blue beret. He had grown a scraggly beard and favoured an elongated ivory cigarette holder. He suggested they drive to a delicatessen on The Main, as in the old days.

"But nobody goes there any more. It's not the style."

Reluctantly, Issy Hersh drove Jake to Hy's Delicatessen on The Main. Smoked briskets were stacked like loaves in the window, red grizzly beef tongues heaped alongside. Salamis rocked on a line when Jake banged the door shut behind him. The aroma was even more maddeningly appetizing than he had remembered.

"It's very *simpático*, this," Jake said warmly.

"Come again."

"It's nice."

"It's a delicatessen. Big deal."

"No. I mean just the two of us, going out to eat again."

"I haven't got any money, if that's what you're after." Mr. Hersh ordered for both of them. Two lean on rye each, sour tomatoes, and knishes — if they were today's. "What sort of camel shit is that you're smoking?" he demanded, irritated.

"Gauloises."

"Feh."

"Do you still read *Northern Miner?*"

"Yes, I still read it. So?"

"What about your stocks, then?"

"What about my stocks? Right off the bat. What about my stocks? The stocks are not so hot. I don't understand it, I really don't. Your uncles have such luck on the market, but with me it never works. If people give me tips, it's out of spite. I've lost maybe eighteen hundred smackeroos, eighteen hundred, in the last year."

"That's terrible. I'm sorry."

"*C'est la guerre.*" Mr. Hersh motioned Jake closer. Narrowing his big frightened eyes, he searched out the farthest corners of the delicatessen for eavesdroppers. "I've got one stock" — his voice fell to an all but inaudible mumble — "Algonquin Mines —"

"Al-what mines?"

"Don't say it, big mouth."

"Say what? I didn't even hear you."

"You have to know the name of the mine? If you don't, your heart will stop ticking over?"

"No. Of course not."

"I've got an ock-stay — X-mines," he said, his voice gathering volume and booming like a bowling ball across the delicatessen, "it's just gone from a dollar nineteen to five ten...IN THE LAST WEEK...."

Immediately Hy switched off his automatic meat slicer. At the next table, an old man's spoon clattered in a bowl of kreplach soup.

"The trouble is," Mr. Hersh said, his voice shrivelling again, "I bought it at eleven fifty-five."

As a boy, Jake remembered, he had used to lie in wait for his father with his grammar text, terrorizing him by demanding help with his homework. Each time his father flubbed a word, Mrs. Hersh laughed, her manner exultant. If not for Rifka and him, Jake realized, they could have been divorced years ago. Issy Hersh needn't have waited. Impulsively, Jake reached across the table to stroke his father's cheek.

Had anybody seen? Mr. Hersh, his eyes shooting in all directions, hastily knocked Jake's hand away. "What's that," he asked, "something you learned at McGill?"

Jake lit another Gauloise.

"Everything's on me," his father added hastily. "Today it's Daddy who pays."

"We should get together more often. I like you."

"I'm your father, for Chrissake. What should you — hate me?"

"When I was a kid, you had a gift for making me laugh. Once you made me lead soldiers on the kitchen stove. You bought the moulds from a junkyard, remember?"

"Well, you're no longer a kid," Mr. Hersh said, bewildered, "and let's face it, it's turned out you're not such a fart smeller. Smart feller, I mean."

But he didn't earn a laugh, not even a smile.

"All right! That's just about enough out of you. Now what did you want to talk to me about? You haven't got the syph or anything like that?"

"No. You don't have to worry about fees any more. I've quit McGill. I'm not going back."

"Why?"

"It no longer suits my *Weltanschauung.*"

Mr. Hersh slapped his cheek. He rocked his head.

"Boy, did you ever turn out a *putz.* You're what-in-shtunk?"

"I'm bored," Jake said hotly. "I didn't like it there."

"What did you ever like? Everything you criticize."

"The movies."

"*What?*"

"I want to get into the movies."

Genuinely amused now, Issy Hersh shook with laughter. "Well, your ears are no bigger than Clark Gable's. That's a start, isn't it?"

Jake laughed too.

"Listen here," Mr. Hersh said, leaning closer, "you don't just decide I-want-to-be-in-the-movies. *You have to be discovered.*"

"I don't want to act. I want to direct."

"You think I like selling. I'd rather own the factory."

"I thought I'd go to New York for a start and look around. It's time I found out who I am."

"What do you mean, who you are? You're Yankel Hersh. You want to bet on it, I'll give you odds."

"The trouble is, I haven't even got the fare."

"I knew we'd get down to brass tacks sooner or later. The movies yet."

Mr. Hersh paid on the way out, scooping up a handful of change. Outside, he screwed up his eyes to glare at each coin before he dropped it into his pocket.

"Anything wrong?" Jake asked.

"Ssh. One minute."

A couple passed. Then a hawkish old lady hugging a parcel of fish, followed by some teenagers sporting shimmering AZA windbreakers. Finally, they were alone. "You see this," Mr. Hersh said.

"Yes."

"It's an American nickel."

"So?"

"So? What were you, born stupid? If this nickel was not a Jefferson but a 1938 Buffalo, with a tiny S and a D...S for San Francisco, D for Denver...it would be worth plenty. Only last summer, Max Kravitz picks up a drunk in his taxi and he drives him to Aldo's. The fare is two ten. The *goy* hands Max a four-dollar bill. Yes, a four-dollar bill. A Bank of Upper Canada note, dated December 1, 1846. You know what that's worth?"

"Oh, Daddy, give up," Jake said fondly. "You're never going to be rich."

"In your books, that's everything, being rich. I'd be your pal then, wouldn't I? We would sit together in a swell restaurant, they have kosher Chinese food now in Snowdon, and you wouldn't be ashamed if your highbrow friends spotted us. Well let me tell you this much, not that you'll listen. What do I know, I'm just your father. Making money isn't everything. The president of the largest steel company in the world, Charles Schwab," he said, numbering him off on a finger, "died a bankrupt and lived on borrowed money for five years before his death. The man who in 1923 was president of the New York Stock

Exchange, Richard Whitney, is still in Sing Sing. The greatest bear on Wall Street, Jesse Livemore, died a suicide. You know what you need? You need a job. Self-respect. Here," he hollered, ramming two ten-dollar bills into his chest, "you know what I am? Crazy."

"One day you'll be proud of me. I'm going to be a great film director."

"Don't shoot me the crap," he protested, appalled. "You want me to be proud? Earn a living. Stand on your own two feet."

—*St. Urbain's Horseman*, pp. 99–103

Mordecai and his father, Moses, 1953.

WOLF RETIRED TO THE DEN. He was a short, skinny man, and his head was crowned by a mass of black curly hair which was forever in need of cutting and always falling over his forehead. When he was nervous or afraid he pushed his hand through his hair, looked at his hand, then pushed it through his hair again. But he was seldom nervous or afraid in the den. The den was his. Wolf wore glasses. When he had to contend with the big drunken Irishmen who came into his office, haggling over prices with them, when he talked back to Leah, or when he was about to ask his father for more pay, he had a trick of wiggling his ears and raising his eyebrows and making his glasses go up and down on his nose. That way, if the others took what he said in the wrong spirit, he could always reply that he had been joking. He worried a lot, but the den was his. It was a clean, well-ordered room with many shelves and a nice smell to the wood. One corner was devoted to his hobby. Woodwork. That wall was lined with tools. The cabinet, which had been nailed to the wall, had many drawers. The drawers were all labelled and contained various sizes of nails, screws, and blades. He had made the cabinet and work-bench and tool chest himself. He knew a lot about construction. Whenever he visited a house that was new to him he asked for a glass of water and set it down on the floor. Later, he would glance at it surreptitiously. That's how he could tell whether the foundation had settled in a level way. One wall of the den was completely taken up by his bookshelves. Here he kept his old copies of *Life*, *Popular Mechanics*, *Reader's Digest*, *True Crime*, and several volumes of scrapbooks. One series of scrapbooks contained his record of the war years, another his collection of data on coins and stamps clipped from the pages of various Montreal newspapers. Most of the drawers to his desk were locked. His diary was kept in the bottom drawer, which also had a false bottom where he kept personal papers and letters. Except for prosaic entries, such as family birthdays, dates of operations, and graduations, the diary was kept in a code of his own invention.

Very often Wolf would lean back in his chair and brood about how much money there must be in the locked box that his father kept in the office safe. That box was very important to him and represented many things. Other times he would worry about the possibilities of another depression or of Noah doing something that would get him in trouble with his father. A depression would not be such a bad thing. A small one, anyway, would certainly fix bigshots like Seigler and Berger who had made a lot of fast money on the black market during the war years. From time to time he fiddled with various ideas for household gadgets. And then there was always the possibility that he might pick up a small packet soon on one of his investments — coins.

Two of the coins issued to commemorate the coronation of King George VI in 1937, a dime and a nickel, had caught Wolf's attention. Studying them with a magnifying glass, Wolf had discovered that the King's nose was slightly crooked on the nickel. So he had invested twenty dollars in the faulty coins. He kept them locked in his desk where, he had decided, they would stay until 1960. I might make a fortune on it, he often thought. And if *I* had money I'd be good. Not like them. Wolf rubbed his jaw. Business was slow. Well, what could you expect? The summer was always like that. Things would pick up in the fall.

—*Son of a Smaller Hero,* pp. 29–30

THE BABY'S PIERCING HUNGRY HOWL jolted Nancy awake, savagely, out of a sleep fathoms deep, her dream cut short.

"Jake, could you please rock the baby until I pee and —"

Not there. Nancy wavered only briefly, between the basinet and toilet — the baby's needs, hers — before she scooped him to her aching swollen bosom lest his screaming wake Sammy.

And Molly.

And Mrs. Hersh.

The very morning of his mother's arrival, Jake, his manner fiendishly sweet, had said, "I suppose we must reconcile ourselves to the fact that you're on one of those twenty-one-day return flights?"

"I'm going to stay here for just as long as I'm needed, *ketzelle*."

Mrs. Hersh had flown over a week before the trial to be with them during, as she put it, "Jake's ordeal," and it fell to Nancy, as if she didn't have sufficient troubles, to obviate an ugly collision between them by filling tense silences with prattle about the children and tedious comparisons between British and Canadian life, the sort of small talk which propelled Jake, liberated but unappreciative, out of the room. Jake's behaviour was atrocious, devious as well. He ricocheted between icy cruelty to his mother and what she, understandably, came to cherish as acts of filial kindness.

Nancy got used to him coming abruptly awake at three a.m.

"Didn't my mother say," he would ask, "that she was going shopping in the West End first thing in the morning?"

"Yes."

Then he would scramble into his dressing gown and shoot outside to make sure that there were no bicycles, scooters, or other potentially treacherous obstacles in her path.

"Imagine," Mrs. Hersh would say to Nancy, "this morning he insisted on helping me across the street to the bus stop. That's some son I've got there."

"He's one in a million, Mrs. Hersh."

And at night in bed, Jake, lighting one cigarillo off another, pouring himself yet another cognac, would say, "You let her go to bed without reminding her to take her medicine. Great, fine. That's a big help. Women her age get strokes just like that. Boom. Heart trouble runs in the family too."

"But she's your mother. In spite of everything she's —"

"You've got to watch her like a hawk. Like a hawk, you hear? All I need is for her to be with us for years...." Bedridden.

Then, only last night, his first question on coming home from the Old Bailey was, "How's my mother?" But once her continued good health was established, he devoted the rest of the evening to tormenting her with Old Bailey lore.

"Things have improved, Maw. I mean these days you can actually plead not guilty." And he regaled her, savouring each *oy*, rising gleefully to her heaviest sighs, about the Press Room that had once been set up beneath the Old Bailey for administering *Peine Forte et Dure*; and how prisoners had been spread-eagled upon the stone-flagged floor, their arms secured, and heavy weights laid upon their bodies until their ribs cracked or they pleaded to the charge on which they were being held. "Mind you," he added, closing in, "even this was tempered with mercy. Prisoners were allowed a wooden spike under their backs to hasten penetration. With the conspicuous exception of one Major Strangeways who, in 1658, refused to admit to the murder of his brother-in-law and was so strong as to withstand the iron and stones that were piled on his chest. Fortunately, Strangeways was blessed with good companions, and a soft-hearted warder gave them permission to stand on him, hastening death. And there, Maw, you have the origin of the expression a friend in need. Like my pal Luke. Isn't that right, Nancy?"

—*St. Urbain's Horseman*, pp. 32–34

MOSES CLUNG TO HIS FATHER, constantly searching for new ways to earn his love. L.B., he noticed, often delayed his morning departure to the dreaded parochial school, blowing on his pince-nez, wiping the lenses with his handkerchief, as he stood by the front window waiting for the postman to pass. If there was no mail L.B. grunted, something in him welcoming the injustice of it, and hurried into his coat.

"Maybe tomorrow," his wife would say.

"Maybe, maybe." Then he would peer into his lunch bag, saying,

"You know, Bessie, I'm getting tired of chopped egg. Tuna. Sardines. It's coming out of my ears."

Or another day, the postman passing by their flat again, she would say, "It's a good sign. They must be considering it very, very carefully."

One ten-below-zero morning, hoping to shave ten minutes off his father's anxiety time, Moses quit the flat early and lay in wait for the postman at the corner.

"Any mail for my father, sir?"

A large brown envelope. Moses, exhilarated, raced all the way home, waving the envelope at his father who stood watch by the window. "Mail for you!" he cried. "Mail for you!"

L.B., his eyes bulging with rage, snatched the envelope from him, glanced at it, and ripped it apart, scattering the pieces on the floor. "Don't you ever meddle in my affairs again, you little fool," he shouted, fleeing the flat.

"What did I do, Maw?"

But she was already on her hands and knees, gathering the pieces together. He kept carbons, Bessie knew that, but these, *Gottenyu*, were the originals.

L.B. went to Moses that evening, removing his pince-nez and rubbing his nose, a bad sign. "I don't know what got into me this morning," he said, and he leaned over and allowed Moses to kiss his cheek. Then L.B. declined supper, retired to his bedroom, and pulled the blinds.

A baffled Moses appealed to his mother. "That envelope was addressed to him in his own handwriting. I don't get it."

"Sh, Moishe, L.B. is trying to sleep."

It would begin with a slight tic of discomfort in the back of his neck, a little nausea, and within an hour it would swell into a hectic pulse, blood pounding through every vein in his head. A towel filled with chopped ice clamped to his forehead, L.B. would lie in the dark, staring at the ceiling, moaning. *One day a floodtide of blood, surging into my head, seeking passage, will blow off the top. I will die drenched in fountains of my own blood.* Then, on the third day, bloated, his bowels plugged, he would shuffle to the toilet and sit there for an hour, maybe more. Afterward he would stagger back into bed, fall into a deep sleep and wake whole, even chirpy, the next morning, demanding his favourite breakfast: scrambled eggs with lox, potatoes fried with onions, bagels lathered with cream cheese.

—Solomon Gursky Was Here, pp. 15–17

AFTER THE FUNERAL, I was given my father's *talis*, his prayer shawl, and (oh my God) a file containing all the letters I had written to him while I was living abroad, as well as carbon copies he had kept of the letters he had sent to me.

December 28, 1959: "Dear Son, Last week I won a big Kosher Turkey, by bowling, when I made the high triple for the week. How I did it I do not know, I guess I was lucky for once, or was it that the others were too sure of themselves, being much better at the game than I am."

February 28, 1963: "This month has been a cold one, making it difficult, almost impossible to work outside. Yes! it's been tough. Have you found a title for your last novel? What can you do with a title like this? 'UNTIL *DEBT* DO US PART'?"

His letter of February 28, 1963, like so many others written that year, begins, "Thanks for the cheque." For by that time we had come full circle. In the beginning it was my father who had sent cheques to me. Included in the file I inherited were cancelled cheques, circa 1945, for $28 monthly child support, following the annulment of my parents' marriage. A bill dated January 15, 1948, for a Royal portable, my first typewriter; a birthday gift. Another bill, from Bond Clothes, dated August 21, 1950, on the eve of my departure for Europe, for "I Sta. Wag. Coat, $46.49."

My own early letters to my father, horrendously embarrassing for me to read now, usually begin with appeals for money. No, demands. There is also a telegram I'd rather forget. March 11, 1951. IMPERATIVE CHEQUE SENT PRONTO MADRID C O COOKS WAGON LITS ALCALA NR 23 MADRID. BROKE. MORDECAI.

Imperative, indeed.

I was also left a foot-long chisel, his chisel, which I now keep on a shelf of honour in my workroom. Written with a certain flourish in orange chalk on the oak shaft is my father's inscription:

Used by M. I. Richler
Richler Artificial Stone Works
1922
De La Roche Street
NO *SUCCESS.*

My father was twenty years old then, younger than my eldest son is now. He was the firstborn of fourteen children. Surely that year, as every year of his life, on Passover, he sat in his finery at a dining-room table and recited, "We were once the slaves of Pharaoh in Egypt, but the Lord our God brought us forth from there with a mighty hand and an outstretched arm." But, come 1922, out there in the muck of his father's freezing backyard on De La Roche Street in Montreal — yet to absorb the news of his liberation — my father was still trying to make bricks with insufficient straw.

Moses Isaac Richler.

Insufficient straw, NO SUCCESS, was the story of his life. Neither of his marriages really worked. There were searing quarrels with my older brother. As a boy, I made life difficult for him. I had no respect. Later, officious strangers would rebuke him in the synagogue for the novels I had written. Heaping calumny on the Jews, they said. If there was such a thing as a reverse Midas touch, he had it. Not one of my father's penny mining stocks ever went into orbit. He lost regularly at gin rummy. As younger, more intrepid brothers and cousins began to prosper, he assured my mother, "The bigger they come, the harder they fall."

My mother, her eyes charged with scorn, laughed in his face. "You're the eldest and what are you?"

Nothing.

After his marriage to my mother blew apart, he moved into a rented room. Stunned, humiliated. St. Urbain's cuckold. He bought a natty straw hat. A sports jacket. He began to use aftershave lotion. It was then I discovered that he had a bottle of rye whisky stashed in the glove compartment of his Chevy. My father. Rye whisky. "What's that for?" I asked, astonished.

"For the femmes," he replied, wiggling his eyebrows at me. "It makes them want it."

I remember him as a short man, squat, with a shiny bald head and big floppy ears. Richler ears. My ears. Seated at the kitchen table at night in his Penman's long winter underwear, wetting his finger before turning a page of the *New York Daily Mirror*, reading Walter Winchell first. Winchell, who knew what's what. He also devoured *Popular Mechanics*, *Doc Savage*, and *Black Mask*. And, for educational purposes, *Reader's Digest*. My mother, on the other hand, read Keats and Shelley. *King's Row*. *The Good Earth*. My father's pranks did not enchant her. A metal ink spot on her new chenille bedspread. A felt mouse to surprise her in the larder. A knish secretly filled with absorbent cotton. Neither did his jokes appeal to her. "Hey, do you know why we eat hard-boiled eggs dipped in salt water just before the Passover meal?"

"No, Daddy. Why?"

'To remind us that when the Jews crossed the Red Sea they certainly got their balls soaked.'

Saturday mornings my brother and I accompanied him to the Young Israel Synagogue on Park Avenue near St. Viateur. As I was the youngest, under bar-mitzvah age, and therefore still allowed to carry on the Sabbath, I was the one who held the prayer shawls in a little purple velvet bag. My father, who couldn't stomach the rabbi's windy speeches, would slip into the backroom to gossip with the other men before the rabbi set sail. "In Japan," my father once said, "there is a custom, time-honoured, that before he begins, a speaker's hands are filled with ice cubes. He can shoot his mouth off for as long as he can hold the ice cubes in his hands. I wouldn't mind it if the rabbi had to do that."

He was stout, he was fleshy. But in the wedding photographs that I never saw until after his death the young man who was to become my father is as skinny as I once was, his startled brown eyes unsmiling behind horn-rimmed glasses. Harold Lloyd. Allowed a quick no-promises peek at the world and what it had to offer, but clearly not entitled to a place at the table.

My father never saw Paris. Never read Yeats. Never stayed out with the boys drinking too much. Never flew to New York on a whim. Nor turned over in bed and slept in, rather than report to work. Never knew a reckless love. What did he hope for? What did he want? Beyond peace and quiet, which he seldom achieved, I have no idea. So far as I know he never took a risk or was disobedient. At his angriest, I once heard him silence one of his cousins, a cousin bragging about his burgeoning real estate investments, saying, "You know how much land a man needs? Six feet. And one day that's all you'll have. Ha, ha!"

Anticipating Bunker Hunt, my father began to hoard American silver in his rented room. A blue steamer trunk filling with neatly stacked piles of silver dollars, quarters, dimes. But decades before their worth began to soar, he had to redeem them at face value. "I'm getting hitched again," he told me, blushing. He began to speculate in postage stamps. When he died at the age of sixty-five I also found out that he had bought a city backlot somewhere for $1,200 during the forties. In 1967, however — riding a bloated market, every fool raking it in — the estimated value of my father's property had shrunk to $900. All things considered, that called for a real touch of class.

I was charged with appetite, my father had none. I dreamed of winning prizes, he never competed. But, like me, my father was a writer. A keeper of records. His diary, wherein he catalogued injuries and insults, betrayals, family quarrels, bad debts, was written in a code of his own invention. His brothers and sisters used to tease him about it. "Boy, are we ever afraid! Look, I'm shaking!" But as cancer began to consume him, they took notice, fluttering about, concerned. "What about Moishe's diary?"

I wanted it. Oh, how I wanted it. I felt the diary was my proper inheritance. I hoped it would tell me things about him that he had always been too reticent to reveal. But his widow, an obdurate lady, refused to let me into the locked room in their apartment where he kept his personal papers. All she would allow was, "I'm returning your mother's love letters to her. The ones he found that time. You know, from the refugee."

That would have been during the early forties, when my mother began to rent to refugees, putting them up in our spare bedroom. The refugees, German and Austrian Jews, had been interned as enemy aliens in England shortly after war was declared in 1939. A year later they were transported to Canada on a ship along with the first German and Italian prisoners of war. On arrival at the dock in Quebec City, the army major who turned them over to their Canadian guards said, "You have some German officers here, very good fellows, and some Italians, they'll be no trouble. And over there," he added, indicating the refugees, "the scum of Europe."

The refugees were interned in camps, but in 1941 they began to be released one by one. My father, who had never had anybody to condescend to in his life, was expecting real *greeners* with side-curls. Timorous innocents out of the *shtetl*, who would look to him as a master of magic. Canadian magic. Instead, they patronized him. A mere junk dealer, a dolt. The refugees turned out to speak better English than any of us did, as well as German and French. After all they had been through over there, they were still fond of quoting a German son of a bitch called Goethe. "Imagine that," my father said. They also sang opera arias in the bathtub. They didn't guffaw over the antics of *Fibber McGee & Molly* on the radio; neither were they interested in the strippers who shook their nookies right at you from the stage of the Gayety Theatre, nor in learning how to play gin rummy for a quarter of a cent a point. My mother was enthralled.

My father was afraid of his father. He was afraid of my unhappy mother, who arranged to have their marriage annulled when I was thirteen and my brother eighteen. He was also afraid of his second wife. Alas, he was even afraid of me when I was a boy. I rode street-cars on the Sabbath. I ate bacon. But nobody was ever afraid of Moses Isaac Richler. He was far too gentle.

The Richler family was, and remains, resolutely Orthodox, followers of the Lubavitcher rabbi. So when my mother threatened divorce, an all-but-unheard-of scandal in those days, a flock of grim rabbis in flapping black gabardine coats descended on our cold-water flat on St. Urbain Street to plead with her. But my mother, dissatisfied for years with her arranged marriage, in love at last, was adamant. She had had enough. The rabbis sighed when my father, snapping his suspenders, rocking on his heels — *speaking out* — stated his most deeply felt marital grievance. When he awakened from his Saturday afternoon nap there was no tea. "Me, I like a cup of hot tea with lemon when I wake up."

In the end, there was no divorce. Instead, there was an annulment. I should explain that in the Province of Quebec at that time each divorce called for parliamentary approval. A long, costly process. A lawyer, a family friend, found a loophole. He pleaded for an annulment. My mother, he told the court, had married without her father's consent when she had still been a minor. He won. Technically speaking, as I used to brag at college, I'm a bastard.

Richler's grandfather, Rabbi Judah Yudel Rosenberg.

Weekdays my father awakened every morning at six, put on his phylacteries, said his morning prayers, and drove his truck through the wintry dark to the family scrapyard near the waterfront. He worked there for my fierce, hot-tempered grandfather and a pompous younger brother. Uncle Solly, who had been to high school, had been made a partner in the yard, but not my father, the firstborn. He was a mere employee, working for a salary, which fed my mother's wrath. Younger brothers, determined to escape an overbearing father, had slipped free to form their own business, but my father was too timid to join them.

"When times are bad they'll be back. I remember the Depression. Oh, boy!"

"Tell me about it," I pleaded.

But my father never talked to me about anything. Not his own boyhood. His feelings. Or his dreams. He never even mentioned sex to me until I was nineteen years old, bound for Paris to try to become a writer. Clutching my Royal portable, wearing my Sta. Wag. coat. "You know what safes are. If you have to do it — *and I know you* — use 'em. Don't get married over there. They'd do anything for a pair of nylon stockings or a Canadian passport."

Hot damn, I hoped he was right. But my father thought I was crazy to sail for Europe. A graveyard for the Jews. A continent where everything was broken or old. Even so, he lent me his blue steamer trunk and sent me $50 a month support. When I went broke two years later, he mailed me my boat fare without reproach. I told him that the novel I had written over there was called *The Acrobats* and he immediately suggested that I begin the title of my second novel with a B, the third with a C, and so on, which would make a nifty trade-mark for me. Writing, he felt, might not be such a nutty idea after all. He had read in *Life* that this guy Mickey Spillane, a mere *goy*, was making a fortune. Insulted, I explained hotly that I wasn't that kind of writer. I was a serious man.

"So?"

"I only write out of my obsessions."

"Ah, ha," he said, sighing, warming to me for once, recognizing another generation of family failure.

Even when I was a boy his admonitions were few. "Don't embarrass me. Don't get into trouble."

I embarrassed him. I got into trouble.

In the early forties, my father's father rented a house directly across the street from us on St. Urbain, ten of his fourteen children still single and rooted at home. The youngest, my Uncle Yankel, was only three years older than I was and at the time we were close friends. But no matter what after-school mischief we were up to, we were obliged to join my grandfather at sunset in the poky little

Gallicianer *shul* around the corner for the evening prayers, a ritual I didn't care for. One evening, absorbed in a chemistry experiment in our "lab" in my grandfather's basement, we failed to appear. On his return from *shul*, my grandfather descended on us, seething, his face bleeding red. One by one he smashed our test tubes and our retorts and even our cherished water distiller against the stone wall. Yankel begged forgiveness, but not me. A few days later I contrived to get into a scrap with Yankel, leaping at him, blackening his eye. Oh boy, did that ever feel good. But Yankel squealed on me. My grandfather summoned me into his study, pulled his belt free of his trousers, and thrashed me.

Vengeance was mine.

I caught my grandfather giving short weight on his scrapyard scales to a drunken Irish peddler. My grandfather, Jehovah's enforcer. Scornful, triumphant, I ran to my father and told him his father was no better than a cheat and a hypocrite.

"What do you know?" my father demanded.

"Nothing."

"They're anti-Semites, every one of them."

My grandfather moved to Jeanne Mance Street, only a few blocks away, and on Sunday afternoons he welcomed all the family there. Children, grandchildren. Come Hanukkah, the most intimidating of my aunts was posted in the hall, seated behind a bridge table piled high with Parcheesi games one year, Snakes and Ladders another. As each grandchild filed past the table he was issued a game. "Happy Hanukkah."

My grandfather was best with the babies, rubbing his spade beard into their cheeks until they squealed. Bouncing them on his lap. But I was twelve years old now and I had taken to strutting down St. Urbain without a hat, and riding streetcars on the Sabbath. The next time my father and I started out for the house on Jeanne Mance on a Sunday afternoon, he pleaded with me not to disgrace him yet again, to behave myself for once, and then he thrust a *yarmulke* at me. "You can't go in there bareheaded. Put it on."

"It's against my principles. I'm an atheist."

"What are you talking about?"

"Charles Darwin," I said, having just read a feature article on him in *Coronet*, "or haven't you ever heard of him?"

"You put on that *yarmulke*," he said, "or I cut your allowance right now."

"OK, OK."

"And Jewish children are not descended from monkeys, in case you think you know everything."

"When I have children of my own I'll be better to them."

I had said that, testing. Sneaking a sidelong glance at my father. The thing is I had been born with an undescended testicle and my brother, catching me naked in the bathroom, had burst out laughing and assured me that I would never be able to have children or even screw. "With only one ball," he said, "you'll never be able to shoot jism."

My father didn't rise to the bait. He had worries of his own. My mother. The refugee in the spare bedroom. His father. "When you step in the door," he said, "the *zeyda* will ask you which portion of the Torah they read in *shul* yesterday." He told me the name of the chapter. "Got it?"

"I'm not afraid of him."

My grandfather, his eyes hot, was lying in wait for me in the living room. Before a court composed of just about the entire family, he denounced me as a violator of the Sabbath. A *shabus goy*. Yankel smirked. My grandfather grabbed me by the ear, beat me about the face, and literally threw me out of the house. I lingered across the street, waiting for my father to seek me out, but when he finally appeared, having endured a bruising lecture of his own, all he said was, "You deserved what you got."

"Some father you are."

Which was when I earned another belt on the cheek.

"I want you to go back in there like a man and apologize to the *zeyda*."

"Like hell."

I never spoke to my grandfather again.

But when he died, less than a year after the annulment of my parents' marriage, my mother insisted it was only proper that I attend his funeral. I arrived at the house on Jeanne Mance to find the coffin set out in the living room, uncles and aunts gathered round. My Uncle Solly drove me into a corner. "So here you are," he said.

"So?"

"You hastened his death; you never even spoke to him even though he was sick all those months."

"I didn't bring on his death."

"Well, smart guy, you're the one who is mentioned first in his will."

"Oh."

"You are not a good Jew and you are not to touch his coffin. It says that in his will. Don't you dare touch his coffin."

I turned to my father. Help me, help me. But he retreated, wiggling his eyebrows.

[....]

In 1954, some time after my return to Europe, where I was to remain rooted for almost two decades, I married a *shiksa* in London. My father wrote me an indignant letter. Once more, we were estranged. But no sooner did the marriage end in divorce than he pounced: "You see, mixed marriages never work."

"But, Daddy, your first marriage didn't work either and Maw was a rabbi's daughter."

"What do you know?"

"Nothing," I replied, hugging him.

When I married again, this time for good, but to another *shiksa*, he was not overcome with delight, yet neither did he complain. For after all the wasting years, we had finally become friends. My father became my son. Once, he had sent money to me in Paris. Now, as the scrapyard foundered, I mailed monthly cheques to him in Montreal. On visits home, I took him to restaurants. I bought him treats. If he took me to a gathering of the Richler clan on a Sunday afternoon, he would bring along a corked bottle of 7-Up for me, filled with scotch whisky. "There'll be nothing for you to drink there, and I know you."

"Hey, Daddy, that's really very thoughtful."

During the sixties, on a flying trip to Montreal, my publishers put me up at the Ritz-Carlton Hotel, and I asked my father to meet me for a drink there.

"You know," he said, joining me at the table, "I'm sixty-two years old and I've never been here before. Inside, I mean. So this is the Ritz."

"It's just a bar," I said, embarrassed.

"What should I order?"

"Whatever you want, Daddy."

"A rye and ginger ale. Would that be all right here?"

"Certainly."

What I'm left with are unresolved mysteries. A sense of regret. Anecdotes for burnishing.

My wife, a proud lady, showing him our firstborn son, his week-old howling grandchild, saying, "Don't you think he looks like Mordecai?"

"Babies are babies," he responded, seemingly indifferent.

Some years later my father coming to our house, pressing chocolate bars on the kids. "Who do you like better," he asked them, "your father or your mother?"

In the mid-sixties, I flew my father to London. He came with his wife. Instead of slipping away with him to the Windmill Theatre or Raymond's Revue Bar, another strip joint, like a fool I acquired theatre tickets. We took the two of them to *Beyond the Fringe*. "What did you think?" I asked as we left the theatre.

"There was no chorus line," he said.

Following his last operation for cancer, I flew to Montreal, promising to take him on a trip as soon as he was out of bed. The Catskills. Grossinger's. With a stopover in New York to take in some shows. Back in London, each time I phoned, his doctor advised me to wait a bit longer. I waited. He died. The next time I flew to Montreal it was to bury him.

—*Home Sweet Home*, "My Father's Life," pp. 56–66, 68–69

UPSTAIRS MELECH ADLER WANDERED ABSENTLY through empty bedrooms that had used to belong to his children. The rooms were draughty and chill and smelled badly. Melech shivered. He tried hard to possess again, if only for a moment, the laughter and the ailments and the play that had used to fill these rooms. Bedsprings had rusted under dust sheets. There were fading marks on the walls where graduation pictures and pennants had used to hang. In Max's old room, opening the cupboard, he stumbled on a pair of boxing gloves and several back issues of sporting magazines. The gloves were mouldy, the pages had yellowed. Melech dropped his find to the floor and stared at his yellowed, shaking hands. He collapsed into a frayed armchair which had been covered by sheets, and stared at the walls. When Ornstein had died his children, according to the Orthodox custom, had covered the mirrors with towels. They had said, according to the modern custom, that their father was better off that way. "He died quick, Mr. Adler. No suffering." Melech Adler held his head in his hands, and sorrowed over what had become of him. He would have rested that way for hours but finally, inevitably, he noticed the white sheet he sat on. He saw the other white sheets that covered the armchair opposite him and the bureau to the right. He backed out of the room, horrified. Suddenly, he heard the radio turned on in Ida's room.

> *It's Make-Believe Ballroom time,*
> *The hour of sweet romance...*

Something stirred within Melech. She is my child, he thought. He was certain that she, his daughter, would comfort him. Her door was opened. Ida, holding an absent partner, glided to and fro before the mirror. Her eyes were shut, her expression dreamy; she wallowed in a smile that said life was good, life was full. She danced naked. Dancing away from him, like the years. His eyes blurred. *Helga, Helga, forgive me.* He saw, more real than her, the rusting springs and the mattress abandoned on the floor. Fading marks on the walls and white, white sheets. Ida opened her eyes and approached the mirror as though she expected to be received by it. She saw an old, bearded man staring at her. She reached for her dressing gown in a panic and whirled about to face her father. I caught him, she thought. Melech smiled and nodded in a friendly manner. Smiled, and saw too late that she misunderstood his intentions. His shoulders slumped. He was surprised and ashamed that his daughter could think of him in such a foul way. So he turned away, hoping to be gone before she could speak things that, once heard, could never be forgotten. But she couldn't understand that either. Besides, he was against Stanley.

"Can't I have privacy in my own room even? Spying on me, eh? I'm going and I'm glad. What are you looking at? Did you ever let me do what I want? Once. Ever ask me how I felt? I'm going. I'm glad, you hear?"

Noah, who at that moment was parked across the street from his grandfather's house, occupied a unique position in the Adler family. He was, to begin with, Leah's son. Leah wasn't liked. He was the grandson of a man whom Melech Adler had deeply respected — Jacob Goldenberg the Zaddik. He was the son of Wolf Adler, who, as far as the others were concerned, had died for the Torah. The Adlers lived in a cage and that cage, with all its faults, had justice and safety and a kind of felicity. I wonder what will happen, he thought, now that I'm leaving? They'll need something to blame me for. Noah stared at the snow. He was immensely happy. He had spent the previous evening with Panofsky. They had sat in the kitchen drinking beer and listening to the music of Vivaldi. Even Aaron had been cheerful. He had given Noah his old suitcase. He had told him stories about Madrid. Panofsky had had lots of beer and had said that he might turn the business over to Karl next summer and come to Europe himself. Aaron had laughed. He had said that the old man was getting lecherous in his last days and that he would be fleeced by the first DP he met up with. Noah had laughed, too. But he had known that Panofsky would never quit City Hall Street. A new crowd is arriving, Panofsky had said. Perhaps this time things will work out better. What do I need Europe for? Noah will write us everything. Remembering, Noah grinned. The cold blue sky was without clouds. There was a dry, clean feeling to the day. Miriam had asked him what he wanted. He hadn't been able to tell her because at that time he had wanted to love her the way he had at first, and he hadn't been able to. He could tell her now, though. He could tell her that he wanted freedom and that innocent day at Lac Gandon and the first days of their love and many more evenings with Panofsky and the music of Vivaldi and more men as tall as Aaron and living with truth and, maybe, sometime soon, a wiser Noah in another cottage near a stream with a less neurotic Miriam. Oh, he wanted plenty. I'm free, he thought. Max can go to hell. You require me to be an alcoholic, he thought. But you'll never get that, Max. Not out of me, you won't. Noah blew on his hands. Remembering his mother, he felt that wire tightening around his heart again. He rubbed his hands together anxiously. She'll be fine, he thought. Now that she knows I'm really going she'll pull through. I'll write every week. Noah dug into his pocket and pulled out two envelopes. One of them contained his rail ticket to New York and his boat ticket. Tomorrow afternoon at four, he thought, I'll be on that train to New York. What can stop me? The other envelope contained Melech's letters and receipts and photographs. Giving it to him will be difficult, Noah thought. Why shouldn't I tell him that Shloime started the fire? He knows that Wolf didn't die for the Torah. He knows.

The door opened.

Noah stood before him confidently. "I'm leaving, *Zeyda*," he said. "I came to say goodbye."

Melech Adler took off his glasses and folded up his paper. "I told you long ago," he began slowly, "that you are no longer welcome here…."

Noah placed the envelope on the arm of Melech's chair. "I brought you this," he said "I'm sorry that I took it. But there were many things that I didn't know then."

Melech ignored the envelope. "I suppose you want a thank you for such a big favour? Maybe you want I should give you a blessing for giving me back what you stole from me? Look at you! A nothing. You would mix into the affairs from your *zeyda*."

"Had I known what was in the envelope I wouldn't have taken it."

Mr. Adler got up. "You are by me de greatest shame I had. Go."

"Did my father know what was in the box?"

Melech stared. He had known that one day Noah would come to ask him that question. A wild, vengeful part of him wanted to tell

Noah the truth. Ever since he had been a boy Noah had denied him the respect that was justly his. The boy was going away. They might never meet again. Melech didn't know that Noah already knew the truth about the box. He rebelled against the idea that Noah should come to respect Wolf and not him. Wolf, who had died for a cash box. Melech walked over to the window. He tugged slowly at his beard. Had I told him about Moore that day, if I had explained it to him first, everything would have been all right. Melech pursed his lips. He remembered that from the first he had always wanted Noah to ask him a favour. He had wanted the boy to be in his debt. He turned to him. "Your Paw knew that I had in the box scrolls. About the other stuff he didn't know. Nobody knew."

Noah turned away from him. A lump formed in his throat. He understood the gift of Melech's lie, and he was speechless.

"You came here another day," Melech said, "and told me I should try to understand. What should I try to understand?"

"I started out here today with anger, *Zeyda*. I came here to tell you things that I've found out. Facts, I guess. But now — you are no longer the same man that I had in mind. I have changed too. I..." Noah paused. He realized gladly that Shloime had been wrong. For Melech, in Noah's place, would have told his grandfather that his youngest son had started the fire. Melech, in his place, would have had God and would have done what was just. "You said you wanted me to be a Somebody. A Something. I've come to tell you that I have rules now. I'll be a human being. I'll..."

"You are going from us?"

"I am going and I'm not going. I can no more leave you, my mother, or my father's memory, than I can renounce myself. But I can refuse to take part in this..."

"I understand that you are going. Finished. Go. Go, become a *Goy*. But have one look first at what the *Goyim* did to your *zeyda*. That girl in the picture had she been willing to become a Jewess, to.... Stones they threw at me, Noah. My heart they made hard against my children. Who burned me down my office? Who murdered my first-born? *Goyim, Goyim*. Now go. Go. Go join, become my enemy."

Melech Adler sat down and picked up his paper again.

Their eyes met briefly. An old man crumpled up in a chair.

Noah reached out and touched his shoulder. "Would you give me one of the scrolls, one of — one of the scrolls you copied...?"

"The scrolls? *You*. I'm not a scribe.... I..."

"I would like to have one to remember — one that you made."

"They are not very well done, child. There are errors. My father now, he...I..."

Melech got up and opened up a drawer. He glanced wordlessly through several scrolls, selected one, and handed it to his grandson.

"I planned so much for you," Melech began falteringly, "I... Money you could have had — anything, but..."

"You have given me what I wanted," Noah said.

Melech sat down again. Noah bent over and kissed him. "I'm sorry," he said.

After he had gone Melech touched his cheek and felt that kiss like a burn. He touched his cheek and felt that he had been punished.

— *Son of a Smaller Hero*, pp. 196–200

Duddy's relationship with his uncle has always been strained. Even Uncle Benjy's cancer fails to leaven Duddy's animosity toward the older man.

UNCLE BENJY WORE HIS ornate silk dressing gown and smoked a cigar. "Sit down and don't stare, please. I know I'm getting thinner. I suppose you expect me to thank you for bringing her back?"

"Will you leave me alone, please?"

"I know what I've got so we won't pretend. I knew before she came back. The day they let me out of the hospital I knew."

"I'm sorry, Uncle Benjy. But — well, where there's life there's —"

"Oh, shettup! Did she fill your head with foolish talk on the train?" Duddy shrugged.

"Don't let me ever catch you making fun of her. I'm warning you. Now there are some favours I have to ask. Why are you smiling?"

"Don't you find it funny?"

"I have lots of money."

"I know," Duddy said.

"If you'll give up those vulgar movies you're making and take over the factory you can have fifty percent. The rest is hers."

"I've got other ambitions."

"You can make more running my factory and you like money so much."

"Why can't Manny run it for her?"

"Manny's a fool."

"You mean I'm not a fool? Thank you, Uncle Benjy. Thanks a lot. I thought you were the only one in the world with brains."

"Why do you hate me so much?"

"I worked for you once. Remember?"

"How long will you hold a grudge, Duddel?" he asked, smiling.

"You think it's funny. Everything about me's funny. I'm a regular laughingstock. You know as a kid I always liked Auntie Ida. But I remember when you used to come to the house you always brought a surprise for Lennie. I could have been born dead as much as you cared."

"Let's not pretend. Everybody has his favourites. There was always the *zeyda* to bring you surprises. He'd never hear a bad word said against you."

"Why," Duddy asked, "did you try?"

"You've developed quite a *chuzpah* since I last saw you. You have money in the bank, I suppose."

"Why did you send for me?"

"A man should arrange his affairs."

"Well, if you can't trust Manny to run the factory you'd better sell out. I'm not interested."

"What is it about us, Duddel, that we can't sit together for five minutes without a quarrel? I really brought you here to say thanks. I'm grateful for what you've done. Aw, what's the use? We bring out the worst in each other."

"We don't pretend but."

"That's true. I wonder what will become of you, Duddel. Well…"

"I'll never be a doctor, that's for sure."

"Now why did you say that?"

"Because Lennie never wanted to be a doctor either. You forced him."

"I did my best for that boy."

"You sure did, Uncle Benjy."

"If I'd left it to your father to bring him up he'd be driving a taxi today."

"I don't like the way you talk about my father. I never have."

"I'll be generous. Max is not very bright. I can't change that with my talk one way or another."

"You're very bright and nobody likes you. I'm sorry, Uncle Benjy. I say things I don't mean. It's just that you make me so sore sometimes...."

"We eat each other up, Duddel. That's life. Take Ida. I know what you think of her. I know what everyone thinks.... But she wasn't always such a foolish woman. She was once so lovely that — I'm not apologizing for her to you. You understand that? It's just — Well, I won't be sorry to die. I'm leaving lots of money. There's some for you too."

"Jeez."

"I thought we didn't pretend?"

"Why didn't you ever have time for me?"

"Because you're a *pusherke*. A little Jew-boy on the make. Guys like you make me sick and ashamed."

"You lousy, intelligent people! You lying sons of bitches with your books and your socialism and your sneers. You give me one long pain in the ass. You think I never read a book? I've read books. I've got friends now who read them by the ton. A big deal. What's so special in them? They all make fun of guys like me. *Pusherkes*. What a bunch you are! What a pack of crap artists! Writing and reading books that make fun of people like me. Guys who want to get somewhere. If you're so concerned how come in real life you never have time for me? It's easy for you to sit here and ridicule and make superior little jokes because you know more than me, but what about a helping hand? When did you ever put yourself out one inch for me? Never. It's the same with all you intelligent people. Except Hersh maybe. He's different. You never take your hand out of your pockets to a guy like me except when it's got a knife in it. You think I should be running after something else besides money? Good. Tell me what. Tell me, you bastard. I want some land, Uncle Benjy. I'm going to own my own place one day. King of the castle, that's me. And there won't be any superior *drecks* there to laugh at me or run me off. That's just about the size of it."

"You're such a nervy kid. My God, Duddel, you're even touchier than Lennie and I never realized it. Take care. Take my advice and take care."

"I don't want your advice."

"You don't want anything from me. Come to think of it, you're the only one in the family who never came here to ask for something. My God, it never occurred to me before. You're the only one. Duddel, I've been unfair to you."

"I can never tell if you're joking. There's such a tricky business in your voice, if you know what I mean?"

"I'm not joking. Lennie, your father, all of Ida's family, nobody has ever come to visit me without the hand outstretched. Except you. Now isn't that something?"

"There was lots of times I needed help."

Uncle Benjy waited.

"No sir. I wouldn't come to you."

"You're hurting me. You know that?"

"I'm sorry."

There was a knock at the door. "That's for me. It's the doctor."

Duddy rose.

"Would you come again?" Uncle Benjy asked.

Duddy rubbed the back of his head.

"Sometimes. When you're free."

"Sure."

But Uncle Benjy knew he wouldn't come. "Was I that bad to you when you worked for me?" he asked.

"You were my uncle," Duddy shouted, "and I thought it was the right thing to tell you the *goy* was stealing from you. I'm no squealer. I wanted you to like me. You treated me like dirt."

The doctor knocked again.

"You always looked for the bad side with me," Duddy said.

"I wish I'd made more time for you. God help me but I wish I'd seen what your *zeyda* saw."

The door opened. "May I come in, please?" the doctor said.

Without thinking, Duddy seized the doctor. "Don't let him die," he shouted. "He's my uncle." And then, embarrassed, he fled the house.

"I'm sorry," the doctor said, "I didn't realize I was interrupting."

Uncle Benjy went to the window and watched Duddy leap into his car and drive off. Run, run, always running, he thought, he can't even walk to his car. "What kind of pills did you bring me today?"

"You mustn't be so cynical, Benjy."

"I can't stand pain, Harry. As soon as it starts for real I want the morphine. Lot's of it."

He won't come again, Uncle Benjy thought. I don't deserve it either.

"Benjy, please. What did the boy say to you? You're so excited."

"We're a very emotional family. Come back later, please."

"Is there anything I can do?"

"Yes. Go away, please," Uncle Benjy said, turning his face away quickly.

— *The Apprenticeship of Duddy Kravitz,* pp. 242–46

JAKE SAT BY HIS FATHER'S BEDSIDE and invited him to come to London and stay with them. They would take in the strip shows in Soho together, hornier than anything the old Gayety had ever dared to offer. But Issy Hersh did not react. So Jake began to ramble on about the old days, trying Tansky's Cigar & Soda for size, evoking the summer shack in Shawbridge, but his father, his eyes turned inward, did not smile. Jake promised to buy him a cane, he offered him a new dressing gown. He reminded his father about Saturday mornings at the Young Israel Synagogue, he chattered about *seders* past, the first time they had been to the steam baths together, but he could bring no spark to his father's eyes. Finally, he helped Issy Hersh into his dressing gown, trying not to stare at the wasted body, his father's hitherto ballooning belly reduced to an empty flap overhanging surgical cuts that circled him like a belt. Supporting him on his paralyzed side, Jake led him into the stuffy, cluttered living room, and the TV set, where father and son watched the Jackie Gleason Show together, Issy Hersh wheezing with laughter, his eyes suddenly sparkling.

"Oh, boy, that Gleason, the crazy fool, the spots he gets into.... Do you get the show in London?"

"No," Jake snarled, and he dared to ask his father a direct question about his mother and the year of their divorce.

"Water over the dam," his father replied, smiling again, his pleasure-filled eyes claimed by Gleason.

"I know him," Jake put in angrily.

"You know Jackie Gleason...personally?"

Jake basked in his father's awe.

"In real life is he...such a boozer?"

"Yes."

Issy Hersh smiled, satisfied, and did not speak again until the commercial break. "Do you get *Bonanza* in London?"

"Yes."

"He's a Canadian, you know, Lorne Green. A Jewish boy." Then, as if it was too much to hope for, he added, "Do you know him?"

"In the old days," Jake said, "I would never use him."

"You mean to say you could have had...Lorne Green...for a part...and you didn't...?"

"Absolutely."

Liar, the old man's eyes replied. "He's a millionaire now, you know. He really made it."

On screen, Bobby Hull tooled down the sun-dappled 401 in a Ford Meteor. Coming on strong.

"You wouldn't know James Bond. What's his name?"

"Yes I do."

"In real life, what's he like?"

"Natural," Jake said vengefully. Then, just as his father's gaze was reverting to the TV screen, Jake retrieved him. "He's after me to direct his next picture."

"Hey, there's a lot of money in that."

"Would you be proud of me?"

"James Bond. Boy."

Jake, embarrassed by his lie, said nothing more, and once Gleason was done he supported his father back to the bed he would never quit again. "The trouble is we never talk," Jake said, "never really talk to each other."

"Who needs quarrels?"

Jake helped his father out of his dressing gown and eased him onto the bed, where he lay briefly uncovered, an old man in a sweat-soiled vest and shorts, smiling dependently. Reaching for his blanket, Jake caught a glimpse of his father's penis curling out of his jockey shorts. A spent worm. Jake's mouth opened, a cry of rage dying in his throat. Years and years ago, he and Rifka used to listen by their bedroom door on Friday nights, hands clasped to their mouths to suppress giggles, as Issy Hersh padded to the kitchen stove in his long Penman's underwear, flung the used condom into the Sabbath fire, where it sizzled briefly, and then retreated to his bed. Matching singles they had, each with a red chenille bedspread. In another bedroom, Jake remembered, a different time, this cock was my maker. He stooped to kiss his father good night.

"Everybody kisses me these days," Issy Hersh said, bemused.

"You're popular."

"Those James Bond pictures are big hits, real moneymakers. You should have seen the lineups here for the last one."

"Yes," Jake said at the door. "I'm sure."

"Oh, Yankel?"

"Yes."

"You get the *Playboy* magazine?"

"Yes."

"When you're through with them, you could send them on to me. I wouldn't mind."

Issy Hersh's wife, Fanny, risen from the basement with a basket of laundry, waylaid Jake in the hall.

"I love your father, he's been a wonderful husband to me, I'm taking excellent care of him."

"I'm grateful. So is Rifka."

"They wanted to put him in an incurable hospital, they said it would be too much work for me, but I said no, he's not going to die there."

"For Chrissake, he isn't deaf. He can hear us."

"It's good you came here. You must be doing very well."

"What?"

"Well, the trip from England is expensive. I'm so glad you're doing well and that we've grown fond of each other. You and your wife will always be welcome here. I'm not one of your aunts, a snob. I don't look down my nose." Now she paused, a hedge-shy horse before the big leap. "Being Jewish isn't everything."

"I'll tell Nancy you said that. See you tomorrow."

— *St. Urbain's Horseman,* pp. 273–75

POETRY COMES NATURALLY to the Panofskys. Take my father, for instance. Detective-Inspector Izzy Panofsky departed this vale of tears in a state of grace. Thirty-six years ago today he died of a heart attack on the table of a massage parlour in Montreal's North End, immediately after ejaculating. Summoned to claim my father's remains, I was taken aside by the visibly shaken young Haitian girl. She had no last words to impart to me, but did point out that Izzy had expired without signing his credit-card slip. A dutiful son, I paid for my father's final squirt of passion, adding a generous tip and apologizing for the inconvenience to the establishment. And this afternoon, on the anniversary of my father's death, I made my annual pilgrimage to the Chevra Kadisha Cemetery and, as I do every year, emptied a bottle of Crown Royal rye whisky over his grave and, in lieu of a pebble, left a medium-fat smoked meat on rye and a sour pickle on his gravestone.

Were ours a just God, which he isn't, my father would now dwell in heaven's most opulent bordello, which would also include a deli counter, a bar with a brass rail and spittoon, a cache of White Owl coronas, and a twenty-four-hour TV sports channel. But the God we Jews are stuck with is both cruel and vengeful. To my way of looking, Jehovah was also the first Jewish stand-up comic, Abraham his straight man. "Take now thy son," the Lord said unto Abraham, "thine only son Isaac, whom thou lovest, and get thee into the land of Moriah; and offer him there for a burnt offering upon one of the mountains which I will tell thee of." And Abe, the first of too many Jewish grovellers, saddled his ass and did as he was told. He built an altar, and laid the wood in order, and bound Isaac his son, and laid him on the altar upon the wood. "Hey, Daddy-o," said a distressed Isaac, "behold the fire and the wood, but where is the lamb for the burnt offering?" In response, Abe stretched forth his hand, and took the knife to slay his son. At which point Jehovah, quaking with laughter, sent down an angel who said, "Hold it, Abe. Lay not thy hand upon thy son." And Abraham lifted up his eyes, and looked, and beheld behind him a ram caught in a thicket by the horns; and Abraham went and took the ram, and offered him up for a burnt offering in the stead of his son. But I doubt that things were ever the same again between Abe and Izzy.

—*Barney's Version*, pp. 46–47

NINETEEN EIGHTY-NINE THAT WAS. I'm jumping all over the place. I know, I know. But seated at my desk these endgame days, my bladder plugged by an enlarged prostate, my sciatica a frequent curse, wondering when I will be due for another hip socket, anticipating emphysema, pulling on a Montecristo Number Two, a bottle of Macallan by my side, I try to retrieve some sense out of my life, unscrambling it. Recalling those blissful days in Paris, in the early fifties, when we were young and crazy, I raise my glass to absent friends: Mason Hoffenberg, David Burnett, Alfred Chester, and Terry Southern, all dead now. I wonder whatever became of the girl who was never seen on the boulevard Saint-Germain without that chirping chimpanzee riding her shoulder. Did she go home to Houston and marry a dentist? Is she a grandmother now and an admirer of Newt? Or did she die of an overdose like the exquisite Marie-Claire, who could trace her lineage back to Roland?

—*Barney's Version*, p. 26

The Last Word

═══════

THE TRUTH IS, I tend to identify more closely with the suddenly sore-armed pitcher — Dwight Gooden, once King of the Ks, now no longer capable of throwing heat. Or Cone, pitching his perfect game in 1999 and, as I write, standing at 3–11 for the 2000 season. Once a novel is finished, my conviction is that I've lost it and will never be able to write another one.

Two years after I published my last novel, *Barney's Version*, a reporter phoned from Toronto. "We're doing a survey," he said. "What are you working on now, Mr. Richler?"

"Hey, I'm sixty-eight years old. Every novelist writes one too many, and that's the one I'm working on now."

— On Snooker, p. 86

Mordecai Richler died in Montreal on July 3, 2001.

Selected Bibliography

FICTION

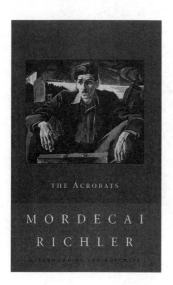

The Acrobats

An expatriate painter in Spain struggles to follow the path of honour in a crass society. The story inclines to melodrama and is marred by occasionally overwrought prose, but the book is salvaged by its energy and passion and by the savage clarity of the author's vision. Richler admitted in an interview that the novel was a pastiche of Malraux, Sartre, and Hemingway — all writers that he admired as a young man.

Diana Athill, Richler's editor at André Deutsch, later marvelled (in her memoir, *Stet*) that she and Deutsch had taken it on. "It really is very bad," she wrote, "but something of its author's nature struggles through the clumsiness, and we were in the process of building a list, desperate for new and promising young writers."

In fact, *The Acrobats* is worth reading — it is a remarkable achievement for a writer barely in his twenties when the book was published. "It was certainly a young man's book, full of passion and romanticism," wrote film director Ted Kotcheff, a longtime friend. "Youthful romanticism is commonplace. What was not commonplace was Mordecai's attempt to deal with profound issues both moral and political."

London: André Deutsch Limited, 1954. New York: Putnam, 1954.
COVER EDITION Toronto: McClelland & Stewart, 2002.

Son of a Smaller Hero

Richler introduces a Jewish protagonist born and raised in Montreal's Jewish ghetto. The relationships between the youthful Noah Adler, his ineffectual father, and his overbearing grandfather are familiar themes in Richler's later work, and are not without poignancy in this early treatment. Some set pieces, including Noah's liberation from Gentile oppressors on a beach in the Laurentians, are striking. (The beach expedition appears in virtually identical form in Richler's collection of stories, *The Street*.)

With this novel, Richler is beginning to come to terms with his roots, even though he is now living abroad. As he told the critic Nathan Cohen at the time: "I am not a European writer and I couldn't become one if I stayed here twenty-five years. All my attitudes are Canadian; I'm a Canadian; there's nothing to be done about it."

London: André Deutsch, 1955.
COVER EDITION Toronto: McClelland & Stewart, 2002.

A Choice of Enemies

As Richler described it himself, "My new novel, very baldly, is about a refugee from East Berlin who falls in with the people who have been blacklisted in America and are living in London. And eventually they treat him in the same way as they were treated, and they treat him that way because of his political beliefs. I believe that the essence of this whole thing was one of power."

Publication of this book marked the end of Richler's apprenticeship as a writer. Ironically, it led the critic Nathan Cohen to write him off. Summing up Richler's output in 1957, Cohen wrote magisterially (and unfairly), "In respect to the ratio of felicities and failings, the book [*A Choice of Enemies*] is if anything a retrogressive step. There are too few virtues; the weaknesses are the same as before. *There has been no improvement*."

Richler responded to this lambasting in a letter to William Weintraub: "only in Canada wd somebody attempt such a long [13 pages] and definitive piece on a young punk who has published a mere 3 bks. Makes me feel like I'm dead, or something."

London: André Deutsch, 1957.
COVER EDITION Toronto: McClelland & Stewart, 2002.

$2.95

The Apprenticeship of Duddy Kravitz
Mordecai Richler

A Canadian classic. This special edition includes 69 stills, cast list and production details from the new feature film.

The Apprenticeship of Duddy Kravitz

Duddy Kravitz, the ambitious son of a Montreal cab driver, is determined to do whatever it takes to get out of the ghetto. His ruthlessness may not be pretty, but he has wit and guts and surprising vulnerability. The protagonists of Richler's previous books were conflicted, but Duddy is more clearly drawn — and far more memorable.

Duddy is Richler's first mature work. The plotting is assured, the prose taut, and, above all, the humour that Richler had kept in check is finally unleashed. Ted Kotcheff suggests that Richler probably felt that humour was inappropriate for a serious writer. With *Duddy*, that youthful misapprehension has been decisively overcome.

This was the last of Richler's books with André Deutsch. Editor Diana Athill commented that before Richler left the publishing house, she "had the delight of seeing him come into his own. *The Apprenticeship of Duddy Kravitz*...was a triumph."

London: André Deutsch, 1959. Boston: Little, Brown, 1959. Toronto: McClelland & Stewart, 1959. COVER EDITION Toronto: McClelland & Stewart, 1974.

The Incomparable Atuk

An Eskimo poet looks for fame and fortune in Toronto in the 1960s. He finds himself surrounded by schemers, mountebanks, and poseurs, some of whom are modeled, however loosely, on Toronto literary figures. If *The Apprenticeship of Duddy Kravitz* is Richler's first mature novel, *The Incomparable Atuk* is something else: not by any means a regression, but a sally in a different direction, toward pure satire.

Richler's Canadian publisher at the time, Jack McClelland, disapproved of the title — *Stick Your Neck Out* — preferred by the American publisher, Simon & Schuster. McClelland argued in a letter to Richler that the only thing going for it was the chance that it would win an award as worst book title of the year.

Mordecai **RICHLER**

The **Incomparable Atuk**

Afterword by PETER GZOWSKI

Toronto: McClelland & Stewart, 1963. London: André Deutsch, 1963.
New York: Simon & Schuster, 1963 (Published in the U.S. as *Stick Your Neck Out*).
COVER EDITION Toronto: McClelland & Stewart, 1989.

Cocksure

This 1960s psychedelic riot-of-a-book reflects Richler's now-established confidence in his powers as a satirist. His targets include Hollywood, the sexual revolution, modish education theory, and the Jewish identity. The hero, Mortimer Griffin, is a Canadian working in London as editor at a prestigious independent publishing house. As Mark Steyn wrote in *The New Criterion*, when the firm is bought up by a Hollywood mogul, the Gentile Mortimer suddenly "finds his life freighted by Jewishness. On the one hand, for the first time in his life, he's the odd one out, because he's not Jewish.... On the other hand, everyone seems to assume he is."

After *Cocksure*, Richler was ready to join his mastery of humour with the serious underlying themes of *St. Urbain's Horseman* and *Joshua Then and Now*.

London: Weidenfeld & Nicolson, 1968. New York: Simon & Schuster, 1968.
Winner (with *Hunting Tigers under Glass*), Governor-General's Award for Literature, Fiction, 1968.
COVER EDITION Toronto: McClelland & Stewart, 1968.

St. Urbain's Horseman

Jacob Hersh, who makes a minor appearance in *The Apprenticeship of Duddy Kravitz*, is a successful Canadian film director working in London. Another of Richler's conflicted and angst-ridden protagonists, Hersh is accused of sexually assaulting a German *au pair*, but the premise chiefly provides the occasion for Richler to send up some favourite targets while exploring serious themes.

Richler struggled with the manuscript of *St. Urbain's Horseman* for much of the 1960s, taking time off to write *Cocksure* in just nine months, before resuming the battle. He had a new American publisher, Alfred A. Knopf, and a new editor, Robert Gottleib, with whom he would remain to the end.

"It does go back and forth, but it doesn't dizzy me," Gottleib wrote to Richler upon receipt of the manuscript. "Whatever it is, it works.... Rest, rest, perturbed spirit."

Toronto: McClelland & Stewart, 1971. London: Weidenfeld & Nicolson, 1971.
New York, Alfred A. Knopf, 1971.
Winner, Governor-General's Award for Literature, Fiction, 1971.
COVER EDITION Toronto: McClelland & Stewart, 2002.

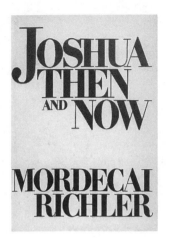

Joshua Then and Now

Joshua Shapiro is a literary cousin of Jake Hersh. He's from the same neighbourhood and, like Jake, he has spent time in Europe. Now he lives in Canada, writing novels and magazine journalism, and narrating documentaries for the CBC. He's famous and prosperous and married to a beautiful, non-Jewish woman. But Jake is plagued by demons that threaten to upset his precariously ordered life.

There are superb comic scenes, especially those involving his father, one of Montreal's few Jewish policemen, and his father-in-law, the senator. But what drives the novel, as a number of critics observed, is its love interest. "What lifts *Joshua Then and Now* from being a very funny novel to being a fine one, however, is the power of its theme," wrote *The Atlantic Monthly*'s reviewer. "Richler has chosen Auden's 'Lay your sleeping head, my love' as his epigram, and it is love that suffuses this book with delight. Love of place, ideas, and friends is rare enough in contemporary literature; married love, the kind that can outlast any sort of trouble, is almost nonexistent. Joshua has it all, in spades."

New York: Alfred A. Knopf, 1980. Toronto: McClelland & Stewart, 1980. London: Macmillan, 1980. COVER EDITION Toronto: McClelland & Stewart, 1980.

Solomon Gursky Was Here

In his review, Bruce Cook of the *Chicago Tribune* wrote: "The texture of this novel is so rich, so completely infused with Mordecai Richler's amazing sensibility and laugh-out-loud humor (mordantly cynical and utterly wacky, by turns) that it is a joy to read. Page for page, there has not been a serious novel for years that can give as much pure pleasure as this one."

Solomon Gursky is an inspired take-off on the family saga. It is also the first novel that Richler researched thoroughly for historical accuracy. It should be noted that the Gursky family bears a passing resemblance to another family that made its fortune selling booze — the Bronfmanns.

Author, dramatist, and man of letters Robertson Davies wrote Richler an admiring letter after reading it: "You pelt along at a cracking pace, as if you did not think you could possibly crowd in all you have to tell — and of course this whips the reader along with it, breathless and spellbound.... Altogether a brilliant performance."

New York: Alfred A. Knopf, 1990. Toronto: Viking, 1989. London: Chatto & Windus, 1990. Winner, Commonwealth Prize, 1990.

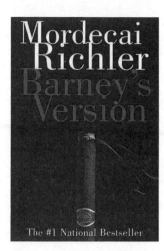

Barney's Version

Barney Panofsky, the disgruntled and aging protagonist of *Barney's Version*, amid rants against topics as diverse as the decline of the Montreal Canadiens and the difficulty of hiring competent assistants for television production company, tells the story of his life and loves. His loves are three: Clara, the suicidally neurotic poet he married while living a Bohemian life in Paris; the Jewish princess known only as The Second Mrs. Panofsky, whom he wedded on his return to Canada; and Miriam, the woman of his dreams, who finally leaves him, out of exasperation, for a younger man. Barney's life, his loves aside, is similarly tumultuous and entertaining.

Barney's Version was an enormous and utterly unexpected bestseller in Italy, where the term "Richleriano" became shorthand for "politically incorrect."

New York: Alfred A. Knopf, 1997. London: Chatto & Windus, 1997.
COVER EDITION Toronto: Alfred A. Knopf Canada, 1997.

STORIES

The Street

A slim volume, unlike any other book in Richler's output, *The Street* is deft and economical in its evocation of the Montreal Jewish ghetto. Richler's longtime friend, William Weintraub, after quoting a passage in which Richler describes a child's experience of the bustle of life on The Main, writes: "When passages like this first appeared in magazines, most Montreal Jews were either furious or, at least, not amused. Was this Richler a self-hating Jew, or what? But as the decades passed, the sons and daughters of those cutters and pressers, now doctors and university professors, could read Richler with amusement and pride, finding not insult but warmth and nostalgia in that world of his."

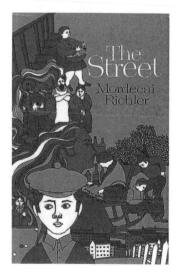

London: Weidenfeld & Nicolson, 1969.
COVER EDITION Toronto: McClelland & Stewart, 1969.

CHILDREN'S FICTION

Jacob Two-Two Meets the Hooded Fang

Toronto: McClelland & Stewart, 1975.
New York: Alfred A. Knopf, 1975.
COVER EDITION Toronto: McClelland & Stewart, 1997.

Jacob Two-Two and the Dinosaur

Toronto: McClelland & Stewart, 1987.
London: André Deutsch, 1987.
New York: Alfred A. Knopf, 1987.

Jacob Two-Two's First Spy Case

Toronto: McClelland & Stewart, 1997.
New York: Farrar, Straus and Giroux, 1997.

NONFICTION

Hunting Tigers under Glass: Essays & Reports

Contents: "O Canada," "Expo 67," "With the Trail Smoke Eaters in Stockholm," "Paper Lion," "Jews in Sport," "The Great Comic Book Heroes," "Writing for the Movies," "Norman Mailer," "Malamud," "The Catskills," "This Year in Jerusalem."

Toronto: McClelland & Stewart, 1968. London: Weidenfeld & Nicolson, 1969.
Winner (with *Cocksure*), Governor-General's Award for Literature, Fiction, 1968.

Shovelling Trouble

Contents: "Why I Write," "A Sense of the Ridiculous," "Gordon Craig," "Bond," "The Holocaust and After," "Making It," "Huckleberry Finklestone," "Starting Out in the Thirties," "Porky's Plaint," "Answering the Ads," "Games (Some) People Play," "Not Me, Leary, Not Me," "Following the Babylonian Talmud, After Maimonides…Rabbi Stuart Rosenberg on the History of the Jewish Community in Canada," "Maple Leaf Culture Time," "Êtes-vous canadien?"

London: Quartet Books, 1972.
COVER EDITION Toronto: McClelland & Stewart, 1972.

Notes on an Endangered Species and Others

Contents: "Why I Write," "A Sense of the Ridiculous," "Gordon Craig," "Writing for the Movies," "Notes on an Endangered Species," "The Great Comic Book Heroes," "The Catskills," "Jews in Sport," "Intimate Behaviour," "Following the Babylonian Talmud, After Maimonides…," "With the Trail Smoke Eaters in Stockholm," "Going Home," "Expo 67," "Êtes-vous canadien?"

New York: Alfred A. Knopf, 1974.

Home Sweet Home: My Canadian Album

Contents: "Home Is Where You Hang Yourself," "Karsh of Ottawa," "A Real Canadian Success Story, or What You Dare to Dream, Dare to Do," "Toronto, Ont.," "Quebec Oui, Ottawa Non," "Bedlam in Bytown," "My Father's Life," "Pages from a Western Journal," "From Roland Gladu, Through Kermit Kitman, to La Victoire Historique and After," "St. Urbain Street Then and Now," "Making a Movie," "The October Crisis, or Issue-Envy in Canada," "On the Road," "'Pourquoi Pas?' — a Letter from Ottawa," "'I'm the Kind of Guy Who Likes to See All the Legs Kick at the Same Time and at the Same Height'," "The Fall of the Montreal Canadiens," "North of Sixty," "Language (and Other) Problems," "O Canada."

London: Chatto & Windus, 1984. New York: Alfred A. Knopf, 1984. COVER EDITION Toronto: McClelland & Stewart, 1984.

Broadsides: Reviews and Opinions

Contents: "Hemingway Set His Own Hours," "Deuteronomy," "From Batman, Through G.A. Henty, to *All Quiet on the Western Front*," "Percolation, Goal-Setting, and Marketing Your Work," "*Debrett's Illustrated Guide to the Canadian Establishment*," "All the Conspirators," "The Road to Dyspepsia," "Impotence," "*Thy Neighbor's Wife*," "Be My Footsie Wootsie, You Buggy Poopoo," "Of Spiritual Guides, Witches and Wiccans," "Mulroney," "Writing Out of Washington D.C.," "Divorce," "Barbara Hutton," "Paid Liars," "Hollywood," "The Screenwriter's Lot," "Journals."

Toronto: Viking, 1990. London: Vintage, 1990.

Oh Canada! Oh Quebec!: Requiem for a Divided Country

Richler was inspired to write an essay on the absurdity of Quebec's language laws when he encountered one of Quebec's "language police" measuring the size of the English chalked inscription ("Today's Special: Ploughman's Lunch") on the blackboard outside his Montreal pub. Initially published in *The New Yorker*, where Robert Gottlieb was editor, the manuscript was subsequently expanded to book length. Certain members of the Parti Québécois, Quebec's separatist party, never forgave Richler for subjecting them to international ridicule.

Toronto: Viking, 1991. New York: Alfred A. Knopf, 1992.

This Year in Jerusalem

Richler combines a travelogue of his journeys to Israel with a critique of Israeli politics (his stance, broadly, that of a Zionist and a liberal) and memories of his own upbringing, with particular emphasis on his exposure to the Zionist movement.

New York: Alfred A. Knopf, 1994.
London: Chatto & Windus, 1994.
COVER EDITION Toronto: Alfred A. Knopf Canada, 1994.

Belling the Cat: Essays, Reports, and Opinions

Contents: "Writing for the Mags," "Mr. Sam," "The Reichmanns," "Lansky," "Woody," "Just Find a Million Readers and Success Will Surely Follow," "Mencken," "Morley Safer's Vietnam," "Supersex," "Saul Bellow," "Sexual Harassment," "The Innocents Abroad," "Germany 1978," "Safari," "Marakech," "Sol Kertzner's Xanadu," "Egypt's Eleventh Plague," "London Then and Now," "Pedlar's Diary," "Eddie Quinn," "Gordie," "Gretzky in Eighty-four," "From Satchel, through Hank Greenberg, to El Divino Loco," "Pete Rose," "Kasparov," "Audrey! Audrey! Audrey!" "Bye Bye Mulroney," "From the Ottawa Monkey House… to Referendum."

Toronto: Alfred A. Knopf Canada, 1998.

On Snooker: The Game and the Characters Who Play It

Richler learned snooker while skipping school in Montreal. Much later in life, when he and Florence acquired a cottage on Lake Memphremagog in the Eastern Townships of Quebec, they had a special wing built to accommodate a pool table. He followed the professional game avidly and wrote on it for magazines. *On Snooker* includes reports on the professional game as well as reflections on snooker and on the Montreal of Richler's youth.

London: Yellow Jersey, 2001.
Guilford, Conn.: Lyons Press, 2001.
COVER EDITION Toronto: Alfred A. Knopf Canada, 2001.

Dispatches from the Sporting Life

Contents: "An Incomplete Angler's Journal," "Jews in Sports," "A Real Canadian Success Story," "With the Trail Smoke Eaters in Stockholm," "Safari," "You Know Me, Ring," "Writers and Sports," "Gretzky in Eight-five," "From Satchel, through Hank Greenberg, to El Devino Loco," "Eddie Quinn," "Cheap Skates," "Maxie," "Paper Lion," "Gordie," "Pete Rose," "Kiss the Ump!" "Soul on Ice," "From Gladu, through Kitman, to the Victoire Historique and After," "The Fall of the Montreal Canadiens," "Playing Ball on Hampstead Heath — An Excerpt from *St. Urbain's Horseman*."

Guilford, Conn.: Lyons Press, 2002.
COVER EDITION Toronto: Alfred A. Knopf Canada, 2002.

ANTHOLOGIES

Canadian Writing Today

Harmondsworth, Middlesex: Penguin, 1970.

ACKNOWLEDGMENTS

THE PUBLISHER would like to thank Michael A. Levine for his unfailing dedication to this project and for his extraordinary support throughout. We are also very grateful to the Richler family for allowing us to present Mordecai Richler's writings in a new light.

Our warmest thanks to Jonathan Webb for his superb editorial instincts and his careful reading and selection from the works. William Weintraub's thoughtful editorial suggestions were also greatly appreciated. Many thanks as well to Terry Mosher, whose illustrations have brought Mordecai's world to life with such energy and wit.

A special note of appreciation to Adam Gopnik for taking time from a very busy schedule to lend his eloquent voice to the Introduction.

We are indebted to Peter Ross for his elegant and thoughtful design of the text, with assistance from Linda Gustafson; and to Angel Guerra for his jacket design. Each brought a love of Richler's work to the project, which has made all the difference.

Many others provided invaluable assistance with images and historical information, among them: Marlys Chevrefils and Apollonia Steele, University of Calgary Archives; Janice Rosen at the Canadian Jewish Congress; Shannon Hodge at the Jewish Public Library; and Gilles Lafontaine at the Montreal Archives.

Shima Aoki, our editor for this title at Madison, has lived and breathed the works of Mordecai Richler for the better part of a year. Innumerable small touches throughout the work reflect her dedication, her good judgment, and her resourceful and imaginative handling of the writings, the archive illustrations, and the work as a whole.

REFERENCED WORKS

FICTION

The Acrobats
  Toronto: McClelland & Stewart, 2002.

Son of a Smaller Hero
  Toronto: McClelland & Stewart, 1989.

A Choice of Enemies
  Toronto: McClelland & Stewart, 2002.

The Apprenticeship of Duddy Kravitz
  Toronto: McClelland & Stewart, 1989.

The Incomparable Atuk
  Toronto: McClelland & Stewart, 1989.

St. Urbain's Horseman
  Toronto: McClelland & Stewart, 1989.

Cocksure
  Toronto: McClelland & Stewart, 1996.

Joshua Then and Now
  Toronto: McClelland & Stewart, 1989.

Solomon Gursky Was Here
  Toronto: Penguin Books, 1998.

Barney's Version
  Toronto: Alfred A. Knopf, 1997.

STORIES

The Street
  Toronto: McClelland & Stewart, 2002.

NONFICTION

Hunting Tigers under Glass: Essays & Reports
  Toronto: McClelland & Stewart, 1968.

Shovelling Trouble
  Toronto: McClelland & Stewart, 1972.

Notes on an Endangered Species and Others
  New York: Alfred A. Knopf, 1974.

Home Sweet Home: My Canadian Album
  Toronto: McClelland & Stewart, 1984.

Broadsides: Reviews and Opinions
  Toronto: Viking, 1990.

Oh Canada! Oh Quebec!: Requiem for a Divided Country
  Toronto: Penguin Books, 1992.

This Year in Jerusalem
  Toronto: Alfred A. Knopf, 1994.

Belling the Cat: Essays, Reports, and Opinions
  Toronto: Alfred A. Knopf, 1998.

On Snooker: The Game and the Characters Who Play It
  Toronto: Alfred A. Knopf, 2001.

Dispatches from the Sporting Life
  Toronto: Alfred A. Knopf, 2002.

ANTHOLOGIES

Canadian Writing Today
  Harmondsworth, Middlesex: Penguin Books, 1970.

EPHEMERA

Robertson Davies
  Toronto: A Harbourfront Reading Series Booklet, 1993.

OTHER WORKS

Christopher, Peter. *Images of Spain*.
  Toronto: McClelland & Stewart, 1977.
  Introduction by Mordecai Richler.

Posner, Michael. *The Last Honest Man: Mordecai Richler, An Oral Biography*.
  © 2004 McClelland & Stewart Ltd. Reprinted with permission of the publisher.

Weintraub, William. *Getting Started: A Memoir of the 1950s*.
  © 2001 McClelland & Stewart Ltd. Reprinted with permission of the publisher.

PICTURE CREDITS

Every effort has been made to correctly attribute all material reproduced in this book. If errors have unwittingly occurred, we will be happy to correct them in future editions.

All illustrations are by Aislin (Terry Mosher).

1: © CP/Toronto Star (Dick Loek).
12: © CP/Toronto Star (Andrew Stawicki).

PART I

22: © George Cree, Montreal Gazette.
27: Mordecai Richler fonds, Special Collections, University of Calgary. With permission of the Richler Estate.
31: Canadian Jewish Congress National Archives.
34: Canadian Jewish Congress National Archives.
39: Canadian Jewish Congress National Archives.
49: City of Montreal. Records Management and Archives.
53: © CP/Toronto Star (Tedd Church).
58: Unknown.
65: © Bettmann/CORBIS.
68: © Christopher J. Morris/CORBIS.

PART II

74: © Jerry Bauer. Mordecai Richler fonds, Special Collections, University of Calgary. With permission of the Richler Estate.
78: Canadian Jewish Congress National Archives.
83: Getty Images.
93: Getty Images.
94: © Time & Life Pictures/Getty Images.
100: © Roger Viollet/Getty Images.
107: © Jerry Bauer. Mordecai Richler fonds, Special Collections, University of Calgary. With permission of the Richler Estate.
111: © Time & Life Pictures/Getty Images.
124: © Bettmann/CORBIS.
133: © CP/Rob Cooper.

PART III

140: © Christopher Morris.
157: © Hulton-Deutsch Collection/CORBIS.
173: © CP/Montreal Gazette.
183: © Thies Bogner, MPA. Mordecai Richler fonds, Special Collections, University of Calgary. With permission of the Richler Estate.
200: Jewish Public Library Archives, Montreal.
203: Jewish Public Library Archives, Montreal.
205: Courtesy of the Richler family.
208: © Courtesy of Peter Ross.

SELECTED BIBLIOGRAPHY

*All covers provided by McClelland & Stewart
unless indicated otherwise. © McClelland &
Stewart Ltd. Reprinted by permission of
the publisher.*

Barney's Version.
© 1997 Mordecai Richler Productions
Limited. Cover design by Spencer Francey
Peters. Cover photo by John Scully.
Reprinted by permission of Knopf Canada.

This Year in Jerusalem.
© 1994 Mordecai Richler Productions
Limited. Cover design by Sharon Foster
Design. Cover photograph by Christopher
Morris. Reprinted by permission of Knopf
Canada.

*On Snooker: The Game and the Characters
Who Play It.*
© 2001 Mordecai Richler Productions
Limited. Cover design by Paul
Hodgson/Spencer Francey Peters. Cover
photograph by Joy von Tiedemann.
Reprinted by permission of Knopf Canada.

Dispatches from the Sporting Life.
© 2002 Mordecai Richler Productions
Limited. Cover design by C. S. Richardson.
Cover photograph courtesy of the Richler
family. Reprinted by permission of Knopf
Canada.

Publisher
OLIVER SALZMANN

Editor
SHIMA AOKI

Book Design
PETER ROSS /
COUNTERPUNCH

Jacket Design
DIANA SULLADA

Production Manager
KELVIN KONG

Vice-President
Business Affairs and Production
SUSAN BARRABLE